From the Vanguard to the Margins
Workers in Hungary, 1939 to the Present

Historical Materialism Book Series

The Historical Materialism Book Series is a major publishing initiative of the radical left. The capitalist crisis of the twenty-first century has been met by a resurgence of interest in critical Marxist theory. At the same time, the publishing institutions committed to Marxism have contracted markedly since the high point of the 1970s. The Historical Materialism Book Series is dedicated to addressing this situation by making available important works of Marxist theory. The aim of the series is to publish important theoretical contributions as the basis for vigorous intellectual debate and exchange on the left.

The peer-reviewed series publishes original monographs, translated texts, and reprints of classics across the bounds of academic disciplinary agendas and across the divisions of the left. The series is particularly concerned to encourage the internationalization of Marxist debate and aims to translate significant studies from beyond the English-speaking world.

For a full list of titles in the Historical Materialism Book Series available in paperback from Haymarket Books, visit:
www.haymarketbooks.org/category/hm-series

From the Vanguard to the Margins
Workers in Hungary, 1939 to the Present

Selected Essays by Mark Pittaway

Mark Pittaway

Edited by
Adam Fabry

Haymarket Books
Chicago, IL

First published in 2014 by Brill Academic Publishers, The Netherlands
© 2014 Koninklijke Brill NV, Leiden, The Netherlands

Published in paperback in 2015 by
Haymarket Books
P.O. Box 180165
Chicago, IL 60618
773-583-7884
www.haymarketbooks.org

ISBN: 978-1-60846-477-7

Trade distribution:
In the US, Consortium Book Sales, www.cbsd.com
In Canada, Publishers Group Canada, www.pgcbooks.ca
In the UK, Turnaround Publisher Services, www.turnaround-psl.com
In Australia, Palgrave Macmillan, www.palgravemacmillan.com.au
In all other countries, Publishers Group Worldwide, www.pgw.com

Cover design by Ragina Johnson.

This book was published with the generous support of
Lannan Foundation and the Wallace Global Fund.

Library of Congress Cataloging-in-Publication data is available.

In memory of our valued colleague Mark Pittaway

Mark Pittaway

Contents

Acknowledgements   ix
Abbreviations   xi

Introduction   1
    Adam Fabry

1 Crisis, War and Occupation   13

2 Building Socialism   34

3 The Reproduction of Hierarchy: Skill, Working-Class Culture, and the State in Early Socialist Hungary   61

4 The Social Limits of State Control: Time, the Industrial Wage Relation, and Social Identity in Stalinist Hungary, 1948–53   94

5 Retreat from Collective Protest: Household, Gender, Work and Popular Opposition in Stalinist Hungary   121

6 The Revolution and Industrial Workers: The Disintegration and Reconstruction of Socialism, 1953–58   156

7 Accommodation and the Limits of Economic Reform: Industrial Workers during the Making and Unmaking of Kádár's Hungary   192

8 Research in Hungarian Archives on Post-1945 History   215

9 Making Peace in the Shadow of War: The Austrian-Hungarian Borderlands, 1945–56   222

10 Workers and the Change of System   245

11 Fascism in Hungary   257

12 Towards a Social History of the 1956 Revolution in Hungary   276

Epilogue 292
 Nigel Swain

References 304
Index 327

Acknowledgements

This book is dedicated to the work of the late historian Mark Pittaway (1971–2010). The essays collected in this volume are revised and updated versions of works that have all been published previously, either as book chapters in individual and edited volumes, articles, or as keynote lectures. The editor would like to thank Mark Pittaway's family and the original publishers of Pittaway's work for kindly granting their permission to republish the essays appearing in this volume. Listed here in order of appearance, the original titles and publishers of texts reprinted in this volume include:

- 'Crisis, War and Occupation' published by Arnold Hodder;
- 'Building Socialism' published by Arnold Hodder;
- 'The Reproduction of Hierarchy: Skill, Working Class Culture and the State in Early Socialist Hungary' published by University of Chicago Press;
- 'The Social Limits of State Control: Time, the Industrial Wage Relation and Social Identity in Stalinist Hungary, 1948–53' published by Wiley-Blackwell Publishing;
- 'Retreat from Collective Protest: Household, Gender, Work and Popular Opposition in Stalinist Hungary' published by Berghahn Books;
- 'The Revolution and Industrial Workers: The Disintegration and Reconstruction of Socialism, 1953–58' published by the Hungarian Studies Association of Canada, the Hungarian Studies Association and the National Széchényi Library of Hungary;
- 'Accommodation and the Limits of Economic Reform: Industrial Workers during the Making and Unmaking of Kádár's Hungary' published by Böhlau Verlag;
- 'Research in Hungarian Archives on Post-1945 History' published by the Center for Austrian Studies, University of Minnesota, MN;
- 'Making Peace in the Shadow of War: The Austrian-Hungarian Borderlands, 1945–56' published by Cambridge University Press;
- 'Workers and the Change of the System' published by Napvilág Kiadó; and finally
- 'Fascism' published by Oxford University Press.

Having said this, the publication of this volume would not have been possible without the initiative, enthusiasm and patience of Steve Edwards. In editing and revising the manuscript, I was also fortunate to draw on discussions and insights from friends and dedicated scholars whose comments and suggestions contributed, however indirectly, to the making of this book: Alexander Anievas, Eszter Bartha, David Broder, Sebastian Budgen, Gareth Dale, György Földes, Tamás Krausz, Nigel Swain, and Peter Thomas. In addition, I would like to thank The Open University and BRILL for providing much needed financial assistance for the publication of the volume. Finally, I would like to thank my family, in particular my mother, father, and my late grandmother 'Ike', for their continual emotional and intellectual support, as well as my beloved Marina Delponti – for without them I would not be writing these lines in the first place.

Adam Fabry

Abbreviations

ÁVH	State Security Agency (Hungary)
CEE	Central and Eastern Europe
ESRC	Economic and Social Research Council
FIDESZ	Alliance of Young Democrats (Hungary)
FKGP	Independent Smallholders' Party (Hungary)
GDR	German Democratic Republic
HSLS	Slovak People's Party
ILO	International Labour Organisation
IMF	International Monetary Fund
KPÖ	Austrian Communist Party
KSČ	Czechoslovak Communist Party
MDF	Hungarian Democratic Forum
MDP	Hungarian Workers' Party
MÉP	Hungarian Life Party
MIÉP	Hungarian Justice and Life Party
MKP	Hungarian Communist Party
MNB	Hungarian National Bank
MOL	National Archives of Hungary
MOVE	Hungarian National Defence Association
MSZDP	Hungarian Social Democratic Party
MSZMP	Hungarian Socialist Workers' Party
MSZOSZ	National Confederation of Hungarian Trade Unions
NAP	Party of National Will (Hungary)
NDH	Independent State of Croatia
NEM	New Economic Mechanism (Hungary)
NEP	National Unity Party (Hungary)
NP	Arrow Cross Party (Hungary)
NSZMP	National Socialist Hungarian Party
NT	Peoples' Economic Council (Hungary)
OECD	Organisation for Economic Co-operation and Development
OT	National Planning Office (Hungary)
PPR	Polish Workers' Party
PSL	Polish Peasants' Party
PZPR	Polish United Workers' Party
SPÖ	Austrian Socialist Party
SZKL	Central Archives of Trade Unions (Hungary)
ÖVP	Austrian People's Party

Introduction

Mark Pittaway (1971–2010) was a prominent scholar on post-war and contemporary Central and Eastern Europe (CEE), with a particular affinity for Hungarian affairs, an outstanding historian of social relations under Soviet-style 'socialism', and a passionate critic of contemporary affairs in post-Soviet CEE. Pittaway was an anti-fascist and socialist, 'of the left', although he was increasingly attracted to the Green Party towards the end of his life. But he adhered to none of the standard revolutionary socialist positions on 'Eastern Europe'. As noted in his obituary, in *The Guardian*, the trademark of Pittaway's work was 'the deft combination of high politics with social history'.[1] Breaking with dominant orthodoxies within mainstream historiography on Soviet-style societies, which remained wedded to the 'totalitarianism' paradigm of the Cold War era, Pittaway developed seminal analyses of the Stalinist state and the conditions of labour under 'real socialism', providing path-breaking theoretical and empirical insights to our understanding of the everyday life of workers in Soviet-style societies.

Although born and raised in Wakefield, Yorkshire, Pittaway was, as Nigel Swain writes in the 'Epilogue' to this volume, a historian who 'crossed borders'.[2] He was equally at home – linguistically, mentally, and culturally – in Wakefield as in continental Europe. He studied history at the University of Warwick and first visited Hungary in 1993, attending a summer school in Debrecen, where many academics who work on Hungary learnt their first smattering of Hungarian. He learnt to speak Hungarian perfectly, with only a hint of his native Yorkshire accent. Apart from English and Hungarian, he also spoke German and Italian fluently, which enabled him to gain a perfect insight into the societies of his studies, and earned him respect from fellow historians and left-wing activists in the East and West alike.

Pittaway's affection for Hungary was to define the rest of his life. From 1993 to 1998 he wrote his doctoral dissertation at the University of Liverpool on the Hungarian working class in the early years of the country's Stalinist dictatorship, spending most of his time in Hungary excavating treasures from obscure local archives. His thesis, entitled *Industrial Workers, Socialist Industrialisation*

---

1 Melvius and Escritt 2010.
2 'Crossing Borders' was the English version of the title of the memorial conference held in Pittaway's memory in Budapest on 24 March 2011. The conference was organised by the Department of East European Studies of the internationally renowned Eötvös Loránd University (ELTE) and the Institute of Political History.

and the State in Hungary, 1948–1958, broke new ground. Turning the totalitarian thesis on its head, Pittaway demonstrated that Hungary's Stalinist regime was not omnipotent, but rather needed to acquiesce to the demands of workers (in particular male manual workers in industry) for its legitimacy. An extended 'book version' of his thesis, entitled *The Workers' State: Industrial Labor and the Making of Socialist Hungary, 1944–1958*, was published posthumously in 2012 with the University of Pittsburgh Press. According to two critics, it is an important contribution to understanding 'the dynamics of early socialist state formation in Hungary', and one that is likely to become 'essential reading for all historians of East-Central Europe'.

Pittaway became a Lecturer at the Arts Faculty of the Open University in 1999, and a Senior Lecturer in 2005. He published widely, producing journal articles and book chapters in both English and Hungarian – an unusual language skill for a scholar of his generation. However, the intellectual path that Pittaway assiduously pursued did not facilitate easy reception of his work. Throughout his scholarly career, Pittaway remained a non-conformist historian, fiercely committed to a 'history from below' in all its messy complexity. While he had no illusions about the pre-1989 Eastern bloc regimes, he believed that these societies remained 'socialist'. This position did not facilitate the acceptance of Pittaway's work, and it also brought him, as Eszter Bartha observes, into controversy with both adherents of the totalitarianism thesis in the East and the West, as well as a significant number of critical Marxists and the wider left, for whom ' "real socialism" did not exist';[3] instead, the latter argued that the Soviet-style regimes represented a particular 'variety of capitalism' known as 'state capitalism'.[4] For Pittaway, the People's Republics were not only a top-down construction, built on Moscow's orders and dominated by local 'communist' parties; workers were able to participate and shape the system. He thus rejected both the totalitarian thesis and the state capitalism thesis, highlighting the 'socialist' features of the pre-1989 Eastern bloc regimes, which contributed to social mobility and cultural ascension hitherto unknown in the region.

As the articles collected in this volume attest, Pittaway was a fervent scholar, devoted to mastering any subject he put his mind to, from Austrian (German) ethnic policy in the 1930s to mining in Tatabánya during the height of the

---

3   Bartha 2011, pp. 130–1.
4   While this is not the place to resume much-heated debates on the nature of Soviet-style regimes, those interested in engaging further with these debates are recommended to consult the following works: Linden 2007; Lebowitz 2012; Krausz and Szigeti 2007 (in Hungarian); Tamás 2007, 2008, pp. 66–75, and 2011, pp. 21–45.

Rákosi regime's accumulation drive in the 1950s. In an 'age of austerity', in which the marketisation of education has become one of the top priorities of governments across the world, irrespective of where they stand on the political spectrum, Pittaway remained committed to the notion that knowledge was a 'common good': he shared his ideas, archival materials and manuscripts without hesitation. On the other hand, he never seemed to have taken himself, academia or politicians too seriously in the first place, 'often jok[ing] with a characteristic mischievous giggle'.[5]

After attending the above-mentioned conference in Budapest to commemorate Pittaway's work, it became clear that Hungarian scholars and political activists embraced him as their equal. He had become a source of inspiration to historians, journalists, political economists, and a large section of what remains of the 'left' in the country, criticising both the corrupt and haplessly incompetent Hungarian socialists, as well as the current neo-conservative government, earning himself an unsavoury reputation in Budapest's corridors of power, which he seemingly relished: 'I have just been denounced by the Hungarian finance minister', he once cheerfully reported.[6]

Themes, Debates, and Contexts

The essays collected in this volume pay homage to Pittaway's work, offering a range of pieces that are representative of his scholarly interests throughout his career. Two central interconnected sets of themes run throughout the following pages: (1) the historical and sociological origins, contradictory nature, and aftermath of the pre-1989 Eastern bloc regimes; and (2) the significance of labour in the politics of post-war and contemporary CEE. The first cluster of themes extend beyond a narrow focus on Hungary to encompass the question of what the Hungarian radical philosopher Gáspár Miklós Tamás has defined as 'the nature of (to use a neutral term for a moment) Soviet-style societies'.[7]

To explain the particularity of pre-1989 Eastern bloc regimes one has to answer a number of related questions. How did 'the transition to socialism' take place in these societies? Who were the key social agents behind this process? How was production organised? What were the aims of production (and, hence, how was the social division of labour organised)? What particular institutional configurations were established to ensure the reproduction of these

---

5 Melvius and Escritt 2010.
6 Ibid.
7 Tamás 2011, p. 25.

societies? Also, what was their relationship to the modern system of sovereign states and global capitalism? These questions are at the centre of the contributions addressed below by Mark Pittaway.

The Origins and Contradictory Nature of 'Real Socialism'

In Autumn 2009, on the eve of the twentieth anniversary of the fall of the Berlin Wall, a Pew Research Center survey revealed that a stunning 72 percent of Hungarians believed that they were 'worse off now than they were under communism'. However, figures showed that Hungarians were not the only ones in the region with a sour taste for capitalism. Of the countries of post-Soviet Central and Eastern Europe (CEE) surveyed, only in the Czech Republic and Poland did the majority of the people believe their economic life to be better now than before the 'transition' to the market. But as the survey made clear, Hungary's malaise was not limited to the sphere of the economy – most people were frustrated with politics too. Indeed, more than three in four (77 percent!) of Hungarians surveyed were dissatisfied with the way democracy was working in Hungary – the highest percentage among the post-Soviet states. (Again, Hungary is hardly the 'odd man out' in the region – only in the Czech Republic, Poland and Slovakia did the majority of the respondents express satisfaction with the functioning of liberal democracy).[8] For mainstream politicians (both liberal and conservative), regional pundits, and scholars of twentieth-century CEE, such figures represent a conundrum. Why is support for liberal-capitalist institutions so weak in Hungary – the supposed 'poster boy' of neoliberal transformation in CEE – as well as elsewhere in the region?

In aftermath of the demise of the Soviet-style regimes in 1989–91, and the revelations of corruption, inefficiency, waste, and mass environmental destruction, scholars often marvelled at how these regimes could have survived for so long. However, 'the fact that they did', as Mike Haynes cogently observed back in the early 1990s, 'points to an important issue – for a long period these systems were both dynamic and viable'.[9] Their dynamism, albeit frequently overestimated with the help of statistical hocus-pocus, was nevertheless real. For all their exaggerations, the fears of Cold War planners in the West were based on the threat of something real. Having said that, 'real socialism' was not without its peculiarities.

---

8 Pew Research Center 2010.
9 Haynes 1992, p. 47.

For Pittaway, the aforementioned figures would hardly have been surprising. As he argues in chapters 1 and 2 of the present book, the origins of Soviet-style 'socialism' in post-war Eastern Europe need to be understood against the background of the economic, political and social tensions that ravaged the region since the end of the First World War. Situating the above question within this broader historical context, Pittaway demonstrates that the formal 'realisation of socialism' in 1947–49, although achieved through the violent overthrow of democratically elected popular front governments by local Stalinist parties operating with the implicit backing of Moscow,[10] resonated with the demands of large sections of the region's population who were tired by the unprecedented scale of economic and human devastation wrought upon them by the Second World War. At the same time, Pittaway notes how the formal achievement of 'socialism' soon proved to be a double-edged sword for the Stalinist leadership. For while the Stalinist regimes 'mobilised workers through the deployment of class war rhetoric and a celebration of manual industrial labour at the ideological level',[11] the increasing drive for industrialisation, entailed by growing economic competition with the West, placed pressures on the state to reshape labour relations in order to mobilise workers to increase productivity. The contradictions and conflicts arising from these policies would manifest themselves in the industrial sphere.

In chapters 3 to 5, Pittaway takes issue with orthodox readings of early Stalinist societies in mainstream historiography, which depict the Stalinist dictatorships that ruled the respective Soviet satellite states of Eastern Europe as 'totalitarian', effectively stripping society at large, and not only the working class, of its 'relative autonomy'. Instead, Pittaway proposes an alternative theoretical framework, building on ideas around 'the limits of dictatorship' (associated with the likes of Sheila Fitzpatrick and Padraic Kenney), and 'factory regimes' (associated with Michael Burawoy and János Lukács). This literature emphasises how the contradictions of Stalinist industrialisation and 'socialist' society allowed social groups, particularly industrial workers, to influence state power.

The third chapter seeks to demonstrate the relative autonomy of the Hungarian working class vis-à-vis the Stalinist state by charting the contradictory and conflict-ridden trajectory of state-society relations within Hungary in

---

10   The only country in the Eastern bloc where the Communist Party did not come to power through a Soviet-backed *coup d'état* was Tito's Yugoslavia. After growing tensions between Belgrade and Moscow, fuelled by Tito's independent ambitions, the Soviet Union broke relations with Yugoslavia in March 1948.

11   See chapter 2 of this volume.

the late 1940s and early 1950s, during which the country's Stalinist regime, under the leadership of Mátyás Rákosi ('Stalin's best Hungarian disciple'), sought to emulate the Soviet Union's programme of industrial transformation. As Pittaway demonstrates, one of the central features of the Rákosi regime's brutal accumulation drive, like its Stalinist counterparts throughout the satellite states of Eastern Europe, was the expansion of the workforce and the contemporaneous introduction of payments-by-results schemes, 'socialist' labour competition, the wider application of scientific management, and increased production targets in workplaces. The hope of the Rákosi regime was that these measures would increase productivity, break down old hierarchies in the workplace – based on divisions between skilled and unskilled, old and young, male and female, and urban and rural workers – as well as transform working class culture and behaviour, thus paving the way to the creation of a 'new communist working class', as epitomised by the Stakhanovite movement. However, building on archival material from factories in a number of different industries throughout Hungary, Pittaway reveals how attempts by the regime to remould the country's working class 'met with considerable opposition rooted in Hungarian shop floor culture'. Hence, although Hungarian central planners had succeeded in increasing the absolute number of the industrial workforce in the late 1940s and early 1950s, by the time of Stalin's death in 1953 their efforts to create a 'new working class' had largely failed. As Pittaway notes, the failure of the Rákosi regime to create a 'new working class' and the persistence of hierarchies in the workplace 'draw attention to the "limits of dictatorship" in the Hungarian case, demonstrating that in Hungarian factories the Stalinist dictatorship's control over social process was far from absolute'.[12]

In chapter 4, Pittaway pursues this argument further by focussing on shop-floor relations in Hungarian factories during the 'high period' of Stalinism between 1948 and 1953. Challenging traditional images of Stalinism as 'collectivist', Pittaway shows how the wage system pursued by the Rákosi regime from 1948 and onwards, known as the piece-rate system [*darabbér*], sought to 'bind workers to the goals of the plan' through the introduction of payment-by-results. This system forced workers to improve their productivity in order to make an adequate monthly wage.[13] However, as Pittaway notes, this led to an 'apparent paradox' at the heart of Stalinist central planning, 'between institutional centralisation and a high degree of individualisation at the point of production'. The problem was compounded by the chronic shortages of labour, materials, and raw materials, which plagued the Hungarian economy in the

---

12 Pittaway, chapter 3 of this volume.
13 For the classical account of the piece-rate system, see Haraszti 1977.

late 1940s and early 1950s, producing a factory regime characterised by informal bargaining between workers and managers. While this meant that the Rákosi regime's efforts to discipline labour were 'strikingly unsuccessful', Pittaway contends that informal bargaining did succeed in undermining solidarity among workers.[14] Pittaway develops this argument further in chapter 5, where he investigates the causes for the absence of major instances of collective protest – whether in the form of strikes, political protests, or bread riots – against the Stalinist regime in Hungary prior to 1956.[15] According to Pittaway, the answer lies in the combination of state repression, severe poverty, and declining living standards (compounded by precarious wages in the state sector and the pervasive shortages in the field of official consumption), which characterised Hungarian society during the Rákosi years. This caused workers to retreat from open collective protest to the private sphere, in order to supplement their incomes and find resources to survive. As Pittaway goes on to show, such a shift from public to private had important implications for gender relations and identities, both in the workplace and the household.

However, in October 1956 popular discontent over Stalinism erupted into the open in Hungary. In chapters 6 and 12, Pittaway traces the origins of the 1956 Revolution to the tensions created by Stalinist rule in Hungarian society. While Moscow's decision to replace Rákosi with the reform-minded Imre Nagy as head of the government in 1953, and the relaxation of repression following the implementation of the new government's 'New Course' programme, went some way towards defusing working class discontent in the short term (in particular among rural workers), continuing economic chaos, together with Nagy's dismissal in 1955 (he was replaced by András Hegedüs, a Stalinist hardliner installed by Rákosi), brought anti-regime sentiment back to the surface in 1956. Throughout the year, militancy against the regime intensified, with students, intellectuals and workers becoming increasingly bold in expressing their resentment for the regime. As Pittaway shows, rising public discontent led to a

---

14 Pittaway, chapter 4 of this volume.
15 As Pittaway notes in chapter 5 of this volume, apart from a one-day demonstration in late December 1951 at the Ikarus bus plant in Budapest by one and a half thousand workers, angry over the government's decision to postpone wages until after the Christmas holidays, 'there were no major instances of open popular unrest [in Hungary] prior to 1956'. In this regard, Hungary was exceptional, as there were significant working class protests elsewhere in the Eastern bloc during this period, especially after the death of Stalin in March 1953. The most well-known disturbances were those that took place in the GDR on 17 June 1953, which saw around one-million people striking in some seven hundred towns, forcing the country's Stalinist regime to impose martial law. For an overview in English, see Dale 2005, pp. 9–37.

'loss of confidence' within the Party in its ability to govern: by September, there was 'a real feeling of panic' among party ranks in Budapest.

In chapters 6 and 12, Pittaway deals a lethal blow to three widespread misconceptions about the 1956 Revolution. First, Pittaway provides a healthy antidote to the Stalinist myth, projected by the Kádár regime and Communist Parties in the West, which depicts the events of late 1956 as a 'counter-revolution', in which anti-socialist agitators, 'reactionaries', and 'agents of imperialism' had stirred up discontent in order to overthrow 'socialism'. In contradistinction to the above, Pittaway shows the crucial role played by workers, in particular young workers, in driving the political Revolution forward by radicalising anti-regime protests, setting up revolutionary organisations in workplaces ('worker's councils'), and 'then spreading disturbances back to the industrial suburbs' of the capital.[16] Second, he challenges the dominant 'Budapest-centred account' of the Revolution that is so pervasive in mainstream historiography, shedding light on the many 'local revolutions', which 'took place before or as the events in Budapest got underway'. Third and finally, Pittaway demonstrates that although armed resistance came to an end within days after Soviet military intervention on 4 November, the quelling of workers' resistance was not achieved overnight. For example, in Tatabánya, located in north-western Hungary and home to the largest of the county's two coal fields, 'Soviet invasion provoked a protracted miners' strike, which dragged on for a full two months, causing coal shortages that closed schools and undermined medical services into early 1957'. In order to break down workers' opposition, the Kádár government and its Soviet allies were forced to manoeuvre carefully between 'a policy of negotiation to one of repression'. Although Kádár's 'two-track strategy' eventually succeeded in defeating the 1956 Revolution, the vivid recollection, backed by meticulous research, that Pittaway presents of the 'dramatic ebb and flow of revolutionary passions, hopes, and disappointments'[17] that characterised the Hungarian Revolution of 1956 not only constitute a significant contribution to the historiography on the 1956 Revolution, but will also be of interest to activists today who are fighting oppressive regimes on the streets of Athens, Cairo, or in the 'red hills' of Marikana in South Africa.

However, the Kádár regime faced a serious crisis of legitimacy, as strikes rumbled on through early 1957. At the heart of this crisis was the apparent

---

16   Official statistics, although they almost certainly underestimate the number of casualties involved in the battles, confirm this claim. They show that in Budapest some sixteen thousand seven hundred were injured and 2,502 were killed. Of those killed a majority were under the age of 30 and were industrial workers; see Hegedüs 1996, pp. 303–5.

17   Marx 1969 [1850], Part 3.

paradox that while Kádár claimed to rule on behalf of the working class, his restoration of 'socialism' hinged on the violent suppression of a revolution driven in large part by workers. In order to consolidate its rule, the Kádár regime pursued a policy of 'social conciliation', which, albeit formally adhering to the institutions of Soviet-style 'socialism', offered (and for a while delivered) material and social improvement to the working class (particularly to the skilled, male, urban workers), and informal compromise on the local level. Chapter 7 explores this argument further by focussing on the contradictions of economic reform, which the Kádár regime embarked upon from the mid-1960s onwards in order to bolster economic performance and thereby maintain the social settlement that had allowed the regime to consolidate its authority in the wake of the 1956 Revolution. Pittaway's rich empirical exposition spans Hungarian economic history and 'workplace politics' from the formation of the Kádár regime in the wake of the 1956 Revolution to its inglorious demise in 1989, illustrating the complex interconnections between the whip of economic reform and working class agency.

As a historian with a voracious appetite to know 'stuff', Pittaway spent much of his time investigating national, regional, and Budapest-based archives – such as those of the now much forgotten old party-state or the trade-union movement. Chapter 8 provides the reader with a succinct exposé of the adventures and pitfalls of doing research on post-1945 history in Hungarian public collections. This short chapter will provide useful insights for anyone intending to undertake any work in Hungarian archives.

Chapter 9 offers a sample of the final research project in which Pittaway was engaged before his premature death, namely, his study of the Austro-Hungarian borderlands. Focussing here on the period between the end of the Second World War and the outbreak of the 1956 Revolution, Pittaway seeks to move beyond an exclusive focus on the 'high' politics of international relations, in which local communities and their residents essentially play a 'passive' role in shaping post-war Austro-Hungarian relations, emphasising instead how 'the reception of the projects of national and international actors at a local level played a central role in their success or failure in constructing legitimate state authority'. Following this argument, Pittaway makes the case that Austria eventually managed to (re)build a state authority, which was considered 'legitimate' by its citizens, whereas Hungary failed. However, Pittaway stresses that this is not due to the inherent superiority of liberal democracy, but rather to the fact that the regime in Vienna managed to 'buil[d] institutions and practices that served to protect local communities in the borderland from a variety of external threats, both real and imagined'. In contrast, the despotism of the emergent Hungarian state not only 'failed to address popular aspirations adequately', hence proving 'unable to build for itself legitimate state authority', but also 'generated real fear outside its borders', which contributed to increasing demands for state protection in those Austrian communities that were Hungary's most proximate neighbours.

From the Vanguard to the Margins: Workers and Post-Soviet Transformation

Shifting to more contemporary events, chapter 10 surveys the trajectory of the Hungarian political economy from 1989 to the present in broad terms. While acknowledging the freedoms – speech, assembly, travel, and the vote – achieved in Hungary and elsewhere in CEE following the 'democratic turn' [*die Wende*] in 1989, Pittaway takes issue with mainstream narratives of the 'transition', according to which archaic economies and closed societies gave way, with the support of Western aid and expertise, to efficient markets and democratic polities. Focussing on Hungary, he paints a dire picture, drawing attention to the country's sluggish economic growth and recurring economic crises, severe poverty, chronically low levels of employment, high levels of indebtedness (private and public), and a conspicuously 'anti-socialist' model of democracy that thrives within the market environment.[18]

As Pittaway notes, one of the conspicuous features of the 'post-socialist' era is the absence of the working class within mainstream academic and political discourse in CEE. According to Pittaway, the reasons for the marginalisation of the working class since 1989 needs to be understood in light of the character of Soviet-style societies, in particular 'the position that workers occupied' within these societies and 'the dynamics of [their] collapse'. Taking issue with critical Marxist assessments of the character of Soviet-style societies, Pittaway defines the regimes that ruled 'Eastern Europe' for over four decades as 'state socialist'. On the basis of this, Pittaway argues that the displacement of the working class 'from the vanguard to the margins' since 1989 is partly due to the fact that 'socialism ended in Hungarian factories and working class communities with a whimper, rather than a bang, as workers concentrated on mitigating the impact of economic crisis on their incomes by working ever longer hours to satisfy material needs, rather than protest'. Another part of the explanation, Pittaway suggests, can be traced to the fact that the working class was 'relatively successfully integrated into the political system under Kádár'.

---

18 For further details of the politico-economic trajectory of post-Soviet CEE transformation economies, see the contributions to Dale 2011, as well as Bohle and Greskovits 2012.

In chapter 11, Pittaway takes up the highly relevant question of Hungarian fascism and national-socialism, and its relationship to the national-Christian conservative Horthy regime, which dominated Hungarian politics during the interwar years. In explaining the historical and social origins of fascist and national-socialist parties in Hungary, Pittaway draws on a combination of social theorists and key texts from the leaders of Hungarian fascist and national-socialist parties in the interwar years, as well as archival material, to cast light on how the explicitly national-socialist Arrow Cross Party (*Nyilaskeresztes Párt*, or NP) eventually rose to power in October 1944. Tracing the roots of Hungarian fascism and the dominant conservative ideology of the interwar years to 'the polarisation of politics that began in the 1890s', Pittaway perceives national-Christian conservatism as a 'counter-revolutionary reaction' to the collapse of the Austro-Hungarian monarchy, institutionalised through the signing of the Treaty of Trianon in 1920. Moreover, there were pressures both *external* – the nascent national projects developing in the countries bordering Hungary – and *internal* – growing polarisation of society along class lines, which culminated in the creation of the brief Hungarian Soviet Republic in 1919 – that followed in the wake of the Treaty. While the Horthy regime that was consolidated in the 1920s was 'institutionally far from fascist', Pittaway identifies and explores three factors that came to be crucial for the later development of fascism and national-socialism: (1) the role of 'counter-revolutionary paramilitarism' within the political system and culture of interwar Hungary; (2) the hegemony of 'anti-liberalism' and 'national-Christian' ideas; and (3) the ideological, political and socio-economic consequences of the Great Depression. In examining the complex interconnections between fascism, national-socialism and national-Christian conservatism in interwar Hungary, Pittaway concludes that the emergence of explicitly fascist and national-socialist parties in the 1930s was made possible through their 'symbiotic relationship to the structures and patterns of social support for the dominant interwar regime'. In a final, evocative note for our current period of crises and monsters, Pittaway warns that although the history of the Hungarian far right and openly fascist movements is complicated, they are 'likely to a have a future'.

Finally, after revisiting the 1956 Revolution in chapter 12 (discussed in detail above), Pittaway's close friend and former supervisor Nigel Swain concludes the collection with an 'Epilogue'.

Mark Pittaway died of heart failure at the age of 39, in London on 3 November 2010. The tragic and premature end to his life was met with sadness and incomprehension by his family, friends and colleagues around the world. Undoubtedly, the Hungarian labour movement and political activists of the left owe a tremendous debt of gratitude to this English historian. While a complete account of Pittaway's contribution to scholarship extends beyond the scope of a single volume, I hope nonetheless that the essays published here provide significant insights into his engagements with labour and the history of post-war and contemporary CEE, and at the same time push these debates forward in new directions.

Adam Fabry
London, 1 November 2012

CHAPTER 1

Crisis, War and Occupation

Most histories of the socialist dictatorships of post-war Eastern Europe begin in 1945, with the end of the Second World War in Europe. Consequently, they focus narrowly on how, in a climate of post-war devastation and reconstruction, Communist parties supported by the Red Army were able to seize power. These histories concentrate on the processes of high politics and neglect the social context in which the dictatorships were formed. However, to place the dictatorships in this social context, it is necessary to recognise, as Jan T. Gross has argued, that 'the Nazi instigated war and the Communist-driven revolution in East Central Europe constituted one integral period'.[1] This broadening of focus entails setting both the wartime and the post-war period in the context of an even longer period in which the societies that came to be ruled as socialist dictatorships in the second half of the twentieth-century constituted, what the Hungarian-born economic historian Iván T. Berend has termed, 'the crisis zone of Europe'.[2]

The outcome of the First World War, and the peace treaties that followed it, remoulded the political map, ending the dominance of multi-national empires like Austria-Hungary over the populations of the region, and either replacing them with 'new' nation states, or reconstructing others and strengthening some of those that had existed in the pre-war years. The new political map of Eastern Europe, however, conformed uneasily at best to the patterns of national, ethnic and linguistic identification across the region. The messiness of this settlement was thrown into sharp relief by the attempts of the nation-builders in the new, reinvented and expanded states to replicate the process of nation-building that had occurred further West during the nineteenth century. This tension was illustrated most starkly in a state like Poland, restored by the post-First World War settlement as an independent state for the first time since the partitions of 1772, 1793 and 1795. In 1921, while Poles – who made up 69.2 percent of the total population in the restored state – were the dominant ethnic group, 14.3 percent declared themselves to be Ukrainians, 7.8 percent were Jewish, 3.9 percent regarded themselves as Byelorussian, and a further

---

* Originally published in Mark Pittaway 2004, *Eastern Europe 1939–2000*, London: Hodder Arnold, pp. 13–34.
1 Gross 1997, p. 34.
2 Berend 1986.

3.9 percent were German. For many of those who advocated Polish independence, like the country's representative at the Paris Peace Conference, Roman Dmowski, Polish nation-building entailed ensuring the political, cultural and economic hegemony of the dominant Polish majority. In expanded Romania, the country's political elite found itself attempting to forge a new state by incorporating a number of diverse territories – previously Austrian-ruled Bukovina, Hungarian-ruled Transylvania, and Russian-ruled Bessarabia – each with their own multiethnic populations. The radical cultural policies employed to do this placed Bucharest on a direct collision course with large sections of the population and regional elites, who often identified with their former governors.[3]

Even the two new, formally, multinational states in the region were riven by similar tensions. Czechoslovakia, probably the most successful interwar state in the region, 'was riven by fault lines of ethnicity'.[4] The attempts of the Prague-based political elite to build a unitary state that rested on a firmly Czechoslovak identity were not only resisted by Slovakia, a junior partner in the project of creating a state for North Slavs, but were also met with the simmering resentment of the country's 3.1 million Germans and 750,000 Magyars. In Yugoslavia, the multinational state of the South Slavs, attempts to create a society based on an all-embracing pan-Yugoslav identity foundered on the persistence of national particularisms among the Croats, Serbs and Slovenes.[5]

The post-First World War settlement not only laid the foundations of internal political conflict around nationality in new states; internationally, it led to the creation of losers who resented the settlement and frequently challenged its legitimacy. Many Germans, furious at the territorial losses mandated by Versailles, provided a social base for revisionist politics in post-war Germany and Austria. Magyars, who attached a notion of Hungary as a one thousand year old kingdom in the heart of Europe, bitterly resented the Treaty of Trianon, which stripped the country of much of its pre-war territory – a resentment that was kept alive by the foreign and cultural policies of the nationalist-conservative interwar regime.[6]

War did not just transform the political landscape of the region; its impact within societies also profoundly subverted hierarchies of class and ethnicity within its states.[7] Social disruption and the transformation of political

---

3 Livezeanu 1995.
4 Sayer 1998, p. 168.
5 Wachtel 1998, pp. 67–127.
6 Várdy 1998, pp. 27–48.
7 Dreisziger 1985, pp. 3–23.

authority produced a revolutionary wave across the region. In Hungary, the frustration of the industrial working class with wartime conditions, and the political collapse of the ruling elite in the face of the fall of the Habsburgs and the Treaty of Trianon, produced a short-lived Soviet Republic – one that alienated the whole of the agrarian population and collapsed in the face of Romanian military intervention, to be replaced by the oligarchic conservative regime of Miklós Horthy. In Bulgaria, the war led to a revolutionary peasant dictatorship that promised a 'third road' between traditional conservative politics and urban socialism. In Bulgaria, as in Hungary, revolution failed in 1923 in the face of a *coup d'état* mounted by the army with the backing of traditional elites.

While the revolutionary governments of Hungary and Bulgaria were exceptional, they were emblematic of a desire on the part of traditionally subordinate groups for both greater participation in politics and an increased share of national wealth.[8] The region's economies were disrupted by war and saddled with the consequences of uneven and peripheral economic development during the pre-war years.[9] The peripheral status of Eastern Europe within the European economy could be seen in the limited impact of industrialisation on the economies and societies of the region. Bohemia and Moravia in the west of Czechoslovakia were the most industrialised parts of the region: 40 percent of those employed worked in industry and trade in 1921, while 31.6 percent worked in agriculture.[10] At the other extreme, some eighty percent of the Albanian population depended on agriculture in 1930.[11] The weakness of the economies of the region was demonstrated during the depression that led to an intensification of the problems of poverty among the rural and, increasingly, much of the urban population.[12]

The tension generated by the clash between state-building projects, ethnic identities, subverted hierarchies of class, and peripheral economic development, formed the backdrop to the retreat of liberal democracy across the region and the apparently inexorable advance of authoritarianism. After the First World War, outside of Hungary where Soviet revolution and violent counter-revolution had led to the creation of Miklós Horthy's conservative-nationalist regime, democratic political systems held sway across the region. By 1938, on the eve of Hitler's violent redrawing of the map of Eastern Europe,

---

8   Király 1983, pp. ix–xv.
9   Radice 1985, pp. 23–65.
10 Teichova 1988, p. 9.
11 Radice 1985, p. 31.
12 Daskalov and Sundhaussen 1999, pp. 123–5; Berend 1998, pp. 253–65.

only Czechoslovakia successfully maintained a democratic system of government. While the retreat of democracy began in the 1920s, with Józef Piłsudski's coup in Poland in May 1926, as well as the rise of royal dictatorships in Albania in 1928, and Yugoslavia the following year, the extinction of democracy in the region occurred during the 1930s.

The retreat of democracy and the rise of authoritarianism, however, was only one of the signs of mounting crisis in the region during the 1930s. The coming to power of the National Socialists in Germany in 1933 threatened to upset the delicate geo-political balance between beneficiaries and losers of the post-First World War settlement. The consolidation and extension of Hitler's power within Germany was met with the politicisation of German minorities within the region's states. This politicisation was most marked in Czechoslovakia where many of the country's 3.1 million Germans had never been fully reconciled to the state; the *Sudetendeutsche Partei* of Konrad Henlein, established with subsidies from Germany, was able to take three of every five German votes in 1935. The politicisation and radicalisation of German minorities, particularly when combined with active political and financial support from Berlin, not only threatened the fragile political balance of power in the region, but also the territorial integrity of some of its states. With Germany's armaments-based recovery after 1933 came increasing German economic penetration of the Eastern European region. Imports from Eastern Europe rose from 9.9 percent of Germany's total in 1933 to 17.7 percent by 1939; over the same period, exports to Eastern Europe increased from 10.7 percent of the German total to 17.7 percent.[13]

The growing influence of National Socialism also fuelled domestic fascism in the countries of Eastern Europe, although this took different forms in different states. In Romania, 'the precariousness and novelty of the democratic institutions; pandemic political corruption; democracy perceived as an urban phenomenon and therefore resented by the proponents of agrarian conservatism; the beleaguered status of ethnic minorities'[14] shaped the social and cultural background of domestic fascism. In neighbouring Hungary, militant opposition to the post-First World War borders institutionalised at Trianon, the political and social marginalisation of many public officials, and growing frustration with the lack of social reform under Horthy, generated similar pressures.[15] These contexts resulted in the formation of distinctive local fascisms. In Romania, domestic fascism was represented by the Iron Guard, which based

---

13   Kaiser 1980, p. 165.
14   Tismaneanu and Pavel 1994, pp. 419–20.
15   Lackó 1966.

its ideology on a mystical nationalism.[16] The Guard's political wing gained 15.58 percent in the 1937 elections, posing a challenge to the established political system – a challenge met by repression on the part of Romania's monarch.[17] In Hungary, the fragmented domestic national-socialist movement crystallised around Ferenc Szálasi's Arrow Cross Party (*Nyilaskeresztes Párt*, or NP). This party would enjoy its finest hour in 1939 in the wake of Hitler's first major steps to remake the political order in Danubian Eastern Europe.[18]

This process began with Hitler's decision to annex Austria in March 1938, which heralded further expansion into Czechoslovakia, where the large German minority, politicised under the influence of both Berlin and the local *Sudetendeutsche Partei*, provided a suitable pretext. The German-speaking areas of the country, the so-called *Sudetenland*, were annexed in October 1938 in the immediate aftermath of the Munich conference where Britain and France had acceded to Hitler's demands that these territories be incorporated into Germany. Thrown into political crisis by both German intervention and the opportunistic decision of Poland to use Hitler's incursion as cover to seize Czechoslovakian Silesia, the multi-national North Slav state survived until March 1939, when it was invaded by Hitler and partitioned.

The Czech parts of the state were transformed into a German protectorate. In the Protectorate of Bohemia and Moravia, as the new entity was known, Germans were given the status of full citizens of the Reich, while Czechs became second-class citizens. Emil Hácha, president of the weakened post-Munich Czechoslovakia, retained a titular position, but real power was held by the Nazi protector, Konstantin von Neurath.[19] In Slovakia, members of the separatist Slovak People's Party (*Hlinkova slovenská ľudová strana*, or HSLS) in co-operation with the Germans, proclaimed an independent Slovak state under the protection of the Reich. Led by Jozef Tiso, the Slovak regime based itself on an authoritarian Catholic ideology, which has led some to characterise the state as representing a 'clerico-fascism'. Its debt to National Socialism could be seen in the power of the paramilitary Hlinka Guard, which represented a centre of power within the new regime.[20] In the new Slovakia, anti-Czech and anti-Semitic sentiment was fused in official propaganda.[21]

---

16 Barbu 1980, pp. 379–94.
17 Hitchins 1994, pp. 418–25.
18 Lackó 1980, pp. 395–400.
19 Mastny 1971, pp. 45–64.
20 Jelinek 1976.
21 Vrzgulová 2000, p. 110.

The impact of Hitler's annexation of Austria and destruction of Czechoslovakia was felt throughout Danubian Eastern Europe. While the dismemberment of Czechoslovakia allowed Hungary to regain territory in both Ruthenia and southern Slovakia, and thus to satisfy, to a limited degree, the domestic appetite for a revision of post-war borders, it created a climate in which the NP was able to mount a serious challenge to the conservative-nationalist regime. The radical right mobilised substantial sections of the urban population in the May 1939 elections, on the basis of hunger for territorial revision and frustration at the lack of social reform inside the country.[22] To defuse the domestic challenge of the NP, which increasingly sought to mobilise industrial workers, the Hungarian political elite pursued a policy of closer links with Germany, as a means of gaining 'lost' territory, to placate the radical right at home. As Romania, alarmed at its loss of Bessarabia to the Soviet Union in 1940, sought closer links with Germany, Hungary was able, with Hitler's support, to secure territorial revision in Transylvania. As a result of the Second Vienna Awards of 1940, the territory was partitioned, with northern Transylvania transferred to Hungary. A large transfer of populations resulted, as two hundred thousand Hungarians left Romanian-ruled southern Transylvania, and a similar number of Romanians departed the Hungarian-ruled territories.[23] The loss of Bessarabia, the enforced transfer of northern Transylvania, and to a lesser extent that of southern Dobrudja demanded by Bulgaria with Hitler's support, created political crisis in Bucharest. In turn, this led to the replacement of the royal dictatorship with that of General Ion Antonescu, whose desire to revise the partition of Transylvania led him to conclude that alliance with Germany was the only viable foreign-policy course for Romania.

The consolidation of German political hegemony over Danubian Eastern Europe combined with economic hegemony. The advent of the Protectorate of Bohemia-Moravia allowed for the exploitation of the industrial plant of the Czech Lands for armaments production, as the German administration of the protectorate integrated the local economy with that of the Reich.[24] Hungary had mandated its own programme for developing heavy industry, in large part to meet demand from Germany, as early as 1938, when it proclaimed the Győr programme that placed the development of armaments and armaments-related production at its heart.[25] The 1930s had seen increasing German economic penetration of Romania's economy, culminating in a 1939

---

22   Pintér 1999, pp. 197–203.
23   Kürti 2001, p. 34.
24   Mastny 1971, pp. 74–80.
25   Berend and Ránki 1958.

trade agreement that effectively sealed the country's integration into a German-dominated economic space.[26] The growing hegemony of Germany could also be seen in the intensification of anti-Semitic legislation across Danubian Eastern Europe. Romania purged its civil service of Jews in 1940 as a prelude to further anti-Semitic legislation.[27] In Hungary, radical anti-Semitic legislation had been passed in 1938 and 1939, which severely restricted the political and economic rights of the Hungarian Jewry and heralded further restrictive measures during the war years.[28]

The remaking of the political, economic and social orders of Danubian Eastern Europe was, however, only the beginning. Germany's invasion of Poland in September 1939 was the precursor to more radical attempts to reshape the societies of the region. The attack on Poland by the Germans was joined by the Red Army who incorporated eastern Poland into the Soviet Union;[29] western and central Poland fell under Nazi occupation. In contrast to the earlier dismemberment of Czechoslovakia, as Hitler's renowned biographer Ian Kershaw has pointed out, the invasion of Poland 'was imperialist conquest, not revisionism'.[30] Poland was transformed into a laboratory for National Socialist attempts to shape, what Hitler termed, 'a new ethnographic order'[31] in the Eastern European region. A swathe of western Poland was incorporated into the Reich, extending the administrative border of Germany almost as far as Warsaw. The Nazi-administrative units [*Gaue*] of the Wartheland and West Prussia-Danzig were carved out of this annexed territory. These territories were marked for 'Germanisation', a euphemism for the mass expulsion of the Polish and Jewish populations in order to make way for the resettlement of ethnic Germans from the Baltic states and the South Tyrol.[32] While in West Prussia-Danzig the authorities sought to achieve the goals of 'Germanisation' through actively seeking the incorporation of Poles into the assimilated German population, in the Wartheland, which centred on the industrial city of Łódź, as the region's Nazi rulers pursued policies of discrimination and deportation towards Poles.[33] In the year following the invasion of Poland, it has been estimated that around four hundred thousand people were deported from the

---

26   Turnock 1986, pp. 59–60.
27   Hitchins 1994, p. 483.
28   Don 1997, pp. 47–76.
29   Gross 1988.
30   Kershaw 2000, p. 239.
31   Aly and Heim 2002, p. 73.
32   Aly 1999, pp. 33–58.
33   Kershaw 2000, pp. 250–2.

annexed western territories.³⁴ In the violent remaking of 'the ethnographic order' in the Wartheland, the origins of later mass genocide can be discerned. The murder of psychiatric patients in Polish port cities in October 1939 to clear space in order to temporarily house German settlers was both an extension of policies of euthanasia practised inside the Reich, and a precursor to extensive genocide to follow.³⁵ The racist policies employed in Wartheland towards the large urban Jewish population, particularly in Łódź, culminated in the closure of the city's ghetto in April 1940, creating 'a sweatshop writ large'.³⁶

While western Poland underwent 'Germanisation', central Poland formed the area under the control of 'the Generalgouvernement' under its Nazi-governor Hans Frank. The population bore the brunt of the National Socialists' anti-Polish and anti-Jewish policies. As early as October 1939, Hitler warned that governing Poland would entail 'a hard ethnic struggle that will not permit any legal restrictions'.³⁷ The Nazis sought to destroy the cultural infrastructure of the Polish nation by targeting its intellectuals. This policy was heralded by the closure of Krakow's higher education institutions in November 1939, and the deportation of 183 of their staff to concentration camps.³⁸ Minus its intelligentsia, Poland was to be transformed into a source of cheap labour for the factories of the Reich. In October 1939, the authorities in the *Generalgouvernement* introduced the obligation to work for all Poles between the ages of fourteen and sixty (and all Jews aged between twelve and sixty). This measure underpinned plans to export large quantities of Polish labour to Germany; indeed, by 1944 between 1.3 and 1.5 million Poles (from a total population of 15 million) had gone to work in Germany.³⁹ In terms of economic policy, the *Generalgouvernement*'s Nazi rulers envisaged its total deindustrialisation. In 1940, Hans Frank stated that 'we shall take away from this land all the valuable machinery, dismantle all the valuable factories, destroy, if possible, all its valuable communication lines'.⁴⁰ However, due to the needs of the German war economy, this policy was never completely implemented, and, indeed, following Barbarossa in June 1941, the policy was partially reversed. Nevertheless, German policies had an impact that was both immediate and catastrophic. It has been estimated that industrial production in the *Generalgouvernement* in

---

34 Paczkowski 1997, p. 25.
35 Aly 1999, p. 37.
36 Burleigh 2001, pp. 593–4.
37 Quoted in Kershaw 2000, p. 245.
38 Paczkowski 1997, p. 26.
39 Gross 1979, p. 78.
40 Quoted in Landau and Tomaszewski 1985, p. 157.

1940 stood at 30 percent of its level prior to the war, and even though it recovered under the pressures generated by the war in the East, it never surpassed 80 percent of its pre-war total.[41] Agriculture was to be bled dry, as Polish peasants faced the compulsory requisitioning of their production in the interest of feeding the Reich.[42]

The effects of Nazi rule on living standards within the *Generalgouvernment* were catastrophic. Unofficial estimates suggested that in 1940–41 the real incomes of ordinary Poles stood at less than forty percent of their 1938 level.[43] Inadequate rations and low standards of living forced many urban residents to rely on a burgeoning and increasingly expensive black market. In the industrial town of Radom in November 1941, black market bread was twenty-five times the price residents had paid in 1939.[44] A sharp increase in the level of repression combined with growing economic impoverishment.[45] The degree of violence against the population accelerated as the war progressed; in 1942 alone, according to one estimate, a total of seven thousand non-Jewish Poles alone were murdered by the Nazi authorities.[46] Poverty and repression engendered resistance, which in turn was fuelled by the fact that the occupation authorities completely ignored the need to legitimate their rule among the subject population. Resistance snowballed, shaping an 'underground' society able, to some extent, to circumvent the mechanisms of Nazi rule, developing an organisation, a press and eventually a military organisation in the form of the Home Army.[47]

Yet it was Poland's Jews who were the greatest victims of the policies pursued by the Nazis in the *Generalgouvernment*. Poland was a laboratory for the radical anti-Jewish policies that culminated in the 'Final Solution'. The invasion of the country in 1939 led to an acceleration of the genocidal logic of the National Socialist regime, as Jews were deported *en masse* from the territories annexed by the Reich, and attempts to create a 'reservation' for deported Jews in southeastern Poland foundered. Many were expelled into the *Generalgouvernment* and others were locked into closed ghettos across urban Poland in appalling conditions: 2.4 percent of the area of the Polish capital

---

41 Radice 1986, p. 431.
42 Landau and Tomaszewski 1985, p. 164.
43 Gross 1979, pp. 97–8.
44 Radice 1986, p. 396.
45 Coutovidis and Reynolds 1986, p. 37.
46 Paczkowski 1997, p. 26.
47 Gross 1979, pp. 213–58.

came to house 30 percent of its population.[48] These measures were envisaged as temporary, as the Nazi leadership searched for a 'final solution' to its 'Jewish problem'. It took the launch of Barbarossa in 1941, and the marked radicalisation of Nazi policies that war in the East brought with it, to begin the extermination of the Jewish population that would take place largely on Polish soil.

The experience of shaping Hitler's 'new ethnographic order' in Poland led to a radicalisation of Nazi policy elsewhere. In the Protectorate of Bohemia-Moravia, Reinhard Heydrich was appointed acting Reich Protector in September 1941, ostensibly with a brief to break Czech resistance to German rule. Heydrich had been a key figure in Nazi attempts to implement Hitler's 'new ethnographic order' in Poland, and his appointment heralded a radicalisation of Berlin's approach to the Czech lands. He tightened German political control over the Protectorate, intensified repression against the Czech resistance and moved to deport Jews.[49] Heydrich combined this with a drive to Germanise fifty percent of the Czech population and to deport the rest, linking this with broader policies to reshape the map of Eastern Europe: '[t]he future of the Reich after the war's end depends on the ability of the Reich and the ability of the people of Reich to meld these newly acquired areas into the Reich'.[50] Heydrich's own rule was short-lived: he was assassinated by Czechs flown in from London by the Special Operations Executive in May 1942. Reprisals were ruthless. The villages of Lidice and Ležáky were destroyed in retaliation, thus fuelling opposition to Nazi rule among the Czech population. Yet, while Heydrich's policies bore the influence of the drive to shape 'a new ethnographic order' that had been pioneered in Poland, Nazi rule in Bohemia-Moravia was immeasurably less destructive than that further north. Hans Frank, Governor of the *Generalgouvernment*, had commented on this while on a visit to Prague in 1940: '[t]here were large red posters in Prague announcing that today seven Czechs had been shot. I said to myself: if I wanted to hang a poster for every seven Poles that were shot, then all the forests of Poland would not suffice in order to produce the paper necessary for such posters'.[51] Repression and arbitrary violence never reached the levels experienced in the *Generalgouvernment* even after Heydrich's assassination. Furthermore, the Nazi authorities in the Protectorate did not seek to pursue the kind of scorched earth policies against Czech industry that were envisaged, if not fully implemented, in Poland. Industry was central to armaments production. After the

---

48   Burleigh 2001, p. 587.
49   Mastny 1971, pp. 184–94.
50   Quoted in Bryant 2002, p. 692.
51   Quoted in Connelly 1999, p. 8.

creation of the Protectorate, the sector was rationalised and the two major arms companies, Československá Zbrojova Brno, the Škoda works and its subsidiaries, were incorporated into the Herman Göring Werke and forced to reorient their production to meet the demands of the German military.[52] The centrality of industry in the Protectorate to the German war effort ensured that the living standards of Czech workers were protected for the first half of the war, despite large increases in the cost of living.[53]

German incursion into south-eastern Europe came on the eve of Barbarossa, brought about by a coup in Yugoslavia in March 1941 launched by officers in the army and the air force who were concerned at the country's drift into the arms of Germany. Hitler's reaction was swift, launching a brutal air assault on Belgrade on 6 April in which up to twenty thousand of the city's residents died. Germany's lightning campaign smashed the country's armed forces, bringing about an unconditional surrender a mere eleven days after the first attack on Belgrade. Following their victory, the Germans set about dismembering the Yugoslav state.

Two-thirds of the territory of Slovenia was incorporated into the Reich and merged into the Nazi *Gaue* of Carinthia and Styria, while Istria was awarded to Italy and a small corner of the north-east of the territory to Hungary. Within dismembered Slovenia the Germans pursued policies that were reminiscent of the attempts of the Nazis to create their 'new ethnographic order' in Poland by expelling Slovenes and replacing them with ethnic Germans transferred from Italian-occupied Slovenia and German-occupied Serbia.[54] The Italians were less harsh, at least prior to the outbreak of widespread partisan activity.[55] The extent of their conquest was not limited to Istria; most of the Dalmatian coast was incorporated into Italy, and ruled, like Istria, in a manner that respected the distinctive nature of the region.[56] Montenegro became an Italian protectorate, extending the power-base in south-eastern Europe it had gained two years previously when it invaded Albania in April 1939. Italy deposed the country's monarch, King Zog, and replaced him with a pro-Italian regime. In December 1941, it tightened its control over the country when it forced Albania to accept the Italian King as its new head of state.[57]

---

52 Hauner 1986, pp. 80–1.
53 Mastny 1971, pp. 80–2.
54 Radice 1986, pp. 320–1.
55 Rogel 1997, p. 18.
56 Pavolwitch 1971, p. 109.
57 Vickers 1999, p. 139.

The dismemberment of Yugoslavia brought Bulgaria directly into the war on the German side. For its co-operation Bulgaria gained Macedonia, long-disputed between Bulgaria and Yugoslavia and (prior to the existence of the multinational Slav state) with Serbia. Serbs and Bulgarians had fought over the ethnic identity of the inhabitants of Macedonia, each claiming that the population was either Serb or Bulgarian. Bulgaria ruled the state as an occupied territory, adopting a radical agenda of Bulgarianising the territory – an agenda that would have important implications for defining Macedonia's place in the second Yugoslavia.[58] The annexation of Macedonia brought Bulgaria into direct military confrontation in Yugoslavia, generating internal political difficulties for the pro-German regime.

Croatia was divided into Italian and German zones of military influence, but the occupying authorities sponsored the established of an independent Croatian state – the *Nezavisna Država Hrvatska* (NDH) – under the leadership of the fascist *Ustaša* and its leader Ante Pavelić. A violent and extreme nationalist organisation, the *Ustaša* had suffered from political persecution under the royal dictatorship of the 1930s. While its leaders had spent the period in exile in Italy, many of its activists filled Yugoslavia's jails.[59] The installation of Pavelić led to the creation of a violent dictatorship that ruled deploying an extreme variant of National Socialism as its ideology. The new regime crushed political opposition and rounded up perceived enemies by mandating the death penalty for infractions committed 'against the honour and interests of the Croatian nation'.[60] Despite the dictatorial nature of the new regime, it was greeted with enthusiasm by many Croats, and received support from large sections of the local Catholic clergy, if not from the Vatican. The Archbishop of Zagreb, Alojzije Stepinac, proclaimed at the beginning of Pavelić's rule that 'we are convinced and expect that the Church in the resurrected state of Croatia will be able to proclaim in complete freedom the incontestable principles of truth and justice'.[61]

Such support was unfortunate, especially given the genocidal nature of the *Ustaša* regime. The dictatorship moved quickly and enthusiastically against the Jewish population on its territory, passing anti-Semitic legislation on the day after the unconditional surrender of the Yugoslav army, and began to intern Jews in June 1941.[62] Yet it was in its attempts to shape its own local

---

58 Troebst 1997, pp. 244–5.
59 Djilas 1991, p. 110.
60 Glenny 1999, p. 499.
61 Quoted in Tanner 1997, p. 145.
62 Malcom 1994, p. 175.

version of Hitler's 'new ethnographic order' on its territory of Croatia and Bosnia that the Pavelić regime gained a distinctive reputation for brutality. The territory of the NDH was a multi-ethnic patchwork – of a total population of 6.3 million, 1.9 million were Serbs. The Serbian population of the NDH were targeted by *Ustaša* attempts to transform the territory into a 'pure Croatian nation'. In the words of one leading *Ustaša* figure: 'there is no method we would hesitate to use in order to make it truly Croatian and cleanse it of Serbs'.[63] The aim of eliminating the Serb population of the NDH was pursued through a variety of means. Zagreb concluded an agreement (later suspended) with the German occupation authorities to deport Serbs living in the NDH to Serbia – around three hundred thousand had either been deported or had fled *Ustaša*-rule by 1945.[64] The regime initiated a campaign to ensure the mass conversion of Serbs to Catholicism in order to integrate them into 'the Croatian nation'. This campaign was violent and frequently accompanied by atrocities. Furthermore, the regime and its supporters relied on 'terrorist' methods against the Serb population, mobilising *Ustaša* militants to attack Serb villages, massacring the population and then destroying the village.[65] Others were rounded up and interned in the network of *Ustaša* concentration camps, the most notorious of which was at Jasenovac, south-east of Zagreb. Attempts to estimate the extent of *Ustaša* genocide have been mired in historical controversy, generated both by the lack of documentation – in itself a legacy of its extreme and random nature – and the subsequent politicisation of the subject.

The vast majority of Serbia fell under German occupation, and was placed for the first few months of that occupation under direct military administration. The collaborationist administration, led by a former Yugoslav-army General Milan Nedić, established in August 1941, was weak. Its own internal security forces – the State Guard, made up of a small number of former Gendarmes – was supplemented by a paramilitary organisation recruited from among Serb fascists.[66]

While, like Poland, Yugoslav society engaged in broad resistance to the new political order imposed on it, what made the South Slav territories unique was the breadth of partisan activity in the face of the collapse of the interwar political order. Partisan activity was triggered initially by the rapidity of the Yugoslav army's collapse as many soldiers abandoned their arms, deserted or simply made for the hills in the face of the German advance across the country.

---

63   Quoted in Djilas 1991, p. 120.
64   Tanner 1997, p. 151.
65   Djilas 1991, pp. 120–1.
66   Pavlowitch 1971, p. 115.

Furthermore, the tenuous hold of the occupation authorities on rural areas created a power vacuum as the Yugoslav state collapsed. In Italian-occupied Istria during the year after occupation, partisan activity in rural areas spread.[67] The moves by the Italian authorities to establish a puppet government in Montenegro provoked an uprising of the former army officers holed up in the mountainous countryside; Montenegro was to form a centre of partisan activity until Italy's withdrawal in 1943. Partisan conflict in the areas annexed by Italy provoked a draconian response, as the Italians interned men across their territories in camps like Rab on the Adriatic coast. According to some estimates, by 1943 internment camps held around fifty thousand inmates.[68] This draconian response only served to increase the intensity of partisan activity along the Adriatic coast. Across Croatia, Hercegovina and Bosnia the genocidal policies of the *Ustaša* regime in Zagreb fuelled partisan activity among Serbs; in Bosnia it frequently led to violence between Serbs, Croats and the Bosnian Muslims, whose position *vis-à-vis* the NDH was ambiguous.[69] In other ethnically mixed regions, such as the Sandžak region of southern Serbia, partisan activity degenerated into internecine ethnic strife, here between Serbs and the local Muslim population.[70]

Principal partisan activity was directed either by the Communists under Josip Broz Tito or the Serbian non-Communist resistance, known as *Četniks*, under the former Yugoslav army officer Draža Mihailović. Partisan activity, by both groups, was at its strongest in western Serbia under German occupation, resulting in ferocious reprisals from the occupying forces. Nevertheless, the Communists were the most militant of the two groups, and little love was lost between them. The Communists were driven out of Serbia in early 1942, re-establishing their headquarters in the Bosnian town of Foča soon afterwards. Embroiled in a three-cornered conflict with local Serbs and the *Ustaša* in Bosnia, the Communists profited by gaining a huge swathe of territory in the region due to the effectiveness of their organisation, the desperate opposition of local Serbs to Croatian genocide, and their advocacy of ethnic co-existence to a population tired of internecine strife. However, these gains were temporary, as the partisans fought a cat-and-mouse game with the Italian and German occupation forces. The eventual withdrawal of the Italians from the war in September 1943 led to German occupation of the whole territory; it also immeasurably strengthened the influence of Tito's partisans across Bosnia,

---

67   Winner 1971, pp. 46–7.
68   Walston 1997, p. 176.
69   Malcom 1994, pp. 178–83.
70   Pavlowitch 1971, p. 128.

Croatia and Slovenia. In Serbia, Mihailović and his supporters dominated the armed opposition – a situation that would remain until the Red Army advanced into the region a year later.

The political fate of the whole of the region would be decided by the outcome of Hitler's war with the Soviet Union. As German troops swept eastwards, the impact of war was felt by the societies of those parts of the region directly occupied by the Reich through the deportation and mass extermination of their Jewish populations, as Poland's ghettos were liquidated during 1942 and 1943. In Bohemia-Moravia, measures to force Jews into ghettos as a prelude to their deportation and extermination began in 1942. Even those areas not directly occupied by Germany came under pressure to deport their Jewish populations in the interests of the Nazis' 'final solution'. In Slovakia, Jews were forcibly deported in 1942, leaving for the camps with their allowance of only seventy-five pounds of baggage per person.[71]

With the turn of the course of the war during 1942 and 1943, as Hitler's advance into the Soviet Union was checked and rebuffed, the strains of waging the war were felt in the societies of the region. In the Protectorate of Bohemia-Moravia, policies towards labour became more despotic, with the lengthening of the working week and forced measures to expand the workforce.[72] In Hungary, industrial expansion had occurred in order to feed the demands of the Nazi war machine – consequently, employment in industry rose from 330,048 in 1938 to 451,032 in 1942. As war rumbled on, policies in the workplace became increasingly despotic, and labour shortages were filled with the increased employment of forced labour.[73] War led to a burgeoning black market and high inflation as the attempts of the state to supply the urban population with food through coercive measures failed.[74] In Bulgaria, these problems had led to spiralling inflation during the first half of the 1940s.[75]

The growing strains on living standards, combined with a growing realisation among the population of eventual German defeat, produced both frustration with and active opposition to Hitler's 'new' order in the region. In the Protectorate of Bohemia-Moravia in 1944, according to one of the small minority who took part in active resistance, 'everyone is united in hatred of the Germans'.[76] While society was gripped by an intense nostalgia for the

---

71 Jelinek 1976, p. 91.
72 Myant 1981, p. 27.
73 Berend 1993, pp. 151–68.
74 Erdmann 1992, pp. 7–13.
75 Lampe 1986, pp. 114–15.
76 Quoted in Bryant 2002, p. 697.

Czechoslovak state, few were prepared to engage in anything more than small-scale individual acts of resistance.[77] Poland's own resistance movement was growing. In March 1943, the Home Army – the military wing of the underground – was estimated to have a membership of around three hundred thousand.[78]

Outside those areas formally occupied by Germany, in territories that were allied to Berlin, both fear of the consequences of Soviet victory and weariness with the social impact of the war resulted in political mobilisation against it by 1943. While the Tiso regime in Slovakia would not be shaken until the Slovak uprising of August 1944, limited partisan activity began in the country's mountainous regions early in 1943.[79] In Hungary, wartime industrialisation, both peasant and worker discontent, and a growing feeling that the war was lost, produced increased support for the labour movement and political parties – such as the Social Democrats (*Magyarországi Szociáldemokrata Párt*, or MSZDP) and the Independent Smallholders' Party (*Független Kisgazdapárt*, or FKGP) – that advocated a more democratic society.[80] For Romania, military disaster at the hands of the Soviets in the Crimea in 1943 likewise strengthened those political actors who had opposed the war.[81] Bulgaria's proximity to Yugoslavia and to the approaching Red Army stimulated partisan activity on its territory. According to some estimates, as many as eighteen thousand participated.[82]

The advance of the Red Army provoked panic among Hitler's East European allies, and some – most notably Romania and Hungary – sought to extricate themselves from the war. In the Romanian case, while General Antonescu's regime continued to fight on the German side, political groups opposed to the war conducted secret negotiations with the Allies to extricate the country from the conflict from the end of 1943. Antonescu's refusal to accept allied terms, and the growing advances into Romanian territory made by the Soviets in 1944, provoked a growing political crisis. Opponents of the war, together with King Michael, mounted a royal coup in the face of imminent military defeat on 23 August, effectively pulling Romania out of the war.[83] Hungary's attempts to negotiate its way out of the war resulted in disaster, as Hitler launched a

---

77   Myant 1981, pp. 28–9.
78   Coutovidis and Reynolds 1986, p. 84.
79   Jelinek 1976, p. 125.
80   Sipos 1988, pp. 209–309.
81   Hitchins 1994, pp. 490–1.
82   Crampton 1987, p. 129.
83   Hitchins 1994, pp. 493–500.

pre-emptive strike by occupying the country in March 1944 and installing the country's radical right-wing ambassador to Berlin, Döme Sztójay, as Prime Minister. Horthy was removed in October and replaced by a national-socialist puppet regime headed by the NP and its leader Ferenc Szálasi. In the last nine months of 1944, an estimated 569,505 of Hungary's 700,000 Jews were murdered as the 'final solution' was implemented in the country. The rest of the population found the country plunged into destructive conflict as Szálasi and the German occupying forces chose to fight to the last.[84] In Slovakia, political upheaval elsewhere undermined support for the Tiso regime. This enabled the Slovak Communists and the non-Communist opposition to form an alliance with elements within the Slovak army. This formed the basis of a short-lived uprising led by partisans in August 1944, which led to the German occupation and reorganisation of the Slovak state.[85]

To the north of Slovakia, the Red Army crossed the eastern border of interwar Poland in June 1944. This was to lead to conflict not only with the country's German occupiers, but also between the Red Army's domestic communist clients who had organised themselves into the Polish Workers' Party (*Polska Partia Robotnicza*, or PPR) in January 1942, and the Home Army, which sought a return of Poland's government-in-exile, based in London. With the 'liberation' of the city of Lublin, the PPR staked its claim to lead post-war Poland, setting up a Committee of National Liberation – an alternative Soviet-backed government.[86] Faced with the prospect of a Communist-dominated government in post-war Poland rather than the return of the London-based government-in-exile, the Home Army attempted to seize the initiative. On 31 July, in the face of Red Army advance, the Home Army led an uprising in Warsaw, anticipating taking the capital as the Germans were beaten back by the Red Army. The uprising failed and the Red Army advance was stopped in its tracks by the Germans, while Stalin failed to provide air support or arms to the uprising – preferring instead that the London government take no credit for the 'liberation' of Poland. The uprising was brutally crushed by Germans. Warsaw was finally 'liberated' by the Red Army on 12 January 1945, but this was not to end the bitter political contest over Poland's future. In Bulgaria, Soviet advance and almost-total Bulgarian capitulation brought swift political change, with a transfer of power to a Fatherland Front government in September 1944. Red Army advance into Bulgaria and Romania strengthened Tito's partisans in Serbia, where they had previously been weak. As the Soviets

---

84   Eby 1998; Braham 2000, p. 153.
85   Jelinek 1976, pp. 125–31.
86   Coutovidis and Reynolds 1986, pp. 113–69.

swept through Hungary, installing a provisional government formed by the Hungarian Communist Party (*Magyar Kommunista Párt*, or MKP) and other democratic parties, German rule in Yugoslavia collapsed, leaving the partisans to sweep away its remnants. Tito's influence ensured the victory of Communist partisans in Albania under Enver Hoxha. The Soviet advance led to the setting up of a new government for a reconstituted Czechoslovakia in the Slovak city of Košice. As Bohemia was liberated by American forces, Soviet troops swept westward taking Prague in the midst of an uprising of the city's population against their Nazi occupiers.

The creation of a new political order to replace the defeated Nazi one was accompanied with enormous political violence across the region. This violence was committed by both retreating German troops and advancing Soviet ones. The most dramatic single German atrocity committed during their retreat was the manner in which they suppressed the Warsaw uprising in 1944. They executed forty thousand people, while two hundred thousand died in the battle in which the Germans reoccupied the city, which in turn destroyed eighty percent of the city's buildings.[87] In the chaos of German-occupied, Arrow Cross-ruled Budapest, prior to the advent of Red Army siege of the city in December 1944, the authorities massacred Jews, rounded up political opponents and sought to dismantle factories to carry them west in a dramatic scorched earth policy.[88] While Red Army atrocities towards the civilian population were less spectacular, brutality was nevertheless extensive. Rape was widely employed as a weapon of war right across the region by its new occupiers. Its extent in Budapest during the first months of 1945 has been particularly well documented.[89] The Soviets, fearful of guerrilla resistance as they advanced, deported large numbers of male civilians. In Transylvania, their measures targeted the ethnic German population whom they regarded as a potential fifth column. According to some estimates, almost one hundred thousand males were deported from Transylvania by the Soviets in early 1945, from a total ethnic German population of just over half a million.[90] In Hungary, measures to deport those 'with German names' resulted in the indiscriminate rounding up and deportation by the Red Army of thousands of male civilians in the first months of 1945.[91] Yugoslav partisans were also guilty of atrocities, as the remnants of the Croatian army with a huge number of civilians in tow attempted

---

87   Burleigh 2001, pp. 754–5.
88   Pittaway 2002, p. 21.
89   Pető 1999, pp. 892–913.
90   Biddiscombe 1993, pp. 210–11.
91   Zielbauer 1992, pp. 270–91.

to cross into Austria at Bleiberg in May 1945. Turned back and handed over to the partisans, tens of thousands were simply massacred at the border.[92]

Yet violence was not merely perpetrated by military forces against a passive civilian population at the end of the war. Parts of that civilian population actively participated in widespread violence. This was particularly marked where Nazi policies had sought to remake the pre-existing ethnic composition of a territory to the advantage of Germans. In these areas, previously subjected populations exacted retribution, directing it against ethnic Germans. In Poland, as the Red Army pushed west, Polish resistance groups began a process of 'wild expulsion' of the ethnic German population. Fighters in the second Polish army were determined to 'treat the Germans in the way that they have treated us'.[93] It was not just fighters who terrorised German populations, but in many cases ordinary Poles. In August 1945, according to local representatives of the Red Army, 'not only does the plundering of the Germans on the part of the Poles not stop, but it gets stronger all the time. There are more and more frequent cases of unprovoked murders of German inhabitants'.[94] This 'wild expulsion' was replicated in the former Protectorate of Bohemia-Moravia, just as it was being reincorporated into a resurrected Czechoslovakia. Probably the most notorious incident in this process was the forced expulsion on foot of twenty thousand Germans from the city of Brno by the new rulers of the Moravian capital.[95] In Istria, as early as 1943 when the Italians withdrew, the Yugoslav partisans pursued a policy of retribution against the Italian population, which heralded eleven years of sustained population transfer.[96] Even in areas like annexed Vardar Macedonia, where ethnic identities were both more fluid and ambiguous than further north-west, reaction to the Bulgarianising policies of the occupiers underpinned political violence against sections of the population perceived to be perpetrators (although far more unevenly than in Poland or Czechoslovakia).[97]

Retribution on the part of previously subjected populations against those associated with the policies of former occupiers was one of the stimulants to enormous movements of people at the end of the Second World War. During late 1944 and 1945, millions of people were on the move across the region. The victims of 'wild transfer' in Poland and Czechoslovakia fled west, those who

---

92 Völkl 1991, pp. 366–70.
93 Ther 1998, p. 55.
94 Quoted in Naimark 2001, p. 127.
95 Glassheim 2000, pp. 475–7.
96 Ballinger 2003, p. 193.
97 Brown 2003, pp. 119–22.

had worked as foreign labour in Germany's industries returned home, the inmates of camps – both Jewish survivors of the 'final solution' and prisoners-of-war – tried to return home.[98] Holocaust survivors invariably found themselves unwelcome in their former hometowns. Anti-Semitism across the region and the harsh post-war economic climate contributed to localised anti-Semitic violence most notoriously at Kielce in Poland and Kunmadaras in Hungary in 1946.[99] Shifts of population were exacerbated by the flight of collaborators and traditional elites in the face of Red Army advance. In the Hungarian town of Szolnok, one observer watched 'the whole of the lordly population of the lands east of the river Tisza' queue to cross the river at the bridge in the town to escape the Soviets in late 1944.[100] The flight of traditional elites resulted in a shift of power to previously subordinate groups. In Czechoslovakia, land seizures by the rural poor and the democratisation of factory administration through the institutionalisation of workers' councils accompanied the Soviet advance – a pattern replicated in Hungary.[101]

The social revolution initiated by war took place against a background of almost complete economic penury across the region. War left the whole of the region economically devastated. Agriculture, industry and infrastructure alike suffered tremendous damage. With cities like Warsaw flattened and the industrial sector across the region ruined, the population was faced with a formidable task.[102] Poor agricultural production in Polish Lower Silesia contributed to desperate poverty, a burgeoning black market and galloping inflation – starvation in 1945 and 1946 was avoided, but the situation resulted 'in widespread malnutrition'.[103] In post-'liberation' Budapest, one factory in the heavy engineering sector could only guarantee food of a calorific value of 35 percent of what they estimated was needed by a manual worker.[104] In Romania, war and Red Army occupation had brought considerable destruction in agriculture, while the unstable political situation had led peasants to hoard grain. This led one American diplomat in Bucharest to note 'a critically short supply' of basic foodstuffs for the urban population in summer 1945.[105]

---

98   Radice 1986, p. 496.
99   Naimark 2001, p. 132; Apor 1998, pp. 601–32.
100 Márkus 1991, p. 87.
101 Bloomfield 1979, pp. 66–7; Pittaway 2002, pp. 18–25.
102 Berend 1996, p. 6.
103 Siebel-Achenbach 1994, p. 179.
104 Pittaway 2002, p. 26.
105 Berry 2000, p. 168.

Alongside widespread violence, mass movements of population, the revolutionary subversion of pre-existing social hierarchies and economic devastation must be set the enormous human cost paid by the societies of the region as a result of the war. According to estimates presented by the historian Bradley F. Abrams, Eastern Europe lost around ten percent of its population during the Second World War, ranging from the 6 million Polish and 1.5 million Yugoslav deaths at one extreme to the relatively small proportionate losses of around 0.5 percent in Bulgaria.[106] This enormous human tally shaped the societies of the region for decades to come. The social dynamics of war, occupation and 'liberation', furthermore, set the context for the politics of the region, defining the social context in which the region's new rulers sought to construct their new socialist political order.

---

106   Abrams 2002, p. 631.

CHAPTER 2

Building Socialism

War wrought economic and human devastation on an unprecedented scale, but it also acted as the midwife of political transformation across Eastern Europe. The nature and direction of this transformation was not immediately clear. The new Soviet occupation forces and their Communist allies proclaimed something they termed 'peoples' democracy' in 1944 and 1945. Until the late 1940s the region (with the exception of Yugoslavia and Albania) found itself in a state of political transition. For most of the region, single-party socialist dictatorship did not emerge until the period between 1947 and 1949. Despite the deployment of considerable repression by the state after 1949, the single-party dictatorships found it difficult to generate circumstances of political stability given the limited nature of the legitimacy on which their rule rested and considerable economic failures, which had become painfully apparent by the mid-1950s. While economic failure stemmed from the radicalism of policies of forced industrialisation and collectivisation that impoverished populations, limited legitimacy had different roots. It stemmed from the way in which Eastern Europe's new rulers attempted to govern post-war society in the region.

The Soviets' policy of initially installing broad anti-fascist coalitions to power across the region, in which the local Communist Party was *primus inter pares*, was rooted in the approach of Communist parties internationally to the threat of fascism. From the mid-1930s onwards, Communist parties across the continent abandoned the strategies of revolutionary sectarianism that had pushed them towards isolation. The shift in policy had been mandated by the *Comintern* (the international organisation of Communist parties) in Moscow due to Stalin's increasing fear of fascism in general, and Germany's National Socialist regime in particular. This shift resulted in Communist parties adopting a 'popular front' approach of unity with all 'anti-fascist' parties. While during the 1930s this included only other left-wing parties, the ideological formula did not explicitly exclude cooperation with some groups on the bourgeois right. While this policy was temporarily abandoned in the face of the Molotov-Ribbentrop pact in 1939, it was renewed with a vengeance following Hitler's invasion of the Soviet Union in 1941. Communist parties were to subordinate

---

* Originally published in Mark Pittaway 2004, *Eastern Europe 1939–2000*, London: Arnold Hodder, pp. 35–62.

revolutionary goals to those of defeating fascism, and thus advocated collaboration with all anti-fascist forces in each country. Georgi Dimitrov, then secretary general of the Executive Committee of the *Comintern*, stated clearly what this shift would mean: 'In Czechoslovakia, we earlier classified Beneš [the pre-war President of Czechoslovakia] as an agent of English imperialism. Now the fire has to be directed against traitors like Hácha'.[1]

As the Red Army occupied Eastern Europe, this policy of cooperation had to be translated into an ideological formula, which would enable Communist parties to govern in broad anti-fascist coalitions. For parties that had argued for the revolutionary transformation of the existing order, this was a difficult manoeuvre to undertake. The concept fashioned was that of the 'peoples' democracy' – a state that rested on a definition of democracy that relied on social equality as much as, if not more than, Western concepts of representative government or a state based on the rule of law. Dimitrov, installed as secretary of the Bulgarian Communist Party, argued in September 1946 that 'Bulgaria will not be a Soviet republic but a people's republic in which the functions of government will be performed by an enormous majority of the people – workers, peasants, craftsmen, and the people's intelligentsia. In this republic there will be no dictatorship of any kind'.[2] His Hungarian counterpart, Mátyás Rákosi, used the term 'new democracy' and defined it through the need to effect radical changes in the balance of class power in Hungarian society. In the villages, 'the acid test of the new democracy is the land question. He who does not want to see land given to the peasants, who wants to retain the system of great estates, is an enemy of Hungarian democracy'. For industrial communities, 'the basic demand of Hungarian democracy is the immediate abolition of any obstacle to the full economic and political realisation of the power of the working class'.[3] This tension between the need for a broad coalition on the one hand, and social radicalism on the other, would dog Communist parties in implementing popular front policies in the region.

Popular front policies based on notions of broad coalitions of all 'anti-fascist forces' were unevenly implemented across the region. This approach was taken least seriously in south-eastern Europe where Communists had taken power through military victory in partisan struggle. In Albania, the Communists under Enver Hoxha governed through a Democratic Front, which maintained the pretence of unifying the Communists and other anti-fascist forces – at least until the Front's 93 percent victory in the rigged elections of

---

1 Quoted in Mevius 2002, p. 36.
2 Quoted in Brzezinski 1967, p. 27.
3 Rákosi 1950, p. 47.

December 1945.[4] Likewise in Yugoslavia, the Communists acted through a Popular Front that was initially a coalition of separate parties – soon after elections in November 1945 it was transformed into a front organisation for the Communists.[5]

Elsewhere, the transition was not so immediate for a variety of reasons. In Bulgaria, the Communists governed from September 1944 through the Fatherland Front, nominally a coalition, which was able to quickly introduce policies of radical nationalisation and anti-fascist purges. The speedy collapse of the collaborationist government and the existence of domestic partisans aided the consolidation of the new regime's authority.[6] In Romania, following the royal coup in August 1944, a National Democratic Bloc government had been created – a coalition in which the Communists were represented. Over the course of the autumn, the country was sharply polarised by political conflict between the Communists and Socialists on the one hand, and the bourgeois National Liberal and National Peasants' parties on the other. Under growing pressure from the left on the streets and the country's Soviet occupiers, the King was forced to appoint a Communist-dominated government under Petru Groza in March 1945. Although nominally a 'popular front' government, the country's two bourgeois parties were excluded from it.[7] In Hungary, a 'popular front' provisional government was formed from four parties, including the conservative Smallholders' Party and the trade unions. While technically a coalition, it was dominated, at least until the November 1945 elections, by the left.[8] In Poland, the road to coalition was a tortuous one and took place against a background of civil war in the country between the Home Army and the Communists, supported by the Soviets. The coalition that emerged was contested by armed resistance in the countryside and by Stanislaw Mikołajczyk and his Peasants' Party (*Polskie Stronnictwo Ludowe*, or PSL) in the political field. At the end of 1945, Communist control in Poland seemed far from secure.[9] In Czechoslovakia, by virtue of their broad base of popular support, especially in Bohemia and Moravia, the Communists had considerable influence over a National Front coalition government, which included the pre-Munich political elite. The country's president was Edvard Beneš, who had headed the London-

---

4   Vickers 1999, pp. 163–4.
5   Lampe 1996, p. 234.
6   Crampton 1987, pp. 145–53.
7   Hitchins 1994, pp. 501–17.
8   Pittaway 2002, pp. 18–45.
9   Coutovidis and Reynolds 1986, pp. 198–228.

based government-in-exile, and his leadership was based on an agreement brokered between that government and Stalin in 1943.[10]

Behind the formal front of coalition, however, the Communists built parallel security states that they would be able to use against present and future opponents. In Czechoslovakia, the Communist Minister of the Interior, Václav Nosek, moved in 1945 to reorganise the country's police to form a State Security Guard in which Communists were quickly promoted to positions of influence. Within this Guard, the State Security division (*Státní Bezpečnost*, or StB) was given the task of rooting out enemies of the republic and given formal independence in 1946.[11] In Poland, the climate of civil war against the Home Army and political forces loyal to the government-in-exile in London was used as cover for the establishment of a parallel security state. The Security Office (*Urząd Bezpieczeństwa*, or UB) was established under the auspices of the Soviet secret police (*Narodnyy Komissariat Vnutrennikh Del*, or NKVD) in 1944. In addition, civil strife was used to justify draconian actions by the new Polish state, including the sentencing of between forty to fifty thousand people by military courts between 1944 and 1949.[12]

In those states that had fought on the side of Nazi Germany, namely, Hungary, Romania and Bulgaria, the power of the Communists was bolstered by Allied Control Commissions. While these nominally represented the interests of the United Kingdom and the United States as well, in each of these countries they were dominated by the representatives of the Soviet Union. This afforded the Communists in each country some protection when building a parallel security state under their control. In Hungary, the task of creating a new political force was entrusted to Communist Gábor Péter, who recruited his new policemen from the ranks of left-wing activists creating a political department initially to round up 'fascists'.[13] In Romania, the Soviets infiltrated the pre-1944 state security services (the *Siguranţa*). With the advent of the Groza government in 1945, the *Siguranţa* was placed under the supervision of the Communist-controlled Ministry of the Interior, and given the task of spearheading the new government's drive against 'fascists'.[14] In Bulgaria, the army was purged and re-organised, while Communist control of the security

---

10   Myant 1981, pp. 25–52.
11   Lukes 1997, pp. 252–3.
12   Micgiel 1997, pp. 91–102.
13   Pittaway 2002, p. 28.
14   Deletant 1999, pp. 114–17.

apparatus was assured through the creation of the People's Militia and People's Courts.[15]

In south-eastern Europe, where lip service had been paid to the principle of popular front coalition, the construction of a security state was closely linked to the overt attempts of local Communists to build a dictatorship over the societies they ruled. In Yugoslavia, the elimination of political opponents merged with the violence that surrounded the end of the war, as the remnants of Mihailović's non-Communist *Četniks* were destroyed militarily in 1945 and 1946. With the liberation of Belgrade, the Communists moved to construct a security apparatus that would serve their needs in peacetime. In 1944, Aleksandar Ranković, a senior Partisan, began to create a security force that would aim at the liquidation of all those who, in Tito's words, did 'not like this kind of Yugoslavia'.[16] As the scope of the security service expanded in 1946, becoming the State Security Administration (*Uprava Državine Bezbednosti*, or UDBa), Ranković recruited in 'every block of flats, in every street, in every village and every barrack room'.[17]

In south-eastern Europe, the development of a police state went hand-in-hand with immediate action against political opponents of the Communists, who often dovetailed the elimination of opponents with retribution against former 'fascists'. In February 1945, the new Albanian government introduced special courts for 'war criminals' right across the country, while it ordered the confiscation of their property.[18] These measures were to herald a wave of generalised repression that led to an estimated eighty thousand arrests of ordinary Albanians for political offences prior to 1956.[19] In Yugoslavia, retribution against those perceived to be 'fascists' or collaborators was severe. The country passed a law to punish 'offences against people and the state', which included provisions against those who had committed what were deemed 'war crimes'.[20] Among the most spectacular measures of 'retribution' in the Yugoslav context was the trial and execution of Draža Mihailović in summer 1946 for war crimes and collaboration with the country's Nazi occupiers. In a similar show trial in the autumn, Alojzije Stepinac, Archbishop of Zagreb, was tried and sentenced to imprisonment with hard labour for his collaboration with the *Ustaša* regime.

---

15 Crampton 1987, pp. 145–7.
16 Quoted in Rusinow 1977, p. 15.
17 Quoted in Lampe 1996, p. 238.
18 Blumi 1997, p. 396.
19 Hamm 1963, p. 53.
20 Völkl 1991, p. 386.

The net was then drawn in to attack non-Communist politicians who were guilty of minor forms of collaboration.[21]

In post-war Yugoslavia, retribution was not simply about reckoning with the immediate past, nor was it about providing a justification for the elimination of political opponents, although both of these elements were present. It was also about constructing a basis of legitimacy for the new state. In the immediate post-war period, in party-propaganda 'fascist' and 'collaborator' came to be used synonymously for those who opposed the policies of the new regime.[22] The state based its legitimacy on the fact that it was the representative of 'the anti-fascist struggle', and promoted this through propaganda and patterns of commemoration. The commemoration of 'uprising days' in each of the Yugoslav republics – in other words, the days when, according to the regime, the partisan struggle began – played an important role in officially promoted commemoration into the post-war period.[23]

While Yugoslavia, with its partisan past, was in many ways unique, anti-fascist measures right across the region combined the three elements of retribution, measures to eliminate potential political opponents and attempts to legitimate the new political system. Because of differing patterns of social reaction to war and of political identification, anti-fascist retribution played out in different ways in the varying national contexts across the region. In Bulgaria, where 10,987 persons were tried under retributive justice and 2,138 executed between September 1944 and March 1945,[24] such measures were used to legitimate the extensive purges that accompanied the Fatherland Front government's consolidation of its power.[25] In Hungary, however, the numbers of those affected were far lower, and the picture in terms of popular reaction was deeply ambiguous. From their establishment up until mid-August 1945, Hungary's retributive courts had arrived at verdicts in 3,893 cases, of which 1,014 had resulted in acquittals and 64 in death sentences.[26] In addition, those deemed to be 'fascists' were interned – 16,949 were interned up to January 1946. 'Verification committees' were set up in factories to prevent those with 'fascist' pasts from returning to white-collar or managerial posts, which continued to function throughout the late 1940s.[27] These measures proved to be a

---

21 Pavlowitch 1971, pp. 181–2.
22 Lilly 2001, p. 87.
23 Roksandic 1995, pp. 256–71.
24 Quoted in Frommer 1999, p. 81.
25 Crampton 1987, pp. 145–7.
26 Karsai 2000, p. 237.
27 Pittaway 2002, pp. 40–1.

poisoned chalice for the regime – internment and verification alienated large sections of the urban middle class who believed that the state had criminalised many for simply working under the interwar Horthy regime. At one and the same time, in the climate of social tension and political division that gripped the country in the immediate post-war years, they also failed to satisfy the regime's working-class base which wanted more radical purges not only of those who had been involved in the brief Arrow Cross regime, but also of those who had undertaken anti-labour measures in the interwar years.[28]

In Czechoslovakia, radical retribution against collaboration was backed by a broad political consensus that stretched from the Communists to the bourgeois parties, and included the non-Communist President, Edvard Beneš. This resulted in the passing of draconian legislation against former collaborators, with little political debate, and an extensive process of retribution. In the Czech lands, up until February 1948, 32,853 persons appeared before retributive courts, of which 22,087 were convicted, while in Slovakia 8,059 received convictions from a total of 20,561 tried. More than seven hundred death sentences were carried out.[29] While retribution received considerable support in the Czech lands in view of their occupied status during the war years, in Slovakia it was regarded with much more suspicion. The trial and execution of Josef Tiso, the wartime leader of the Slovak state, in 1946 provoked strong feelings among Catholic and nationalist opinion in Slovakia, which underlined political differences between the two component parts of the Czechoslovak state.[30] The politics of retribution in Czechoslovakia provided cover for the extension of undemocratic measures that supported the parallel security state constructed by the Communists. Paradoxically, in punishing patterns of behaviour that had sustained an illegitimate and repressive regime in the war years, they allowed those same patterns of behaviour to reproduce themselves in new post-war circumstances. According to the journalist Jiří Bilý, in 1947, 'the vice called denunciation, which was born on 15 March 1939, lives on'. For him, the witch-hunt climate promoted by retribution ensured that 'a new army of denouncers is already being born among us'.[31]

Retribution was often directed not just at individuals but at entire ethnic groups, particularly Eastern Europe's German population. Here the concerns of the region's new rulers intersected with the strong desire for revenge on the part of those who had suffered from the plans of the Nazis and their clients to

---

28 Pittaway 2002, pp. 40–5.
29 Frommer 1999, p. 2.
30 Abrams 1996, pp. 255–92.
31 Quoted in Frommer 1999, pp. 95–6.

shape 'a new ethnographic order' in the region. In the newly liberated Czechoslovakia, the language of left-wing politicians fanned the flames of Czech anger that manifested itself during the process of wild expulsion that accompanied liberation. In May 1945, Zdeněk Nejedlý, Minister of Education, proclaimed that the country's new rulers 'will purify Prague and the border districts [of Germans] and we are in a position to do so, because we have a great helper in doing this – the Red Army'.[32] The preparations for the organised expulsions, due to begin in January 1946, occurred against the background of continued 'wild transfer' that was incited by representatives of the state. One publication in the Bohemian town of Ústí nad Labem warned local Czechs that ' "social relations" with Germans are also punishable; don't forget that there are still people who want not only to interact with Germans far more than is necessary, but who even want to marry German women'.[33] As a result of organised deportation, an estimated two-and-a-half million Germans left. Despite war losses, expulsion accounted for most of the 25.5 percent drop in population in Bohemia between 1937 and 1947, and the 21 percent fall in Moravia and Silesia.[34] Deportation from Poland was more radical as it was combined with the geographical shift as the country moved one hundred and fifty miles west of where it had lain in 1939. In addition to the 'wild expulsion', the new Polish state began the transfer of millions of Germans westwards. In the chaos of the immediate post-war months, with Poland itself racked by nigh-on civil war, 'the transports of the settlers were sent over the borders in an unorganised and unplanned manner', a situation that began to improve in the second half of 1946.[35] Transportation was carried out in a manner that increased the suffering of those expelled: at the assembly points in Poland at the turn of 1947, German 'women, the elderly, and children are in an exceptionally difficult predicament. They are literally half dead with hunger'.[36] The organised transfer of 2.2 million Germans from Poland was combined with an estimated four million who had left the western territories ceded to Poland during the period of 'wild expulsion'.[37]

The post-war expulsion of Germans from Poland and Czechoslovakia was but the most spectacular act in a wave of population transfer and ethnic retribution, which swept Eastern Europe in the late 1940s. Over two-million Poles

---

32   Quoted in King 2002, p. 192.
33   Quoted in Frommer 2001, p. 226.
34   Spulber 1957, p. 32.
35   Ther 1998, p. 59.
36   Jankowiak 2001, p. 98.
37   Spulber 1957, pp. 30–1.

were forced from their homes in the former east of the country as the territory was annexed by the Soviet Union.[38] Germans were expelled across the region: an estimated half a million were thrown out of countries in the region other than Poland and Czechoslovakia.[39] In Vojvodina, in northern Yugoslavia, the expulsion of Germans smoothened land reform policies, inasmuch as their land swelled the land fund, which in turn was distributed to 'colonists' (poor peasants from elsewhere in the federation, 71.97 percent of whom were Serb, altering the ethnic balance of the local population).[40] In 1947, Czechoslovakia and Hungary agreed to an 'exchange of populations', in which substantial numbers of Magyars were expelled from southern Slovakia, while members of Hungary's Slovak minority were removed to make room for them.[41]

The profound ethnic conflicts of the 1940s demanded that the region's new rulers pay close attention to issues of nationality during reconstruction. This was at its most marked in those regions that had borne the brunt of post-war campaigns of expulsion. In August 1948, an official in the British Embassy in Prague commented on the impact of expulsion on the landscape of northwestern Bohemia in striking terms: '[a] traveller entering Czechoslovakia by road from Germany is struck by the contrast between the rich and well-kept fields and busy villages through which he has just passed and the desolate weed-grown wastes and empty dwellings which are his first sight of Czechoslovakia'.[42] Policies of reconstruction had been pursued in this borderland for three years when the official made this observation. Under the auspices of a Resettlement Office set up by the state, the region was to be rebuilt as an industrial heartland, but one populated by Czech and Slovak settlers, not by Germans. Nation-building and industrial reconstruction went hand-in-hand.[43] Similar policies were pursued in western Poland annexed from Germany, as Poland's Ministry for the Regained Territories bolstered ethnic homogeneity by resettling Poles in the areas vacated by Germans. While the total population in the post-war territories never matched the pre-war population, the influx of settlers created new Polish population centres. Wrocław, formerly Breslau, capital of Lower Silesia, saw its population increase from 170,700 in 1946 to 308,900 by 1948.[44] One settler in the city described the urban

---

38   Ther 1998, p. 53.
39   Spulber 1957, p. 31.
40   Bokovoy 1998, p. 50.
41   Tóth 2001, pp. 177–208.
42   Public Records Office (PRO) Foreign Office (FO) 371/71352, p. 1.
43   Radvanovský 2001, p. 243.
44   Siebel-Achenbach 1994, p. 196.

landscape he found in terms that would have been familiar to contemporary travellers in north-western Bohemia: 'Endless ruins, the stink of burning, countless huge flies, the clouded faces of occasionally encountered Germans, and most important, the emptiness of desolated streets'.[45]

The policies pursued in Poland and Czechoslovakia aimed at rebuilding the countries around the hegemony of dominant ethnic groups. In other states, new rulers pursued policies based on nation-building strategies. In Albania during the late 1940s, Enver Hoxha's regime pursued policies that combined the standardisation of language and campaigns of repression to advance a version of Albanian identity that rested on the culture of Tosks, who inhabited the south of the country, and aimed at the marginalisation of the Ghegs, who inhabited the north.[46] However, Albania was somewhat exceptional. Outside of Poland and Czechoslovakia, the most dramatic attempts to pursue policies of nation-building were in multi-ethnic Yugoslavia. Because of the bloodletting of the war years in the multinational south Slav state and the appeal of its Communists to sections of the populations tired of the violence that accompanied the politics of ethnic exclusivity, the re-making of both state and nations was essential to the survival of the regime. The Communists promoted a revival of Yugoslavia based on a 'supranational "universal" culture' that could exist together with the separate 'national' cultures of the constituent peoples of the state.[47] This pushed the country's new rulers down the road of a federalism based on 'the brotherhood and unity' of the state's constituent parts. As the first article of the 1946 constitution stated: 'The Federal People's Republic of Yugoslavia is... a community of peoples with equal rights'.[48] Six constituent republics were created by the constitution: Bosnia-Herzegovina, Croatia, Macedonia, Montenegro, Serbia and Slovenia. At the same time, five 'nations' were recognised – Croatians, Macedonians, Montenegrins, Serbs and Slovenes. Defined by culture, one could be a member of any of these 'nations' regardless of the republic of which one was a citizen. This political formula allowed a Yugoslav identity to be promoted based on, in the words of a statement of principles to be used to define the post-war school curriculum, 'the building of socialism in our homeland, fraternity among the Yugoslav peoples, pride in the achievements of the War of National Liberation'.[49] On the other hand, it enabled the republics to pursue cultural policies of nation-building, albeit

---

45   Quoted in Kenney 1997, pp. 137–8.
46   Blumi 1997.
47   Wachtel 1998, p. 131.
48   Quoted in Djilas 1991, p. 162.
49   Quoted in Wachtel 1998, p. 137.

within the political limits imposed by the regime and of 'Yugoslavism'. This was at its most evident in Macedonia, where language and education were used to promote a Macedonian identity distinct from the Serb and Bulgarian identities that had been frequently ascribed to the populations of the territory.[50]

Reconstruction everywhere was accompanied by nationalist rhetoric, often appropriated by the Communist parties and their leaders. Hungary's Communists, for example, cast themselves as 'the heirs of Kossuth, Petőfi and Táncsics' in order to bolster their legitimacy.[51] Reconstruction was in part about 'national' reconstruction and recovery from the devastation of war, but it was also about radical change that would increase the role of previously subordinate groups in each national society. It was at its most radical in Yugoslavia and Albania, where the politics of reconstruction were virtually synonymous with those of socialist transformation, and at its least radical in Hungary where a substantial private sector in commerce and industry was allowed to survive until 1948. Right across the region, the politics of reconstruction meant the expropriation of large landholdings and their distribution to peasantries and the rural poor, in many cases simply legalising land seizures and occupations that had occurred as the Red Army advanced westward.

In the factories, the politics of reconstruction posed more acute problems for the region's rulers, because at one and the same time the industrial working class provided the most secure base of support for the 'popular front' regime, and yet also demanded political change that was often more radical than, and differed starkly from, that envisaged by governments. The factory committees and works' councils that sprang up in the face of the Red Army advance were quickly incorporated into the trade-union bureaucracies and given the task of ensuring a degree of control over enterprises. In the words of Czechoslovakia's trade-union leader Antonín Zápotocký, 'the aim of the control activity of the works' councils is to inspect production, trade and administration so that it is not abused against the interests of employers and the state'.[52] Workers were to maintain 'discipline' in the interests of reconstruction, even if this meant cooperation with private owners. As far as Hungarian Communist theorist Aladár Mód was concerned, workers and their representatives should 'abandon the kind of behaviour that big capital expects of them'.[53] In the desperate post-war conditions of penury, shortage and hyperinflation, workers believing in the promise of a better, more socially just future, struggled in the interests of

---

50   Troebst 1997, pp. 250–5.
51   Mevius 2002, p. 117.
52   Quoted in Bloomfield 1979, p. 98.
53   Mód 1945, pp. 4–5.

reconstruction. In the Polish industrial city of Łódź, in the first post-war months 'no-one asked about pay, but everyone s[tood] resolutely at his post'.[54] Yet frustration across the region soon set in. In Hungary, miserable living conditions created by hyperinflation, the failure to conduct extensive purges of managerial and supervisory personnel, and unpopular collective agreements, all stoked sporadic labour conflict in the second half of the 1940s.[55] In post-war Łódź, working-class protest was often stimulated by management authoritarianism and labour policies, which were seen as a threat to traditional shop-floor cultures in the city's factories.[56]

Industrial workers provided an insecure base of support for the post-war regimes of the region, but there were many others who opposed 'popular front' rule. Only in Czechoslovakia, where the Communists won 38 percent of the popular vote in elections in May 1946, were the Communists able to legitimate their rule through fair elections. Even this result revealed the limited nature of the left's legitimacy, inasmuch as the Communists captured the Czech lands, winning 40.17 percent in Bohemia and Moravia, but failed dismally in Slovakia.[57] Here a large rural majority attached to individual landholding, and thereby suspicious of Communist egalitarianism, and the existence of a strongly Catholic political culture in the villages, hampered the left's advance, creating a situation in which they were trounced by the centre-right Democratic Party (*Demokratická Strana*, or DS), which took 61.43 percent of the Slovak vote against the 30.48 percent polled by the Communists.[58] The constellation of forces that emerged in Slovakia in 1946 replicated that which had appeared in Hungary the previous November. Beneficiaries of land reform attached to property, the prevalence of political Catholicism in the centre and west of the country, middle-class distrust of the new state and the decision of the Allied Control Commission to ban other right-wing parties from contesting the election, combined to hand the conservative FKGP a landslide victory in parliamentary elections with 57.03 percent of the vote. The MKP emerged with a mere 16.95 percent. Only by rallying a fragmented left and using Soviet support to maintain a key position in the government was the MKP able to recover the situation, mobilising its supporters and using its control over the security services to destroy the Smallholders' Party in 1946 and 1947. It recovered its

---

54   Quoted in Kenney 1997, p. 78.
55   Pittaway 2002, pp. 57–63.
56   Kenney 1997, pp. 74–134.
57   Myant 1981, p. 125.
58   Abrams 1996, pp. 258–66.

position at the head of a 'popular front' coalition only through the semi-rigged elections of August 1947.[59]

Nowhere else in the region were the elections in the mid-1940s as fair or as free as those held in Czechoslovakia or Hungary. Outside Albania and Yugoslavia, which have already been discussed, Communist-dominated 'popular front' governments held power despite the considerable opposition of large sections of the societies they ruled. In Romania, where Petru Groza's government had ruled without the support of the country's non-socialist majority, elections in November 1946 were conducted against the background of intimidation, political tension and attacks on the non-Communist press. The landslide election victory of Communist-dominated Bloc of Democratic Parties was produced, according to observers, through widespread electoral fraud.[60] In Bulgaria, while widely discredited elections had been held in November 1945, the real electoral contest between the Communist-dominated Fatherland Front and the opposition led by Nikola Petkov was held in October 1946; the Front's victory was a product of an ugly and polarised political climate.[61] In Poland, the government in Warsaw faced opposition both from the armed groups formed from the Home Army, and from the political opposition of the PSL around Stanislaw Mikołajczyk, which attempted to organise the anti-Communist majority in the country. This majority was underlined when, in a climate of generalised political polarisation, the government held a referendum on 30 June 1946 on the issues of constitutional reform, nationalisation and the new borders. Although the referendum resulted in 'yes' votes on all three counts, fraud disguised the degree of hostility among ordinary Poles towards the PPR. Consequently, the PSL judged that it could defeat the PPR and its Socialist allies in forthcoming elections held in January 1947. The elections were far from free and fair: members of the PPR dominated electoral commissions, and in much of the country there was no secret ballot. PSL scrutineers were denied access to the counting of the votes across the country. Officially, the Democratic Bloc dominated by the PPR won 80.1 percent to the 10.3 percent recorded for the PSL.[62]

Some commentators have regarded the post-war 'popular front' regimes as little more than a stage in the drive of Eastern Europe's Communist parties for absolute power.[63] This understates the distinctiveness of the immediate

---

59 Pittaway 2002, pp. 45–66.
60 Hitchins 1994, p. 533.
61 Crampton 1987, p. 155.
62 Coutovidis and Reynolds 1986, pp. 229–310.
63 Brzezinski 1967, pp. 3–64; Seton-Watson 1961.

popular front period, when the economies of the region were characterised by mixed forms of ownership and multi-party systems were permitted, save in Yugoslavia and Albania, even where elections were not free and fair. Yet to term the period a 'democratic interlude' as others have done[64] is to overstate the case. The Soviets and their Communist allies ensured close control over politics either through the Allied Control Commissions in those states, which had fought alongside Hitler, or through parallel security states. The manner in which Communists used policies of anti-fascist 'retribution' to strengthen their position, or their undemocratic tactics when their hold on power was threatened by electoral defeat, attest to the limits of democracy in the post-war states. 'Popular front' rule was the Eastern European product of the wartime alliance between the Western powers and the Soviet Union. As the wartime alliance itself broke down, 'popular front' rule was destined to disappear with it.

The breaking of the wartime alliance was partly precipitated by tension generated by the undemocratic behaviour of the Soviets and their Communist allies in 'popular front' Eastern Europe. American concern over the 'communist threat' prompted the United States to offer Western European states Marshall Aid. The anti-communist nature of politics in post-war Western Europe was cemented with the expulsion of the powerful communist parties of France and Italy from the coalition governments in those countries in 1947. The Soviets responded with the foundation of the Cominform, a new international organisation of Communist parties, which heralded greater coordination. The founding meeting of the organisation, held in the Polish town of Szklarska Poręba in September 1947, sounded the death knell for the wartime alliance internationally, but also for 'popular front' policies domestically.

This was underlined most dramatically in the months following Szklarska Poręba by events in Czechoslovakia. Prior to September 1947, the Czechoslovak Communist Party (*Komunistická Strana Čekoslovenska*, or KSČ) had committed itself to an electoral road to socialism in view of its success in the 1946 elections. Its secretary, Klement Gottwald, had set the Party the goal of winning 51 percent in the next elections.[65] In an atmosphere of growing tension between the coalition parties over KSČ control of the police, Stalin's ban on the country applying for Marshall Aid, and a deteriorating economic situation, popular support slipped away from the Party in 1947.[66] Political crisis erupted as twelve non-Communist ministers walked out of the government over KSČ control of

---

64 Gati 1986, pp. 13–123.
65 Myant 1981, p. 140.
66 Kaplan 1987, pp. 148–9.

the security forces in February 1948. A majority of ministers stayed, and Gottwald, bolstered by support from the unions, was able to force President Beneš to accept a single-party KSČ government. The security forces and KSČ supporters rolled into action, setting up 'action committees' that took over the non-communist parties and set themselves up in 'the civil service, in all large enterprises, in the professions, and in all towns and villages' to conduct purges and thus consolidate the Party's power.[67]

The 'Prague Coup', as the Czechoslovak events became known, was only the most spectacular in a series of processes that characterised the region's slide into overt dictatorship. In Hungary, where Communist power over a 'popular front' government was only fully consolidated in August 1947, the year of 1948 saw the liquidation of the non-socialist opposition, the enforced merger of the Communist and Social Democratic parties to form the Hungarian Workers' Party (*Magyar Dolgozók Pártja*, or MDP), and the creation of the personal dictatorship of Mátyás Rákosi.[68] Where Communist power had been consolidated earlier, similar shifts from 'popular front' to overt dictatorship were underway. In Poland, the PPR deployed increasingly radical class rhetoric throughout 1948, culminating in the merger between it and the Socialists in December that established the Polish United Workers' Party (*Polska Zjednoczona Partia Robotnicza*, or PZPR), which established a political system in which one party enjoyed 'the leading role'.[69] In Romania, non-Communist political opposition had been all but eliminated by early 1948, while the Communist Party swallowed the Social Democrats in September 1947 and then purged its membership, expelling around three hundred and forty thousand between 1948 and 1950, thus laying the foundations of the personal dictatorship of Gheorghe Gheorgiu-Dej.[70]

In Yugoslavia, where socialist dictatorship had been institutionalised as early as 1946, the changes of 1948 initiated a new phase in the development of the state. Because of its roots in partisan warfare, rather than Red Army occupation pure and simple, the Communist regime proved immune to Moscow's control. Growing tension between Belgrade and Moscow, fuelled by the independent behaviour of Tito, led Stalin to break links with the regime in Yugoslavia in March 1948.[71] The break led to an increased drive for Communist political control in Yugoslavia, or what the historian Stevan K. Pavlowitch has

---

67 PRO FO 371/71264, p. 1.
68 Standeisky, Kozák, Pataki and Rainer 1998.
69 Kenney 1997, pp. 189–236.
70 King 1980, pp. 72–3.
71 Lampe 1996, pp. 241–9.

termed 'Stalinism without Stalin'.⁷² Yet this drive was, paradoxically, justified by anti-Stalinism and the need for unity in the face of a sea of hostile states.⁷³ For Albania, whose independence had been threatened by Yugoslavia, Tito's split with Stalin was an opportunity – one that was grasped wholeheartedly by Hoxha who aligned Albania closely with the Soviet Union.⁷⁴

The construction of overt dictatorship in much of the region, and the intensification of that dictatorship in Yugoslavia and Albania, meant above all an escalation of repression against opponents (both real and imagined). Building on the foundations of the parallel security states laid in the 'popular front' era, the dictatorships dramatically expanded their internal security services during the late 1940s and early 1950s. In Hungary, the political department of the police was reorganised several times, eventually becoming the State Security Agency (*Államvédelmi Hatóság*, or ÁVH) in 1948. The numbers it employed rose from 9,000 in 1949 to 28,000 a year later.⁷⁵ In neighbouring Romania, the internal security services were renamed the *Securitate* in August 1948. Employing a relatively small number of officers and a vast army of informers, they gathered evidence on an astounding 417,916 people by 1951.⁷⁶ In Poland, the UB had become a vast organisation by 1951, while in Bulgaria it was estimated that some seventy thousand were employed in police-related activities, compared to a mere 25,000 at the end of the 1940s.⁷⁷ In Yugoslavia, Ranković's security services also grew and new forms of detention camps were opened for 'political' detainees – the most notorious of which was on the island of Goli Otok, off the Croatian coast.⁷⁸ The expansion of detention camps accompanied the creation of overt dictatorship across the region. A law passed in Czechoslovakia in 1948 that established 'educational working centres' legalised the practice, in force since February, of sending political prisoners from Prague's Pankrac prison to work camps in the towns of Kladno, Karlovy Vary and Pradubice.⁷⁹

The escalation of repression, like the expansion of the security state, was built upon the foundations of the campaigns of anti-fascist 'retribution' pursued in the popular front era, in that it combined retribution – although on this occasion the scope of retribution was dramatically widened to include

---

72   Pavlowitch 1971, p. 211.
73   Wachtel 1998, pp. 132–3.
74   Vickers 1999, pp. 173–5.
75   Ormos 1991, pp. 64–8.
76   Deletant 1999, pp. 118–26.
77   *News from Behind the Iron Curtain* 1952, pp. 13–14.
78   Pavlowitch 1971, pp. 214–15.
79   PRO FO 371/71265, p. 1.

those who had opposed the Communists – with the elimination of political opponents, in addition to its propagandistic motives. At one and the same time, however, it represented a dramatic break from earlier practices, most especially in terms of its scale. It also rested on notions that society was divided into 'supporters' and 'enemies' of socialist construction, a practice derived directly from that of Soviet Stalinism. Most especially, the range of 'enemies' identified by the state and security apparatus was enormous. The first targets of the escalation of repression were the representatives of non-Communist political forces and their supporters. In Bulgaria, the show trial and execution of Petkov in summer 1947 initiated a process by which non-communist political forces were eliminated, while many of their members and representatives were arrested and tried.[80] In Czechoslovakia, the post-Prague Coup suppression of non-communist political forces extended beyond the ranks of non-communist parties to include representatives of the press. In the aftermath of February 1948, 'the Union of Journalists ... expelled a large number of its members on political grounds', while in the country's universities 'action committees' 'deprived the rector and a large number of professors of their offices and all their functions. Some students have been expelled'.[81] The scope of the repression of former members and representatives of non-communist parties was extended to those who had belonged to the region's socialist and social democratic parties prior to their liquidation. In Hungary, arrests and show-trials of former Social Democrats, including that of the country's president Árpád Szakasits, took place in 1950.[82]

The show trial – in which a senior public figure was tried often for a conspiracy against the state that was fabricated by the security apparatus and signed under torture – became a symbol of the wave of repression that spread across the region during the early 1950s. The most striking of these show trials were those in which senior Communists themselves were tried and executed on trumped-up charges of treason against both the system they had helped to create and their country. The early show trials directed at senior Communists involved rooting out assumed 'enemies' within the Party who had, according to the fabricated charges they faced, conspired with Tito to betray their comrades to the capitalist West. This was easiest to implement in Albania where Hoxha was keen to cooperate with Soviet attempts to identify and root out 'Yugoslav deviationism', resulting in the trial of the former Interior Minister, Koçi Xoxe,

---

80   Crampton 1987, pp. 160–6.
81   PRO FO 371/71264, p. 2.
82   Kádár 1999, pp. 163–9.

in May 1949.[83] The trial in Hungary of another former Interior Minister, László Rajk, on similar charges in September 1949, and his execution the following month, began a wave of arrests and trials that convulsed the Hungarian Party throughout the early 1950s.[84] In Bulgaria, the trial and execution of Traicho Kostov, the former Communist Deputy Prime Minister, followed for membership of the 'Titoist' conspiracy.[85] While the 1949 wave of show trials was intended to send a message to party members, activists and the population that Tito was little more than the 'chained dog' of Western imperialism, Yugoslavia's split with Moscow had initiated a wave of purges inside the South Slav state. Tito had liquidated all non-Communist opposition by the time of the split, and when it initiated a new wave of repression in 1948, this was against pro-Moscow elements inside the Party, in a purge which was a mirror-image of those underway elsewhere. According to Ranković, between 1948 and 1952 around thirteen thousand five hundred persons had been punished for their pro-Moscow stance.[86] The waves of trials on the other side of the divide in Soviet-dominated Eastern Europe rumbled on throughout the early 1950s. The secretary general of the KSČ, Rudolf Slánský, in one of the most notable show trials in the region, was tried and executed for 'treason' in 1952.[87]

The intended message of the show trials of senior party figures was that internal enemies and traitors were to be found everywhere. This bolstered the escalation of repression, as its objects shifted from political opposition to society. Organised religion was increasingly one object of escalated repression during the late 1940s and early 1950s. This was partly due to the natural suspicion with which the Communists regarded the churches, given the anti-clericalism of the region's rulers. It was also due to the fact that in much of the region churches had sustained anti-Communist political activity during the popular front period and continued to do so as the dictatorship was built. In Slovakia and Hungary, for example, political Catholicism in rural areas had shaped a political culture, which propelled centre-right parties to victory in elections during the mid-1940s. In the latter state, the reaction in the country to the arrest of its Catholic primate and prominent conservative critic of the regime, Cardinal József Mindszenty, in December 1948, underlined popular Catholicism's continued hold among sections of the population, particularly women and those living in rural areas. Even in industrial areas like the town of

---

83 Hodos 1988, pp. 28–35.
84 Zinner 1988.
85 Crampton 1987, p. 171.
86 Pavlowitch 1971, p. 214.
87 Pelikán 1971, pp. 101–14.

Újpest, women textile workers who commuted from rural areas greeted Mindszenty's arrest with dismay.[88] In Slovakia, the period after the Communist assumption of power in Prague was accompanied by a wave of arrests of priests who used their position to make anti-Communist statements. By the summer of 1949, there were reports of violence in a number of villages as residents attempted to defend their priest from arrest by the security services.[89] In rural Poland, rumours that the state would arrest priests provoked considerable opposition. The way in which political opposition and popular Catholicism fused in the Polish context was illustrated by reactions to the supposed sighting of the weeping of the statue of the Virgin in Lublin cathedral in 1949. This 'miracle' was interpreted by many believers as a sign of the illegitimacy of Communist rule.[90]

It was not only in predominantly Catholic central Europe that the state responded to church activity with repression. In western Yugoslavia, where Catholicism was tied to Croatian nationalism, and thus to the issue of collaboration with the NDH, and to Slovene anti-Communism, Catholic priests had been targets of state repression as early as 1946.[91] Albania saw increasing measures to limit the influence of Islam and to curb Catholicism.[92] In Romania during the early 1950s, the focus of the state's attacks on organised religion were Catholic priests and the Uniate church, which it tried to effectively suppress, deploying considerable brutality.[93]

In the handling of organised religion, the limits as well as the extent of dictatorship became apparent. In view of the importance of both organised and popular religion among the region's rural majority, the regimes sought not simply to suppress, but also to incorporate certain elements of organised religion into the official power structure. In Yugoslavia, while the Serbian Orthodox Church, like the Catholics, had been victims of politically inspired repression during the late 1940s, from 1950 there was a gradual reconciliation based upon the church promising to support the regime's efforts to achieve 'brotherhood and unity', in exchange for the state extending social insurance to priests and regularising the legal status of churches.[94] In Romania, a bargain had been

---

88 Magyar Országos Levéltár (The National Archives of Hungary, hereafter MOL) M-Bp.-95f.3/69ö.e, pp. 120–1.
89 PRO FO 371/77248, p. 2.
90 Jarosz 1999, pp. 70–1.
91 Alexander 1979, pp. 53–94.
92 Skendi 1956, pp. 294–9.
93 Deletant 1999, pp. 89–103.
94 Alexander 1979, pp. 196–201.

struck between the regime and the Orthodox Church in 1949, but it was a highly unequal one. It agreed to the nationalisation of its assets, making it financially dependent on the state. While this bargain ensured that Orthodox priests did not face the level of persecution met by Catholics and Uniates, it effectively accepted incorporation into the power structure.[95] In Hungary, where the anti-Communism of both Catholic and Protestant clergy, as well as the jailing of Mindszenty, made a durable institutional settlement between church and state nigh-on impossible, the regime sought to incorporate the clergy into the power structure through the official party-sponsored peace movement, limiting their freedom of action and giving them a defined political role.[96] In Poland, a concordat between church and state had been signed in April 1950, but relations between the two remained tense throughout the early 1950s, given the anti-Communism of much of the clergy and of many religious believers. This failure of the state to stem opposition resulted in a further turn to repression, culminating in the arrest of the Polish primate, Cardinal Stefan Wyszyński, in 1953.[97]

The escalation of repression was not merely about the drive for political control, nor was it strictly motivated by the desire of the region's rulers for retribution against groups that had sustained opposition. Rather, it was necessitated in large part by the radicalism of the regime's policies in the economic and social sphere, as it moved to explicitly row back from the conciliatory tone of the 'popular front' period and pressed ahead with 'the construction of socialism'. This was accompanied by a rhetorical attack on social classes perceived to be hostile to socialism, as 'an intensification of the class struggle' was demanded by the region's leaders. This shift was already visible in 1947, on the eve of the onset of overt dictatorship through campaigns like Poland's Battle over Trade, in which the PPR's and later the PZPR's economic supremo Hilary Minc launched campaigns against 'speculators', which added up to a generalised attack on private enterprise in the retail sector.[98] In Czechoslovakia, campaigns directed against the 'hoarding of goods' and 'speculation' by retailers, manufacturers and wholesalers in the textile and clothing sector immediately preceded the political crisis of February 1948.[99] The drive against the private sector sometimes resulted in economic show trials. Hungary's oil fields had provided a source of political conflict between their American owners and the

---

95   Deletant 1999, pp. 90–1.
96   Gergely 1977, p. 275.
97   Kersten 1999, pp. 84–9.
98   Kenney 1997, pp. 192–8.
99   PRO FO 371/71264, p. 1.

Ministry of Industry throughout the 1940s. With the advent of overt dictatorship in 1948, they were simply confiscated by the state while their senior management were put on trial for 'sabotage' of the national economy.[100] These offered political cover for the liquidation of private ownership in industry, finance and trade through policies of radical nationalisation: by 1952, between ninety-seven and one hundred percent of industrial output came from the socialist sector of the economy across the region, and between seventy-six and ninety-eight percent of all retail turnover was generated in socialised enterprises.[101]

The 'class war' rhetoric and practice of the dictators was directed not only at businessmen, but also at the rural population, as the state moved to socialise the agricultural sector and grab as much of the agricultural surplus as possible to feed urban populations. The attack on the individual landholder that resulted was justified through references to the incompatibility between individual patterns of land ownership and socialism. In the words of Romania's dictator Gheorgiu-Dej: '[w]e have in the villages an ocean of small individual farms (over 3 million), which after the celebrated saying of Lenin, generate capitalism'.[102] In order to prevent the 'generation of capitalism' in the countryside, the state targeted the 'proto-capitalist' class in the countryside by identifying the wealthier farmers and labelling them 'kulaks'. Although the term was used throughout the region, its precise meaning varied from country to country, while its implementation often varied from village to village. The term had entered official discourse in 1946 – two years before it became widely used in the rest of the region. It is hard to disagree with Yugoslavia's chief ideologist, Edvard Kardelj, who noted that 'the kulak is a political concept'.[103] The countryside was subjected to increased taxation and an intensification of the state requisitioning of agricultural produce that had been introduced in most of the region during the war years. Those identified as 'kulaks' were subjected to more punitive taxation and quotas of requisitioned produce than their fellow farmers, as the state aimed to drive them out of farming entirely. These policies produced penury in many villages across the region, as smallholders struggled to preserve their family landholding in the face of pressure from the state. In western Hungary in late 1952, 'the farmer got less for his produce, than his seed had cost him', causing 'general hunger ... the rural population had to wait in long queues for bread and flour, whilst the family who could get hold of half a

---

100   Srágli 1986, pp. 295–307.
101   Brus 1986, p. 8.
102   Quoted in Cartwright 2001, p. 67.
103   Quoted in Bokovoy 1998, p. 90.

kilo of flour was delighted'.[104] This climate provoked both resentment and passive resistance to state attempts to collect taxes and enforce the requisitioning of produce. In one Polish village in 1952, the residents adopted:

> what might be called a solid anti-political front. The government inspectors who occasionally visit the place are given identical information at each house. Obviously all the people in the hamlet know who has hidden potatoes or illegally slaughtered a hog, but they keep quiet. The inspectors are unable to break through the wall of silence.[105]

Attempts to force peasants into agricultural-producer cooperatives – new large-scale agricultural enterprises, which were in theory owned by the workers, but saw production take place on an industrial scale under state direction – went together with the increase in deliveries. This was attempted everywhere in the region, including Yugoslavia, where there were concerns over guaranteeing food to its cities. Smallholders across the region were largely hostile to state steps to end their independence. The Polish countryside was marked by a wave of protest that accompanied collectivisation campaigns. These protests included arson, sabotage and demonstrations.[106] Poorer smallholders tended to join cooperatives, but where they did so disorganisation and underinvestment led to miserable living conditions. Remuneration in one Bulgarian cooperative, paid in kind, was so low in late 1950 that the members 'tired of all the vain promises, and armed with spades and forks ... attacked the cooperative, taking back their cattle and implements'.[107] Opposition rarely turned into open revolt, but where it did so, the resulting protests could be spectacular. The largest anti-collectivisation uprising occurred in the Bihač region of north-western Bosnia in May 1950, which affected five villages and resulted in 714 arrests.[108] The strength of feeling across Eastern Europe did not result in compromise, at least until Yugoslavia's permanent abandonment of collectivisation in 1953, and Hungary's temporary suspension of the process following the death of Stalin in the same year. The countryside was where the dictatorships could be seen at their most brutal, and where anti-regime feeling was at its strongest.

---

104 Open Society Archives (OSA) 300/40/4/22, Item No. 3242/54, p. 1.
105 *News From Behind the Iron Curtain* 1953, pp. 20–1.
106 Jarosz 1999, pp. 64–5.
107 *News From Behind the Iron Curtain* 1952, p. 17.
108 Bokovoy 1998, pp. 136–7.

Anti-regime sentiment was also marked among large segments of the pre-socialist middle class, especially among those dispossessed by radical nationalisation. In the western Hungarian town of Nagykanizsa in 1949, dispossessed former businessmen waited for a war with the United States that they hoped would bring 'the liberation of the country'.[109] Members of these social groups were subject to routine discrimination in employment and faced the pressure of deportation, particularly when they lived in politically sensitive regions. The 40,320 inhabitants deported by the Romanian state from the Banat region on the western border in 1951 included 'kulaks and inn keepers', as well as 'former landowners and industrialists'.[110] Yet those targeted by such measures were more than just former capitalists; they included professionals, civil servants and a range of middle-class groups. This could be seen in 1951 when several thousand 'class enemies' were removed from Budapest, in part to ease pressure on housing in the capital as the industrial workforce expanded.[111] Members of the former middle classes were discriminated against in terms of access to education. The future Czech president Václav Havel was among those denied educational opportunity in early socialist Czechoslovakia due to his 'bourgeois' origins.[112] As the state changed the social roles of many in intellectual occupations in academia and areas like the arts and journalism, political control increased and non-communists were purged.

Yet strangely enough, despite the policy of purges and restrictions on the numbers of those of 'bourgeois' origins who could gain access to higher education, middle-class social groups preserved their social positions to a remarkable extent. In Hungary, it was estimated in 1956 that of those employed in professional positions, as many as sixty to seventy percent had occupied similar social positions in the pre-socialist period.[113] In some countries, the reason for this lay in the fact that attempts to promote workers and peasants to higher education courses that served as the entry-point to such professions never achieved success. This was the case in the Czech lands where working-class students continued to be grossly underrepresented in higher education throughout the 1950s.[114] The demands of the economy for technical expertise in a climate of industrialisation created such a demand for educated labour that opportunities were opened for children of former middle-class groups to

---

109 Zala Megyei Levéltár (Zala County Archive, hereafter ZML) 57f.1/17ö.e.
110 Deletant 1999, p. 142.
111 Dessewffy and Szántó 1989.
112 Keane 2000, p. 88.
113 Mark 2003, p. 1.
114 Connelly 2000, p. 266.

enter new professional jobs. This seems to have been the case in Hungary,[115] as well as in Poland, where discriminatory practices were relaxed in 1950, and where the family members of an applicant were 'important to production and politically valuable'.[116] Thus, while they were an object of repression, the limits and the extent of dictatorship were clearly visible in how the state dealt with members of the middle class.

Both the limits of dictatorships and protest against its policies could be seen at their starkest in the industrial sphere. Just as industrial workers provided a base of (albeit conditional) support for the regimes in the popular front era, Stalinist dictatorships mobilised workers through the deployment of class war rhetoric and a celebration at the ideological level of manual industrial labour. At the same time, the state began to prepare the ground for comprehensive economic planning pursued with the objective of expanding the industrial sector: Yugoslavia began its first five-year plan before the break with Moscow in 1947, but elsewhere in the region five- and six-year plans commenced in 1949 and 1950.[117] In order to prepare workplaces for planning, the state reshaped labour relations in factories, mines and on construction sites, replacing existing wage systems with standardised ones that were designed to strictly reward production as set out in the plan.[118] In order to mobilise workers to increase productivity, labour competition campaigns and the decoration of 'outstanding' workers, known as Stakhanovites, began during the late 1940s.[119] Such campaigns brought the state into direct confrontation with working-class culture. The reaction of one Łódź union official to textile workers mobilised in the labour competition was typical: '[w]e are fighting for [the right] to work on only one loom, and you work on two looms and take bread away from the others'.[120] The marked unpopularity of these campaigns was underlined when they were combined with increases in production targets for workers that resulted in cuts in wages. In Hungary, such increases resulted in a wave of industrial unrest in August 1950.[121]

The industrialisation drive that central planning entailed brought enormous increases in the size of the industrial labour force across the region: between 1948 and 1953 the numbers of people employed in mining and

---

115   Mark 2003.
116   Connelly 2000, p. 239.
117   Spulber 1957, p. 280.
118   Pittaway, chapter 4 of this volume.
119   Satjukow and Gries 2002.
120   Quoted in Kenney 1997, p. 252.
121   Pittaway, chapter 4 of this volume.

manufacture rose from almost 1.4 to over 1.6 million in Czechoslovakia, from 0.4 to 0.9 million in Hungary, 0.4 to over 0.7 million in Romania, and from under 0.5 to 0.6 million in Yugoslavia.[122] The industrialisation drive also brought economic chaos. It was based on Soviet demands to expand sectors, such as machine manufacture, in order to feed its arms capabilities, so that Moscow would be able to fight a third world war – something leaders in the region believed to be imminent given the deteriorating relations between the superpowers and the conflict in Korea, which broke out in 1950.[123] Industry expanded quicker than the production of energy and raw materials to support it. The result was that production was frequently plagued by shortages of tools and raw materials that undermined the attempts of enterprises to fulfil the plan. These combined with severe shortages of labour: by 1952, the Polish trade unions warned that industry was short of around two hundred thousand workers.[124] As managers attempted to meet plan targets in a climate of endemic shortage and widespread working-class discontent, a range of informal compromises between workers and lower management resulted, which subverted wage policies that sought to tie workers' performance to the goals of the plan.[125] Given the chaos that reigned, as industrial production was hit by frequent stoppages, earnings became increasingly insecure. Absenteeism and labour mobility in industry rocketed: by 1953 around twelve percent of Czechoslovakia's industrial workforce changed jobs annually.[126] The state unsuccessfully responded to its increasing lack of control over the working-class with repression. Attempts in Hungary in 1952 to criminalise both job-quitting and absenteeism failed to stem the tide of 'work indiscipline'.[127]

Discontent of both the working class and the urban population more generally was fuelled by the impact of forced industrialisation, and the economic chaos that accompanied it, on living standards. In Hungary, working-class real wages fell by an estimated 16.6 percent between 1949 and 1953.[128] In Czechoslovakia, real wages in 1951 stood at only 86.6 percent of their 1937 level.[129] Poverty combined with endemic food and goods shortages that had been a near-permanent feature of everyday life in the region since the late

---

[122] Spulber 1957, p. 386.
[123] Birta 1970, pp. 125–8.
[124] *News from Behind the Iron Curtain* 1953, p. 19.
[125] Pittaway, chapter 4 of this volume.
[126] Heumos 2001, p. 349.
[127] Pittaway 1998, p. 225.
[128] Pittaway 2003, p. 109.
[129] *News From Behind the Iron Curtain* 1953, p. 20.

1940s. As early as 1949, discontent caused by food shortages had rumbled in Slovak urban centres like Bratislava, Nitra and Zilina.[130] By 1952, Western observers commented regularly on shortages of food and consumer goods across the bloc: 'food shortages were attributed by refugees to many causes; drought in Poland, changeover from agriculture to industry in Czechoslovakia, food exports from Bulgaria to other nations... peasant unwillingness to fulfil compulsory delivery quotas'.[131] Such shortages fed a burgeoning black market, which prospered across the region, despite its criminalisation and the vigilance of the security services. In Romania in mid-1952, 'certain people' brought 'anything needed to the houses of those they know and trust, on condition that the black market price, which is about three times the free market price, be paid'.[132]

While working-class protest had bubbled beneath the surface throughout the early 1950s, where it had been concerned with workplace issues it was met with repression. This contributed to a situation in which large numbers of industrial workers languished in the region's jails and work camps – for example, workers made up 31.6 percent of those held in Czechoslovak prisons for 'political' crimes in 1950.[133] Continued economic chaos, declining living standards, and attempts by the state to further reduce the purchasing power of the population to keep forced industrialisation on track, caused a breach between the state and the working class. This became painfully apparent in 1952 and 1953, as governments responded to growing shortages, suppressed inflation, and generalised economic chaos, by implementing currency reforms that effectively confiscated the savings of populations. Imitating a reform introduced in Poland in October 1950, reforms were introduced in Romania in January 1952, Bulgaria in May 1952, and Czechoslovakia in May 1953. The Czechoslovak currency reform provoked not only a wave of strikes across the country, but also one of the most spectacular acts of working-class protest in the region during the early socialist years. In Plzeň, strikes at the Škoda works in the town in June 1953 erupted in generalised rioting, which led to the occupation of the town hall by demonstrators. The uprising was only put down by military force brought in from Prague.[134]

Three months before the Plzeň revolt, however, an era had come to an end with the death of Stalin. While this was not clear at the time, Stalin's death

---

130   PRO FO 371/77264, p. 1.
131   *News from Behind the Iron Curtain* 1952, p. 16.
132   *News from Behind the Iron Curtain* 1952, p. 31.
133   Pelikán 1971, p. 56.
134   Ulc 1965, pp. 46–9.

would usher in a period of fraught, conflict-ridden consolidation of the regimes that ruled the region. That consolidation would be so problematic for the regimes' rulers because of the deep-seated weaknesses of the socialist states. Industrialisation and collectivisation had brought economic turmoil, while the policies the regime had pursued had alienated almost every section of society. While the states had lost control of the economy, they were dogged by widespread peasant and working-class protest at many of their policies. Despite their repressive nature, socialist dictatorships were as far away from establishing a stable basis for their rule as the popular front regimes had been in 1945.

CHAPTER 3

The Reproduction of Hierarchy: Skill, Working-Class Culture, and the State in Early Socialist Hungary

Introduction

In November 1951, on a night shift in pit number XII of the Tatabánya coal trust, Sándor Hajósi, one of the most experienced coal hewers, worked at a poor position at the coalface and was unable to make his quota. As the hopelessness of his task dawned on him, he became demoralised, slackening his work pace and growing increasingly angry. Finally, he threw down his pick in frustration. He confronted the deputy responsible for his section, arguing that as a 'good worker' with experience he deserved a better work area in which he would easily be able to fulfil his quota. His superior retorted that he should not argue, and should return to work. Rather than standing in solidarity with him, Hajósi's workmates were far from united as to whether his treatment had been just. One coal hewer new to the mine, Lajos Szabó, was heard to remark, reiterating the view of the deputy, that had Hajósi not put down his tools and argued, he would have been able to fill two carts in the time he had wasted.[1]

The incident was reported in the newspaper of the party organisation that covered the coal trust. Party officials, under pressure from their superiors in Budapest, were anxious to exhort ordinary miners to maintain work discipline even as management lost effective control of production.[2] Although party-propagandists were eager to use tensions within the workforce for their own ends, such conflicts were not merely products of their wishful thinking. The more experienced miners regarded newcomers recruited in early 1951 as inferior to them. Such attitudes were related to conflicts between workers based on notions of skill and hierarchy that came to the fore when the regime put recruits to work after crash training courses created to replace traditional apprenticeships. Few of the experienced miners expressed their opposition to

---

* First published in Mark Pittaway 2002, 'The Reproduction of Hierarchy: Skill, Working-Class Culture, and the State in Early Socialist Hungary', *Journal of Modern History*, 74, 4: 737–69.
1 'Azt hallotuk...', *Harc a Szénért*, 29 November 1951, p. 4.
2 For more on the actual conditions of production in the coal mines during late 1951, see Pittaway 1998, pp. 110–49.

these changes publicly. There were exceptions though: in a meeting in pit number VI, one miner stated that he did not regard it as just 'that somebody could become a coal hewer after only one year'. Instead, he argued that 'a miner should only be able to join a brigade after a good six to eight years' apprenticeship under a master'.[3] The state was aware of widespread conflict over skill at Hungarian coalfaces. In 1953, one policy-maker writing in the party's theoretical journal criticised more experienced coal miners for their 'skill-based chauvinism, the way they look down on new workers who have come straight from the village and on female workers'.[4]

The disputes over skill and hierarchy in Hungary's coal mines during the early 1950s shed light on the conflicts over working-class identity that were generated by the state's programme of industrial transformation. This programme formed one plank of the drive to reshape Hungarian society along socialist lines that was initiated by the Stalinist dictatorship of Mátyás Rákosi in the late 1940s and early 1950s.[5] We know very little about the reactions of society as a whole to this programme of transformation. This is because the bulk of recent research on the Rákosi era has focused on the destruction of civil society at the beginnings of the dictatorship, the show trials, and the mechanisms of repression employed by the state. Much of this work has reified state power, arguing that the Stalinist dictatorship was effectively able to strip society of its autonomy. Social groups, private business, religion and independent associations have often been seen as passive victims of socialist despotism.[6]

That Rákosi's dictatorship, like its Stalinist counterparts across Eastern Europe, was despotic is beyond doubt. It is undeniable that it employed considerable repression in the pursuit of its policies. It is also clear that it initiated radical social change that was bitterly opposed by many of those affected. Agricultural cooperatives were created; peasants were subjected to extraordinary taxation, coercion and police supervision; private industry was decimated

---

3   Komárom-Esztergom Megyei Levéltár (Komárom-Esztergom County Archive, hereafter KEML), *Magyar Szocialista Munkáspárt Komárom Megyei Bizottság Archívium iratai* (Papers of the Archive of the Komárom County Committee of the Hungarian Socialist Workers' Party, hereafter MSZMP KMBA ir.) 32f.4/150.e, p. 26.

4   Kürti 1953, pp. 1024–5.

5   For an introduction to the social history of post-war Hungary, see Valuch 2001. The best recent general overview of the Stalinist years is provided in Romsics 1999, pp. 333–82. See also Gyarmati, Botos, Zinner and Korom 1988.

6   For a sample of this literature, in both English and Hungarian, see Hankiss 1990; Szakács and Zinner 1997; Standeisky, Kozák, Pataki and Rainer (eds.) 1998; Róna-Tas 1997; Belényi and Varga 2000, pp. 13–52; and Szakács 1998, pp. 257–98.

and large numbers of people were forced into industrial jobs. However, this picture is one sided. The Stalinist collectivisation drives were abandoned in Hungary in 1953, and although they were half-heartedly revived in 1955, Hungarian agriculture was not fully collectivised until 1961.[7] Despite the state's apparent grip on industry, large black markets – fuelled by the failure of the state sector and endemic corruption – undermined the functioning of socialised enterprises. Large numbers of people were forced into industrial jobs, but informal wage bargaining, labour mobility, and behaviour termed 'labour indiscipline', meant that the state lacked authority over them.[8]

These processes are similar to those identified by research in social history on socialist dictatorships in the Soviet Union and Eastern Europe outside Hungary. This research has examined 'the limits of dictatorship', and thus has allowed the degree to which state power influenced social process to be investigated as a problem.[9] The issues of how the power of the socialist state affected industrial workers, and how workers responded to state power, have been identified by some of this research as central to an understanding of the nature of the 'limits of dictatorship' and thus of socialist society. In the Soviet context, although individual scholars differ on the question of the extent of the power of industrial workers vis-à-vis the Stalinist state, there appears to be a consensus that the industrial workforce was endowed with a degree of countervailing power. Furthermore, social histories of industrial labour have shown that socialist industrialisation utterly transformed the workforce, as industry absorbed huge numbers of migrants from the countryside. During the 1930s, a Soviet working class was made that was very different in terms of its culture and behaviour from the workforce that existed during the 1920s.[10]

At the end of the 1940s, the institutions of the state and economy in Eastern Europe were transformed along Soviet lines as the Stalinist model was exported westward. When socialist industrialisation began in these countries, the scope for the transformation of the industrial workforce was much smaller than it had been in the Soviet Union two decades earlier. While much less research

---

7   For agriculture, see Lampland 1995, pp. 109–66; Rév 1987, pp. 335–50; and Varga 2001.
8   For industry and industrial labour, see Pittaway, chapter 4 of this book.
9   The phrase 'the limits of dictatorship' is borrowed from the title of an edited collection dealing with the GDR; see Bessel and Jessen (eds.) 1996. Research in Soviet social history has explored 'the limits of dictatorship' for some time. For a recent anthology of new research, see Fitzpatrick (ed.) 1999. For some of the best work on post-war Eastern Europe, see Bokovoy 1998; Connelly 2000; Kenney 1997; Kopstein 1997; and Lilly 2001.
10 For a sample of this literature, see Filtzer 1986; Kuromiya 1988; Siegelbaum 1988; Siegelbaum and Grigor Suny (eds.) 1994; Kotkin 1995; Straus 1997; and Fitzpatrick 1999.

has been conducted on the transformation of industrial labour and working-class community life in Eastern Europe than in the former Soviet Union, the work that has been done suggests that pre-socialist working-class culture remained resilient. For Poland, Padraic Kenney has argued that attempts during the very early post-war years to reshape the shop floor met with considerable resistance rooted in Polish working-class culture. Kenney suggests that the Stalinist state's transformation of Poland's industrial workforce was, at best, highly uneven.[11] In the German Democratic Republic (GDR), a working-class culture – one that survived the transformations in work and everyday life that the creation of socialist dictatorship brought in train – provided a basis for certain forms of collective behaviour that placed real limits on state action.[12] For Czechoslovakia, Peter Heumos has suggested that 'trade unionist' attitudes inherited from the interwar period survived and motivated worker behaviour throughout the early socialist years, which, in turn, limited the power of the state.[13]

In Hungary, as the institutions of dictatorship were built during 1948 and 1949, the country's new rulers attempted to transform industrial production, adapting models derived from Soviet practice, in order to lay the foundations for comprehensive economic planning. Wages tied to individual performance, socialist labour competition, the wider application of scientific management, and increased production targets, were introduced.[14] These measures were more than simply the instruments of centralised economic planning; they formed part of a programme to create a class-conscious socialist working class out of the fragmented and divided pre-socialist workforce. Such societal goals were often captured in party propaganda. When the Stakhanovite movement emerged in Hungary in early 1950, the Party daily hailed the new Stakhanovites as the 'vanguard' of a 'new working class.' It proclaimed that 'in the Stakhanovite movement a new kind of worker has appeared; the first signs of the new communist working class have emerged'.[15] As the mentality of the 'vanguard' spread throughout the workforce, a 'new working class' would be forged: '[f]rom the practice of their everyday life the toiling masses learn the truth of what theory tells us, that the construction of socialism ... is tied to an increase in the welfare of the workers'.[16]

---

11 Kenney 1997.
12 Kopstein 1997; Hübner 1995.
13 Heumos 1999, pp. 119–28.
14 Pittaway, chapter 4 of this volume.
15 'Új munkásosztály születik', *Szabad Nép*, 5 March 1950, p. 1.
16 'Erősödő munkásosztály – emelkedő életszinvonal', *Szabad Nép*, 5 February 1950, p. 3.

But attempts to transform Hungary's working class using instruments such as payment-by-results and socialist labour competition met with considerable opposition rooted in Hungarian shop-floor culture, where industrial workers jealously protected their on-the-job control. This was a particular issue among skilled workers who, through their unions, exercised considerable control over job rates. The conflict between the Stalinist revolution in production and shop-floor culture was captured in the official biography of the Budapest Stakhanovite, József Kiszlinger. Kiszlinger, a skilled worker in the highly unionised heavy-engineering sector, had 'endless problems with the older [workers]' when he tried to improve his own work performance. 'Sometimes he worked with a different knife and managed to over-fulfil his quota. The older ones attacked him: "Are you insane? You're undermining us!" Even one of the union officials came to warn him: "Watch yourself, son. This isn't a good idea. Don't go for too high a percentage".[17] As the institutions of the dictatorship were strengthened, the state dealt with endemic shop-floor opposition by subordinating the trade unions to party policy – a process completed in early 1949.[18] The suppression of independent organisations in the workplace was, however, insufficient, given that the state needed to mobilise substantial numbers of workers behind labour competition if they were to break the influence of traditional working-class culture.

Pre-socialist working-class culture was underpinned by notions of hierarchy, with the experienced, urban, skilled worker at the top. Hierarchies of skill were not merely connected to knowledge and experience, but were also overlain with deeply held ideas about gender and generation. Working-class cultures were often both deeply masculine and based upon seniority. Furthermore, political, economic and cultural tensions between urban and rural dwellers, which were often shrouded in assumptions about skill, were endemic.[19] The state deliberately subverted existing hierarchies to mobilise workers. In the early days of the labour competition, the party-leadership targeted younger workers and apprentices to considerable effect.[20] The state's use of the young to bust rates and pave the way for the transformation of production led to considerable tension. At the Bánhida power plant, the authority of older stokers

---

17 Varga 1951, p. 20.
18 Varga 1995, pp. 13–94.
19 For some useful surveys of the pre-socialist industrial workforce and shop-floor culture, see Berend in Lengyel (ed.) 1993, pp. 151–68; Földes 1980, pp. 309–19; Gereblyés 1959; Lackó 1989, pp. 3–44; Paládi-Kovács 2000, pp. 239–308; Rézler 1940 and 1943.
20 A clear example of this kind of propaganda is *Harc a Másodpercekért! Kézikönyv az Országos Termelési Versenyhez* 1948.

and boiler men was challenged in 1949 by less experienced younger colleagues through the Stakhanovite movement. Although production relations were remade, this did not result in the creation of a 'new working class'; instead, the state's subversion of generational hierarchies exacerbated pre-existing divisions between workers. Tension between the two groups still persisted in 1951, when it was reported that 'the older stokers still regard the experiences and methods of the younger Stakhanovites with contempt'.[21] Rather than creating the basis for the transformation of working-class culture, as the state had intended, the implementation of its policies produced conflict, as many older workers sought to defend that culture and the traditional hierarchies embedded within it.

These conflicts set the stage for the growth of tension that accompanied the increase in the size of the labour force. With Hungary's first five-year plan, begun in 1950, a process of industrialisation was initiated that demanded a huge expansion in the labour force. The state viewed this as an opportunity to complete the task of creating its 'new working class'. For one senior party-official, charged with leading political work on the country's largest construction site, increased employment under socialist conditions would allow 'fearful, passive, insecure village labourers to be transformed into class-conscious, fighting workers'.[22] In order to achieve this, the state combined expansion of the workforce with a drive to open industrial employment to previously excluded groups, and in so doing it directly challenged the hierarchical nature of working-class culture. Traditional apprenticeships were abolished as young people were recruited *en masse* into key skilled positions through crash training courses that challenged older notions of apprenticeship and seniority.[23] Women were encouraged to regard socialist labour as a potential career, as campaigns were initiated to recruit women into the industrial workforce as men's equals.[24] Planners exhorted enterprises 'not to place women into occupations that have been generally filled by women... Women should

---

21 Politikatörténeti és Szakszervezeti Levéltár (Archive of Political History and Trade Unions, hereafter PtSzL), A Volt Szakszervezetek Központi Levéltár anyaga (Papers of the former Central Archive of the Trade Unions, hereafter SZKL), Komárom Szakszervezetek Megyei Tanácsa (Komárom County Council of Trade Unions, hereafter Komárom SZMT) 80d./1951, 'Jegyzőkönyv felvétetett a Vas- és Fémipari Dolgozók Szakszervezete Komárommegyei Területi Bizottság helységében Tatabányán megtartott Megye Bizottsági ülésről', p. 5.

22 Quoted in *A Szocializmus Épitésének Útján: A Magyar Dolgozók Pártja II, Kongresszusának Anyagából* 1956, p. 276.

23 Darvas 1983, pp. 59–75.

24 Goven 1993, pp. 30–108; Lampland in Kruks, Rapp and Young (eds.) 1989, pp. 306–22.

be directed to every occupation ... except those which their physical strength prevents them filling'.[25] This move also directly challenged gendered hierarchies on Hungarian factory floors, provoking considerable resistance. The state introduced labour recruitment drives in poorer rural areas to find future skilled workers who could be trained in Hungary's industrial centres, thus directly undermining perceived hierarchies based on notions of an urban-rural divide.[26]

Despite these efforts, the state did not get its 'new working class', as challenges posed to hierarchy by regime policies met with ferocious resistance. Labour competition and wages based on payment-by-results were never embraced by Hungarian workers. They were only ever accepted insofar as they led to increased earnings, and acceptance often came at the cost of considerable tension between workers. As the first five-year plan was implemented in 1950, production targets were increased and wage levels fell, destroying even the limited consent on which the state's partial mobilisation of the workforce had rested. Furthermore, the introduction of the plan led to the emergence of Hungary's early socialist 'factory regime', which had profound effects on shop-floor culture.[27] Collectivist centralisation at the national level was combined with individualised production targets for each worker to which wages were explicitly tied. Remuneration was linked to making the rate for a given job. At the same time, bottlenecks and shortages generated by the breakneck speed of socialist industrialisation reshaped the rhythm of production, producing periodic shortages of work on factory floors. This environment only exacerbated the tensions between workers that had been generated by state attempts to subvert traditional hierarchies.[28] The number of workers in industry (excluding construction) rose from 412,590 in 1949 to 616,544 in 1953, while those in construction increased from 121,888 in 1950 to 194,827 in 1953.[29] Despite this increase, skilled experienced labour was in short supply. Foremen, largely promoted from the ranks of skilled workers, believed in the hierarchies embedded in working-class culture. The demands of plan targets, combined with the chaos of socialist production and submerged yet widespread working-class

---

25 Magyar Országos Levéltár (Hungarian National Archive, hereafter MOL), MDP-MSZMP Központi Szervek iratai (Papers of the Central Organs of the Hungarian Workers' Party-Hungarian Socialist Workers' Party, hereafter MKS) 276f.116/430.e, pp. 15–17.
26 MOL XIX-A-16b/138d, p. 1.
27 For more on the concept of 'factory regimes', in both socialist and capitalist contexts, see Burawoy 1985; Burawoy and Lukács 1992.
28 This is explored in much greater depth in chapter 4 of this book.
29 Központi Statisztikai Hivatal 1951, p. 13, and 1954, p. 27.

resistance, forced management to cooperate with older skilled workers. This created the space for the reproduction of traditional hierarchies in the context of early socialist factories and mines as pre-socialist working-class culture remained resilient. Skilled workers reasserted their preeminent position, however, in opposition to members of previously marginal groups. Conflict around generation, gender and social origin accompanied the reproduction of hierarchy in the context of socialist industrialisation.

This article shows how the hierarchies that had underpinned pre-socialist shop-floor culture were defended and reasserted by skilled workers in the context of Hungary's early socialist factory regime. It begins by describing the material environment in which such hierarchies were reproduced by tracing the emergence of the early socialist factory regime in one industrial plant, paying particular attention to the patterns of dependence that grew between more experienced skilled workers and lower management. The focus is then broadened to examine industry as a whole, in order to show how such patterns of dependence created space for pre-socialist hierarchies to reassert themselves in socialist factories. Finally, it proceeds to examine the reproduction of pre-socialist hierarchies by concentrating on shop-floor conflict around generation, gender and social origin.

Popular Opposition, Collective Action, and Informal Bargaining: The Case of the Danube Shoe Factory

The experience of the Danube Shoe Factory sheds light on the changing patterns of conflict and cooperation in Hungarian industry during the early years of the first five-year plan. It provides a case study of how working-class opposition and the environment of socialist production generated informal cooperation between management and experienced skilled workers. This cooperation was a crucial precondition of the reproduction of hierarchy. By 1952, the Danube Shoe Factory was the largest shoe factory in the country. It produced over 2.5 million pairs of shoes during the year and employed 2,513 people.[30] It became an independent enterprise in 1948, and before that it had been the shoemaking division of a larger leather-working plant. At the beginning of the first five-year plan, it relied on handicraft methods and largely

---

30   MOL Magyar Szocialista Munkáspárt Budapesti Bizottság Archivium irarai (Papers of the Archive of the Budapest Committee of the Hungarian Socialist Workers' Party, hereafter MBp) 176f.2/190/100.e, p. 43.

outdated technology.³¹ Over the next three years, the plant was dramatically extended and modernised. In 1949, the existing workshops were closed and transformed. Production was completely reorganised through the creation of vertically integrated workshops dealing with leather cutting and stitching. In each shop, production was centred on production lines, with each worker performing specialised and narrowly defined tasks. New machinery was imported from the Soviet Union and Czechoslovakia. The factory expanded as new workshops were added, allowing production to increase fivefold between 1948 and 1952. The intentions of economic planners in organising work around a series of production lines were clearly stated by one Stakhanovite in the factory. As far as he was concerned, 'with a production line it's possible to produce much more than before and one can really pay more attention to quality ... The whole process is so unified and continuous that the shoes can be looked at individually'.³²

The transformation of the Danube Shoe Factory reflected the broader industrial programme of the new socialist state. Workers from smaller, older factories, alongside newly nationalised artisans, were concentrated in large-scale enterprises in which production was 'scientifically' organised. This proceeded alongside state attempts to speed up production through socialist labour competition, to create 'scientifically' determined individual work targets, or quotas, and to tie remuneration explicitly to them.³³ These policies, implemented from 1949 onward, met with hostility from skilled workers who were more used to on-the-job control, considerable autonomy and the ability to regulate their own pace of work.³⁴ Party-officials dismissed this discontent as 'political backwardness that is closely connected with skill-based backwardness'.³⁵

Workers outside the Danube Shoe Factory were also suspicious of the intentions of the state in production. In the workplace, industrial workers developed a strictly instrumental attitude toward payment-by-results and socialist labour competition. Workers only participated where direct material benefits resulted.³⁶ Fortunately for the regime, the late 1940s were a period of real and

---

31 *Duna Híradó* 10 June 1950, p. 3.
32 For this comment, see ibid. For the rising production of the new factory as it was modernised, see MOL MBp 176f.2/190/100.e, p. 43. On the expansion of the production line system throughout the factory, see *Futószalag* 5 March 1952, p. 3, and 19 April 1952, p. 4. For information on the extent of the transformation of the plant, see *Futószalag* 25 September 1952, p. 1.
33 Pittaway, chapter 4 of this volume.
34 Budapest Főváros Levéltára (Archive of the City of Budapest, hereafter BFL) XXIX/553f./1d.
35 MOL MBp 95f.4/1470.e, p. 74.
36 Garai 1948, pp. 14–15.

rapid wage increases.³⁷ When wages fell, or when the state attempted to raise productivity by increasing production quotas, a wave of shop-floor protest resulted.³⁸ In the second half of 1949, the regime launched a drive to tie workers' wages to individual work targets to prepare for the beginning of the first five-year plan in 1950. Individual forms of labour competition were aggressively promoted in a bid to pave the way for individualised quotas, and thus remuneration. In the run-up to the so-called 'Stalin shift' – the campaign to celebrate the Soviet leader's seventieth birthday in December 1949 – the Stakhanovite movement was introduced in Hungary.³⁹ The new Stakhanovites were widely distrusted, since workers feared that increases in production targets for all would follow from the exceptional performance of a few.⁴⁰ There was, however, little general discontent, as high quota fulfilment led to increased wages across industry in the first months of 1950.⁴¹ This tacit compromise was broken by sharp increases in production targets during the summer. These led to increased work intensity and reduced wages, and provoked one of the largest waves of open worker unrest in the post-war period. The state responded to the slightest signs of discontent with repression. Even individual acts of protest were ruthlessly crushed by the state security services.⁴²

The effects of increased production targets on workers in the Danube Shoe Factory were not dissimilar to those experienced elsewhere. The new quotas were difficult to fulfil: a majority of workers in the plant failed to meet them in the second half of 1950, and wages fell accordingly.⁴³ Older workers in the factory unfavourably compared working conditions and wages under socialism to those that existed prior to nationalisation in 1948. Such older workers told their newer colleagues that 'under Wolfner [the previous capitalist owner] they had

---

37 'A magyar munkásosztály fejlödése' 1954, p. 20.
38 MOL MKS 276f.116/180.e, p. 6.
39 For the background to the changes of late 1949, see Hevesi 1950a, pp. 30–2, and 1950b, pp. 85–103.
40 Zala Megyei Levéltár (Zala County Archive, hereafter ZML), Magyar Szocialista Munkáspárt Zala Megyei Bizottság Archivium iratai (Papers of the Archive of the Zala County Committee of the Hungarian Socialist Workers' Party, hereafter MSZMP ZMBA ir.) 57f.1/520.e, p. 20.
41 MOL MKS 276f.116/180.e, pp. 22–3.
42 MOL MBp 95f.4/1200.e, p. 214; PtSzL SZKL Komárom SZMT/42d./1950, p. 1; PtSzL SZKL Komárom SZMT/43d./1950, p. 1; PtSzL SZKL Komárom SZMT/43d./1950, p. 1.
43 MOL MBp 95f.4/1200.e, p. 252.

a better life'. They complained that the basis of the system was 'the enslavement of the worker'.⁴⁴

Manifestations of nostalgia for pre-socialist conditions – although those conditions had often been poor – were fed by the deep sense of betrayal many workers felt when faced with the results of the policies of the socialist regime. Workers in industry as a whole believed themselves to be exploited by 'a bloodsucking government'.⁴⁵ These perceptions of exploitation helped to ensure that pre-socialist working-class identity persisted in early socialist factories and mines. Many of the complaints about low wages, high work intensity, and despotic management, which had provided the backdrop to working-class political activism in the interwar and immediate post-war years, persisted.⁴⁶ Such complaints after 1950 came to be directed against the state. In the Tatabánya mines during the early 1950s, 'there was a great deal of discontent among the miners; they denounced the system and grumbled that despite the difficulty of their work pay was low'.⁴⁷ Deep-seated discontent with working conditions and the system in general persisted in the Danube Shoe Factory throughout the early 1950s. Because of the threat of repression, it rarely took the form of open collective action, and, when it did, fear of the state security services blunted its impact. One former worker who escaped to the West recounted: '[I]n 1953 there were grumbles about the quotas. One time the workers went out on an unofficial smoke break to protest. Work stopped for ten minutes. Because the workers didn't want to risk any more, management simply forgot the incident, and no one felt the consequences'.⁴⁸

Working-class opposition to the regime, and the solidarity it generated, sustained a whole range of practices that subverted management intentions in production and partially substituted for more open forms of collective protest. Industrial workers engaged in widespread albeit concealed acts of protest – as one former worker remembered, 'psychologically the situation was...that they [the workers] were happy if they could harm the Communist system'.⁴⁹ Workers cooperated to subvert the quality-control systems in the factory.

---

44 Open Society Archives (OSA), Radio Free Europe Hungarian Collection (RFE Magyar Gy.), Interviews with Escapees (6)/Item no. 3677/56, p. 3.
45 PtSzL Szakszervezetek Országos Tanácsa (National Council of Trade Unions, hereafter SZOT), Bérosztály (Wage Department)/33d./1953, p. 1.
46 For a survey of working-class political activism in interwar Hungary, see Sipos 1988; for the immediate post-war years, see Habuda 1986.
47 OSA RFE Magyar Gy. 6./Item no. 8083/54, p. 12.
48 Ibid./Item no. 3677/56, p. 2.
49 Ibid./Item no. 08794/53, p. 1.

The plant newspaper criticised workers for accepting and passing on without question the poor-quality shoes made by others.[50] Discontent also manifested itself through widespread theft by workers.[51] This provided the basis for participation by workers in informal and often illegal economic activity outside the factory.[52] Former artisans stole raw materials to manufacture and repair shoes within the framework of the black economy. In 1955, one worker who had been fined on five occasions for theft was finally dismissed and prosecuted for stealing twenty-thousand forints' worth of leather, sole and other related materials.[53] There was, however, almost no scope for expressions of working-class discontent outside the factory, and solidarity between workers behind the factory gates was severely limited. This was due not only to repression, but also to a particularistic climate that grew on the factory floor as a result of the circumstances of socialist production.

Across the economy, and in the Danube Shoe Factory, the individualisation of production and remuneration increased wage differentials between workers – often between workers who had the same job description. Furthermore, the implementation of the regime's policy of rapid industrialisation led to the emergence of widespread shortages of materials, labour, machinery and tools in Hungarian industry during the early 1950s.[54] This meant that production and earnings were at the mercy of the operation of the planned economy. The Danube Shoe Factory constantly struggled with unpredictable deliveries of raw materials that completely depended on the situation of its supplying enterprise. As one manager put it, 'if the leather factory is only making 70–80 percent of its plan target, then we'll never make 100 percent'.[55] The result was considerable fluctuation in earnings. The monthly pay of one typical worker stood in September 1952 at 981 forints; this figure rose to 1,124 forints in October, and then fell back to 822 forints in November.[56] Along with this fluctuation in earnings, take-home pay in the shoe industry was well below the industrial average. In 1953, thirty percent of workers were in the lowest wage categories, while sixty percent were in the median wage category for industry as a whole. Hourly wages were lower in shoe production, category for category, than the industrial average. This led to low wages for skilled workers;

---

50   *Futószalag* 29 August 1953, p. 3.
51   OSA RFE Magyar Gy.6/Item no. 3677/56, p. 3.
52   MOL MBp 176f.2/190/60.e, p. 204.
53   Szabó 1955, p. 3.
54   Pittaway, chapter 4 of this volume.
55   MOL MBp 176f.2/190/60.e, p. 242.
56   MOL MBp 176f.2/190/70.e, p. 73.

the lowest wages for the skilled were as little as 500 forints per month. Unskilled shoemakers earned between 450 and 580 forints.[57]

Low and fluctuating wages led to high labour turnover in the plant and a problem of permanent labour shortage.[58] The quality of the shoes produced declined. This was partly due to the poor quality of much of the leather supplied to the plant. The effects of shortage on the production lines led to a loss of managerial control over the shop floor. The strict vertical integration of tasks within the factory that the introduction of a system based around production lines entailed created the space for small groups of workers to resort to crude though highly effective forms of shop floor bargaining around wages. Informal bargaining often occurred in the stitching shops where the shoes were assembled. Workers seeking an easier quota for a given job, and who had tasks that were crucial to the assembly of the shoe, would perform their jobs sluggishly. This caused work stoppages further down the line, leading in turn to discontent among the affected workers that lower management had to deal with. This was especially effective as a strategy where it endangered plan fulfilment. While the authorities were far from inclined to give in to this kind of action, management had little alternative when faced with severe labour shortages.[59]

Informal bargaining of this kind reshaped shop-floor relations in the factory, leading to what management termed 'disorganisation' of the wage system, as struggles on the production lines increasingly determined wage levels and differentials.[60] Certain groups of workers – namely, older and more experienced skilled workers – benefited disproportionately from informal bargaining. This was because socialist production had created circumstances in which management developed a dependence on certain workers to solve problems in production. The initiative and skill of these workers thus, paradoxically, became crucial to a labour process designed to develop greater control over them. They were able to manipulate this situation and turn it to their own advantage, demanding better working conditions and higher levels of remuneration for their work. This was illustrated by one production run in the leather cutting shops in late 1951. Low-quality leather was delivered to the shop that could not easily be cut on the production lines by the inexperienced new workers. As a result, shop-management reorganised production. It concentrated the small number of experienced workers into brigades of five, separating

---

57 PtSzL SZKL SZOT Bérosztály/3od./1953, pp. 4–5.
58 MOL MBp 176f.2/190/100.e, pp. 6–13.
59 *Futószalag* 22 March 1952, p. 3.
60 *Futószalag* 28 April 1952, p. 3.

them from the rest and giving them special lower quotas, and allowing them to perform the best work. Lower paying, discontinuous work was given to the other workers.[61]

Informal bargaining generally benefited more experienced skilled workers because of the patterns of cooperation and mutual dependence that developed between the skilled and lower management. This characteristic of informal bargaining created the material backdrop to the reproduction of traditional hierarchies because of the connections that existed between notions of skill and such hierarchies. These patterns of dependence and cooperation between experienced skilled workers and lower management were not merely a characteristic of shoe manufacture; they existed across industry, construction and mining. They arose not only as a result of the imperatives of production, but also of foremen, shop managers and experienced skilled workers sharing certain common values and attitudes inherited from pre-socialist working-class culture. Such patterns of bargaining, therefore, contributed to the reproduction of hierarchies that had been rooted in that culture.

The Meaning of Skill: Hierarchy, Working-Class Culture, and Socialist Production

In spring 1953, the regime began to pay attention to the skill level of the industrial workforce. This was because of the poor quality of much production. In 1952, the calorie content of the coal mined in the Nógrád field for export to Czechoslovakia was so low that it could not be sold. In the machine industry, the parts for coal-cutting machinery were so poorly cast that they often broke.[62] The authorities blamed the low skill level of the workforce for the poor quality of production. Despite figures showing that the percentage of skilled workers in industry increased from 32.1 percent in 1949 to 48.2 percent in 1953,[63] questions were raised as to whether such figures reflected the true skill level of the workforce. One party-investigator, examining work methods in the machine industry, was horrified by the methods used by many 'young workers'. He reported:

---

61   MOL MBp 176f.2/190/20.e, p. 139.
62   MOL MKS 276f.94/5910.e, pp. 110, 127–37.
63   See footnote 37 above.

[T]he workers are not clear about even the most basic questions. For example, in the repair and assembly shop one worker used a tool that should never have been used for that particular process... or he just put a run through the machine as fast as possible without caring what came out, or used such a large drilling bit that he could not possibly have drilled a hole with regard to any technical specifications at all.[64]

Similar conclusions had been reached by managers, if not by the authorities, long before 1953. During the early years of socialist industrialisation, the state had been deeply suspicious of such arguments. Many foremen had been directly criticised for allocating good work to more experienced workers on these grounds and neglecting newer workers.[65] They had, in fact, done this for two reasons. The first was practical: experienced skilled workers were in short supply. The poaching of skilled labour and labour turnover were widespread, and state regulations to prevent this, despite being draconian, proved ineffective.[66] Second, there was considerable social solidarity between foremen and the best skilled workers across industry. Most foremen had been promoted from the ranks of the skilled workers, and this connection had been accentuated by the purges initiated in 1950 and 1951 against foremen with a 'capitalist' past. The result in one large Budapest factory, which was far from atypical, was that in 1951, '95 percent [of foremen] had worked in their current positions for under a year, and prior to that they had been skilled workers or semiskilled machinists in the factory'.[67] Skilled workers had been able to use their positions to secure for themselves preferential access to raw materials, unofficial wage rates or quotas that were easier to reach than those officially handed down. This had often been achieved at the expense of workers who were either less skilled or less experienced, or even excluded for other reasons from the small groups of workers able to use their skill as a bargaining chip with lower management.

Skill was a contested category on Hungarian shop floors during the early 1950s. To be a skilled worker in pre-socialist Hungary meant having attained skill in and experience of a given production process during a long period of

---

64 MOL MKS 276f.94/5910.e, p. 62.
65 These kinds of criticisms can be seen in: PtSzL SZKL Fejér Szakszervezetek Megyei Tanácsa (Fejér County Council of Trade Unions, hereafter Fejér SZMT) 72d./1951, pp. 1–3.
66 For evidence of the poaching of skilled labour in heavy industry, see ZML MSZMP ZMBA ir. 57f.1/520.e., pp. 47–9; on labour mobility, see Belényi 1993, pp. 106–9.
67 Quoted in Varga 1984, p. 71.

apprenticeship. As part of its bid to rapidly expand the workforce, the state replaced apprenticeships with crash training programmes. Older skilled workers bitterly resented younger, newer workmates being given the same wage rates when they had only completed short training programmes that were deemed inferior to traditional apprenticeships.[68] Skill was not only a matter of experience or training, although it was, of course, very much tied to these; it was also a social and cultural construct bound to hierarchies based on gender, generation, and social origin, which had been inherited from pre-socialist working-class culture.

The identification of 'good', 'experienced' or even 'skilled' workers was as much linked to such perceived hierarchies as it was to actual attributes of skill or experience. These perceived hierarchies could exclude others from the highly particular groups upon which informal bargaining was based. The Party Committee of the fourth district of Budapest conducted an investigation into poor third-quarter plan fulfilment in the Danube Shoe Factory in October 1952. They found that one workshop received worse raw materials than the others. Its plan fulfilment was consistently poor. Management dumped inexperienced workers there. The wage affairs officer of the factory trade-union branch told investigators that 'across the factory this production line is nicknamed "the agricultural cooperative conveyor". In part the workers use this term because of the large number of workers from rural areas who are on it, and also because of the number of beginners'.[69] The introduction of women to certain jobs in heavy industry was fiercely resisted by male skilled workers and foremen. This was crucial in determining the gender composition of the industrial workforce. In the Óbuda Gas Factory, skilled workers told women that 'they should leave their jobs, because they aren't suitable for them'. In the Bázakerretye Oil Drilling Plant, male skilled workers were accused of not regarding their female colleagues as proper workers. Persistent problems of intimidation were reported.[70] Foremen reserved the best work for male skilled workers, while allocating the worst to women. In the Elzett Factory, 'the female employees were put on different machines each day, hindering their chances of making their rate'.[71] The rapid promotion of young workers taught their skill on crash training schemes provoked opposition from older skilled workers on the grounds that this challenged seniority and perceived generational

---

68 Pittaway 1998, pp. 170–6.
69 MOL MBp 176f.2/190/70.e, p. 244.
70 For the incident in the Óbuda Gas Factory, see PtSzL SZKL Fejér SZMT/72d./1951, p. 3; for the various incidents at Bázakerretye, see ZML MSZMP ZMBA ir. 61f.3/3/ PTO/60.e, p. 1.
71 PtSzL SZKL Fejér SZMT/72d./1951, p. 3.

hierarchies. Older skilled workers often complained that their younger colleagues were inept, undisciplined, and corrupt.[72] Many foremen shared these opinions. This led to active discrimination against many recently trained young workers. In the Ganz Wagon Factory, one young worker was allocated the jobs that no one else would take on a regular basis, and which, in some cases, were judged by union investigators to be physically impossible.[73]

Generations of Skill: Work, Youth, and Bargaining

Struggles around skill and hierarchy were most evident where generational tension on the shop floor was marked. Seventy-five thousand young workers who entered industry between 1948 and 1953 trained as skilled workers in the crash training programmes instituted after the abolition of the apprenticeship system.[74] By 1953, it was clear to economic planners that workers trained in these crash programmes were insufficiently skilled. When newly trained workers went into productive life, they were only able to fulfil their quotas if they were given work that fell into low wage categories, thus leading to a problem of low pay.[75] The authorities gradually became aware of this problem. The evidence often quoted by official inspectors for the poor skill levels of many younger workers was their frequent recourse to highly unorthodox work methods, or their blatant lack of concern for the quality of what they produced. One inspector examining shop-floor production in the machine industry clearly stated he was convinced that many of the younger workers were 'unable to judge their own work'.[76]

The poor quality of state-sponsored mass training schemes placed young workers at a disadvantage when they entered productive life. Yet the low wages of young workers and their use of questionable work methods were not exclusively the result of poor training. Before 1953, their older colleagues noticed a marked difference between themselves and younger workers in their attitudes toward work. This led them to complain about undisciplined young workers. In the United Lighting and Electrics Factory, an older Stakhanovite complained:

---

72 BFL XXIX/321/1d, p. 3.
73 PtSzL SZKL Fejér SZMT/72d./1951, p. 1.
74 Note 37 above.
75 PtSzL SZKL SZOT Bérosztály/30d./1953, p. 5.
76 MOL MKS 276f.94/5910.e, p. 61.

In our workshop there are sixteen Stakhanovites, of whom six are young. From them it seems that work with the younger ones is not satisfactory. It's not only us; the young ones are to blame too. They go to get the high percentages, ignoring the fact that they should first look to the quality of what they produce, and only then the quantity. There are those who just ignore our warnings, and answer back, saying they'll pay a few forints penalty for producing scrap if in the end they get higher earnings.[77]

In the neighbouring Duclós Mine Machinery Factory, these differences fed generational tension. One party member described a piece of work completed by a young worker that the quality-control department had sent back: 'I was curious as to why and looked at it... The whole of the part was not properly cut. I don't know how such people can get work'. Another recounted an incident in which 'Simon [the young worker] asked for two knives. I gave him two knives that the foreman had cleared as being good for the job... Simon replied that they were not usable and in the middle of this swore at me'. Another blamed young workers for destroying grinding machines by employing unauthorised methods to make their quotas.[78]

Behind this generational tension lay deep-seated resentment on the part of older skilled workers at the role that the growth in the number of young workers trained on crash courses had played in subverting the traditional generational hierarchies that had characterised pre-socialist shop-floor culture. This resentment manifested itself in the form of complaints about the nature and behaviour of the young workers who had entered productive life through such training schemes. In the United Lighting and Electrics Factory, one skilled worker complained that 'there are trainees who have absolutely no interest in the skill that they train for. It would be better to send them elsewhere, because all they do is destroy work discipline'.[79] In the same factory, older skilled workers simply 'did not want to accept' new trainees as skilled workers.[80] In the early 1950s, this attitude was condemned officially by the regime as 'skill-based chauvinism', and was regarded as a manifestation of the 'underground work of right-wing Social Democrats'.[81]

---

77   BFL XXIX/321/2d, p. 6.
78   MOL MBp 176f.2/191/40.e, pp. 138–9.
79   BFL XXIX/321/1d, p. 3.
80   MOL MBp 134f./220.e, p. 172.
81   For some examples of reports that show the regime's concern about 'right-wing Social Democrats' in Budapest, see the documents in MOL MBp 95f.2/168/b0.e, and MOL MBp 95f.3/3450.e.

The foremen often identified with older workers, from whose ranks many of them had been drawn and whose attitudes they shared. In 1952, the factory party-committee of the United Lighting and Electrics Factory believed that many of the plant's engineers and foremen were 'former Social Democrats' with little attachment to socialist work methods. It accused them of enjoying 'good relations with members of the aristocracy of labor' – code for older skilled workers in the plant.[82] On the socialist shop floor, the distribution of work affected individuals' abilities to make their quotas. The solidarity that existed between older workers and foremen often helped to ensure that older workers received more of the highly lucrative work available than did their younger workmates. In the tool-making shop of the United Lighting and Electrics Factory, newly qualified apprentices 'almost never received decent jobs ... Some workers are able to take only work that they judge to be advantageous to themselves'.[83] In the Vacuum Technology division of the factory, the plant director drew attention to the effects of informal bargaining in May 1953: '[t]he informal selection of work has still not disappeared. As a consequence of this the large, long batches are given to the key workers and for this reason young, promising workers are just not able to develop'.[84] In the Danube Shoe Factory, their unfavourable situation within the internal division of labour of the plant led young skilled workers to quit their jobs in greater numbers than any other group in November 1953.[85]

Job-quitting was a criminal offense, and while the laws against it were unevenly applied, it was still potentially dangerous.[86] Young workers often had to resort to other strategies. In the Duclós Mining Machinery Factory in 1954, the only good work, according to many young workers, was that 'where the quota could be fulfilled by 170 percent, or enough to get the desired amount of money'. When work was issued without the right quota or rate of pay, 'an endless amount of scrap was produced'.[87] In 1952, in one textile factory, underperforming workers frequently submitted blatantly fraudulent time sheets to the factory administration, counting on the negligence of the foremen to pass them. A query from the quota office, or a failure to pay the claimed amount,

---

82 MOL MBp 176f.2/194/190.e, p. 14; MOL MBp 176f.2/194/230.e, pp. 82–9.
83 MOL MBp 176f.2/194/190.e, p. 17.
84 BFL XXIX/321/4d.
85 MOL MBp 176f.2/190/110.e, p. 202.
86 On the application of the law to prevent job-quitting in the early 1950s, see Gyekiczky 1989, pp. 25–89.
87 MOL MBp 176f.2/191/90.e, pp. 27–8.

resulted in small groups of workers abandoning their machines for ten minutes to complain, disrupting production on an entire floor.[88]

Party-inspectors who entered factories in 1953 reported that the reasons for the poor quality of much production were to be found in the inadequate skill level of 'new' skilled workers, but this gave only part of the picture. The problem of training skilled workers, along with the short supply of experienced skilled labour, provided part of the material background to generational conflict on the shop floor. Such conflict was as much related to notions of how skill was acquired, and how it was connected to perceived generational hierarchies, as it was to actual skill levels. Older workers used their ideas about skill – something that could only be transferred through long and careful study on the shop floor under a master, and was closely related to age and experience – as a bargaining chip. In factories across the country in the early 1950s, the key to maximising earnings was to gain sufficient work to make the quota. Older workers were able to use their ideas about skill being intimately tied to experience, length of service, and generation, to secure a monopoly over such work. As a result of younger workers' allocation to frequently impossible jobs, abuse of machinery was often a rational response to their position within a structure of shop-floor bargaining that was heavily skewed against them.

By 1953, policy makers had come to accept the assumptions of older workers about skill, retreating from earlier notions that had branded those who held such ideas as 'skill-based chauvinists'. In 1951, an official report had attacked a factory manager for discriminating against a young worker.[89] By 1954, such reports were discussing the percentages of young workers who had an 'insufficient command of their craft'.[90] These retreats by policy makers underlined the extent to which hierarchies that had underpinned pre-socialist working-class culture had been able to reassert themselves in the environment of the early socialist factory.

Gendered Conflict: Women, Men, and the Politics of Work

Open gender conflict in Hungarian industry was much rarer than open generational conflict, although gendered hierarchies played a central role in shaping working-class identities during the early 1950s. As industrial employment expanded, women were encouraged to regard socialist labour as a calling and,

---

88   MOL MBp 143f./100.e, pp. 84–7.
89   PtSzL SZKL Fejér SZMT/72d./1951, p. 1.
90   See footnote 37 above.

consequently, to enter jobs previously closed to them.[91] The women who tried to do so met with obstacles similar to those faced by younger male workers in attempting to establish themselves in their workplaces, especially when they took skilled positions. Margit Fekete arrived in the male-dominated construction sector as an aspiring skilled worker. On 4 May 1951, she took work at Sztálinváros, where a steel plant and new town were to be built, as a trainee reinforced-concrete fitter. On completing her course in November, management assigned her to Site XII. Site XII, she later complained, 'didn't take me on; they said the work was not suitable for women. I then asked why our state taught me if that was the case'. The refusal to employ her happened at a time when the site was short of ten reinforced-concrete fitters.[92]

It was not merely management, nor was it the undoubted physical difficulty of the work, that represented a barrier to women establishing themselves as construction workers, although both of these factors played their part. By early 1952, there were 2,541 women at Sztálinváros, where a total of 14,708 were employed.[93] Some women recruits undoubtedly found the work difficult and actively sought reassignment to easier jobs. Management on the Sztálinváros construction site, closely monitored by the party leadership in Budapest, made stronger efforts to integrate women into the workforce than at any other establishment in the country. Sztálinváros was conceived as a showpiece of the new socialist society that the state set out to build.[94] Furthermore, the construction site was at the forefront of the attempts of economic planners to eliminate the 'artisanal nature' of Hungary's construction industry and to transform it along modern socialist lines.[95] Given the stress placed by the state on equality for women in socialist labour, management sought to provide ways to integrate women into what was essentially a male industry. It attempted to do this by creating a women-only work site, which was heralded as a pioneering measure by officials. This was to be one small part of construction at Sztálinváros. The aim of the work site was to ensure that women were given appropriate tasks and that they were adequately prepared for work at other locations in Sztálinváros. To this end, they were assisted by a team of full-time trainers who

---

91   Lampland 1989.
92   Fekete 1951, p. 2.
93   Fejér Megyei Levéltár (Fejér County Archive, hereafter FML), Magyar Szocialista Munkáspárt Fejér Megyei Bizottság Archiviuma (Archive of the Fejér County Committee of the Hungarian Socialist Workers' Party, hereafter MSZMP FMBA ir.) 17f.2/220.e, p. 1.
94   Erdös 2000, pp. 243–80; Horváth et al. 2000; Miskolczi and Rózsa 1969; Weiner 1959, pp. 17–88.
95   Hámor 1951, p. 628.

were given the task of educating the female bricklayers and unskilled workers in new, Soviet-inspired work methods.[96] According to party reports, after several months a majority of female workers had become accustomed to their work and were able to fulfil their quotas easily.[97]

The women-only work site was also created to protect newly recruited female construction workers from the sexism of their male colleagues. Male construction workers refused to accept the presence of women in their industry. With the creation of the women-only work site, these attitudes manifested themselves in the form of rumours about the performance of the female skilled workers employed there. In one case in early 1952, a rumour that a chimney built by an all-woman brigade had collapsed led to an investigation by site management, who quickly concluded that the rumour was unfounded.[98] Outside the women-only work site, the men subjected female construction workers to campaigns of verbal, and sometimes physical, harassment. One all-women brigade, formed in late spring 1951, faced frequent taunts from male workers, who shouted: '[b]rooms are more suitable for your hands than filthy wheelbarrows'. They were derided publicly by the men as 'weak girls'.[99]

The women-only site provided a space on the larger construction site in which women could train for and work in jobs that had traditionally been regarded as the exclusive province of men. Some on the all-women work site, like Klára Czavrik, replied to the taunts of men who urged her to return to housework with the response: 'at home I would have accepted that, but I came here to build'. She came to regard it as a matter of pride that she proved the men wrong, and thus persevered in the face of their derision, earning the praise of party propagandists anxious to combat sexism on the site.[100] Despite these achievements, the women-only work site was marginalised on the larger construction site, and failed to become a school for female skilled workers who would later take their place alongside men in building the new socialist city. Management and the Party tried to integrate male and female labour by creating mixed brigades, but these were almost impossible to establish. This was not because of the lower ability of the women, but because of resistance among the men. According to one party secretary, '[i]t would be impossible to put men into mixed brigades because the men would not readily join them, and of

---

96 Belényi and Varga 2000, p. 172.
97 FML MSZMP FMBA ir. 17f.2/230.e, p. 1.
98 'Több megértést a női dolgozóknak', *Sztálin Vasmű Épitője*, 22 February 1952, p. 3.
99 'Női dolgozóink élen járnak a termelésben', *Sztálin Vasmű Épitője*, 23 November 1951, p. 1.
100 Ibid.

those who would, only the weakest men would go'.[101] The masculine culture of construction workers clashed sharply with attempts to integrate women into the industry's workforce. In part, this culture associated masculinity with physical strength, thus identifying work in construction as male work. Male hostility contained another dimension tied to gendered notions of hierarchy shared by male workers outside construction. In a climate of shortages and frequent work stoppages, men believed it illegitimate that women were allowed to take work on the construction site. The memory of the high unemployment experienced by construction workers in the immediate post-war years was keenly felt.[102] As bottlenecks and shortages of raw materials led to some workers lying idle waiting for work, many construction workers saw the work stoppages as a shortage of work akin to the unemployment of the late 1940s. Newspapers in Sztálinváros carried complaints urging the authorities to 'end unemployment among skilled workers'.[103] One of the roots of male hostility to the introduction of female labour into construction in this context was identified by one woman who made it into a mixed brigade: 'Women couldn't really work in construction when there wasn't enough work for the men'.[104] The resistance of men to working alongside women in construction was a manifestation of deeply held notions about the relationship between gender and work across industry. Gendered notions of hierarchy, which claimed that men were breadwinners and therefore had a greater right to work than their female workmates, manifested themselves on the site. Consequently, men sought to maintain a monopoly on work, and thus on earnings, in the disorganised shortage-ridden economy of the construction site. It was not only construction where the introduction of women to male-dominated jobs confronted working-class masculinity and similar gendered notions of hierarchy. In the Zala oil fields in 1951, workers on one drilling site instituted a work slowdown. Investigations revealed that it had been incited by two workers who claimed that 'it wasn't worth working hard because new women workers earn more than us and we have to make a stand on this issue'.[105] This revealed a perceived gendered hierarchy between workers that asserted a male worker's right to earn more than a woman in the same job.

---

101   FML MSZMP FMBA ir. 17f.1/220.e, p. 6.
102   The memories of the construction workers on the site of the poverty and unemployment of the late 1940s were recorded in the interviews collected in Dobos 1958.
103   Fekete 1951.
104   'Ma már Sztahanovista vasbetonszerelő vagyok', *Sztálin Vasmű Épitője*, 19 August 1952, p. 2.
105   ZML MSZMP ZMBA ir. 61f.4/3Agit/30.e, p. 1.

Sztálinváros demonstrated at a local level what happened in industry as a whole to the state's attempts to integrate women into the industrial labour force. Nationally, the state planned to recruit seventy-six thousand women into industry over the course of the first five-year plan. This drive to recruit women was combined with a campaign to subvert older gender hierarchies by breaking the male monopoly over certain skilled trades. A policy of affirmative action was introduced to ensure that a minimum of thirty to fifty percent of training enrolments for skilled work were filled by young women.[106] This policy had all but failed in its first year. Although women were recruited into the workforce in greater numbers, pre-socialist patterns of gender differentiation within the workforce persisted. During 1951, the Light Industry Ministry, which covered industries where the workforce was already feminised, succeeded in fulfilling its plan, integrating 7,145 women into production, over and above the 7,000 set as its initial goal. In the male-dominated heavy industry, however, egalitarian policies made few inroads. In the sector covered by the Steel and Machine Industry Ministry, only 18,740 new female employees had been taken on, compared with a target of 29,000.[107] Despite the introduction of affirmative action at the national level – and, unevenly, at the local level, through initiatives like Sztálinváros's women-only construction-site – gendered hierarchies quickly reasserted themselves.

Why did this happen? Part of the answer is provided by the persistence of gendered notions of the division between public and private in post-war Hungary, as well as poor working conditions and the substantial demands made on the household as a result of poverty and goods shortages.[108] The furious resistance of male skilled workers rooted in gendered notions of hierarchy that were woven into working-class culture, and the sympathy this resentment found in foremen and site managers, provides the largest part of the answer to this question. Sectors where masculinity and physical strength were associated proved to be unfriendly ground for female workers. Gendered notions of hierarchy – defining men as breadwinners more deserving of both work and higher wages than women – proved extremely powerful across industry and construction.

While the state attempted to challenge gendered hierarchies on Hungarian shop floors, it never came close to breaking them down. Unlike generational conflict, gender conflict was largely submerged, except in several exceptional cases. Claims to be skilled or experienced rested on foundations that were

---

106   MOL MKS-276f.116/430.e, pp. 15–16.
107   MOL MKS-276f.116/430.e, pp. 70–1.
108   See chapter 5 of this volume.

often interconnected with material conflict around gender identities. Such connections were rarely direct ones, however, and gendered notions of hierarchy were not merely the exclusive province of the skilled elite, but were also to some extent shared by all male workers. The belief that men ought to earn more than women, and had a right to preferential access to employment when work was scarce, was deeply ingrained in working-class culture. In some sectors, notions that associated masculinity and physical strength were superimposed onto this. Consequently, gendered hierarchies on Hungarian shop floors proved remarkably persistent.

Workers and Worker-Peasants: Small-Scale Agriculture, Industrial Work, and Shop-Floor Tension

Perceived hierarchies based on a divide between the urban and the rural, as well as hierarchies between those with agricultural smallholdings and those without, were as interconnected with skill and working-class identity as were gendered hierarchies. In early 1953, according to party reports, skilled workers on the oil-drilling platforms at Lovászi looked down on their unskilled colleagues. This led to serious tension between the two groups. Behind this tension lay two separate factors. The first was that the skilled oilmen resented the fact that their unskilled colleagues could begin training as skilled workers after working for only one year on the site. The second was that many of the unskilled workers were so-called *kétlaki*, that is, they laboured both in industry and agriculture. According to the skilled oilmen, such workers 'did not know how to work... It isn't worth spending time with these workers, because they don't know how to learn anyway'. This led the skilled oilmen to refuse to work alongside them, and to request that they be allocated to different tasks at the drilling rigs.[109]

The divide between the skilled oilmen and the unskilled worker-peasants was not simply the product of the first five-year plan. Lovászi was one of the drilling sites in the Zala oil fields in the far south-west rural area of the country. It had been established as recently as 1937, and consequently the culture of its workforce in the pre-socialist years was fused with the agrarian culture of the region in which it was located.[110] Dénes Vidos, who arrived in the Zala oil fields as a trainee engineer in 1947, wrote at the time: 'just about every oil worker was

---

109   ZML MSZMP ZMBA ir. 61f.4/3PTO/220.e.
110   On the beginnings of oil drilling in Zala, see Budai, Ferenc and Kovács 1987, pp. 9–46; on the agrarian nature of pre-socialist Zala county, see Vaska 1979.

kétlaki. They had land, a garden, kept animals, and worked for one of the companies in the oil fields'.[111] Given the close links that existed between agriculture and industry, therefore, the growth of tension between workers and worker-peasants requires explanation.

Vidos exaggerated when he stated that 'just about every oil worker was *kétlaki*'. Oil drilling in south-west Hungary was initially the result of investment by Standard Oil in 1937. They recruited their labour from the rural poor of the surrounding area, using high wages and a draconian disciplinary code to induct their new workers into the oil industry.[112] This was later combined with the construction of housing at the drilling rigs for a proportion of the workforce, which led those workers to leave the land behind. Others also gave up their land, keeping only a garden to grow food, and concentrated on work in the factory. A sizable proportion, however, retained their family landholding.[113] In 1950, an officer in the state security services reported that of all Lovászi's workers '60 percent come from the neighbouring villages ... and also farm ... They are therefore not strictly speaking industrial workers ... but work on the oil fields to guarantee a fixed income for themselves'.[114] With this differentiation among the workforce, a hierarchy of skill was established. The *kétlaki* workers tended to be underrepresented in the key skilled positions in oil drilling: at Lovászi in 1952, only three percent of them were drilling masters – the key skilled workers who supervised the drilling process. Most occupied semi-skilled or unskilled positions. Where they were skilled, they tended to be carpenters or truck drivers on the site.[115] Although the division between those with smallholdings and those without was not directly a division between the skilled elite and the less skilled, skill was superimposed onto the divide between workers with agricultural smallholdings and those without.

The division between workers with no connection to the land and the *kétlaki* was smaller at the onset of socialist industrialisation in the oil fields than in other industrial sectors. In the heavy-engineering establishments situated in the industrial suburbs of Greater Budapest, hierarchies of skill were even more starkly superimposed onto perceived hierarchies based on an urban-rural divide. In one factory in the environs of the capital at the end of the 1930s, workers who lived in the industrial community surrounding the plant enjoyed

---

111   Vidos 1990, p. 40.
112   Srágli 1985, pp. 169–81; Budai et al. 1987, pp. 194–5.
113   Budai et al. 1987, pp. 204–5.
114   ZML MSZMP ZMBA ir. 57f.1/770.e., p. 41.
115   ZML MSZMP ZMBA ir. 57f.2/Olajipar/250.e.

a monopoly of the highest-paid skilled positions. Rural commuters, who came from as far as twenty kilometres away, were largely unskilled and semi-skilled workers.[116] This was also true in smaller provincial industrial centres where a permanent workforce lived in company housing, or in urban centres near the workplace, while *kétlaki* commuters took work on a seasonal basis.[117]

The new socialist state was deeply suspicious of *kétlaki* workers in general, and of Zala's *kétlaki* oil workers in particular. These suspicions had several roots. At the national level, in 1948 the state began its collectivisation drive in the countryside and sought to force all rural smallholders into agricultural producer cooperatives.[118] Alongside the collectivisation drive it questioned the commitment of *kétlaki* workers to industrial labour, arguing that such workers would undermine production by concentrating on their smallholdings. It consequently sought to eliminate land ownership among industrial workers.[119] In Zala, the oil workers were a politically suspect group in their own right. The oil fields had been under American ownership until their confiscation, and this alone made the workforce politically suspect, but there had also been a marked lack of support for the Communist Party among the workers prior to 1948.[120]

The Party initiated national campaigns in 1950, and again in 1952, to force *kétlaki* workers to give their land to agricultural cooperatives.[121] The campaigns in the Zala oil fields were far from successful. When land was surrendered, local councils and state farms refused to accept it. A small minority of *kétlaki* workers took the view that the 'land, which I've had to farm alongside work, has been a pain in my family's neck and in mine'.[122] The overwhelming majority of *kétlaki* workers, however, were hostile to state attempts to make them hand over their land. In part, this stemmed from the deep-seated hostility felt in many rural communities toward collective agriculture. During the very early stages of the collectivisation drive in the county in 1949, the state security services noted that many village-dwellers who worked in the oil fields 'took positions openly hostile to agricultural producer cooperatives'.[123] This hostility persisted throughout the early 1950s. One such worker, Sándor Bertok, 'sought

---

116   Lackó 1989, pp. 3–44.
117   Szabó 1938, pp. 127–67; Magyary and Kiss 1939, p. 99.
118   Donáth 1977, pp. 101–56.
119   PtSzL SZKL Zala Szakszervezetek Megyei Tanácsa (Zala County Council of Trade Unions, hereafter Zala SZMT)/31d./1949.
120   On the circumstances of nationalisation, see Bencze 1980, pp. 34–5; Srágli 1986, pp. 295–307.
121   *Kétlakiság* 1952.
122   ZML MSZMP ZMBA ir. 61f.2/Agit/70.e; ZML MSZMP ZMBA ir. 57f.2/Olajipar/250.e.
123   ZML MSZMP ZMBA ir. 57f.1/780.e, p. 34.

to prove to the working peasantry that surrendering land to collectives harmed the workers'.[124] As food shortages spread and wage levels fell, many workers remained attached to their land because it gave them a degree of security in the face of the shortages generated by the malfunctioning of the socialist economy. One oil worker refused to surrender his land, telling the party committee that his wife had told him that 'it [the land] is there to help us live, because of it we have not starved, but if it is taken away from us we will [starve]'.[125]

Severe shortages of goods – including bread, fat, eggs and soap – seriously affected daily life in the oil fields from 1951, as the effects of state policies toward agriculture began to be directly felt in industrial areas.[126] These shortages caused a marked deterioration in relations between the *kétlaki* workers and those who had cut their ties to the land. Resentment grew because workers regarded it as unjust that their *kétlaki* workmates were able to make purchases in state shops even though they often had access to pigs, chickens, vegetables and corn at home. Those without land had to go into the neighbouring villages to buy their food on the black market.[127] Workers complained that their *kétlaki* workmates refused to bring them food, yet expected to be able to purchase goods in the state shops on the site.[128]

These tensions fuelled conflicts that grew at the drilling platforms during the early 1950s. Furthermore, growing labour shortages in the oil fields, and the pressures of collectivisation on rural households, drove a reconstitution of the oil industry's workforce that in turn shaped the social makeup of the *kétlaki* workforce. Rural households in Zala responded to high taxation, the collectivisation drive, and the poverty these measures induced, by sending their sons to work as unskilled labourers in the oil industry.[129] In 1952, enterprise management surveyed those members of the workforce at Lovászi who belonged to a household with agricultural land. Only 45.6 percent of such workers held the land in their own name; in 53.4 percent of all cases, it was the parents of the worker who actually held the land.[130] Newer *kétlaki* workers, it was said, lacked

---

124 ZML MSZMP ZMBA ir. 57f.2/Agit/100.e.
125 ZML MSZMP ZMBA ir. 61f.2/Agit/70.e.
126 Vidos 1990, pp. 94–9; the documents in ZML MSZMP ZMBA ir. 57f.2/Agit/100.e, and ZML MSZMP ZMBA ir. 57f.2/Agit/110.e.
127 Vidos 1990, p. 94.
128 ZML MSZMP ZMBA ir. 61f.4/2/40.e.
129 See chapter 5 of this volume.
130 ZML MSZMP ZMBA ir. 57f.2/Olajipar/250.e.

the disciplined ethos of those who had worked under the former capitalist owners of the oil wells.[131]

The decline in real wages across industry and the spread of food shortages reshaped worker attitudes toward their work. Smallholders were faced with onerous compulsory deliveries and a struggle for survival in agriculture. Food shortages underlined for *kétlaki* workers the importance of land, while falling real wages sharpened their discontent with working conditions in the oil fields. At the Bázakerettye drilling plant, *kétlaki* workers slept on the night-shift during the harvest season, allegedly as a result of working in the fields during the day.[132] Many were absent altogether during the harvest period, leading to a lack of manpower in the factory, and thus disruption in production.[133]

The disruption of production, different attitudes toward labour, and conflicts over consumption and notions of skill, all fed tensions between different groups of workers based on social origin. Oil workers complained in 1951 that among their colleagues, 'there are many who have land... It is possible to see this in their work, especially in the summer, when the agricultural season is at its peak'.[134] In 1953, workers complained about those of their workmates who owned land. According to the complainants, the *kétlaki* workers 'come to our factory to relax and earn their money there, and then go home and work on the land'.[135]

Tension between urban workers and their *kétlaki* colleagues was not restricted to the Zala oil fields, but because of their specific rural working-class culture these workers provide an especially useful vantage point from which to view the issue. Tensions existed in factories and industrial communities up and down the country. In Tatabánya, urban miners complained that *kétlaki* workers 'take loaves and loaves of the bread from the town dwellers; the same happens with the flour that they take packets of... and [they] hinder our shopping for food'.[136] These tensions strengthened distinctions based on notions of a hierarchy between the urban and the rural. The cases of the 'agricultural cooperative production line' in the Danube Shoe Factory, and the *kétlaki* workers

---

131 For some of the differences between pre-socialist and socialist oil workers, see Mocsár 1970, pp. 212–13.
132 ZML MSZMP ZMBA ir. 57f.2/Ipar/70.e, p. 1.
133 ZML MSZMP ZMBA ir. 61f.4/2/70.e, pp. 4–6.
134 ZML MSZMP ZMBA ir. 57f.2/Agit/100.e, p. 1.
135 ZML MSZMP ZMBA ir. 61f.3/3/Agit/40.e.
136 PtSzL. SZKL SZOT Szociálpolitikai Osztály (Social Policy Department, hereafter Szociálpolitika) 21d./1952, p. 1.

in the Zala oil fields, illustrate the degree to which such perceived hierarchies did not disappear, but rather adapted to socialist conditions.

Conclusion

By the time of Stalin's death in March 1953, and the effective beginnings of de-Stalinisation in Hungary that followed at the end of June, it had become clear that the regime's attempts to create a 'new working class' had failed. The industrial workforce had grown substantially, yet pre-socialist working class culture and the hierarchies embedded in it had reproduced themselves under socialist conditions. The attempts to train large numbers of new skilled workers through crash training schemes had largely failed. Likewise, attempts to recruit substantial numbers of women into the industrial workforce as men's equals had been frustrated. Workers from rural areas, or those who were members of families with agricultural smallholdings, remained culturally distinct from urban industrial workers. The hierarchical relationships between the urban, experienced, skilled elite and the traditionally subordinate groups had reproduced themselves despite Hungarian Stalinism's revolution in production and the expansion of the workforce that had taken place between 1948 and 1953. Furthermore, although the workforce was internally divided along lines of skill, gender, generation and social origin, it was deeply antagonistic to the regime due to the poverty and repression that characterised Hungary's early socialist years. However, it was not until the upheaval of the 1956 Revolution that the regime came to recognise the extent of its failure. In 1958, the Party initiated an investigation into 'the political, economic, and cultural situation of the working class', in order to ascertain why the Party had been deserted by its supposed working-class constituency during the Revolution.[137] In an unpublished written submission to those conducting the survey, the party-secretary of the industrial Budapest district of Kőbánya identified both working-class antagonism toward the regime, and, in a more confused fashion, the internal divisions that characterised the workforce. 'One part of the workforce does not agree with us', he wrote. '[I]t does not accept this system'. This group consisted of 'toolmakers, turners, etc.', who had lost their prestige and high wages. Consequently, they took an openly anti-regime stand. Alongside the skilled workers were 'declassed' groups, which acted to spread rumours and

---

137   For the background to the survey and some of its published results, see Vass and Ságvári 1973, pp. 272–7.

informal political information on the shop floor, thereby confusing the 'honest' and 'diligent' workers.[138]

Both the failure of the state to create its 'new working class', and the remarkable persistence of hierarchy, draw attention to the limits of dictatorship in the Hungarian case, demonstrating that in Hungarian factories the Stalinist dictatorship's control over social process was far from absolute. Indeed, they suggest that the popular experience of Rákosi's dictatorship in Hungary's factories, mines and construction sites was not shaped according to a script prepared in party headquarters in Budapest. Party and government policies were only one very important influence in shaping the experiences of industrial workers. The climate generated by the circumstances of socialist production, the resilience of working-class culture, and particularly the importance of skill to production and notions of hierarchy, were at least as important in moulding working-class identity during these years.

The reproduction of hierarchy, and the resilience of working-class culture in the face of state-initiated social change, point to continuities in the country's social history that have hitherto been little explored. Working-class identity remained strong throughout the socialist era, while the industrial workforce continued to be marked by hierarchies of gender, generation and social origin. The temporary collapse of the socialist regime during the 1956 Revolution brought to the surface the depth of working-class discontent, as workers demanded greater democracy in both the political system and the workplace. Workers, however, were not united in their behaviour during the Revolution. Working-class youth formed the backbone of many of the mass demonstrations and provided the revolutionaries who turned those demonstrations into an armed uprising. Skilled workers, with foremen and engineers, dominated the workers' councils that emerged during the Revolution. The *kétlaki* workers returned to their villages, leaving the factories behind.[139]

Following the Soviet intervention in November 1956, the new regime of János Kádár sought to generate long-term stability through a reconstruction rather than a restoration of the socialist system.[140] As far as Hungary's industrial workers were concerned, this entailed a concerted attempt by the regime

---

138   MOL MKS 288f.21/1958/190.e, p. 301.
139   Much has now been written on the social history of 1956. On workers in the revolution, the best account is still Lomax 1976. For the role of youth, see Eörsi 1997; on the workers' councils, see Kozák and Molnár 1994. Information on *kétlaki* workers during the Revolution is more fragmentary; see Lomax and Kemény 1986, p. 202. For the observations of the police immediately following the Soviet intervention, see Kajári 1996.
140   Kalmár 1998.

to accommodate working-class culture. The ruling Party sought to restore its legitimacy among workers by recasting its identity as that of a 'workers' party'. This meant that improvements in working-class living standards and social policy measures became central to its programme.[141] The consolidation of Kádár's rule led to the emergence of a tacit settlement in the workplace during the 1960s, in which the regime accepted the preeminent position of the skilled elite in the workplace. This tacit settlement both implicitly acknowledged hierarchies within the workforce, and granted the skilled elite considerable informal countervailing power vis-à-vis management.[142]

Despite the accommodation of the Kádár regime to working-class culture, however, perceptions of discontent and exploitation that formed the basis of the persistence of working-class identity survived well into the Kádár era. In the mid-1970s, one writer reporting on working-class opinion and life in a Budapest factory recorded one of the workers complaining that the workers 'get everything we have with such difficulty in this country'.[143] Tensions between different groups of workers based on notions of hierarchy within the workforce seem also to have persisted throughout the socialist era. In the aftermath of the 1968 economic reform, conflict between rural workers in the factories and the urban 'core' of the workforce was reported, and it was skilfully used by opponents of economic reform within the party apparatus.[144] Class identity and the hierarchies embedded in working-class culture proved remarkably persistent even in the face of radical social change. Therefore, the question of continuity in the labour and social history of the socialist era in Hungary is one that requires further exploration.

The social history of industrial labour in post-war Eastern Europe is a relatively undeveloped field. This examination of industrial labour in Hungary suggests some ways in which this history might be approached. It is clear from the Hungarian case, and from research on workers in the GDR, Czechoslovakia and Poland, that in the Central European socialist states at least, presocialist working-class cultures remained resilient. Stalinist regimes in these countries did not remake working-classes anew. Socialist institutions and the environment of production, however, did reshape the context in which such working-class cultures reasserted themselves and were in turn remoulded. This has been shown in this article for the Hungarian case. For the GDR, Peter Hübner has demonstrated how shop-floor institutions – such as socialist work

---

141   Földes 1993, pp. 57–73.
142   Kemény 1992 [1978], p. 208.
143   Halmos 1978, pp. 131–2.
144   Soós 1988, pp. 89–110.

brigades – provided the scope for certain continuities in working-class culture to emerge in a socialist context.[145] We know relatively little, however, about the shifts in working-class identity in these countries. The forces that shaped worker identity in each of these states were similar to those examined in this article for Hungary. In all countries of Eastern Europe, the state attempted to challenge hierarchies in the workplace based on skill, gender, generation and social origin, although the timing and nature of these attempts varied from country to country. The workforce expanded across the region in the context of an industrialisation drive that generated widespread shortages, transforming the environment in which production took place. This article suggests, therefore, the need for studies of all the countries of the region that would examine shifting worker identities in conjunction with the development of socialist factory regimes and state policies to break down traditional hierarchies on the shop floor.

---

145   Hübner 1995, pp. 211–45.

CHAPTER 4

The Social Limits of State Control: Time, the Industrial Wage Relation, and Social Identity in Stalinist Hungary, 1948–53

Introduction

In the very early months of 1950, the management of Magyar Pamutipar, a leading Budapest textile factory, began to alter the system through which the factory maintenance staff were paid. Prior to that date, staff had been paid according to work targets that were established at the level of the group; thus, the collective rather than the individual was measured in order to establish the basis of remuneration. The authorities were especially keen to see that the individual became the unit on which the wage was established. The rhetoric of their justification for this shift was surprisingly anti-collectivist – without individual norms, or work targets, individual contributions to the economy could not be measured. Furthermore, work discipline could not be maintained if good workers within a group were to be remunerated at the same level as the bad and the lazy.[1]

It has been widely assumed that Stalinism was highly collectivist in both its ideology and practice. It has been seen as being at the extreme end of a state socialist paradigm characterised by the elimination of individual civil rights, property rights and, in some variants, the abolition of a distinction between public and private spheres altogether. The contradiction between the apparent assumption of 'individualisation' that characterised socialist wage systems, and the collectivist ideology of the regime in Hungary, was noticed in the later socialist period. Miklós Haraszti noted:

> [I]n one newspaper, a Hungarian expert on 'management science' claimed that payment-by-results was the ideal form of socialist wages. It was, he said, the embodiment of the principle 'from each according to his capacity, to each according to his work'. But in another issue of the same

---

* First published in Mark Pittaway 1999, 'The Social Limits of State Control: Time, the Industrial Wage Relation and Social Identity in Stalinist Hungary, 1948–1953', *Journal of Historical Sociology*, 1999, 12, 3: 271–301.

1 *Pamutújság*, 1 January 1950.

paper a veteran communist who now holds a high position warmly remembered a former comrade in arms who had been prominent before the war in the organisation of workers' demonstrations against the Bedeaux system – the 'scientific' system of payment by results then in force.[2]

A large number of sociological studies of shop floor relations have drawn attention not merely to the contradiction between the collectivism of regime ideology and the wage systems it endorsed for the late socialist period in Hungary, but also to the lack of control the state exercised over the conditions of production. According to such accounts, the dynamics of shop relations during economic reform in Hungary were determined by the phenomena of shortage, informal bargaining, widespread participation in the informal economy, and managerial attempts to create 'hegemonic' factory regimes based on a range of unofficial rules partially hidden from the eyes of the state.[3]

While none of this literature explicitly dealt with the situation on the shop floor during the period of Stalinist rule, much of it implicitly assumed that the spread of informality on Hungarian shop floors was a product of gradual yet progressive waves of economic reform, as a highly despotic state conceded power to actors at local level. István Kemény, for example, argues that informal bargaining over norms was a creation of the climate in the factories following the 1956 Revolution.[4] Michael Burawoy and János Lukács imply, based on their research in Hungary, that 'despotic' factory regimes under state socialism are replaced by 'hegemonic' ones, founded around informal bargaining and cooperation between management and workforce, when 'the market provision of consumer goods and services' associated with economic reform destroys the basis on which the state is able to discipline and mobilise labour.[5]

In these accounts, therefore, economic reform under state socialism creates space in which workers are able to exercise considerable countervailing power on the shop floor. This assumption is maintained through an implied contrast between the reformist state of the late socialist period, and the despotic state

---

2 Haraszti 1977, p. 21.
3 There is an enormous social-scientific literature describing these phenomena in the 1970s and 1980s. For an excellent overview of the research, see Swain 1992, chapter 6. For a sample of the more important studies, see Burawoy 1985, especially chapter 4; Burawoy and Lukács 1992; Galasi and Sziráczki (Eds) 1985; Héthy and Makó 1972 and 1978; Kemény 1985 and 1990; Róna-Tas 1997; Stark 1985, 1986 and 1989.
4 See Kemény 1985, pp. 15–16.
5 Burawoy and Lukács 1992, pp. 32–4.

of the Stalinist years, which is able to subordinate industrial workers to its political programme on the shop floor. Such accounts seem to contradict much of the recent historical literature dealing with Stalinism in both Eastern Europe and the Soviet Union. This work has demonstrated that industrial workers were endowed with a considerable degree of countervailing power vis-à-vis the early socialist state. It has demonstrated – in contexts ranging from the Soviet Union in the 1930s, through Poland in the late 1940s, to East Germany in the 1950s and 1960s – that labour was mobilised by the state, and that in turn workers were able to subvert state intentions and, in doing so, remake the institutions of socialism at the local level.[6]

This article demonstrates that 'hegemonic' factory regimes, characterised by a high degree of cooperation between at least a core of the workforce and management, dominated industry in the Stalinist years, as much as they were to characterise the conditions of production in a climate of economic reform. Furthermore, it shows that they emerged from economic tensions created by the Stalinist state and by worker responses to them. An examination of how such 'hegemonic' factory regimes arose suggests a major revision of the traditional image of Stalinism as collectivist. The state attempted to use systems of remuneration on the shop floor to bind workers to the goals of the plan. These systems of remuneration were individual rather than collective, suggesting that at the heart of classical central planning lay an apparent paradox between institutional centralisation and a high degree of individualisation at the point of production.[7] Embodied in wage systems was a specific attempt to discipline the individual worker through using a specific 'politics of time'. This aimed to force workers to use every minute of working time to produce goods as laid out in the plan, to accelerate their work, improve their productivity and constantly surpass the goals of the plan. The implementation of this system led to a breakdown of social solidarity between workers, as the industrial workforce became increasingly fragmented. It was not, however, the state's 'politics of time' – something similar to the concept of time described by Stephen Hanson in the Soviet context – that determined the factory regime on

---

6 For the early literature dealing with the role of workers in the Soviet industrialisation drive in the 1930s, see Kuromiya 1988; Andrle 1988; Siegelbaum 1988; and the contributions to Rosenberg and Siegelbaum (eds.) 1993, and Siegelbaum and Grigor Suny (eds.) 1994. For two recent excellent contributions to the literature, see Kotkin 1995, and Straus 1997. For Poland in the late 1940s, see Kenney 1997. For East Germany, see Kopstein 1997.

7 The case made here is close to that argued by Rév 1987.

Hungarian shop floors.[8] The remaking of wage systems and the institutionalisation of central planning was combined with an industrialisation drive that generated what János Kornai has conceptualised as an 'economy of shortage'.[9] The combination of shortages of labour and materials, combined with the disciplines of the plan on both workers and managers, produced a regime characterised by informal cooperation between the two. This resulted in a loss of control of the shop floor by the state as early as 1953, while social solidarity among workers was further undermined by the practices of informal bargaining.

The Institutionalisation of Central Planning and the Shop-Floor

On 20 August 1949, the People's Republic of Hungary sealed its transition to a state that sought to embark on 'the construction of socialism' with a new constitution. This constitution stated clearly that 'the basis of the social order of the Hungarian People's Republic is work'. In addition, it laid down the principle that all citizens of the new state had an obligation 'to work according to their ability', in order to participate in 'the construction of socialism'. In assessing the particular obligation of each citizen, 'the Hungarian People's Republic attempts to realise the socialist principle "from each according to their ability, to each according to their need"'. This obligation to work amounted to the participation of each citizen in the economic life of the country. The constitution clearly stated that 'the economic life of the Hungarian People's Republic is determined by the state people's economic plan'. Therefore, the economic plan was, at least in theory, the institution that regulated the labour obligation of each and every citizen in the new state. As such, it was to be much more than a means of regulating the performance of the economy, although, of course, it was certainly this too. It aimed to calculate the contribution of every citizen to the generation of the social product.[10]

This entailed considerable institutional centralisation, as a hierarchical system of central planning – copied from the Soviet model – was introduced.

---

8   Stephen Hanson has shown the way in which a specific concept of time was central to the design of Soviet economic institutions; see Hanson 1997. The conception of time, which Hanson describes in the Soviet context, was in many ways similar to that which informed the design of Hungarian wage systems.
9   Kornai 1992.
10 *A dolgozó nép alkotmánya: a Magyar Népköztársaság alkotmánya* 1949, pp. 37–9.

Decision-making authority within the system would be vested in the government through the Council of Ministers, and in the People's Economic Council (*Népgazdasági Tanács*, NT) established in 1949 as an overall coordinating body. This set the framework within which planning was to take place. The planning process itself was overseen and conducted by the National Planning Office (*Országos Tervhivatal*, OT). As the institutions of central planning were consolidated, it assumed the role of nerve centre within the economy, translating the directives of both the Council of Ministers and the NT into general quantitative plans for the economy as a whole and its individual sectors.[11]

Each sector of the economy was supervised by a branch ministry. Within each branch ministry there were a number of industrial directorates that devised the plans for each enterprise within the appropriate sub-sector.[12] Following the pioneering study by János Kornai in 1955 of the operation of the system of planning devised in 1949 in light-industry, those seeking to critically examine the system have sought to examine the tension within it between excessive centralisation and the requirements of the enterprise unit. Analyses based on this approach tend to conceptualise the enterprise as the basic unit in socialist production, and as the organisation that sought to respond to the mixture of instruction, incentives and regulations that were issued by higher authorities. Such an assumption would, of course, seem to contradict the view that running almost in parallel to the process of collectivist centralisation was a process of individualisation. While for a variety of reasons enterprises responded as units to the instruction of planners in practice, the structure of the central planning system was based on the assumption that the individual producer – not the enterprise unit – was the basis of the plan.[13]

Comprehensive Soviet-style economic planning sought to redefine the role of the enterprise, turning it from the legally autonomous entity of capitalist society into a mere administrative level within the planning process. The first manifestation of this shift was the beginning of the process of 'profilisation' in 1948. This essentially meant that every enterprise should have a 'profile', so that

---

11   On the broad outlines of classical Soviet central planning in its Hungarian context, see Swain 1992, pp. 55–8; Berend and Ránki 1985, pp. 208–10; Pető and Szakács 1985, pp. 104–20. On the importance of quantitative targets in Hungarian economic planning, see Lampland 1995, especially chapter 5.

12   On the creation of the branch ministries, see Pető and Szakács 1985, pp. 110–12; Swain 1992, p. 55; Berend 1974, pp. 86–7; and Spulber 1957, p. 76.

13   The classic study is Kornai 1994 [1954]. For an example of an analysis of classical Stalinist central planning, which erroneously identifies the enterprise as the basic unit of the central planning system, see Berend 1974, pp. 87–93.

its production range would be transparent to central planner; the profile being a range of products for which it had exclusive or near-exclusive responsibility. Enterprises lost production units that produced goods, which came under different industrial directorates or even ministries.[14]

The state aimed to decentralise the implementation of the plan to units below that of the enterprise, often combining this with the principle of 'profilisation', to produce a series of reorganisations across industry during the early 1950s. This process of reorganisation in order to secure more effective control of production took the form of the creation of Trusts in industry. This was clearly illustrated by the example of the Tatabánya coalmines, where such a Trust was formed in early 1952. This acted as a strategic planning unit for the whole of the mines with considerable responsibility for labour management and social policy. It drew up and monitored the performance of the separate production plans for factory and workshop units under its control.[15] Though the Trust was the general model of sub-enterprise planning in Stalinist Hungary, it could never be applied to the whole of industry. In textiles, the implementation of the principle of 'profilisation' led to planners bypassing the enterprise level in some plants. In the heavy-engineering sector, enterprises were divided into 'self-accounting units' [*önelszámoló egységek*]. These units each had their own distinct profile and contained all of the technical administration necessary for the production of the goods in each unit's 'profile'. Each unit was responsible not only for fulfilling its plan, but also for controlling its production costs.[16]

The basic subject of the plan was not the factory unit or workshop, but rather the individual producer. From 1949 onwards, attempts were made to individualise economic plans – for each individual worker there would be, at least on paper, an individual Five Year Plan. This process was known as the 'breaking down of the plan' [*tervfelbontás*], and was attempted in a large number of enterprises and factory units. The breaking down of the plan to individual producers was far from uniformly achieved. Very little information exists on the proportion of workers working to an individual plan, and such figures would make little sense in examining the practice of labour relations in the socialist economy simply because of the disorganisation of production. The

---

14   On the process of 'profilisation', see Pető and Szakács 1985, pp. 112–14; Berend 1964, pp. 17–19; and Swain 1992, pp. 57–8.
15   The best source for the various organisational changes to the mines in Tatabánya can be found in Rozsnyói 1972.
16   For a description of how 'profilisation' worked in other cases, see Hanák and Hanák 1964, pp. 314–15 and Szekeres and Tóth 1962, p. 266.

regime's intentions are identifiable through an examination of the situation in individual factories. In the workshop of the United Electrics Factory that made radio components, for example, in summer 1951, 582 of 1,341 employees worked to individual plans, even though 767 employees had individual labour competition records. Given the complexity of individualising factory plans, management often adopted a more indirect method: the total maximum working time of an individual worker over five years would be calculated, and anyone who completed the work that was supposed to have taken that amount of time, as defined by the work norms, was judged to have completed their plan. On this basis the state drew attention to the achievements of individual Stakhanovites who, according to regime propaganda, had completed their individual First Five Year Plans in fewer than five years.[17]

The individual producer was central to the planning process. In particular, the individual was central to the process of labour planning. In an economy that was not driven by fully autonomous firms subject to the discipline of the market (at least on a theoretical level), alternative criteria had to be devised against which enterprises determined how many workers should be employed. The major criterion was that of the degree of labour power needed to produce a particular product. The level of employment would then become a matter of simple calculation for the planners. They would determine what needed to be produced, after which the amount of labour power required to produce those goods could be calculated through scientific norms, and from this calculation the total level of employment in the economy could be determined.[18]

These systems profoundly affected social relations on Hungarian shop floors. The individualisation of production heralded by central planning was reflected in the reshaping of the systems of remuneration and, indeed, the organisation of production itself. Such a raft of measures and systems – ranging from norms to piece rates, through to labour competition campaigns – directly tied workers to the system of centralised economic planning. Focus will now turn to the reshaping of production on the shop floor as central planning was implemented, and the reform of the system of remuneration.

---

17   Budapest Főváros Levéltára (Archive of the City of Budapest, hereafter BFL) XXIX/321/2d. For the best-known example of 'breaking down the plan', see Déri 1952, p. 3.

18   This system of labour power planning was effectively incorporated into the yearly economic plans in 1950 – for example, for the 1951 Peoples' Economic Plan. For an explanation of this principle, see *Munkaerőtartalék* 1951, pp. 251–7.

The Industrial Wage Relation and the Individualisation of Production: 1948–50

From 1948 onwards, the state sought more direct control over production, as the authorities began to introduce the institutions of comprehensive economic planning across the economy. Wage policy shifted as the authorities began to move towards greater dependence on so-called precise 'norms', calculated by scientific means, which by their nature were heavily standardised. This entailed, firstly, a reform of the system of payment-by-results, and, secondly, a move to reform the organisation of production itself.

The reform of the system of payment-by-results began in January 1948 with the so-called second supplement to the collective agreements of that year. Norms had been in existence since 1945, but these were linked to statistical estimates of previous production in a given plant. In many cases, they had been informally established on a decentralised basis at the point of production. As far as the authorities were concerned, this was a problem because they sought to control the ways in which the norms were established. It called for the introduction of new so-called *szabatos* or precise norms, calculated on the basis of 'scientific' principles. Where such norms were not brought into being, earnings would be cut by revising the statistical norms downward, and the average norm-fulfilment in November 1947 would act as the baseline used to determine 100 percent fulfilment.[19]

The introduction of 'scientifically' established precise norms met with one major obstacle from the shop floor, namely, the high degree of control of the job and remuneration enjoyed by certain groups of skilled workers. This control had been largely exercised through the skill sections of certain unions (particularly the Metalworkers' Union), so that a high degree of union control over job rates could be exercised. This was paralleled by a high degree of control on the shop floor, especially where piece-based systems were in force, by the shop stewards over pay claims in order to regulate the rates of skilled workers. The case of how union control of the labour process and remuneration worked in a workshop of a railway repair shop in the late 1930s and early 1940s describes this process well. The shop steward had to approve of the rate for a specific job before it was given to the turners in the workshop. The fulfilment of rate was measured neither individually nor directly by management, but instead by the shop steward in order to preserve a 'solidaristic wage policy' operated by the union on behalf of its members. There is considerable evidence that such practices had not merely survived, but in fact remained

---

19   The best account of the policy background to these attempts is Rákosi 1985, pp. 202–4.

widespread in many sectors, particularly in heavy engineering and machine manufacture, at the end of the 1940s. In the machine manufacture shop of the United Electrics Factory in 1948, there were frequent complaints that the shop-stewards controlled the performance of turners, instructing them to make no more than 135 percent of their norm, when they could easily have made 170 percent.[20]

The state attempted to break these solidarities by generalising labour competition, thus mobilising all workers to bust rates, and as such they needed to secure the consent of large sections of the workforce. The state also aimed to pave the way for planning production at the shop floor level. From 15 March until 31 August 1948, the first National Labour Competition was held. Each enterprise and shop formed a competition committee in which the social organisations, management and, to an extent, the workforce were to discuss changes in work organisation necessary to improve productivity. All enterprises and shops were then to be assessed through various criteria based on production, productivity and good work discipline. Rewards were then distributed to those units in each sector with the highest point scores, which were in turn distributed among the workers. Central to this was an attempt to modify work practices, and fundamental to the attack on traditional shop floor solidarities was the launch of the brigade movement and brigade competition. This aimed to unify all workers engaged in a given production process into a unit that would then compete using centrally defined criteria with other units, or brigades, for which they would be given rewards. This would be measured against newer and more explicitly decentralised economic plans. As labour competition was continued throughout 1948, brigades spread throughout industry.[21]

Workers participated in the labour competition for purely instrumental reasons. In the Magyar Pamutipar cotton plant, for example, throughout the summer of 1948 the semi-skilled and largely female machine-operators were mobilised behind the labour competition through the tangible increases in pay brought about by the competition. This instrumental support for the competition was very much a two-edged sword for the regime. Firstly, such

---

20   For the case of the railway repair shop, see Tóth 1994, pp. 72–3. On the United Electrics Factory in 1948, see Magyar Országos Levéltár, MSZMP Budapesti Bizottság Archiviuma (Hungarian National Archives, Archive of the Budapest Committee of the Hungarian Socialist Workers' Party, hereafter MOL M-Bp.) 134f/4ö.e, p. 104.

21   The 1948 labour competitions are described in *Társadalmi Szemle* 1948a, pp. 299–315; *Társadalmi Szemle* 1948b, pp. 513–36; and Politikatörténeti Intézet Levéltára (Archive of the Institute for the History of Politics, hereafter PIL) 274f.20/23ö.e, pp. 73–6.

instrumental attitudes allowed the regime to mobilise support around the notion of a reshaping of labour organisation and of the institutions of production, which smoothed the introduction of comprehensive central planning at factory level. Secondly, it made this support conditional on the continued growth in workers' earnings. The degree to which support for the competition was dependent on the growth of earnings, however, was demonstrated to some extent by the way in which the competition led to abuses in terms of work practices, and in the use of machinery and raw materials in the constant struggle to drive up production. The productivist emphasis of the competition, combined with the pressure to over-fulfil norms, led to an 'overly intense worktempo, which went together with disadvantages in terms of quality'.[22]

From the middle of 1949, the state began to explicitly individualise production. The focus of labour competition began to change to fit this emerging economic model. The state increasingly began to criticise the enterprises for giving insufficient weight to what it saw as 'the most important basic condition of the labour competition movement, the individual labour competition'. Such an individual labour competition movement was regarded as a fundamental part of the individualisation of production obligations, given that in the forms of labour competition that had existed hitherto, 'whilst the factories had globally joined one stage in the labour competition, the degree to which the implementation of particular tasks helped the totality of an enterprise fulfil its work'. Not only was individual labour competition designed to provide planners with information on how plans could be individualised, it also formed part of an intensification of the state's drive against traditional work practices. The state aimed to promote particular individuals within production in order to measure particular work methods that they could then record and use to reorganise production in other factories and base newer, more scientific norms upon such methods.[23]

During the autumn of 1949, the focus of regime policy was on promoting individual competition and identifying those individuals capable of achieving real changes in their own work methods to improve productivity. The whole phenomenon assumed the role of a campaign leading up to the seventieth

---

22   *Pamutipari Értesitő*, 1 June 1948; MOL M-Bp.-136f./3ö.e, p. 65; and MOL M-Bp.-136f./3ö.e, pp. 79–80.

23   Szakszervezetek Központi Levéltára (Central Archive of the Trade Unions, hereafter SZKL), Szakszervezetek Országos Tanácsa (National Council of Trade Unions, hereafter SZOT), 46d/1949; *A Magyar Munkaverseny Mozgalom Fejlődése*, p. 4. On the plans and processes by which individual competition was to be (and was) used to make new norms, see SZKL SZOT, 3d/1949; *Kiváló teljesitmények vizsgálatáról készült összefoglalás*.

birthday of Stalin on 21 December 1949. Between the beginning of September and the middle of November, participation in individual labour competition increased enormously as a result of the campaign, with the numbers of declared individual competitors increasing fivefold in some factories. Again, it was those factories in which traditional work practices predominated that were the focus of the introduction of individual competition like the United Electrics. In this firm, the number of individual competitors rose 75-fold, from six at the end of August to 450 by the end of October.[24]

Faced with endemic worker control over the job, the authorities across the country sought to identify candidates to become a new kind of individual competitor. They would seek to break rates spectacularly. This process gave birth to the Stakhanovite movement in Hungary. In the United Electrics, the machine manufacture shop was the focus of this campaign. The future Stakhanovites were carefully picked from among the workforce of the plant by management and the authorities, which carefully exploited the social, political and personal tensions in the shops in order to persuade and coerce workers into the movement.[25]

During the shift held to commemorate Stalin's birthday on 21 December 1949, in the United Electrics machine shop – as in other plants up and down the country – production was explicitly reorganised to ensure that the new Stakhanovites achieved exceptional levels of production. The factory newspaper celebrated 'the good organisation of production' and the fact that 'the preparation of tools and raw materials was decisive', while 'the tool room worked like never before'. Rising wages, as a result of increased production during the campaign, created considerable enthusiasm for the competition across the country and not just in the plant. In Újpest, there were reports of individuals arriving at work an hour before the start of their shift. In one Győr factory, the party secretary described the feeling during the 'Stalin shift' as being like that felt at a football match. The state's aim of individualising production relations had been significantly advanced by the spread of individual labour competition. Production was reorganised while workers had been encouraged to regard their contribution to production as an individual rather than collective act. Onto the individualisation of the labour competition was

---

24 For the national picture with individual competition, see MOL M-Bp.-95f.2/296ö.e, p. 157; MOL M-Bp.-95f.4/147ö.e, p. 42.
25 For the intentions of the organisers of individual competition in the factory, see MOL M-Bp.-95f.2/295ö.e, p. 224. On its beginnings, see *Tungsram Híradó*, 8 September 1949 and *Tungsram Híradó*, 5 December 1949.

superimposed a wage system that explicitly tied remuneration to the value of a worker's production as set out in the plan.[26]

This system was the *darrabér*, or piece rate, which was introduced across Hungarian industry in 1950. While this form was never fully comprehensive, it did become the hegemonic wage form in industry during the early 1950s. The central component of the system was that the work done, and *not* the individual worker, was the subject of remuneration. In this way the principle was established that payment should reflect the amount and value of what was produced by a worker as laid out in the plan.[27] This opened up the possibility of a worker working on several different hourly wage rates on the same shift. In many ways, it came to resemble a kind of fee for work done, which made it very different from many of the piece rates existing in capitalist factories. There were several important differences, however, between the piece rate and a simple contract fee. The first was that the rate was received within the context of an employment relation; theoretically, the recipient was not self-employed, but was legally a waged worker-citizen. The second was the dual nature of the incentive. Work was divided into different categories depending on their difficulty, and this determined the rate. This rate would then be paid on the basis of the worker's fulfilment of their production norm. The interaction of the piece-rate and the norm created a pressure for the worker not only to complete a given number of pieces in order to make an adequate monthly wage, but also to constantly strive to complete every piece in the shortest time possible. The intention behind the system was to completely subordinate the worker to the dictates of 'clock time',[28] in order to force the workers to improve their productivity according to the terms set out in the plan. As such, it aimed to force workers to maximise the amount of their working time spent performing productive labour. The third difference was that the worker did receive an hourly wage when they were not working, although the rate was often set at a miserably low level by the foreman and was linked to the category of work a worker could expect to obtain.[29]

By the spring of 1950, through labour competition and the wage system, the state had largely succeeded in individualising work relations. A worker's

---

26 *Tungsram Híradó*, 5 January 1950; MOL Bp.-95f.4/147ö.e, pp. 134–6; MOL M-Bp.95f.2/296ö.e, p. 81; MOL M-KS-276f.65/76ö.e, pp. 30–1.

27 For an explanation of the piece rate principle, see Dékán 1950, p. 7. For important documents on the design of the piece rate, see SZKL SZOT 3d/1949; *Tervezet a darrabérrendszerre való áttéres előkészítésére*.

28 For this term, see Thompson 1993 [1967], pp. 352–403.

29 On the process of *besorolás*, see SZKL SZOT 3d/1949, pp. 6–7; Dékán 1950, pp. 8–9.

performance was measured strictly on the basis of their individual contribution to the economy, and they received their reward as a result of the value of that contribution. Work on the shop floor was, therefore, formally tied to the plan. Despite this, the new systems had been accepted by workers only on the basis that they led to direct wage increases, a situation which undermined attempts by the state to increase productivity. Consequently, in mid-1950, the state sought to clamp down by revising the norms in order to 'close the damaging difference between the wage system and the production fulfilments achieved in the labour competition'.[30]

The tightening succeeded in increasing productivity by cutting the wage funds (the amount of money given to enterprises by the central apparatus to cover wage-related expenses). In heavy industry, wage funds fell by 13.5 percent, and in light industry they fell by 11.4 percent, as the new system was introduced in August 1950. Yet the increase in productivity was bought at the cost of huge reductions to workers' nominal wages at a time of accelerating inflation, which smashed any of the trust that had existed between workers and 'their' new state. Nominal wages fell by 14.3 percent in heavy industry, 12.5 percent in light industry, and 19.4 percent in over-ground construction. Furthermore, the introduction of the new norms was met by one of the largest waves of worker unrest in the post-war period, although open discontent was ruthlessly crushed by the regime.[31]

In the medium-term, the major effect of the 1950 norm revision was to create norms that were very difficult for workers to make, a situation that was clearly borne out by the statistics from late-1950 on the proportion of workers not making their norms. In Újpest, in November there were thirteen factories in which more than twenty percent of the workforce failed to make 100 percent of their norms. In the district's textile factories, a majority of the workforce failed to make their norms; in one factory, the proportion of those failing to reach their norm stood at 73.6 percent. In the Danube Shoe Factory, where 32

---

30   For this, see *Munkaerőtartalék*, August 1951, pp. 251–7; Magyar Országos Levéltár MDP-MSZMP Központi Szervek Iratai (Hungarian National Archive, Papers of the Central Organisations of the Hungarian Workers' Party-Hungarian Socialist Workers' Party, hereafter MOL M-KS), 276f.116/18ö.e, p. 34.

31   For a more detailed description of the 1950 norm revision campaign, see Pittaway 1998, pp. 99–104; MOL M-KS-276f.116/19ö.e, pp. 129–30; MOL M-KS-276f.116/19ö.e., pp. 220–3; MOL M-KS-276f.116/18ö.e, pp. 180–3; MOL M-KS-276f.116/18ö.e, pp. 197–9; MOL M-KS-276f.116/19ö.e. p. 1; MOL M-KS-276f.116/19ö.e, p. 5; MOL M-KS-276f.116/19ö.e, p. 58; MOL M-KS-276f.116/19ö.e, pp. 43–5.

percent failed to reach their norms, another 20 percent only just made them. The whole process of norm revision did not lead to undifferentiated cuts in wages nor in performance. Indeed, it seems that the process rather led to the sharpening of inequalities between individual workers and between brigades, almost independent of their skill or formal position within the division of labour. On one construction site in the capital soon after the introduction of the new norms, the average fulfilment rates of the bricklayers varied between 70 and 169 percent, with the range for carpenters being between 53 and 139 percent, while for unskilled workers it stood between 32 and 130 percent. This was also true of other sectors. In the Danube Shoe Factory, where the majority of the workforce were either unable or only just able to make their norms, there were just over ten percent of the workforce who were able to achieve rates of over 150 percent, and a small number who were able to achieve rates as high as 180 percent.

This inequality existed partially as a consequence of keeping Stakhanovism alive. With the fall in support for the labour competition that accompanied norm revision, the high performances of a small number of workers were maintained by granting them preferential access to machines, tools and materials. One former worker in a textile factory near the capital recalled:

> [T]he wages were not great and permanently fluctuated ... a large proportion of the weaving machine operators earned between 500 and 800 Forints, it was very difficult to get a wage of over 1,000 Forints a month, only party members and Stakhanovites could get that. Of course they got the best machines and the 100 or 200 Forint wage supplement.[32]

The individualisation of production had led to the fragmentation of the workforce, a phenomenon exacerbated by the preferential treatment of certain workers by management. This process, however, was given enormous impetus by the rise of a shortage-economy immediately following the norm revision of 1950. This in turn undercut the attempts of the regime to use monetary incentives in order to enforce their 'politics of time' on the shop floor.

---

32   MOL M-Bp.-95f.4/120ö.e, p. 252; MOL M-Bp.-95f.4/120ö.e, p. 238; MOL M-Bp.-95f.4/120ö.e, p. 58; Open Society Archives, Radio Free Europe, 'Interviews with Escapees', hereafter OSA RFE Magyar Gy. 6/Item No. 5898/54, p. 2.

Forced Industrialisation, Shortage, and Socialist 'Flexibility': The Effects of Systemic Problems on the Shop Floor

At the heart of the failure of the regime to subordinate workers to the goals of the plan through remuneration attached to their 'politics of time', was a wage-system that rested on the assumption of continuous production. In reality, the interaction of the plan and the shortage generated by the plan created its own peculiar rhythm of production, with serious effects on the shop floor and the earning potential of industrial workers. The plan established a calendar for the enterprise as the First Five Year Plan was broken down into quantitative annual plans, and from there into quarterly plans, then monthly plans, and finally even daily plans. Within this tight system of deadlines, a hierarchy was established. Non-fulfilment of the daily plans alone was not an especially serious matter; failure to fulfil a monthly plan might be a cause for concern, while non-fulfilment of a quarterly plan might provoke serious state intervention and would definitely mean the loss of premiums for managers and technical staff.[33]

The other determining factor of the rhythm of shop floor production was not planning *per se*, but the nature of the First Five Year Plan in place during the period. This plan had been passed as a law in 1949, and it was geared to the rapid development of heavy industry, especially of the machine manufacturing sector. The plan was constantly revised, with more ambitious targets constantly set for the growth of heavy industry at the expense of living standards, agriculture and other light-industrial sectors. Furthermore, the plan sought to expand heavy-industrial production without appropriately investing in supporting industries.[34]

The consequences of this kind of production for the economy were very clear, as enterprises became trapped in a vicious cycle of plan under-fulfilment followed by severe shortages of raw materials, which in turn led to further shortages. This environment of shortage had taken hold in some sectors by the second half of 1950, but by spring 1951 it had become a general trait. This tendency was at its most extreme on the sites of major investments – such as the construction of new towns at Tatabánya, Komló and Sztálinváros. The building of the Budapest metro and the reconstruction of the Diósgyőr steel plants had

---

33 See Kornai 1994 [1959], pp. 1–27, for a discussion on how the plans were broken down temporally into quarterly planning units, and how non-fulfilment at various points was regarded by the authorities.

34 For general information on the First Five Year Plan, see Pető and Szakács 1985, pp. 151–67; Berend 1964 and 1974, p. 76; and Birta 1970, pp. 113–51.

been constantly plagued by severe shortages of raw materials. This was very much a symptom of the problem: certain sectors, especially those supplying raw materials to the fastest growing sectors, faced unrealistic and unrealisable plans. In electrical power generation, for example, the late delivery of turbines to the Tatabánya power plants led to the under-fulfilment of the electrical production plan by early 1952. The growth of shortage goods was fed by the more general fact that in the first 48 months of the plan, on nine occasions the monthly quantity-based plan had been under-fulfilled leading to an increase in shortage products in each case.[35]

These economic problems manifested themselves on the shop floor in three different ways. The first was the shortage of raw materials; the second was the shortage of labour; and the third was that of tools and other kinds of machinery. Because of the dependence of wages on finished production, shortages of raw materials had direct and catastrophic effects on workers' wages. This can be seen by examining the situation in some factories over the summer of 1953, when the problem of raw material shortages grew across industry. For example, in the Cog Wheel Factory, the assembly shop was unable to start work on the monthly plan until 20 July, while by 22 July it had only 45 percent of the materials to reach its target.[36] In the Gábor Áron Iron Foundry and Machine Factory, the failure to guarantee the workers a continuous supply of raw materials led the workers' monthly pay to decline from 1,100–1,200 forints to 500–550 forints.[37] Severe disorganisation of production caused by persistent raw material shortages led to continual work stoppages in textiles as well. In the Cotton Textile Spinning Plant, these accounted for 9.31 percent of total working hours in June, 9.98 percent in July, and 12.87 percent in August.[38]

The second of these phenomena was that of labour shortage. This shortage differed from that of raw materials in that it was driven by low wages. This can be shown via the situation in coal mining, which was a particularly extreme example of the problem. The wage department of the National Council of

---

35   On the plan in general, see Pető and Szakács 1985, pp. 189. For a brief contemporary discussion by a senior party-economic expert, see *Társadalmi Szemle*, 1953, pp. 143–4. For the problems this caused on some construction sites, see the example of the Budapest metro as discussed in Prakfalvi 1994, pp. 31–6; for a discussion of similar problems on the Sztálinváros construction site, the biggest single investment of the First Five Year Plan, see Miskolczi and Rózsa 1969, p. 41; for a discussion on the situation in the cement industry, see Gerő 1952, p. 303; and for Tatabánya, see *Harc a Szénért*, 25 January 1952.

36   SZKL SZOT 18d/1953; *Jelentés a munkaverseny, munkafegyelem és a munkavédelem alakulásáról a kormányprogram elhangzása óta* p. 2.

37   MOL M-KS-276f.53/145ö.e, p. 28.

38   SZKL SZOT 28d./1953.

Trade Unions reported in late 1953 a constant shortage of 6,500–6,800 workers in the mines. While the Council reported that labour recruitment campaigns could successfully recruit eight to ten thousand new workers monthly, it stated that this had been undermined by a greater level of labour turnover, as worker-peasants went back to work in agriculture during the summer months.[39] Feeding this high labour turnover were the low wages of the unskilled coal haulers and cart loaders, among whom worker-peasants were overrepresented. Most of these workers left work after approximately two weeks.[40] Coal haulers' wages were particularly low for the work they undertook. One worker, Károly Németh, working in mine number XV in Tatabánya, earned 18.40 forints daily, after working 25 shifts, and with a 20 percent supplement for working underground he took 552 forints home at the end of the month – about half the industrial average. A lack of workers able to carry away the coal after it had been cut led to the severe disorganisation of production in the mines, which hindered the coal cutters from producing, and thus prevented them from fulfilling their norms.[41] The Csolnoki II mine was forced to stop production outright because of a lack of such workers. In Ormospuszta, many of the mines were forced to cope with the shortage by allocating coal hewers to clear the coal, thus leading to temporary stoppages of work at the coal face.[42] This led to a situation in which only around fifty percent of skilled workers at the coal face could fulfil their norms.[43] In an examination of wage problems in the Petőfi Coal Mine in May 1953, it was reported that it 'was a really rare case if a worker could gain a percentage at the coal face sufficient to make him a Stakhanovite'.[44] This fed a growing problem of worker absenteeism. In June 1953, the number of shifts missed in the sector was 10,241 – a figure that rose in July to 13,101.[45] Indeed, so great was the labour shortage that the authorities often deployed prison labour to make up the numbers at the coal face. In Tatabánya in 1953, the enterprise reported that some 405 prisoners were working in the city.[46] Although mining was an extreme case, this

---

39 SZKL SZOT 15d/1953, p. 1.
40 MOL M-KS-276f.53/145ö.e, p. 36; SZKL SZOT 2d/1953, p. 3.
41 SZKL SZOT 30d/1953, p. 1. (It is interesting to note that the Mineworkers' Union, who submitted the report, did not believe that a monthly wage of 700–800 forints was sufficient to cover a miners' living expenses, let alone 522 forints. See ibid., p. 2.)
42 MOL M-KS-276f.53/145ö.e, pp. 35–6.
43 SZKL SZOT 28d/1953, p. 3.
44 SZKL SZOT 30d/1953. For more detail on the findings of the investigation, see MOL M-KS-276f.94/588ö.e, p. 130.
45 SZKL SZOT 18d/1953, p. 3.
46 Tóth 1992, p. 127.

phenomenon manifested itself to a greater or lesser extent in other branches of the economy. In the leather industry, generally low wages amid a tight labour market inevitably led to severe labour shortages, especially of unskilled workers. At the Táncsics Leather Factory, it was reported that when the factory managed to recruit new workers, almost without exception they would leave the job within two days.[47]

The third problem related to the over-exploitation of machinery and the shortages of tools in the plant itself. The poor maintenance of machinery and plants was a severe problem, and one that was gravely exacerbated by labour shortages, as management directed as many workers as possible away from maintenance into production. In the Tatabánya mines, the adoption of this policy by mine-management was blamed for poor safety conditions.[48] Often the incentive structures discouraged enterprises from adequately maintaining machinery. They were not credited for maintenance work in the calculation of plan-fulfilment indicators, yet the expenditure related to such work represented a drain on the enterprise wage fund. Such an incentive structure led managers to exploit ageing machinery to its limits, creating huge backlogs of maintenance expenditure. In metalworking, the poor state of machinery particularly affected workers on tight norms. In the Esztergom Tool and Machinery Factory, workers on small machines complained that they were in such bad condition, and the motors inside them so weak, that it was impossible to make 100 percent of their norms using them.[49] Added to this was a very serious shortage of work tools. In the Esztergom Tool and Machinery Factory, piece-rate workers spent on average thirty to thirty-five percent of their working time in search of the tools and materials to finish their job.[50]

The cumulative effect of each of these essentially systemic problems was that even with very lax norms, the percentage of those failing to reach 100 percent in ministry controlled industry was always high: it stood at 15.5 percent in June 1953.[51] More importantly, however, the constant pressure of the plan target combined with a persistent problem of shortage to change the way in which management attempted to utilise labour. This had profound implications for workers' own experiences of work, and for the rhythms of production. Management attempted to 'flexibly' deploy labour across the territory of an enterprise, forcing workers to take varied jobs, with different wage rates

---

47 SZKL SZOT 30d/1953, p. 2.
48 MOL M-KS-276f.53/145ö.e, p. 44.
49 MOL M-KS-276f.53/145ö.e, p. 30.
50 MOL M-KS-276f.53/145ö.e.
51 SZKL SZOT 18d/1953, p. 2.

depending on the state of production. In the Northern Hungary Chemical Works, a new enterprise, one hundred skilled workers had been trained, but due to raw material shortages they could not be given work appropriate to their training. As a result, they were shifted to different jobs within the enterprise. Such 'flexibility' had negative consequences for their earnings. It was estimated that, in October 1953, instead of earning the standard wage of 800 forints per month, they earned only 400–500 forints instead. This, it was reported, severely hindered the smooth operation of the internal labour market within the enterprise.[52] Such strategies met with serious worker discontent. In the Ózd Metallurgical Works, one skilled worker complained to a party committee that 'there are shops where, because of material shortage, they transfer work group leaders, brigade leaders, and outstanding workers. That means that they get unskilled workers wages, they can't even earn 800 or 900 Forints'.[53]

There was another side to the problem of stoppages. When the raw materials arrived, or when the deadline for plan fulfilment neared, management would need to draw on reserves of time and labour to make up the previous shortfall. This would often be done through the use of campaign-style methods. In sectors producing for export, because of the poor quality of much of the production, forty to fifty percent of the quarterly plan would be produced in the last month; and of this around fifty-five to sixty percent was produced in the last ten days of the last month.[54] Forms of the labour competition and related 'work' movements could be used to help the enterprises cope with the problem. In the Danube Shoe Factory, the reorganisation of the export warehouse was done on Sunday and classified by the enterprise management as 'social' work, so that overtime payment could be avoided.[55]

During such periods, overtime increased – and, in many factories, unlawfully increased. In the construction sector, the total expenditure on overtime pay increased by 200,000 forints from July to August 1953. In the Láng Machine Factory in September of that year, plan fulfilment of the monthly plan in the first ten days stood at 10 percent, yet it made up the production lag in the second ten days with the aid of overtime, which had averaged over the year at 30,000–50,000 hours every month.[56] At such times, the demand for overtime fell on different categories of workers, with high working hours being particu-

---

52   SZKL SZOT 30d/1953, p. 6.
53   MOL M-KS-276f.53/145ö.e, p. 7.
54   For this case, see Pető and Szakács 1985, p. 195.
55   SZKL SZOT 30d/1953, p. 10.
56   MOL M-KS-276f.53/145ö.e, p. 25.

larly demanded of those workers whose position in the internal division of labour of the plant meant that the maintenance of continuous production was dependant on them. For some workers, overtime became a constant part of working life. In the KISTEXT Textile Factory, the demand for overtime fell disproportionately on both administrative workers and manual workers in the maintenance shop.[57] In sugar production, the shortage of engineers meant that it was often necessary for technical workers to work for eight hours on Sunday without a rest day, in order to guarantee the conditions for production during the following week. In spite of this situation, the central authorities refused to allow overtime to be paid for such work, creating enormous problems for the enterprise.[58] In those sectors where this was required, the enterprise became dependent on the 'flexibility' of certain categories of workers and this relationship of dependence was sometimes successfully exploited by the workers concerned.

Above all, the unpredictable and uneven rhythms of production, combined with the pressure of the wage system, undermined remuneration as a mechanism for binding the worker to the plan. Indeed, the operation of the 'shortage' economy that had come into being during the early 1950s had a rhythm and a calendar of its own that was impenetrable to the will of the worker, one governed by the dialectic of shortage and at the end of plan cycle, the rush, as raw materials arrived. This was to form the context against which workers were able to exercise a degree of countervailing power, even at the height of Stalinism in Hungary.

Informal Bargaining and the Particularisation of Working-Class Identity

By the end of the Stalinist era in 1953, the attempt to use the wage system to persuade the worker to produce more quickly had been destroyed by the different rhythms of production created by the operation of the economy at shop floor level. The demands that the plan imposed upon enterprise management, combined with the environment of shortage, created a chaotic situation in production, but simultaneously gave a degree of countervailing power to the workforce. The environment in which production occurred, and the strategies workers adopted to exercise this countervailing power, had consequences for the social identities adopted by industrial workers. The workplace had become

---

57   MOL M-KS-276f.94/590ö.e, p. 43.
58   SZKL SZOT 30d/1953, p. 2.

an arena for considerable shop floor bargaining fed by management's need to accommodate workers to cope with the demands of production in a shortage economy and worker rejection of the official wage system.

Many of the more blatant forms of bargaining were simply called 'norm cheating' by the central apparatus. One form was the abuse of the innovation movement, which was often found in the metalworking sector, to disguise shortcuts in the production of each piece – a practice that often led to declining quality. Such 'norm cheating' often took the form of the abuse of elements of the labour competition. In the Diósgyőr Steel Mills, unskilled workers supplying the furnace were able to earn wages that were fifty percent higher than usual by engaging in 'shock work'. These workers officially left their workplace and were simply re-employed by the enterprise as shock workers, performing their original job, in order to gain higher wages. There were cases reported of workers abandoning the enterprise completely and simply living as shock workers as a result. In other cases, 'cheating' took the form of the foreman changing the size of the job done on paper in order to raise the wages of the workforce. In the Sztálinváros Brick Factory, the foreman simply reported that two to three hundred tons more bricks had been produced than was actually the case. On the Nagyatádi construction site, the wage fund had been overspent by 147,000 forints in August 1953. This was due largely to enterprise management that had paid for 2,500m² of plastering, as well as the haulage of 770,000 bricks, 825m³ of mortar, and 390m³ of concrete. This work had only ever been completed on paper.[59] This more blatant form of wage manipulation was exceptional, in that 'norm cheating' generally occurred during rushes at the end of the month or quarter in order to fulfil the plan.

Another more subtle form of informal bargaining was the exploitation by management of ambiguities in the work categorisation system to give workers higher wages than the central authorities stipulated. Indeed, bargaining between managers and workers over the categorisation of jobs for which there was a particular shortage of labour had become endemic by the early summer of 1953. At that time, the Ministry of Heavy Industry and the trade unions intervened to prevent an informal reduction of the norms in the Mátyás Rákosi Pipe Factory. The result was a debate between the central and the enterprise-level organisation about the appropriate categories into which warehouse workers should be placed, with the enterprise arguing that they should go into a higher category than that proposed by the central authorities. The union reported that in steel mills the enterprise management commonly shifted maintenance workers, fitters and turners into higher wage categories

---

[59]   SZKL SZOT 28 d/1953.

than those centrally stipulated. Among maintenance workers in the textile factories, such modifications seem to have been quite common and were made in order to give workers in these industries wages comparable to those in the metalworking sector in order to prevent labour mobility.[60]

The classic form of shop floor bargaining, however, was over the norms. One of the most notable features of the norms was how certain groups of workers could use their position in the production process to informally bargain with management to secure norm relaxation. This differed from 'norm cheating', in that the latter consisted of blatant attempts to defraud management, while other forms of bargaining around the norms were more subtle. Initially, the introduction of unpopular norms was met by a series of exaggerated complaints. In the Mátyás Rákosi Machine Factory, some eighty percent of the complaints were described as unrealistic and as a tool in the bargaining process between workers and management.[61] If this failed to have any effect, then the next step was for workers to withhold production. In one machine factory, the workers regulated the pace of their work in order to under-fulfil their norms over a twenty-day period (fifty to sixty percent fulfilment). Over the next ten days, the enterprise management converted them to 'shock work' wages, in order to fulfil the monthly plan, which led to norm fulfilment of two to three hundred percent. Often such behaviour led to norm relaxation. In the metalworking sector, this strategy simply took the form of underestimating the capacity of technology to cope with high work intensity.[62] This also seems to have been the case with semi-skilled workers operating machines or working on automated assembly lines in food processing.[63] In construction, crane-operators had been able to bargain to relax the norms. This led to them earning as much as 2,500–3,000 forints monthly, while many of their workmates on the site could only earn around eight hundred Forints.[64]

Some workers were better able than others to successfully secure norm relaxation, and this led to a reshaping of the wage system. In the metal industry, at the Mátyás Rákosi Machine Factory the differing importance of the various shops in the production process led to wage differentials opening up between the skills, depending on their area of employment in the factory. Turners' average hourly wages varied from between 5.01 forints in the lowest paid shop to 6.27 forints in the highest. The biggest difference was among the

---

60   SZKL SZOT 28 d/1953, p. 2.
61   SZKL SZOT 31d/1953, p. 1.
62   SZKL SZOT 28 d/1953.
63   SZKL SZOT 30d/1953, p. 16.
64   SZKL SZOT 31d/1953, p. 2.

grinders – the lowest paid earned 4.28 forints per hour, while those working in the maintenance section could earn 9.88 forints.[65] In textiles, lax norms were experienced in enterprises where skilled work by hand was required. In areas such as flax, hemp, yarn, silk and ready-made hosiery production, the norms for those jobs requiring handicraft production were considerably more lax than those for machine workers, with handicraft norms fulfilled by 150–180 percent.[66]

Maintenance workers were generally able to exploit their position to secure wage advantages through norm relaxation and informal bargaining over the categorisation of jobs. In the metal industry, the result of such bargaining was to create large wage differences between enterprises. In most large enterprises in light industry, the maintenance staff accounted for some fifty to one hundred workers. The work was not paid according to a standardised norm, although wages were generally set according to the rates for skilled work in heavy engineering.[67] The consequences of this lack of standardisation can be illustrated by the problem of the labour mobility of maintenance workers between the Almásfűztő Aluminium Smelter and the Almásfűztő Oil Refining Enterprise. In the aluminium smelter, the maintenance staff were paid according to the heavy-engineering rates, while in the oil refinery they were paid on the basis of the lower chemical-industry rates. The consequence of this was that the latter enterprise had serious problems recruiting and retaining maintenance staff.[68] In mining, low pay for maintenance workers relative to other sectors was a major cause of discontent among the workers. Monthly wages were as low as five to six hundred forints for some workers in the sector.[69] Such a lack of standardised payment gave workers considerable scope to employ informal bargaining strategies to increase their wages. In one pharmaceuticals plant, for example, maintenance workers simply refused to complete work when the enterprise management refused to offer them pay for supplementary time.[70] The ability of maintenance workers to participate in informal bargaining could lead to serious problems. Indeed, in light industry the superior capacity of maintenance workers over even skilled workers to bargain informally with management led to distortions in the wage distribution. In the Budapest Conserves Factory, for example, in August 1953, machinists earned

---

65 SZKL SZOT 31d/1953, p. 1.
66 SZKL SZOT 30d/1953, pp. 3–4.
67 SZKL SZOT 30d/1953, p. 3.
68 SZKL SZOT 30d/1953, p. 4.
69 SZKL SZOT 30d/1953, p. 2.
70 SZKL SZOT 30d/1953, p. 3.

between 1,079 and 1,098 forints, while unskilled workers in maintenance could earn between 1,146 and 1424 forints monthly.[71]

Those workers responsible for supplying, loading and unloading materials, were particularly successful in achieving norm relaxation, because of their ability to determine the pace of production, through regulating the speed of their work. At the Békés County Flour Mills, for example, average norm fulfilment varied between 90–105 percent, while loading workers could fulfil their norms by 135–140 percent. At the Szabolcs County Flour Mills, in the third quarter of 1953, average norm fulfilment varied between 103–104 percent, guaranteeing an average monthly wage of 671 forints. In this enterprise, one loader was able with 20 days' work to earn 1,175.90 forints, while one milling grinder in 15 days with 150 hours' work earned 847.37 forints, and a flour siever with 17 days and 190 hours' work could only make 487.60 forints. Often the skilled millers earned less than the unskilled loaders.[72]

Such informal bargaining contributed enormously to the fragmentation of the industrial workforce that had been set in train by the implementation of new systems of remuneration during 1949 and 1950. Informal bargaining strategies could only be employed successfully by small groups of workers, and in many factories they were generally secured at the expense of other workers. In one Budapest machine factory, informal bargaining had undermined relations between the workers on the shop floor to such an extent by early 1951 that one union official stated that 'the biggest problem ... is the lack of good relations between work mates, we should have a friendly atmosphere between work groups like that we had a year ago, when we didn't throw insults at each other'.[73]

Superimposed onto the fragmentation of the industrial workforce was a process that can best be described as the particularisation of worker identity, which contributed to and was partly driven by the process of informal bargaining.[74] This resulted from the combination of informal cooperation between management and the workers, with the re-composition of the workforce arising out of the considerable proletarianisation that came with forced industrialisation. This transformation was documented by a survey of twenty enterprises located in Budapest, in October 1953, employing a total of 93,000 workers. Of these only 62.8 percent had been workers in 1949, 10.8 percent were of peasant origin, a further 8.8 percent had been housewives on the eve of the

---

71   SZKL SZOT 30 d/1953, p. 2. The information on the tightness of the norms for machinists in light industry can be found in ibid., p. 3.
72   SZKL SZOT 30d/1953, pp. 12–13.
73   MOL M-Bp.-176f.2/191/4ö.e, p. 146.
74   For a more detailed description of this process, see Pittaway 1998, pp. 243–86.

Five Year Plan, and 4.2 percent had either been self-employed or had white-collar jobs four years previously. The survey also indicated that, in the provinces, the extent of the re-composition had been much greater.[75]

Growing official concern over the indiscipline and low skill levels of the many new recruits had created spaces in which small groups of workers could secure preferential treatment from management. One union official in a western Hungarian mining town admitted giving preferential treatment to small groups of more experienced workers when applying work discipline regulations. He stated:

> [because] new workers are the ones who absent themselves ... if an old worker with 18 to 20 years' service to the pit came to the factory management almost crying to ask that they don't penalise him for being absent, then of course with such an old and honest worker we wouldn't use a severe penalty, but with new workers who go absent, we are strict.[76]

Such spaces were exploited by small groups of workers to bargain informally with management over wages, access to tools and raw materials, and the implementation of work discipline regulations using attributes of skill and experience to secure favourable treatment. Such attributes were cultural constructs, and their successful deployment served to exclude workers on the basis of gender, generation, and social origin from access to favourable positions within informal wage bargaining. Needless to say, this process was deeply subversive of class solidarity among industrial workers, although it also did not allow the state to enforce its authority on the shop floor.

Conclusion

This examination of the attempts of the Stalinist regimes in post-war Hungary to discipline labour – by binding industrial workers to economic plans through individualised systems of remuneration underpinned by a specific 'politics of time' – demonstrates that such policies were strikingly unsuccessful. Instead, the major determinant of work rhythms appears to have been the operation of the 'shortage economy' itself. Despite this mismatch between state-led intervention and the actual operation of the economy, the institutions the state

---

75 'A magyar munkásosztály fejlődése' 1954, p. 14.
76 SZKL Bányász (Mineworkers' Union), 922d/1955, p. 4.

used, that is, the wage system, to ensure that 'time' acted as a stick in order to raise productivity, remained in place. As a result, these attempts became the basis for a (largely informal) struggle on the shop floor, as workers attempted to find ways to reconcile the time embodied in the wage system with the 'rhythm' of the shortage economy as a means of boosting their earnings.

This discussion of wage determination and factory regimes in the context of early Socialist Hungary has three important implications for how Stalinism is studied, both generally and in its East-Central European context. The first and most important implication is that the analysis presented here suggests that approaches that stress the dominance of the state in socialist society have misread reality. This article argues for the primacy of the realm of the material over the intentions of the political, given the way in which the intentions of state rationalisers foundered on the reality of the shortage economy. While this economy was undoubtedly the consequence of state action, it is difficult to maintain that its perverse functioning was an intended goal of this intervention. These 'rhythms' caused state-led rationalisation to founder at a shop floor level. The focus on the material, as opposed to the political dimensions of the Stalinist order, also points out how a repressive state was able to prevent the tensions created by this failure from assuming a 'formal' nature. The struggles on the shop floor around remuneration were not public, but rather informal. What is more, bargaining tended to accept the rules of the game on the shop floor; it was often about bargaining over the right to maximise earnings from scarce work, rather than protesting about the scarcity of work itself.

This point feeds through into the second major implication of the analysis presented here. In opposition to the traditional view of Stalinism as collectivist and monolithic, this article has shown how state policy could – at least in the realm of the economy – seek to individualise social actors. This process of individualisation occurred at the level of policy, in the way that the economic plan was designed to be broken down to the individual producer, at the level of institutions, through the wage system or labour competition, and to some extent at the level of social response. The actions of the state in the realm of production undermined social solidarity. This outcome was reinforced by the operation of the shortage economy and worker responses to it, which heightened fragmentation of the industrial workforce, undercut the appeal of social solidarity, and provided the material base for the particularisation of worker identity.

The third implication of the analysis presented here is more historical, and applies explicitly to Stalinism in its Eastern European and, more particularly, Hungarian context. It has been widely assumed that during the 1960s and

1970s, a monolithic Stalinism gave way to a more liberal and less despotic regime, which allowed greater room for autonomous social action. The emergence of a tolerated informal economic sector and greater economic freedom has been attributed to this wave of reform, something that, it is commonly argued, affected the system changes in the region in 1989–90. In some accounts, informal cooperation between workers and managers within the context of 'hegemonic' factory regimes, to use Michael Burawoy's term, was a product of reform. The account presented here suggests that such institutions emerged under high Stalinism itself and were due not to reform from above, but rather the need to survive at a local level in the face of an environment of endemic shortage. This points to a need to re-examine the history of post-war Eastern Europe in a new light, in a way that utilises the perspectives of social history and pays close attention to the material world in which individuals both produced and consumed. Such a re-examination would question many assumptions about the nature of state socialism and recast our understanding of the relationship between Stalinism, post-Stalinism and the events of 1989–90.

CHAPTER 5

Retreat from Collective Protest: Household, Gender, Work and Popular Opposition in Stalinist Hungary

Introduction

In mid-December 1951, in an attempt to prevent absenteeism on the days immediately after Christmas, the government announced that it would end the practice of paying wages before the holiday. Instead, workers would receive their wages on 27 December. This resulted in considerable discontent. In the Ikarus bus plant in Budapest, both the union and the party organisation were deluged with complaints. Management and the factory organisation received assurances from the ministry that wages could be paid on 23 December despite the decision. The factory party-committee immediately issued a statement to that effect to the discontented workforce. On 23 December, payment of wages commenced to workers on the morning shift. However, at 11am the ministry intervened to prevent the payments to those scheduled to receive their wages at 1:30pm. Management objected, resulting in a dispute between enterprise and the ministry. Ernő Gerő, second in the Stalinist party leadership and its economic policy supremo, was called in to arbitrate. He ruled that no more of the wages should be paid. By this time it was 3.30pm and some fifteen hundred workers were waiting impatiently. As the decision was announced, the fifteen hundred staged an angry demonstration, occupying the offices of management and the factory party organisation. It was only broken up with the use of force. The ÁVH – the Stalinist secret police – took 156 people into custody for their role in the demonstration.[1]

This demonstration was the largest single act of collective protest by industrial workers in Hungary during much of the period. It was an exceptional event during the Stalinist years in Hungary, unlike its neighbours; there were

---

* Originally published in Jan Kok (ed.) 2002, *Rebellious Families: Household Strategies and Collective Action in the Nineteenth and Twentieth Centuries*, New York, NY: Berghahn Books, pp. 198–228.
1 Magyar Országos Levéltár, MSZMP Budapesti Bizottság Archíviuma (Hungarian National Archive, Archive of the Budapest Committee of the Hungarian Socialist Workers' Party, hereafter MOL M-Bp.) 95f.4/118ö.e, pp. 81–7.

no major instances of open popular unrest prior to 1956 – whether strikes, political protest or bread riots.[2] This apparent lack of open collective protest existed alongside considerable poverty, declining standards of living, extreme repression and increasing work intensity across industry. Despite this, even open attacks on workers' incomes met with only sporadic opposition.[3]

As collective protest became more sporadic, members of 'working-class' households began to centre their activities increasingly on the private sphere. There was a considerable desire on the part of many to seek a relative degree of household self-sufficiency in the production of foodstuffs, rather than depend on the unreliable state sector. In mining areas, the state began to sponsor a programme of subsidised private house building. This proved to be highly popular, simply because a house with a garden offered 'working-class' households greater opportunities for producing food independently of the state sector.[4]

In other words, as collective protest declined, industrial workers increasingly began to centre on the private sphere. Why was this so? The seemingly obvious answer is that it was as a result of a high degree of political repression. This undoubtedly played a partial role. Yet this seems to ignore the fact that collective protest was more prevalent in the rest of Eastern Europe than in Hungary, while the populations of these other states were subject to a similar degree of political repression. The severe poverty of the Stalinist years provides another plausible explanation. It might be said that this fails to account for the precise dynamics of the retreat from open collective protest that occurred. While poverty and political repression provide part of the solution to our

---

2 On protest elsewhere in the socialist states during this period, there was substantial working-class protest in the GDR in 1951, see Port 1998, pp. 145–73. In Yugoslavia, the Tito regime's attempts to collectivise agriculture met with substantial and violent peasant opposition; see Bokovoy 1998, pp. 134–40. The death of Stalin in 1953 led to substantial open protest in many states, but not in Hungary. In May, tobacco workers in Plovdiv rioted; see Crampton 1987, p. 176. In Czechoslovakia, there were riots in Plzeň; see Ulc 1965, pp. 46–9. The best-known disturbances that followed Stalin's death were those of 17 June 1953 in the GDR. The best English language account is in Fulbrook 1995, pp. 177–87.

3 For some examples of sporadic opposition, see Szakszervezetek Központi Levéltára (Central Archive of the Trade Unions, hereafter SZKL), Szakszervezetek Országos Tanácsa (National Council of Trade Unions, hereafter SZOT), Közgazdasági Osztály (Economics Department, hereafter Közgazdaság), 13d./1952.

4 For the general point, see Pittaway 1998, pp. 305–9. For my exploration of the meanings that the state and mineworkers' families attached to the limited private house building campaigns of the early 1950s, see Pittaway 2000.

puzzle, the processes that reshaped the boundaries between public and private in Stalinist Hungary were more complex and subtle.

The retreat of open collective protest recast gender relations both within industrial production and the household. Although political scientists and others frequently sought to analyse the occasional explosions of popular protest that periodically characterised socialist societies across the region, there has been little work since 1989 on the nature of the more everyday forms of collective action.[5] There has been virtually nothing on the gender dimensions of such protest – an analytical framework that can reveal much about the shifting boundaries between the household and place of work. In a study of the gender dimensions of resistance and protest in Communist Poland, Padraic Kenney has argued that a gendered division between the public and private spheres played a decisive role in structuring the patterns of men's and women's protest.[6]

The argument presented here identifies a clear similarity between gender ideologies in both Poland and Hungary – at least for the early socialist period. The notion of a gendered split between a male public realm and a female private realm permeated society. Despite the superficially egalitarian rhetoric of the labour mobilisation campaigns of the Stalinist regime, this notion was reinforced rather than challenged by the new state.

The argument presented here suggests that 'working-class'[7] women's and men's experiences of socialist industrialisation created an ideal of social privatisation and household self-sufficiency. Increasingly, a world of poverty and insecure wages from the state sector combined with the pervasive shortage in the field of official consumption to transform the state-dominated public realm. This public sphere, for many working-class households, became an arena in which needs could not be satisfied. A moral economy developed in which the household strove for autonomy from the state-dominated public realm. This was never completely achievable; indeed, in many cases it was completely unachievable. Households, insofar as they were self-sufficient, were so because of the complex links between the public and private sphere. The ideological effects of an ideal of social privatisation should not, however, be underestimated; they legitimised a gradual withdrawal, albeit initially

---

5   Probably the best overview of such events from the pre-1989 period in English is Montias 1981, pp. 175–87.
6   Kenney 1999, pp. 399–425.
7   I use the term 'working class' rather than simply working class (that is, without quotation marks) simply to indicate my scepticism as to whether industrial workers constituted a class. For greater elaboration of this point, see Pittaway 1998.

prompted by state repression, from forms of public protest in the factory or community. They did not eliminate popular opposition, but rather served to channel it. In the workplace, protest was channelled into more covert forms of resistance, such as pilfering, which further supported informal economic activities centred on the household.

Such a shift from public to private had important implications for gender relations within both the workplace and the household. While the Stalinist state advocated gender equality at work and expanded female employment, women, paradoxically, invested more in the maintenance of the household. This was reflected in patterns of collective protest, as well as in survival strategies. Furthermore, male bargaining within the workplace reflected the redrawing of the boundaries between the public and private realms. Informal bargaining around wages tended to be underpinned by assumptions that reflected shifting gender relations.

The argument is developed thematically throughout the chapter. The first section deals with the notion of the public and private during the post-war years in Hungary. The second considers the changing patterns of collective protest within the workplace. The third section deals with the realm of consumption, while the fourth examines the household.

The Gendered Dimensions of Public and Private in Post-War Hungary

As the Hungarian Workers' Party (*Magyar Dolgozók Pártja*, or MDP)[8] began to construct the formal institutions of Stalinist dictatorship in Hungary in 1948, the state initiated labour competition in the factories. Labour competition was intended to mobilise workers to increase production. Furthermore, as far as the more idealistic of the builders of the 'new' state were concerned, it was to herald a revolution in production and 'working-class' attitudes towards their work. Propagandists reacted with concern at opinion-poll evidence, collected in 1948 in the industrial suburbs of the capital, which showed that 37 percent of factory workers' wives did not know whether their husbands participated in the labour competitions. These propagandists recognised that factory workers' wives, however, were concerned with the affairs of the home and their

---

8 Created in 1948 as the result of a forced union of Hungary's Social Democratic and Communist Parties, the MDP was to become the ruling party for much of the 1950s. It was dissolved as a result of the 1956 Revolution, and reconstituted as the Magyar Szocialista Munkáspárt (Hungarian Socialist Workers' Party, or MSZMP) on 1 November 1956.

immediate community. They were thus 'separated from the factory, factory work and the labour competition'.[9]

The compilers of opinion-poll surveys about the attitudes of household members to changes that were occurring in the factory were revealing the traces of an ideal of a gendered separation of the public and private in industrial Hungary. Urban industrial workers subscribed to an ideal of the male worker as breadwinner and the married wife as manager of the household. These attitudes were reflected in the attitudes of factory committees, which – in heavy industry at least – were dominated up until 1949 by the representatives of the skilled, male worker elite. In the Lampart Factory in 1948, women were systematically moved from the best paying jobs to lower ones by the committee. This was justified on the grounds that the family 'responsibilities' of their male colleagues should be taken into account when distributing work. In the Ganz Ship Yards, the factory trade union only distributed potatoes and other benefits paid in kind to 'the men and their families', explicitly excluding female labour from having direct access to them.[10]

While 'working-class' masculinity conferred the role of the breadwinner on male workers, the female role of household management conferred several responsibilities on women. While this included housework, the management of 'house-keeping' money, and shopping for the household,[11] it could also lead to the adoption of other forms of unpaid work for the household outside the home itself. During the period of poverty that accompanied post-war reconstruction, many urban households were given an allotment on which chickens were kept or vegetables grown. In many industrial areas, the wives of factory workers worked the allotments, while their husbands laboured for wages. Consequently, when school holidays arrived, enterprises were inundated with requests from families with children for child care to allow the mothers to work on the allotments.[12] Such a division of responsibilities was commonplace in worker-peasant households where the men commuted to work in neighbouring industrial centres, while women assumed the management of the

---

9 Garai 1948, pp. 14–15.
10 SZKL A Magyarországi Vas- és Fémmunkások Központi Szövetség iratai (Papers of the Federation of Metalworkers of Hungary, hereafter VASAS)/520 d/1948.
11 Personal interview with B. P-né, Dunaújváros 8 February 1995.
12 For such a request from wives of Tatabánya mine workers, see MOL Magyar Általános Köszénbánya Személyzeti Osztály iratai (Papers of the Personnel Department of the Hungarian General Coal-Mining Company) Z254/10cs/38t, p. 493.

farm.¹³ This gender division of household labour could lead to alternative forms of female participation in the public sphere, at least prior to Stalinism. Ethnographer Erzsébet Örszigethy traced the fortunes of a series of worker-peasant households, examining the strategies they adopted from the 1920s onwards. The husbands took jobs in the Budapest public transport company. The women took responsibility for the landholdings – given that their means of subsistence were guaranteed they used their landholdings to produce for the market. This enabled them to enter the public sphere as market gardeners, albeit on a small scale.¹⁴

With the advent of Stalinism, the new state offered a vision of social transformation characterised by sociologist Zsuzsa Gille as 'metallurgical socialism'.¹⁵ Heavy industry was expanded, as Hungary became 'a country of iron, steel and machines'.¹⁶ As elsewhere in Eastern Europe, this vision of socialist industrialisation was sharply gendered. It celebrated male productive labour and promoted the development of heavy industry – a sector that largely employed men.¹⁷ As the aims of the First Five Year Plan were announced, the gendered nature of the vision of social transformation upon which it was based was not lost on many women in industrial areas. They failed to see how an expansion of heavy industry would directly benefit them, preferring instead a plan that raised living standards, and improved housing and community services. In Újpest, when the plan was popularised, male workers supported the aims of the plan even though some questioned its feasibility. Among women the picture was entirely different. They questioned 'why so many construction sites are needed, [when] it would be better to give higher wages'.¹⁸

Despite the ambivalence of many 'working-class' women, the First Five Year Plan seemed to offer a radical restructuring of gender relations by allowing women to fully participate in the socialist labour force. In 1950, labour planners envisaged introducing 123,000 new women employees into the labour force during the course of the First Five Year Plan. Of these, 40,000 were to come from the ranks of young women, 43,000 from agriculture, and 40,000

---

13 For pre-Second World War evidence on the importance of the existence of the worker-peasant household in certain regions of the country, see Erdei 1977, pp. 53–4; Szabó 1938, pp. 48–52. Useful evidence on the gender dimensions of worker-peasant households in the immediate post-war period is provided in Markus 1946 pp. 251–61.
14 Örszigethy 1986.
15 Personal conversation with Zsuzsa Gille, July 1998.
16 The phrase is that of Ernő Gerő; see Gerő 1952.
17 Kenney 1999, pp. 403–4.
18 MOL M-Bp.-95f.3/55ö.e, pp. 46–7.

from urban households. Fifty-four thousand were to go into industry and 22,000 into construction. Of this seventy-six thousand, 20,000 were to be directed to the machine industry, and fifteen hundred to the mines.[19] The National Planning Office pursued an egalitarian policy in the workplace. On training schemes for skilled workers, it called for a policy of affirmative action. This policy stipulated that a minimum of thirty to fifty percent of the training places be filled by young women.[20] To this end, it explicitly called for a 'reorganisation of male labour' to facilitate the entrance of women into previously male-dominated occupations. It explicitly instructed enterprises 'not only to place women into occupations that have generally been filled by women, but they have to take the line that women should be directed to every occupation.'[21]

Even this policy – which did not have much success – did not challenge established gender ideologies, insofar as they related to the boundaries between public and private. Instead, the policy envisaged 'freeing women from their domestic duties' through the expansion of crèches and day-care centres for children, and the growth of factory and communal eating facilities. Furthermore, the regime envisaged the growth in the availability of labour-saving devices – such as washing machines – and, most ambitiously, the industrialisation of housework.[22]

Assumptions about a gender division between a male public realm of work and a female private realm formed the backdrop to the retreat from collective protest. Such assumptions were shared by 'working-class' men and women themselves, and played an important role in structuring their attitudes and actions. In some ways, paradoxically, they were reinforced by the new socialist state.

The Retreat from Collective Protest in the Workplace

Hungary's Stalinist turn heralded a revolution in production. The dependence of the practice of comprehensive economic planning on the application of principles derived from scientific management has been much neglected by those who have analysed it. In the Soviet Union and Eastern Europe, its

---

19 MOL Magyar Dolgozók Pártja-Magyar Szocialista Munkáspárt Központi Szervek iratai (Papers of the Central Organs of the Hungarian Workers' Party-Hungarian Socialist Workers' Party, hereafter M-KS-) 276f.116/43ö.e, pp. 15–16.
20 MOL M-KS-276f.116/43ö.e, p. 17.
21 MOL M-KS-276f.116/43ö.e, p. 16.
22 The documents contained in the dossier MOL M-KS-276f.116/43ö.e, are full of such plans.

implementation entailed considerable institutional centralisation, along with an individualisation of responsibility for the achievement of the production targets it laid down. Hungarian economic planning was characterised by this apparently paradoxical combination of collectivist centralisation and an individualised production regime on the shop floor. The organisation of production and systems of mobilisation and remuneration were explicitly individualised and tied to goals laid down in the plan.[23]

The institutions that resulted from the introduction of comprehensive economic planning were far from popular. In the workplace, industrial workers developed a strictly instrumental attitude towards payment-by-results and labour competition. Workers only participated where direct material benefits resulted.[24] Fortunately for the new regime, in the late 1940s real wages rose rapidly.[25] When wages did not rise, the state met with a wave of shop-floor protest from both male and female workers, just as it had done with its attempts to increase production norms in 1949.[26]

In late 1949, work was explicitly individualised with the promotion of individual participation in labour competition and the introduction of the Stakhanovite movement in Hungary. Wages rose not just for the new Stakhanovites – or outstanding workers – but also for the workforce in general. Despite distrust of the new Stakhanovite workers, the workforce was generally content as a result of their increased wages.[27] The individualisation of production entailed by central planning was completed with the transformation of the wage-system accompanied by a norm revision for the vast majority of the workforce. The first major step was to change the basis on which worked was rewarded. A piece-rate system was introduced for the majority of the workforce in March 1950. The central component of the system was that the work done, and *not* the individual worker, was the subject of remuneration. In this way, the principle was established that payment should reflect the amount and value of what was produced by a worker as laid out in the plan. Alongside this development, new and tighter production norms were to be introduced in the summer of 1950.[28]

The introduction of the new norms met with one of the largest waves of worker protest in the post-war period. As early as July, before the introduction

---

23 Pittaway, chapter 4 of this volume.
24 Garai 1948.
25 'A magyar munkásosztály fejlődése' 1954, p. 20.
26 MOL M-KS-276f.116/18ö.e, p. 6.
27 MOL M-KS-276f.116/18ö.e, pp. 22–3.
28 Pittaway, chapter 4 of this volume.

of the new norms worker anger took the form of workers ignoring and cold-shouldering union- and party-officials on the shop floor. In one Szeged factory, a well-organised 'go-slow' was used. In Kecskemét, one worker was detained by the secret police for publicly comparing the regime to that of the Nazis. In a neighbouring factory, a norm-setter was physically assaulted. He had argued that their 200 percent fulfilment was the result of the laxness of workers' production norms. In one textile factory, the factory committee president stated that a new norm revision would follow if the new norms were systematically over-fulfilled. In the Hoffher tractor factory, the electricians broke into the factory on a Sunday and wrecked one of the most expensive machines in protest. The discontent across industry was only defused through the Korea-week labour competition campaign in early August, which management organised to allow workers to fulfil the new norms.[29] Despite this, the damage had been done, and any shaky legitimacy still possessed by institutions like the labour competition had now been destroyed.

This was to be made clear to the regime through the pattern of much of the worker protest that emerged. Labour competition was blamed directly by many workers for the norm revision, and in many cases the 'heroes of labour' were personally attacked for class treachery. In many Budapest factories, angry workers held the Stakhanovites responsible for what had happened. In Kiskunfélegyháza, construction workers destroyed a wall built by Stakhanovites after they called workers to a labour competition to over-fulfil the new norms. In many cases, the pressure many Stakhanovites experienced forced them to fall back with their workmates and oppose the new norms publicly. One Stakhanovite in the construction industry openly attacked the new norms as being too tight. In the textile industry, at the Magyar Pamutipar cotton factory, one Stakhanovite was forced – under pressure from workmates – to formally request the norm office to base norms on average and not Stakhanovite fulfilment.[30]

The state, however, was prepared for labour unrest and showed a willingness to use repressive measures against those who protested. In the United Lighting and Electrics Factory, management working in close cooperation with the secret police were able to identify and quash discontent before it

---

29   MOL M-KS-276f.116cs/19ö.e, pp. 129–30; MOL M-KS-276f.116cs/19ö.e, pp. 220–3; MOL M-KS-276f.116cs/18ö.e, pp. 180–3; MOL M-KS-276f.116cs/18ö.e, pp. 197–9; MOL M-KS-276f.116cs/19ö.e, p. 1; MOL M-KS-276f.116cs/19ö.e, p. 5; MOL M-KS-276f.116cs/19ö.e, p. 58; MOL M-KS-276f.116cs/19ö.e, pp. 43–5.

30   MOL M-KS-276f.116cs/18ö.e, pp. 180–3; MOL M-KS-276f.116cs/19ö.e, p. 5; MOL M-KS-276f.116cs/40ö.e, pp. 77–82.

grew. Only two workers were sacked for 'oppositional behaviour' in connection with the tightening, while four were arrested by the secret police for 'spreading rumours' likely to lead to discontent. This policy was replicated right across the country. In one Felsőgálla factory, a worker was sacked after publicly stating that only the norms of those workers with fulfilment rates of over five hundred percent should be cut. Management was sometimes able to avoid the intervention of the secret police. In the machine shop of the Tatabánya mines in July, a work stoppage was halted after twenty five minutes simply as a result of management threatening to report those participating to the authorities. Even individual acts of protest and attempts to informally bargain with management over the new norms were dealt with brutally. Attempts by brigades on one western Hungarian construction site to institute a go-slow in order to secure better norms met with police intervention.[31]

Norm revision and reductions in living standards fed a negative solidarity against the state among workers. From 1950 onwards, they were united in feeling exploited by a 'bloodsucking government'.[32] This opposition was expressed in the way that workers collaborated to beat factory systems designed to control them. In the Danube Shoe Factory, there was a degree of solidarity between all workers when it came to getting poor output past the quality-control systems in the factory. In 1953, the plant newspaper criticised workers on production line 301 for being prepared to accept and pass on the poor quality shoes made by other workers without question.[33] Such forms of solidarity were common across industry and had an important political dimension. Upon his escape to the West in 1953, one former worker in a heavy-engineering factory, in answer to the question of why workers collaborated to keep the quality of their work at a low level, or to use more materials than was strictly necessary,

---

31   MOL M-Bp.-95f.4/120ö.e, p. 214; SZKL Komárom Szakszervezetek Megyei Tanácsa (Komárom County Council of Trade Unions, hereafter Komárom SZMT)/42d./1950; Szakszervezetek Országos Tanácsa Esztergom-Komárom Megye Bizottság, Tatabánya, 1950 augusztus 24 (National Council of Trade Unions Komárom-Esztergom County Committee, Tatabánya, 4 August 1950), p. 1; SZKL Komárom SZMT/43d./1950, p. 1; SZKL Komárom SZMT/43d./1950; Szakszervezetek Országos Tanácsa Esztergom-Komárom Megyei Bizottság, Tatabánya, Jelentés, 1950 augusztus 29 (National Council of Trade Unions Komárom-Esztergom County Committee, Tatabánya, Report, 29 August 1950), p. 1.

32   This phrase is taken from the response of a worker to the beginning of the New Course, quoted in SZKL SZOT Bér-Munkaügy Osztály (Wage-Labour Department, hereafter Bér-Munkaügy)/33d./1953, p. 1.

33   *Futószalag*, 29 August 1953.

answered that 'psychologically the situation was . . . that they [the workers] were happy if they could harm the Communist system'.[34]

The culture created by workers' negative solidarity against the state provided a basis for concealed acts of collective protest to continue. Elek Nagy, later a workers' council leader in Csepel during the 1956 Revolution, stated:

> there were a whole series of hidden strikes under Rákosi and then under Imre Nagy, which were generally caused by wage issues. The norm-setter gave us the time [for a given job]. Then a workmate went to complain . . . then we decided to organise a 'black' strike.[35]

One worker in the Danube Shoe Factory recalled:

> [I]n 1953 there were grumbles about the norms, at one time it came to the workers going out on an unofficial smoke break to protest. Work stopped for ten minutes. Because the workers didn't want to risk any more, the management simply forgot the incident, and no-one felt the consequences.[36]

Underneath these forms of concealed collective protest lay another level at which discontent was expressed. Much worker resistance took an 'infra-political' form – a form that was concealed from the direct view of those in power and consisted of individual acts such as jokes, persistent rumour-mongering, and the expression of anti-regime statements through graffiti.[37] Many of these actions revealed deep discontent with the low living standards of industrial workers. Young workers from Tatabánya, who escaped to the west in 1953, recounted how under cover of darkness they would go from the worker's hostel into the town to tear down posters inviting them to produce '[m]ore coal for the homeland', or to 'sign up for peace loans, build a future for your family and your children', and replaced them with their own home-made posters with slogans like 'Long live the Americans!', and 'Don't work for such low wages!'[38] Negative solidarity against the state made possible

---

34 OSA RFE Magyar Gy.6/Item No. 08794/53, p. 1.
35 Quoted in Kozák and Molnár 1994, p. 13.
36 OSA RFE Magyar Gy.6/Item No. 3677/56, p. 2.
37 For a discussion of the whole nature of 'infra-political' resistance as a concept, see Scott 1990, especially chapter 7. For an examination of such kinds of 'resistance' in the Hungarian context, see Rév 1987, pp. 335–50.
38 OSA RFE Magyar Gy.6/Item No. 06687/53, p. 5.

widespread theft by workers from their employers during the early 1950s. This often provided the basis for participation by workers in informal, sometimes illegal, economic activity beyond the scope of their employment.[39]

Shop-floor opposition to state policy has been characterised as negative solidarity against the state for the reason that it coexisted with an extraordinary decline in solidarity between workers at the point of production. The individualisation of production increased wage differentials between workers – often between workers who had the same job description. Despite the collectivism of regime ideology, this individualisation of production was highly visible by late 1950. Furthermore, the implementation of the regime's policy of rapid industrialisation led to the emergence of widespread shortages of materials, labour, machinery and tools in Hungarian industry during the early 1950s. Although the precise impact of such shortages varied from sector to sector, enterprise to enterprise, and often workshop to workshop, they decisively reshaped the rhythms of production and the shop-floor experience of industrial labour. The level of earnings became more unpredictable. Industrial workers increasingly began to compete with their workmates for scarce work in order to make out.[40]

This competition was given enormous impetus by informal bargaining between lower management – desperate to meet plan targets in an unpredictable economic environment – and a discontented workforce. Workers in a favourable position within the division of labour of a given plant were able to use their bargaining power to gain advantage by manipulating wage systems or securing preferential access to remunerative work. As the state became concerned about the rapidly declining quality of industrial production, skilled experienced workers were also able to argue for preferential treatment.[41] At the same time, older skilled workers, who on the whole had worked prior to 1948, were able to shape the division of power, work and earnings on Hungarian shop floors. Their opposition to certain consequences of state labour policies pursued during the early years of socialist industrialisation was to play an important part in a phenomenon best characterised as the 'particularisation of worker identity.[42] The gender implications of this process of particularisation of worker identity are of particular interest to us here. As the 1950s went on,

---

39 MOL M-Bp.-176f.2/190/6ö.e, p. 204.
40 For this analysis, see Pittaway, chapter 4 of this volume.
41 Ibid.
42 For an in-depth examination of this phenomenon, see Pittaway 1998.

women were increasingly marginalised on the shop floor, as they enjoyed less countervailing power in informal bargaining than their male colleagues.

This was illustrated most clearly in those sectors like textiles where the workforce was largely female. In textiles, the introduction of new norms in 1950s had led to increased work intensity and low wages. A high proportion of the largely female machine operators in the spinning and weaving halls could not make out. In the Magyar Pamutipar, one of the capital's largest textile factories, during 1951 many of the machine operators complained that 'it just isn't possible to maintain this tempo for much longer' and 'it's a wonder that the workers can manage this'. With this high work intensity, in textiles a higher proportion of the workforce failed to make out than almost anywhere else in industry. In July 1951, the proportion of the workforce failing to fulfil their norms in the two spinning shops were 21.7 percent and 46.72 percent, while in the weaving shop 31.53 percent of the workers failed to reach 100 percent. In addition, the average wages in the factory stood at 645 forints per month in October 1951. This was well under the industrial average.[43]

Some of the female machine operators did gain preferential treatment. This was not based upon the kinds of informal bargaining seen elsewhere in the economy. In textiles, this took place entirely within the boundaries of the labour competition. The management of the Magyar Pamutipar, rather unusually for a large industrial enterprise in 1952, was able to report that 'the norms are firm' – a sign that very little, if any, bargaining over job rates occurred. Among the machine operators in the weaving shop, preferential treatment was granted to those workers who operated the most machines simultaneously. The quality of the cotton they received was the best, ensuring that they did not have to cope with the thread snapping. This provoked tension between those who operated eight machines and those who operated sixteen machines. Normally the latter earned twice as much as the former, but a decline in the quality of the cotton had led to lower earnings among those operating eight machines, while preferential treatment in the distribution of the raw materials had ensured that those working sixteen machines had stable earnings. Such practices caused complaints; in 1951, one young worker complained that 'there

---

43   For a more in-depth examination of working conditions in the textile industry in the early 1950s, see Pittaway 1998, pp. 133–43. On the increase in work intensity in the plant over the course of 1951, see *Pamutújság*, 31 January 1952; MOL M-Bp.-143f./14ö.e. p. 222; MOL M-Bp.-176f.2/236/2ö.e, p. 247. On low norm fulfilment in early spring 1951, see *Pamutújság*, 16 April 1951. For the average worker's wage in the factory in late 1951, see MOL M-Bp.-176f.2/236/4ö.e, p. 69.

are materials of variable quality. The good quality ones are taken by the "good" workers ... it's easy to work well when you have good materials'.[44]

Among the largely male skilled workers who maintained the machinery, informal bargaining of a kind visible elsewhere was endemic. They were far more willing to resort to the tactics of go-slow and of non-cooperation than their female colleagues in order to secure preferential treatment. Rumours of imminent norm revision were frequently used in order to ensure that at such times the workers did not 'go too fast with their work'. Such strategies were often accompanied by intimidation of norm-setters who complained that 'the maintenance staff were putting pressure' on them. Increasingly, as work intensity increased and the demands on the machinery rose with it, male skilled workers were able to translate their relative autonomy, at least when compared with the machine operatives, and management's dependence on them to their advantage. It was this small group of workers that gained countervailing power to informally bargain with management to secure better earnings.[45]

The differential access of male maintenance workers and female machine operators to informal bargaining strategies can be, to some extent, attributed to the differences in their position within the division of labour in a socialist textile enterprise. What is difficult to explain is the lack of female protest at their subordinate position within the workplace. The changing patterns of collective protest in the textile industry help illustrate the more general problem. There is no evidence that women workers were any less inclined than men to engage in collective protest in the pre-Stalinist period; indeed, the reverse is true. Women machine operators led a two-day strike in one Budapest plant in 1949 against the introduction of higher production norms. The strike closed the factory, making it the most serious single strike in the country prior to the outbreak of the 1956 Revolution.[46] In spring 1950, when piece-rate wage systems were introduced across industry, once again female machine operators in textiles were more militant than almost any other group in industry, engaging in a series of strikes (of several hours each) right across the capital.[47]

---

44   MOL M-Bp.-176f.2/236/7ö.e, p. 151; MOL M-Bp.-95f.3/56ö.e, p. 101; SZKL Textilipari Dolgozók Szakszervezetének iratai, 1949–1955 (Papers of the Textile Industry Workers' Union 1949–1955, hereafter Textiles-a)/140d./1949–1955; Magyar Pamutipar. Jegyzőkönyv amely készült 1951 november 10-én az olvasó teremben megtartott Ü.B. értekezleten (Magyar Pamutipar. Minutes of a factory committee meeting held in the reading room on 10 November 1951), p. 2.
45   MOL M-Bp.-95f.3/345ö.e, p. 8; MOL M-Bp.-176f.2/236/4ö.e, p. 268; MOL M-KS-276f.116/40ö.e, p. 74.
46   For this strike see SZKL Textiles-a/129d/1949.
47   MOL M-Bp.-95f.4/2/168/b, ö.e, p. 37.

The crushing of worker protest against norm revision in the summer of 1950 seems to have represented an even more radical turning point in textiles than in industry as a whole. Despite a huge increase in work intensity and a large fall in earnings, collective protest disappeared. Increasingly, machine operators reacted to their working conditions by taking up and leaving. In the Magyar Pamutipar, in 1951 party officials noticed that 'a large number of workers quit and seek work at factories where they don't have to work Sundays or at night. Neighbouring factories are hiring those that left without permission'. Labour turnover stood at around eighteen to twenty percent over the course of the first five months of the year. Such labour mobility fed an absolute problem of labour shortage. Party officials frequently requested the recruitment of more labour, while management replied that it could not be found.[48] Many married women left the textile industry – machine operators were recruited from the ranks of female school-leavers in rural areas who, in turn, would leave the industry when they married.[49]

Where open protest did occur, it did not relate to the questions of working conditions or wages, although considerable discontent with both did exist. Instead, it directly addressed questions of working time and the attempts of the state to extend it, limiting the time available to women for the management of the household. In textiles, the state expanded the number of working days by cutting down the number of public holidays and tentatively introduced seven-day production. This provoked considerable opposition because they attempted to redraw the balance that the largely female workforce made between work in the factory and in the private sphere. These attempts began in 1950. The first step was to force workers to work on the Saturday before Easter. In deference to the moral economy of the machine operators who regarded their Saturday afternoon as one for making preparations for the Easter Sunday holiday, they had been previously allowed the afternoon off. Attempts to make them work the full day were met with vociferous protests throughout the factory and a problem of considerable absenteeism for every year thereafter. The extension of the working week to include Sundays in 1951 was met with similar protests. While party agitators suspected that this opposition was due to

---

48   *Pamutújság*, 2 August 1951; MOL M-Bp.-95f.4/6oö.e, p. 133; MOL M-Bp.-143f./9ö.e, p. 308; MOL M-Bp.-176f.2/236/4ö.e, p. 130; MOL M-Bp.-143f./6ö.e, p. 49.
49   For concern at this pattern, see *Pamutújság*, 27 June 1952; OSA RFE Magyar Gy.6/Item No. 08794, p. 2; MOL M-Bp.-95f.4/6oö.e, pp. 133–4; PIL 867f.1/d-50, p. 76.

'religious agitation', they could never prove this. Machine operators saw this measure as an attack on both family and household.[50]

In addition to the effects of state repression, gendered notions of a split between public and private realms were also reshaping collective protest. State attempts to extend working time for women, and thereby restrict the amount of time to be devoted to the household, provoked open protest, while reductions in wages and working conditions provoked job-quitting. Furthermore, much bargaining over remuneration and work seemed to be deployed by skilled male workers only, and was often at the expense of women. This provoked surprisingly little protest or open complaint. The argument presented here is that this was in part because the formal state-controlled economy was failing to satisfy the economic needs of Hungarian households. Given that a repressive state had closed off the avenues to collective protest, improvements in wages and incomes could not be achieved through collective action. Severe poverty and shortage in the sphere of consumption fuelled the growth of an ideal of social privatisation that women had more to invest in than men. It is, however, 'working-class' poverty and the problems of consumption to which we will turn our attention now.

The Economy of Shortage in Everyday Life

Problems with the supply of goods were first noticed in Hungary's mining areas. In Tatabánya, the problems began in September 1950 with shortages of sugar that led to workers queuing for supplies. The shops ran out of potatoes, onions and other fresh vegetables. By early October, the city council responded by distributing daily supplies from 6:00am onwards in the marketplace.[51] Official organs received complaints about consumers having to queue for sugar, especially from households where both partners worked and as a result were unable to queue, forcing them to go without sugar supplies for weeks on end.[52] As far as workers in pit number VI of the mines were concerned, the fact they 'had to run around' after groceries was a sign that the regime 'continually

---

50   MOL M-Bp.-95f.4/143ö.e, p. 2; MOL M-Bp.-95/4/62ö.e, pp. 55–6; MOL M-Bp.-95f.4/60ö.e, pp. 119–20.

51   Tatabánya Városi Levéltár (Archive of the City of Tatabánya, hereafter TVL) Tatabanya VB ülések jegyzőkönyvei (Minutes of Tatabánya City Council meetings): 29 September 1950, Item No. 4; 6 October 1950, Item No.2/b.

52   SZKL Komárom SZMT/42d./1950: Titkári jelentés 1950-év november hóról (Secretarial report about the month of November 1950), p. 1.

talks about rising living standards and gives us nothing'. Another stated that living standards were declining because 'on the market there aren't any goods'. The shortages meant that the workers 'only earn salt and paprika now'.[53]

The shortages in towns like Tatabánya were to spread quickly to all industrial areas. As a result, 'shortage' became not only a fundamental determinant of life within the sphere of socialist production, but also in consumption. Shortages fundamentally reinforced the perception that the formal economy was incapable of satisfying material need. The chaos that characterised it shaped the search of many households for a degree of autonomy. Despite the fundamental importance of the experience of socialist consumption in shaping popular attitudes toward the state, the private and the public, as well as the formal and informal, it has received little attention in critical social-scientific investigation of the patterns of everyday life in state-socialist societies.[54] Shortages of goods undermined the legitimacy of the regime, and for many 'working-class' consumers it called into question the relationship between work and reward. Problems in the realm of consumption fundamentally reduced the willingness of industrial workers to respond to the work incentives that were designed to improve their performance in the realm of socialist production. The problems of consumption were to create the space for a large parallel economy, alongside that of official socialist production, which operated independently of the latter without being entirely separate from it.

Labour histories of proletarianisation and industrialisation under capitalist conditions have underlined the role of increased working-class consumption in improving work discipline. More recently, historians of scientific management have seen high consumption as having stabilised Fordist production regimes in the capitalist West.[55] The state in early socialist Hungary aimed to

---

53   SZKL Komárom SZMT/43d./1950; Szakszervezetek Országos Tanácsa Esztergom-Komárom Megye Bizottság 393/1950 sz. hangulat jelentés (National Council of Trade Unions, Esztergom- Komárom County Committee, Report on the climate of opinion 1950/303), pp. 1–2; SZKL Komárom SZMT/43d./1950; Szakszervezetek Országos Tanácsa Esztergom-Komárom Megye Bizottság 419/1950 sz. hangulat jelentés (National Council of Trade Unions, Esztergom- Komárom County Committee, Report on the climate of opinion 1950/419), p. 2.

54   The exception to this has been anthropological work on Romania during the 1980s. Katherine Verdery has argued that the regulation of consumption through shortage was part of the attempt of the state-socialist regime in the country to 'confiscate' the time of its citizens, forming part of the general process that she identified as the 'bureaucratisation of time'; see Verdery 1996, chapter 2.

55   For a useful synthesis of these arguments, insofar as they have been made for early industrial England, see Pahl 1984. On scientific management, see some of the contributions in Shiomi and Wada 1995.

mobilise Hungarian society behind its policy of proletarianisation and its individualisation of production relations within factories with the promise of higher consumption. In 1953, in a party-propaganda pamphlet the regime made increases in living standards and in consumption central to its appeal. While it admitted there had been 'difficulties' in the field of food supply, it argued that 'the free market prices of many foodstuffs have fallen and a state of general plenty has been created in the provision of industrial goods'.[56]

The reality of early socialist consumerism in this regard fell short of state intentions or its propaganda. Although the number of shops increased substantially, the conditions in them were often inadequate. In Újpest, during the course of the 1950s the number of shops selling spices doubled. Between 1951 and 1958, the number of butchers increased from 29 to 40. Despite this rise, even as late as 1958 officials judged that 'alongside modern and pleasant shops there are those which are old-fashioned and give cause for concern on health grounds'. Furthermore, while the centre of the district was well provided for, 'goods supply to outlying areas' was 'inadequate',[57] disadvantaging the residents of those parts of the district. In the new town of Sztálinváros, despite its privileged position as far as state investment in services was concerned, similar problems were experienced. In 1954, the local representative of the Ministry of Internal Commerce admitted that 'the development of commerce has been pushed into the background in recent years', and that this had led to poorly designed and often inadequate shopping facilities in the town.[58]

Even though the provision of shops and basic services for consumers in the industrial centres left much to be desired, it was at least considerably better than in the surrounding villages from where many workers commuted. In the villages surrounding Tatabánya, there was a simple lack of basic facilities and services; a grocer's shop only existed in those villages where a marketing cooperative for agricultural produce had survived the collectivisation drive, although most villages had a small pub.[59] In rural Zala county, which because of the oil industry contained a significant number of village-dwelling commuting workers, the situation was similar. In 1953, there were 31 villages without a shop, and of these one had a population of between five hundred and one thousand, while the remaining thirty had populations under five

---

56 *Mit adott a népi demokrácia a dolgozóknak?* [What has the Peoples' Democracy Given the Workers?] 1953, pp. 12–13.
57 MOL M-KS-288f.21/1958/20ö.e. p. 272.
58 *Sztálin Vasmű Építője*, 19 March 1954.
59 SZKL Komárom SZMT/61d/1950: Jelentés a bányász falvakról (Report on the mining villages), pp. 1–2.

hundred. As a result, some village dwellers were often four kilometres from the nearest shop.[60]

In theory, however, from 1951 onwards 'working-class' consumers were able to turn to the 'free markets' where producers directly sold their goods to consumers at market prices. Such a market was created in Sztálinváros in 1952, but was not used as widely as was hoped for by 'working-class' consumers. One official reported that 'in the morning it is the housewives who live locally, after work the workers come down to get necessary things. The real situation is that very few use it'.[61] 'Free markets' suffered from a problem of legitimacy, as in many consumers' minds they were often associated with speculation and a poor deal. Many consumers incorrectly referred to the 'free market' as the 'black market' implicitly refusing to recognise its officially tolerated status.[62] Because of the shared reliance on agricultural production, food supply in both state shops and on the 'free markets' suffered from the same problems. Where agricultural production was of a high quality and quantity, the markets tended to be well stocked.[63] In industrial areas they tended to be poor.[64] Furthermore, during times of agricultural dearth they tended to be poorly stocked.[65]

At least in urban households, because of their strict gender division of labour, the 'working-class' consumer was often the woman within the household. It was her responsibility to negotiate the problems of food shortages and poor standards of service and design in the shops. This task was often made more difficult by both the acute poverty in many 'working-class' households during the early 1950s and the gender division of household income. Poverty and declining living standards were serious problems in the early 1950s. According to trade-union figures, real wages were 16.6 percent lower in 1953

---

60   ZML MSZMP ZMBA ir. 57f.2/Ipar/66ö.e: Kedves Nagy elvtárs! [Dear comrade Nagy!]; ZML MSZMP ZMBA ir.57f.2/Ipar/66ö.e: Kedves Elvtársak! [Dear comrades!], p. 1.

61   FML MSZMP FMBA ir. 17f.1/24ö.e: Jegyzőkönyv felvétetett 1952 június 3-án megtartott pártbizottsági ülésen, a PB tanácstermében [Minutes of a meeting of the party-committee held on 3 June 1952 in the party-committee meeting room], p. 2.

62   SZKL SZOT Szociálpolitika/9d/1951: Kereskedelmi és Pénzügyi Dolgozók Szakszervezete, Feljegyzés a kenyér és húsjegyek bevezetésével kapcsolatos hangulatról [Report of the Commerce and Finance Workers' Union on the climate of opinion in relation to the rationing of bread and meat], p. 2.

63   OSA RFE Magyar Gy.300/40/4/43/Item No. 8349/56.

64   FML MSZMP FMBA ir. 17f.1/24ö.e: Jegyzőkönyv felvétetett 1952 június 3-án megtartott pártbizottsági ülésen, a PB tanácstermében [Minutes of the party-committee meeting held on 3 June 1952 in the party-committee meeting room], p. 2.

65   SZKL SZOT Szociálpolitika/22d/1952: A 1952 második negyedév kiskereskedelmi forgalomról [About retail sales in the second quarter of 1952], p. 5.

than in 1949. The average income of households living from wages and salaries had fallen by 8 percent over the same period. This was reflected in changing patterns of household expenditure. Groceries accounted for 45.9 percent of the budget of an average household in 1949, a figure that had risen to 58.8 percent by 1953. The share of expenditure on clothing had fallen from 18.2 percent to 10.4 percent. Furthermore, the average household's consumption of meat, fat and milk was lower in 1953 than in 1938.[66] These averages concealed the desperate poverty of many households; one young worker who had escaped to the West recalled that many of his neighbours had 'gone every six weeks to give blood to get a supplementary income'.[67] In the early 1950s, the sight of large numbers of people scouring Budapest's rubbish dumps for scraps of food or assorted bric-a-brac to sell on was very common.[68]

In addition to this absolute poverty, severe pressure was brought to bear on 'working-class' household budgets. In urban households with very few dependants, living standards were low. For larger households, the situation was desperate. One miner's wife, who fled to the West in 1952, described the problem of budgeting given the low level of industrial wages and the relatively high level of prices:

> My husband gave me the whole of his wage to manage the household . . . At the beginning of the month the mine paid the first instalment that was always about 320 Forints, and I had to budget with it so that it would last until the middle of the month, when my husband got the second instalment of his monthly pay. During that time I only bought the most necessary things, like fat, oil, flour . . . then came the second part . . . from that with the most basic living standard I managed to save 100 to 120 Forints, though that was only done because my husband, instead of resting, did extra shifts . . . so that sometimes I could buy material to make clothes for the children.[69]

Often, however, the husband or male partner refused to give all his earnings over to his wife or partner, insisting that he keep sufficient income for leisure, while he expected his wife to maintain the household. Often women were

---

66 SZKL SZOT Szociálpolitika/13d./1953: Adatok és példák a Szakszervezetek Országos Tanácsa III. teljes ülésének beszámolójához [Data and examples for the third full sitting of the National Council of Trade Unions], pp. 1–5.
67 OSA RFE Magyar Gy. 6/Item No.11555/55, p. 4.
68 Földes 1994, pp. 22–9.
69 OSA RFE Magyar Gy.6/Item No. 08371/52, p. 1.

severely disadvantaged by this distribution of the household budget. An extreme example of a situation that was by no means uncommon was that of a young woman who lived with her fiancé in a poor Budapest district. While her fiancé was a skilled worker, he 'drank and gambled on the horses', which resulted in her getting '600 or 700 Forints' of the '1,100 to 1,200 Forints' he earned monthly, and from this housekeeping allowance he would 'often ask for money back'. Because of high prices she was often unable to buy food for herself or afford to heat the flat during the day in winter. She ate only bread and jam, and stayed in bed simply to keep warm when not out shopping for the household.[70]

Even where women were able and willing to ease the income problems of their households by participating in the labour force of the socialist sector, the burden of homemaking fell upon them. This, in a world characterised by shortage, unresponsiveness and inefficiency, was far from an easy task. One Budapest consumer who did not work described the daily shopping routine when the supply of food and goods was not interrupted by shortage accordingly:

> Every morning I got up at six and went to the *Tejért* [the dairy shop] to buy necessary things for breakfast... I had of course to queue, but at least in the week I could buy as much milk as I wanted, or as much as I could afford. It was only on Saturday there was a restriction on how much I could buy, just a litre per person... I had to buy bread at the Közért [the general grocery store]... after my fiancé had gone to work I would do the shopping for lunch and dinner, by this time one did not have to queue.

Consumption was frequently characterised by many small trips to the shops in the industrial districts, simply because 'the wives of workers didn't have enough money to buy large amounts'.[71]

For working women, especially for those on morning shifts, shopping had to be done before or immediately after work. Because of the lack of capacity of many of the shops and the frequent late deliveries of many foodstuffs, there was a problem of queuing. In Sztálinváros in 1952, queues frequently developed in the morning hours before work and then in the afternoon at the end of the first shift at 2 p.m. It was reportedly common to have to queue for 'hours' while the bread was delivered, shelved and distributed. This forced many to

---

70 OSA RFE Magyar Gy.6/Item No. 10820/54, pp. 1–5.
71 Ibid., pp. 4–5.

wait for up to two hours in the morning, and then to wait again in the afternoon, before they were able to buy what they wanted.[72]

Commuters from rural areas, even those with no land, were in a more unfavourable position as consumers in the socialist economy. In rural households, where one member or more worked in urban industry, the gender division of labour had been modified, with women likely to remain in the village and work in agriculture.[73] In such cases it was the men who would combine their work with shopping for the goods that could not be cultivated at home (if the family owned land) or were scarce in the village generally. This division of labour within a household unit existed where the men commuted over a long distance, returning home only every few weeks, and where the worker commuted on a daily basis. In both instances, commuters' consumption habits differed significantly from their urban counterparts, albeit for different reasons. The major difference was that commuters did not go to the shops frequently, but tended to go infrequently and buy noticeably large amounts. In the case of long-distance commuters, this was in order to take large quantities of goods that were scarce in their home villages for their families over the time that they were away. In 1953, in Sztálinváros the long-distance commuters were said to be taking advantage of the favourable supply of meat to the town, alongside 'customers who do not work here', causing a run on meat supplies on the day before the free Saturday when they were off work.[74] Those who commuted on a day-to-day basis would buy larger amounts than urban residents for another reason, namely, that they would buy for friends and relatives in their home village who had no other connection to the urban world. One commuter to the mines in Tatabánya was challenged on the train home by a trade-union official as to why he had ten loaves of white bread, to which the commuter replied that he had been asked to buy them for his neighbours.[75]

---

72 FML MSZMP FMBA ir. 9f.2/PTO/48ö.e: A Sztálinvárosi Tanács végrehajtó Bizottságának [To the implementation committee of Sztálinváros City Council], p. 1.

73 For evidence of this kind of gender division of labour in areas characterised by commuting, see the example of Tárnok, close to Budapest, in OSA 400/40/4/43/Item No. 7095/54. For allusions to this as a reason for the 'weakness' of agricultural cooperatives in the rural mining areas in Esztergom-Komárom, see SZKL Komárom SZMT/168d/1956: Jelentés a Falusi Osztályharc Helyzetéről [Report on the state of the class struggle in the villages].

74 FML MSZMP FMBA ir. 17f.1/29ö.e: Jelentés a város közellátásának helyzetéről és az üzlethálózat fejlesztéséről [Report on the state of public supply and the development of the network of shops in the city], p. 1.

75 SZKL SZOT Szociálpolitika/21d/1952: Szénszállító és Szolgáltató Vállalat Szakszervezeti Bizottsága, Tatabánya – Jegyzőkönyv Társadalmi ellenőrök részére megtartott értekezletről, p. 2.

Commuting workers' consumption patterns led to accusations that they hoarded goods. This contributed to a climate in which commuters were actively discriminated against. In Tatabánya in 1952, one trade-union official instructed the director of the local shop to 'give out the white bread at midday when the buses to the villages depart'. He justified this on the basis that 'the commuters take loaves and loaves of the bread from the town dwellers, the same happens with the flour ... and so hinder our shopping for food'.[76] This kind of discrimination was widespread and led to considerable anger among commuting workers. One village youth described his day-to-day experience of such discrimination, stating that in his village 'meat was not available; if someone wanted to buy meat they had to go to town. In the town, if they knew you were from the village and wanted to buy, they very unwillingly gave you fat, let alone meat, because it was commonly said, why do the villagers come to the town, when in the village they have plenty of everything'.[77]

The considerable difficulties created by the inadequacy of the state shops and 'free markets' intensified during the periods of extreme food and goods shortage. The experience of this phenomenon had two effects: the first was to encourage 'working-class' consumers to resort to a series of measures designed to mitigate the situation; the second was a more long-term process that led to the development of a trend towards reduced dependence on the wage packet from the socialist sector and the goods available in the state shops. This led workers to strive for greater household self-sufficiency. Even the most successful households who tried to become more self-sufficient never managed completely to achieve this objective.

Firstly, let us consider the various forms of immediate adjustment to shortages, which 'working-class' consumers attempted to deploy. The most common response among those with sufficient cash available to them was to buy up goods when they became available and to hoard them. Because of the financial constraints on most 'working-class' households, it was reportedly those with spare money – who had either an extra source of income or food through land, and were not dependent on their low wages from industry for survival – who were able to employ such a strategy. In February 1952, as fat and eggs reappeared in the shops in two counties it was reported that 'largely villagers' bought up the goods with the intention of hoarding them; from one shop five-thousand eggs were sold in two hours.[78] Some families sought to buy up goods

---

76   Ibid., p. 1.
77   OSA 300/40/4/43/Item No. 6700/54, pp. 1–5.
78   SZKL SZOT Szociálpolitika/22d/1952: Feljegyzés a dolgozók hangulatáról [Report on the opinions of workers], p. 3.

by sending all the family members to queue. In one case in Tatabánya, five members of the same family had stood in one queue and each had bought flour.[79] In 1951, rumours of food shortages often provoked waves of panic buying.[80]

Shortages and hoarding significantly reshaped buying patterns among those who had the ready cash to do so, and severely disadvantaged those who did not. Food and goods shortages often forced consumers to resort to informal, unofficial and often illegal solutions to their problems. Certain 'working-class' consumers were able to secure privileged access to goods through kin and friends who worked in the stores. In February 1953, it was reported that staff in the state shops in Tatabánya were secretly reserving scarce supplies of flour for their friends and relatives.[81] There is very little direct evidence of bribery, but the existence of bribery seems likely given that overcharging by staff in shops – with staff pocketing the surplus – seems to have been a common practice throughout industrial Hungary during the early 1950s.[82]

The other form taken by informal, unofficial and illegal strategies was that of buying through the 'black' market. Due to administrative control, access to goods could be extremely restricted. Many people came into contact with unofficial economic activity through itinerant sellers from rural areas who would offer food in exchange for used clothes or industrial goods.[83] Given the need for extra cash, 'working-class' consumers themselves sought to exploit shortages in order to supplement their own incomes. In Miskolc in 1951, cases were reported of workers who had bought boots that were in short supply and were selling them illegally for prices higher than those in the state shops.[84]

Households sought a degree of autonomy for the household as a long-term response to the problem of shortage. This strategy was well illustrated by the problem of bread production and consumption in the mining areas. Much

---

79   SZKL SZOT Munkásellátás/15d/1953: Tatabánya, Ótelepi gépüzem, 1953 január 31 [Tatabánya, the machine factory on the old site, 31 January 1953], p. 4.
80   ZML MSZMP ZMBA ir.57f.2/Agit/10ö.e: Nagykanizsa Városi Pártbizottság, 1951 január 2, délután 4.30 [Nagykanizsa City Party Committee, 4.30pm, 2 January 1951].
81   SZKL SZOT Munkásellátás/15d/1953: Tatabánya, VIII akna, 1953 február 9 [Tatabánya, pit no. VIII, 9 February 1953], p. 2.
82   FML MSZMP FMBA ir.9f.2/PTO/48ö.e: A Sztálinvárosi Tanács végrehajtó Bizottságba..., p. 1; SZKL SZOT Szociálpolitika/21d/1952: Szénszállító és Szolgáltató Vállalat Szakszervezeti Bizottsága, Tatabánya – Jegyzőkönyv Társadalmi ellenőrök részére megtartott értekezletről, p. 2.
83   OSA RFE Magyar Gy.6/Item No. 11699/52, p. 1.
84   SZKL SZOT Szociálpolitika/9d/1951: Jelentés a Miskolc, Diósgyőr munkásellátási kérdésekről [Report on workers' provision in Miskolc and Diósgyőr], p. 1.

state-produced bread was not only frequently late, but was also of extremely poor quality. As a result of this poor quality, 'working-class' consumers demanded the freedom and the goods to make the bread themselves by 1953. Many miners told a party committee investigating their living conditions that 'they wanted to eat homemade bread, as the factory-made bread was of appalling quality', and demanded that the appropriate flour and yeast be made available in the shops.[85]

Household Autonomy: Ideals and Realities

With the beginning of socialist industrialisation, the state became concerned about those it termed *kétlaki* – in other words, those workers who were members of households with land and, therefore, incomes from agriculture. The state saw this as a central obstacle to 'new' workers' acceptance of socialist work discipline. A campaign was implemented in 1951 and 1952, which had two parts. The first part aimed to use propaganda to make the *kétlaki* existence socially unacceptable in the eyes of other workers. Regime propaganda portrayed the worker-peasant existence as detrimental to all of the workers, including the worker-peasants themselves, because it prevented the development of a purely socialist consciousness. In the words of one propaganda booklet, 'the *kétlaki* miner is his own enemy'. Furthermore, by concentrating on their own land it was inevitable that they would betray their work colleagues, by undermining the earning potential of their workmates by going sick. The second part was to launch a programme of agitation among the workers to persuade them to sell their land, at a favourable price, either to the local council or to join the cooperative.[86] In areas where a worker-peasant had deep roots, this campaign engendered considerable opposition from the wives who managed the smallholding while their husbands went to work. Women did not want the land sold, nor did they want to join cooperatives, even when their husbands were willing to agree to state demands. From their vantage point, as managers of the household, they saw land as giving the household a degree of independence from the shortages of the socialised retail sector and the unreliability of their husbands' earnings. In the villages in the Zala oil fields, wives were said to have threatened their husbands with divorce and suicide if they joined the cooperatives. They had refused to cook for their husbands where

---

85   MOL M-KS-276f.53/145ö.e: Tájékoztató az üzemi dolgozók és az üzemi vezetők által felvetett szociális és kultúrális problémákról, p. 40.

86   *Kétlakiság* 1952. For the programme, see Rákosi 1997, p. 845.

they had signed away their land. One oil worker told the authorities what his wife had told him: 'it [the land] is there to help us live, because of it we have not starved, but if it is taken away from us we will [starve]'.[87]

Despite the pressures to which agricultural households were subjected in the early 1950s, in the face of shortage the worker-peasant existence represented an ideal to which many workers – and especially 'working-class' women – subscribed.[88] With the limited liberalisation that followed a change of government in 1953, those workers – normally worker-peasants – with sufficient resources to build a private house did so.[89] The growth of private house construction fed a growing parallel economy as the state sector, hit by power-cuts and shortages, failed to meet the material demands of the population.[90] Materials pilfered from their official workplace formed one major source of construction materials for such houses. A journalist who escaped to the West in 1956 cynically commented that 'the villages surrounding the "great constructions of socialism" contain the most new peasant cottages, built from excellent materials, and of sound construction ... of course the material "removed" from the site of the socialist constructions'.[91]

Household autonomy in early socialist Hungary was, in the minds of many, premised upon the private ownership of land, a family house, or access to some source of income outside of an unreliable state sector. The household was at the centre of an informal economy that grew up in the cracks created by the malfunctioning of the state. The repression and poverty prevalent in the official realm during the 1950s led to the creation of a household-centred and partially visible economy. Paradoxically, however, this economy was based on an interaction between worker experiences of the state sector – both in production and consumption. It drew on and reinforced notions that property conferred independence, which were far from unique to Hungary.[92] Not all households, however, were autonomous in any sense, although those that were

---

87 ZML MSZMP ZMBA ir. 61f.2/Agit/7ö.e: Hangulat jelentés [Report on the climate of opinion], p. 1; ZML MSZMP ZMBA ir.61f.2/Agit/7ö.e: MDP MAORT Lovászi üzemi pártszervezet titkársága jelentés [Hungarian Workers' Party, MAORT Lovászi factory party-organisation secretariat report].
88 Pittaway 2000.
89 For the situation in one poor county in 1954, see ZML MSZMP ZMBA ir.57f.2/63ö.e: Kimutatás a Zalamegyében engedélyzett . . . [Figures on family house construction approved in Zala county].
90 Pittaway 1999.
91 Quoted in Lomax 1981, p. 32.
92 For a useful description of the ideological role private homeownership has played in the United Kingdom, see Hunt 1995, especially pp. 310–12.

relatively less independent of the state sector suffered the greatest poverty. The differentiation that opened up between 'working-class' households on the basis of access to resources, other than those provided by the state, fuelled the spread of an ideal of social privatisation.

For households dependent on wages alone in urban Hungary by the mid-1950s, living conditions were poor. Even according to a poverty line set at a miserably low level, the National Council of Trade Unions estimated that in 1956 thirty-five percent of households dependent on wages from the state sector lived in poverty. Among urban households it discovered that the key determinant of poverty was the ratio of earners in a household to dependants. This left young families – with one earner where the mother could not find any work – in dire poverty.[93] Low household earnings went together with poor housing conditions; in 1957 it was still common in industrial towns that 'a five member family live in a one room flat'.[94] In such families where incomes could not be increased through younger family members taking work in industry, rising prices cut into household incomes during the early 1950s.[95]

The large number of young urban households with children had several options open to them. The male earner could attempt to increase his income through moonlighting if the sector in which he worked gave him skills that could be deployed in the informal economy. Where the worker provided a service, the route to extra income was easy to find. Household electricians' wages were around 1,000 Forints a month, but they could often make another four to five hundred Forints monthly through, what one former electrician described as, 'black work'. The charges for repairs made by his employers – the local housing repair cooperative – were high, and often the electrician could pocket the money for the job by charging the customer lower rates. In one case, the customer 'eagerly agreed, but after she had to call the cooperative to say the work hadn't needed doing'.[96]

Access to incomes from 'black work' was not open to everybody and depended either on the nature of their state job or personal connections. The second possibility open to a low-paid worker would be to take a second job. This possibility, however, was circumscribed by legal regulation. These provisions were commonly sidestepped, which led workers to take up secondary employment unofficially. In 1953, wages among railwaymen varied from four-hundred and twenty to seven-hundred Forints monthly. Of these employees,

---

93   MOL M-KS-276f.66/36ö.e, p. 31.
94   MOL M-KS-288f.23/1957/21ö.e, p. 54.
95   Ibid., p. 49.
96   OSA RFE Magyar Gy.6/Item No.1646/55, pp. 1–8.

some eight thousand failed to earn more than 570 Forints. In such cases, many workers spent their spare time undertaking additional employment – most commonly informal agricultural work – to guarantee a basic standard of living for their families.[97] Access to such informal work was often dependent on contacts secured through workmates in the socialised sector of the economy. This was especially true of casual labour in agriculture during harvest periods. As early as summer 1951, the local authorities had noticed that the Sztálinváros construction site was being used as an informal labour market to recruit casual labour.[98]

The third possibility for poverty-stricken urban families was for other adult household members – usually the wife and mother – to seek work. It was, nevertheless, difficult for a woman to find work in Hungary during the early 1950s.[99] From 1953, female unemployment was privately recognised as a problem by the authorities, as opportunities for women to enter manual employment were extremely restricted. In Budapest in 1955 and 1956, the labour exchanges reported a problem in finding industrial work for women, leading local authorities to state that there was a problem of hidden unemployment among women, the extent of which 'can only be estimated'.[100]

A fourth option was to spend less money by recycling clothes. Bodies such as trade unions noted that 'large families restrict their expenditure on children's clothes through handing them down from the older to younger children'. In doing this, however, they came up against the problems of the poor quality of the clothing sold in Hungarian shops. Mothers were thus forced to 'ensure they remained usable through continual repair and restitching, whilst they continued to keep a stock of really inferior clothes'.[101]

Lastly, such households could attempt to reduce their expenditure by becoming more self-sufficient. This attempt to shift towards greater self-sufficiency took a number of forms that were generally more open to those who lived in or close to rural areas than to workers in Budapest. Often this led to the theft of certain goods that were in short supply in the socialised chains

---

97 SZKL SZOT Bér és Munkaügyi Osztálya (Wage and Labour Department)/21d/1953: Közlekedés és Postaügyi Minisztérium Vasúti Főosztálya levél Varga Jánosnak, Szakszervezetek Országos Tanács titkára, 1953 november 21 [Ministry of Transport and Post, Railway Department, Letter to János Varga, Secretary of the National Council of Trade Unions, 21 November 1953].

98 FML MSZMP FMBA ir.18f.2/1ö.e: Jelentés a Dunai Vasmű Pártbizottság augusztus havi munkájáról [Report on the August work of the Danube Steel Works party-committee], p. 1.

99 Personal interview with T. J-né, Dunaújváros 6 May 1996.

100 MOL M-KS-276f.94/886ö.e, p. 141; MOL M-KS-276f.94/886ö.e, p. 230.

101 MOL M-KS-288f.23/1957/21ö.e, p. 59.

of shops. This was the case with firewood of which there was a significant shortage in the winter of 1952. In areas close to woods and forests, this led to a significant problem of the illegal felling of trees. One miner's wife, who escaped to the West in 1952, remembered that 'because my husband wasn't a member of the trade union, we didn't get wood' at concessionary prices. This meant that 'wood cost 280 Forints for a cubic metre', and was in short supply. Instead, they went to the nearby woods to cut wood, which was only possible to do 'on Mondays and Fridays, when no-one was there to look after the wood', since they faced a heavy fine if they got caught.[102] In some rural areas, a growing problem of poaching was experienced as many workers in both industry and agriculture illegally hunted to ensure that they gained an adequate supply of meat.[103] Another sign of this shift was the growth of unofficial fishing. During the early 1950s, the state reorganised fishing clubs, placing them under the control of the enterprises and banning those who were not members of a club from buying either fishing tackle or obtaining a fishing licence. Furthermore, the state ordered anglers to keep a record of every catch, so that when their records were inspected the authorities would be able to see that the angler had caught only the amount of fish that was deemed necessary to feed the family. Yet unofficial fishing was widespread.[104]

Rural dwellers enjoyed considerable advantages over their urban workmates in pursuing strategies based on household self-sufficiency. At many industrial establishments, the expansion of the workforce during the early 1950s had led to many of the rural poor escaping underemployment in their home villages by taking unskilled industrial work. These workers commuted and were able to use their gardens as a hedge against unreliable earnings and chaos in the state sector.[105] Alongside this, the *kétlaki* phenomenon existed. This was not unique to the socialist period. The evidence suggests it expanded as a result of the parallel pressures of collectivisation campaigns and socialist industrialisation. The first official post-war estimate of the extent of this phenomenon, offered in 1957, suggested that of households attached to agricultural producer cooperatives 29 percent had permanent non-seasonal income from wages. Of households that owned family farms, 35 percent had some income from industry.[106]

---

102   OSA RFE Magyar Gy.6/Item No. 08371/52, p. 2.
103   OSA 300/40/4/24/Item No. 8183/55, p. 5.
104   OSA 300/40/4/25/Item No. 9394/54; OSA 300/40/4/25/Item No. 09153/53.
105   Pittaway 1998, pp. 150–229.
106   MOL M-KS-288f.23/1958/27ö.e, p. 19.

The expansion of the *kétlaki* lifestyle cannot be understood without some reference to rural communities' experiences of the various strands of Stalinist agricultural policy. From 1948 onward, the intensification of 'class war' politics by the state, increases in taxation and compulsory deliveries, as well as the attempts to socialise agriculture, transformed rural life. The combination of high taxation of land and the sharp increases in compulsory deliveries severely squeezed the incomes of individual landholders by 1951. Even before compulsory deliveries, amounts of goods that had to be sold to the state at fixed prices were levied and taxation of smallholders was high. The son of one landholder recalled that in the early 1950s, 'under normal circumstances tax was 250 Forints per month, but in many cases rose to 300 Forints, because if we couldn't give anything to the state it was put into tax'.[107]

Compulsory deliveries were often punitive, while the arbitrary methods used to enforce them were bitterly resented. One young farmer remembered that the local supervisor of agricultural procurement

> strictly ensured that the correct amount was collected . . . at the latest milk had to be brought to them (the authorities) by quarter past six in the morning. The calculation took place monthly . . . the yearly delivery of milk was 660 litres from our first cow, 380 litres from the second one. They didn't take into account that we also used them as beasts of burden and so the poor, tired animals hardly produced any milk on the days we worked with them. For this reason we were happy if a single cup of milk was left for us in a day.

In response to such pressure, many smallholders resorted to the blatant avoidance of regulations.[108]

The taxation and compulsory deliveries had pushed many small farmers close to starvation by late 1952 and early 1953. As a result of compulsory deliveries, 'the farmer got less for his produce than his seed had cost him', causing 'general hunger in western Hungarian villages. The rural population had to wait in long queues for bread and flour, whilst the family who could get hold of half a kilo of flour was delighted'.[109] Living conditions for members of the new agricultural cooperatives were little better. Many were extremely disorganised and their production levels were low. Taxes ate into the low earnings of the agricultural cooperatives. One member of a cooperative recounted that by 1952

---

[107] OSA 300/40/4/22/Item No. 8027/55, p. 2.
[108] OSA 300/40/4/22/Item No. 04759/53, p. 3; OSA 300/40/4/22/Item No. 8501/55, p. 1.
[109] OSA 300/40/4/22/Item No. 3242/54, p. 1.

'the older members did not have a fillér for pocket money or a cigarette had their children not gone out and found some other work'.[110]

Faced with this misery, the younger members of many agricultural households were sent out to work. The way this worked was illustrated by the experience of one smallholder family in the predominantly rural Tolna county:

> M.K. could not maintain his independence any longer, and his daughter Ilonka went to work for the post office. She helped at home in the morning, and collected and delivered letters in the afternoon. She gave her money to her father, couldn't buy herself clothes from it, and stole food from work so that her mother and younger sister could have something decent to eat.

The needs of family members often led to changes in the gender division of labour in smallholder households. One escapee from a south-western Hungarian village stated that 'the women have never worked as much as they do now. Nobody employs anyone else in the village because there aren't applicants, and it's impossible to accept them anyway. Women have to leave the housework to work in the fields'.[111]

It was predominantly the poor rural youth which took jobs in industry. The lack of any security of income for the rural poor was the major motivation for such young people. This forced families to send one or more of its young members out to earn a secure income. The household unit could use this as a hedge against the failure of the agricultural producer cooperative to pay out at the end of the year, a bad harvest, a severe tax or compulsory delivery collector. One such worker who took up employment on a large construction site lived on a farm of 8kh (about four hectares), and as a result of the farm's inability to guarantee an income for the family, he had to go to work. He remembered that twice a month he could go home for one-and-a-half days and had to spend half a day of free time travelling. He gave his family 200 Forints of his monthly earnings and had to live from the rest. In some cases where there was no child of working age, it was the head of the household who went to work: 'the private farmers were attached to their small amounts of land and were not willing to enter the cooperative. The majority of private farmers couldn't live from their land and were forced to go and work away. The peasants in general went to the construction sites to get work, the women and children farmed the land'. Many were driven by the notion that for work the wages 'were paid in cash that you

---

110   OSA 300/40/4/23/Item No. 267/54, p. 3; OSA 300/40/4/41/Item No. 12232/53, p. 3.
111   OSA 300/40/4/22/Item No. 14271/52, pp. 8–9; OSA 300/40/4/22/Item No. 4154/55, p. 7.

receive in your hand. Furthermore in the town they take the effort to provide bread to the people'.[112]

The earliest surveys of the phenomenon from 1957 confirm that those who took up industrial employment came from the ranks of poorer villagers. Of agricultural households with less than 1kh[113] of land, 51 percent had one or more family members working in industry, with 15 percent having two or more members. For households with between one and three kilo hectares, the respective proportions were 37.6 and 9.1 percent. Among households with more property, the phenomenon was virtually non-existent: of those farming between twenty and twenty-five kilo hectares of land, the proportions stood at 8.8 and 0.9 percent.[114]

It is important not to idealise the worker-peasant lifestyle. Many households were pushed into it by dire poverty. Furthermore, it was premised on a particular configuration of gender and generational relations within the households, which were often profoundly exploitative. In a climate of low wages and shortages, many of these new worker-peasants refused to accept the demands of their jobs in the socialist sector when they conflicted with those of the household. This was despite the fact that unauthorised absenteeism was a criminal offence during the early 1950s and offenders were often prosecuted. This concerned many in the party leadership, including Mátyás Rákosi – Hungary's home-grown Stalinist dictator – who stated:

> [T]hese workers during the harvest go absent from their factories, and disrupt the rhythm of production. At the same time because of their work in the factory they don't pay enough attention to their land, which shows itself in their production. These *kétlaki* workers in one go disrupt industrial and agricultural production.

Many local functionaries shared the views of their leaders, and, indeed, many worker-peasants strongly defended their way of life. One such worker in one western Hungarian construction enterprise bluntly told his superior that 'the democracy secured for him 7kh of land, and he had to work it. First came his land and second came the factory'. Indeed, at harvest time a large number sought to leave the factory to perform agricultural work on their land. In July

---

112   Pálfalvi 1958, pp. 149–155; RFE Magyar Gy. 6/Item No. 06852/53, p. 5; OSA 300/40/4/42/Item No. 7929/54, p. 1; OSA 300/40/4/41/Item No. 12232/53, p. 3.
113   A measurement equivalent of 0.58ha (or 5,800m^2).
114   MOL M-KS-288f/23/1958/27ö.e, p. 54; ZML MSZMP ZMBA ir.1f.1958/12ö.e: A tapasztalatok összefoglalása (A summary of our experiences), p. 9.

1951, in the Mátyás Rákosi Works around two-thousand workers asked for unpaid leave to work on their land. In machine manufacture, absenteeism was high among these *kétlaki* workers who 'at the beginning of the spring agricultural season leave work for a longer or shorter period or quit completely... during the harvest season labour turnover becomes a mass phenomenon'. Of those that remained employed in industry, *kétlaki* workers came to work fatigued, given that in their 'free time' they had needed to perform agricultural labour. In light of a relative lack of supervision, those on the night shift in the oil industry often went to sleep in order to conserve their strength for work during the day in the fields.[115]

Nevertheless, as the weight of taxation and compulsory deliveries declined after 1953, the members of such households had a degree of independence and countervailing power that was envied by many of their workmates. In the post-1953 period, the incomes of individual landholders increased at a faster rate than those of industrial workers. In the Tatabánya coal fields, in 1954 officials in the local branch of the state savings bank began to notice that worker-peasants were becoming less dependent on their wages. Increasingly their wages would be left in the bank and not be touched for months on end as they lived from their agricultural incomes and produce. After a reasonable amount had been accumulated, it would be spent on consumer goods or on luxury items (like a motorcycle).[116] The relative affluence of worker-peasants fuelled considerable resentment among poorer urban workers who lacked access to alternative sources of food and income.[117]

---

115 Rákosi 1997, p. 845; SZKL Komárom SZMT/59d/1950: Épitők Szakszervezet Komárommegyei Bizottsága Havijelentés [Monthly report of the Komárom County Committee of the Construction Workers' Union], p. 2; MOL M-KS-276f.116/7ö.e, p. 28; MOL M-KS-276f.116/7ö.e, p. 99. On tiredness, see ZML MSZMP ZMBA ir.58f.3/4ö.e: MDP Olajüzemi Szervezet Nagylengyel, jegyzőkönyv felvétetett a Nagylengyeli Olajüzem MDP szervezetének kibővitett vezetőségi ülésen, 1955 augusztus 22-én [Hungarian Workers' Party Nagylengyel Oil Factory Organisation, minutes of an expanded leadership meeting, 22 August 1955], p. 3; ZML MSZMP ZMBA ir.61f.4/2/26ö.e: Feljegyzés a Pártbizottság megbizásából a kapott feladatot – a pártszervezet munkája a fegyelem megszilárditása érdekében [Report on the fulfilment of tasks allocated by the Party – the work of the party organisation in improving work discipline], p. 1.

116 KEML MSZMP KMBA ir.32f.4/53ö.e, pp. 10–11.

117 MOL M-KS-288f.21/1958/20ö.e, p. 260.

Conclusion

It has been argued throughout this chapter that industrial workers responded to socialist industrialisation and the consolidation of the Stalinist state in the factories through investing in an ideal of social privatisation. The brief sketch of the fortunes of various kinds of households outlined above demonstrates that all of them were unable to manage from the wages provided by the state sector alone. As a result of this shortfall, they sought to some extent to compensate for this. The extent to which they were able to do this was based on whether they could combine wages with some other means of satisfying material need. Some households managed better than others: those split between agriculture and industry were the best placed to do so, while the dire poverty of those households entirely dependent on wages demonstrated their disadvantage.

The sources of income on which households drew were very diverse. Their extent is impossible to estimate precisely because of the lack of reliable information. Nevertheless, there is evidence of a multiplicity of different sources of income and resources ranging from wages, expanding employment within households, moonlighting, theft, hunting and fishing, growing vegetables, keeping chickens and combining farming with an industrial wage. In years of severe 'working-class' poverty, differential access to sources of income not derived simply from the state sector stratified 'working-class' households. Furthermore, as the jealousy of worker-peasant incomes attests, all workers were acutely aware of how household circumstance divided them.

The Stalinist state crushed collective expressions of protest, action and organisation. Its vision of creating a class-conscious working class that could be mobilised around the goals of building socialism was not realised either. Instead, poverty and shortage forced industrial workers to supplement their incomes and find resources outside the formal state sector in order to survive. Hidden discontent fuelled informal bargaining and moonlighting, legitimised theft from the workplace, and increased absenteeism during the harvest period.

For many industrial workers, the state sector became a realm of poverty and shortage where needs could not be satisfied. State repression meant that the public sphere could not be used to express discontent, improve living conditions or to protest. Shortage in production and consumption created tension between individuals and groups, as the discussions of consumption and the particularisation of worker identity aptly show. Poverty was felt to be a household problem, and this drove an ideal of greater social privatisation. The lack of collective protest in Stalinist Hungary was, therefore, much more than simply a response to considerable state repression. The circumstances of socialist industrialisation promoted a withdrawal into the household. Not all, indeed only a minority of, households pursued this strategy with significant success. Yet the fact that some households could mitigate their poverty by combining industrial work with agricultural activity, striving for greater household self-sufficiency, or engaging in informal economic activity, helped to legitimise social privatisation as an ideal. The spread of an ideal of social privatisation as an ideal led to a marked decline in social solidarity.

The subtext of the argument presented here is one that deals with the consequence of socialist industrialisation for gender relations and identities. Given the sharp gendered split between public and private that much gender ideology assumed in Hungary, ideals of social privatisation would have deeply conservative implications. Despite its apparent egalitarianism, the state never challenged established ideologies of gender directly, but rather accommodated itself to them. The evidence seems to suggest that women had a deeper investment in ideals of social privatisation, and the protection and maintenance of the household, than their male workmates. This led to an apparent paradox. Although women were supposed to assume a central role in the socialist labour force according to Stalinist ideology, they were less willing than men to protest as workers. After 1950, they withdrew more substantially than male workers from collective protest concerning workplace issues. Where they did protest, it was over an extension in working time. Women, it would seem, invested much more so than men in ideals of social privatisation. This was because they coped with the consequences of socialist industrialisation not only as workers, but also as homemakers and consumers.

It would be an overstatement of the case made here to say that Hungarian society was 'atomised' by the Stalinist state. Such arguments are often premised on a myth of an all-powerful state. The argument presented here suggests that although the state prevented collective protest, it did not control social process. In fact, were studies of Stalinism to focus more on the material world and less on the political, a picture would emerge of a weak state confronting a weak society. The state was repressive, but it could not control the shop floor; nor, indeed, could it control how people made their living more generally, despite attempts to reshape agricultural production and enforce proletarianisation. The state was confronted by a privatised society – one that, at least until the outbreak of the 1956 Revolution, was characterised by the pursuit of an ideal of household self-sufficiency and independence from the state.

CHAPTER 6

The Revolution and Industrial Workers: The Disintegration and Reconstruction of Socialism, 1953–58

Introduction

Just over three weeks after the arrival of Soviet troops in Budapest to remove the revolutionary government of Imre Nagy in November 1956, the party newspaper for the industrial county of Esztergom-Komárom announced to local miners that 'the workers' councils (the revolutionary organs in the factories) had been given responsibility for the economic life of the country'. In negotiations with the new Soviet-imposed government of János Kádár, the authorities signalled a willingness to make marked concessions to the demands of miners, a key group within the workforce of the county. The 'restoration of certain old privileges', like 'the annual coal entitlement, rent-free accommodation and lighting, the reintegration of factories that had belonged to the mining enterprises with the mines', and 'an expansion in family housebuilding' featured on the agenda of such discussions.[1] Talk of such concessions occurred against the background of a miners' strike that supported the political goals of the Revolution and which paralysed the Hungarian economy. In Tatabánya, the centre of the largest of the county's two coal fields, the Revolution had been ignited by a combination of a sympathy strike of the city's bus drivers with the demonstrators in Budapest and a major demonstration led by younger miners. While the local Party in the city and the mines did not collapse to the same extent as in the rest of the country, the implosion of the regime at the national level allowed the demonstrators to seize control of the mines locally, set up anti-communist workers' councils, and effectively organise a strike in support of the political demands of the Revolution. While they returned to work for three days in early November, believing the political demands of the Revolution to have been accomplished, the Soviet invasion

---

* Originally published in Mark Pittaway 2007, 'The Revolution and Industrial Workers: The Disintegration and Reconstruction of Socialism, 1953–1958', *Hungarian Studies Review*, 34, 1–2: 115–54.

1 'A bányászok nehéz munkájukhoz méltó bért kapnak', *Komárom Megyei Hírlap*, 27 November 1956, p. 1.

provoked a protracted miners' strike, which dragged on for a full two months, causing coal shortages that closed schools and undermined medical services into early 1957.[2]

The targeted use of repression was at least as central to breaking the strike in the coalfields as was the promise of concessions. Yet repression often proved to be counter-productive. In Tatabánya, the local police were forced to concede that the operations of the reconstructed state-security agencies throughout December had not only provoked open demonstrations, but had in fact bolstered support for the strike.[3] Where local state-security forces intervened to arrest the organisers of demonstrations and strikes, it was forced to legitimate their actions. When in December one attempt to arrest a group of such organisers provoked an explosion of armed conflict in one of the city's neighbourhoods, the party newspaper found it necessary to argue that the members of the new state-security agencies were ordinary mine workers dedicated to meet the demands of the 'people' who 'wanted to live in peace and quiet'.[4] As the post-revolutionary regime was consolidated, it was forced to build on the fiction that no 'honest' worker had anything to fear from repression. The only groups targeted were 'counter-revolutionary' agitators. The myth, projected by the Kádár regime, of the events of late 1956 as a 'counter-revolution' – in which anti-socialist agitators, 'reactionaries' and 'agents of imperialism' had stirred up discontent in order to overthrow socialism – had its local counterpart.[5] In Tatabánya, the overwhelmingly working class character of the Revolution posed problems for the 'revolutionary government of workers' and peasants'. Therefore, the local myth of the 'counter revolution', underpinned by the most

---

2   Országos Szechényi Könyvtár, Kézirattár (National Széchényi Library, Manuscripts Collection, hereafter OSZK Kt.), 1956-os gyűjtemény, Komárom-Esztergom megye (1956 Collections, Komárom-Esztergom county, hereafter 412.VIIf),7d, Tatabánya Városi Tanács VB. Tárgy: Az 1956 oktober 23-i és követő ellenforradalmi események leirása. Hiv.rsz: T.260/1957. On the strike and its impact, see OSZK Kt. 412.VIIf.6d, Komárom Megyei Tanács VB 1957: Beszámoló az 1957 május hó 16-i tanácsülésre, a véggrehajtóbizottság munkájáról, pp. 2–3; on the nature of the strike in the mining enterprises, see OSZK Kt. 412.VIIf.1d, Komárom Megyei Bíróság, Elnökségi iratok 1958: Az Esztergomi Megyei Bíróság Elnökétől, Esztergom, Kossuth Lajos u. 6, I em., tel: 212. 1958.El.IX.22 szám. Tárgy: 1958 évi áprilisi havi jelentés, pp. 1–3.
3   Kajári 1996, pp. 478–9.
4   'Kik és miért félnek a tatabányai karhatalomtól?', *Komárom Megyei Hírlap*, 22 December 1956, p. 3.
5   For the official presentation of the events of 1956 and how they were represented in official propaganda, see the five volumes of the so-called 'white book': 1957, *Ellenforradalmi erők a magyar októberi eseményekben, I–V kötet*; and 1958, *Nagy Imre és bűntársai ellenforradalmi összeskűvése*.

significant political trials, sought to attribute the events to the most anti-communist activists in the factories, and more significantly to local professionals, who despite holding key positions in the city's revolutionary committee, were in reality either marginal or had been unable to control the consequences of the explosion of working class anger.[6]

While repression was far from successful as a tool for consolidating the regime, the wave of working class anger was beaten back through other means. The fear rather than the fact of political retribution had encouraged many of those who joined the demonstrations in the city to leave Hungary outright. In Tatabánya's mine number XI, at the end of January 1957, only 60 percent of those who had been employed there before October continued to work there – some had left for other parts of the country, others had joined the flight from Hungary.[7] Furthermore, forms of moral coercion were deployed by the regime concerning the shortages of coal that arose following the miners' strike, with particular emphasis given to the effects the shortages had on schools, hospitals, and the economy in general. These proved highly effective in mobilising the workers who remained.[8] These were often backed by more overt forms of blackmail: in December 1956, the county party paper warned that 'if there is no coal, then Tatabánya's food provision will be in danger'.[9] The failure of protest to remove the regime, and intensifying economic hardship, provided

---

6   For local representations of the 'myth' of the 'counter-revolution' in propaganda, see 1957, *Az ellenforradalom Komárom megyei eseményeiből*; and the series of articles in the county party-newspaper – the first of which was 'Hogyan Történt? Az ellenforradalom tatabányai napjaiból', *Komárom Megyei Hírlap*, 26 January 1957, p. 4. On how the particular local construction of this 'myth' shaped the post-revolutionary political trials, see the indictments and/or verdicts in the two most important of the political trials that concerned the events in the city, OSZK Kt., 1956-os gyűjtemény, Győri Megyei Bíróság Népbírósági Tanácsának anyaga (1956 Collection, Material of the Győr Peoples' Court, hereafter 1956-os gy., Gy.NB.) 1127/1957,1d: Győr Sopronmegyei ügyészség, Győr, 1957.Bül.372 szám. 'Vádirat népi demokratikus államrend megdöntésére irányuló szervezkedés vezetésének büntette miatt, dr. Klébert Márton és társai ellen inditott bünügyben'; OSZK Kt. 412.VIIf.4d, Győri Népbíróság B.0027/1957/16, Mazalin György és társai; A. Magyar Népköztársaság Legfelsőbb Bírósága Népbírósági Tanácsa, Nbf.I.5198/1958/31 szám.

7   'Újra az élen! Ismét elsők a tatabányai XI-es aknák', *Komárom Megyei Hírlap*, 26 January 1957, p. 3.

8   OSZK Kt.412.VIIf.2d, Esztergom Megyei Bíróság, 429/1957: B.429/1957/5 szám. 'Jegyzőkönyv készült a Nép. d.áll. rend. megdönt. ir. mozg. Való részv. btte. miatt Kovács Imre és társai ellen inditott bűnügyben az Esztergomi Megyei Bíróság, Tatabányai bíróságnál, 1957 évi szeptember hó 2-ik napján tartott zárt tárgyalásról', p. 13.

9   'Ha nincs szén, veszélyben Tatabánya élelmiszerellátása', *Komárom Megyei Hírlap*, 15 December 1956, p. 1.

the central motivating factor for miners to return to work.[10] Yet breaking the strike alone did not translate into support for the regime; a sullen mood in the mines in early 1957 masked a climate of deep-seated but silent anger, which occasionally broke through and was carried in rumours of imminent strikes and protest.[11]

The regime consolidated its authority in Tatabánya and among the working class nationally by following through promises of directly addressing the material grievances of workers. Most miners expected the reimposition of socialist rule to lead directly to the return of despotic policies of plan-based mobilisation in the workplace and those that had produced goods shortages and penury before the Revolution outside of the workplace. During the year following the Revolution, the apparent openness of the Party to working class opinion in the city generated 'surprise'.[12] Measures like the large increases in wages, the initiation of a housing construction programme, and other welfare measures, underpinned this at national level; meanwhile, more locally unpopular systems of remuneration at the coalface were abolished and certain benefits-in-kind were restored.[13] Through such measures, a year after the end of the strike party officials were able to record – displaying some surprise – a degree a cautious optimism: 'it seems', commented one, 'that there is trust in the Party and the government'.[14] This popularity was conditional and to some extent belied the fact that few accepted the official arguments about the nature of the Revolution when questioned by propagandists about their attitudes to what had happened in 1956, while miners began referring to it as the 'counter revolution', they often slipped into describing it as 'a revolution'. Most took the stance that 'you should give us an honest wage, I'm not bothered with the rest'.[15]

The defeat of the Revolution and the consolidation of the Kádár regime in Tatabánya, as in other working class communities across Hungary, presented

---

10 Komárom-Esztergom Megyei Önkormányzat Levéltára (Archive of the Government of Komárom-Esztergom County, hereafter KEMÖL), Az MSZMP Tatabánya Városi Bizottságának iratai (Papers of the Tatabánya City Committee of the Hungarian Socialist Workers' Party, hereafter XXXV.2f.)3/1957/8ö.e, pp. 7–15.
11 'A Tatabányai bányászok válasza a sztrájkra, a munkanélküliségre', *Komárom Megyei Hírlap*, 6 January 1957, p. 3.
12 KEMÖL XXXV.2f.2/2ö.e, p. 28.
13 On wages, see 'A szakmány bérezésről', *Komárom Megyei Hírlap*, 6 January 1957, p. 2.
14 KEMÖL XXXV.2f.3/1958/17ö.e, p. 2.
15 KEMÖL, Az MSZMP Komárom Megyei Bizottságának iratai (Papers of the Komárom County Committee of the Hungarian Socialist Workers' Party, hereafter XXXV.1f) 3/1957/23ö.e, pp. 4–5.

an ambiguous picture of an event defeated through the highly selective, rather than the very widespread, use of force. Moral and economic coercion played a larger role, on which were laid substantial concessions in the workplace and the community. While this produced a degree of popularity and support for the Kádár regime by the end of 1957, this coexisted with profound awareness of its deeper illegitimacy as a regime imposed through force of arms by the armies of a foreign power. This outcome points to the need to look at the 1956 Revolution in a new light. It was certainly not 'the first domino', which led irreversibly to the decay, decline and collapse of state socialism thirty-three years later, as many have suggested.[16] While the revival of the memory of the 1956 Revolution played a fundamental role in the events of 1989 in Hungary, because of the way it symbolised the illegitimacy of the regime,[17] in the short- and medium-term it led to the regime's consolidation. Yet this consolidation occurred on the basis of a very different pattern of socialist governance to that which had characterised its rule during the early 1950s, and which drew lessons from the outbreak of the 1956 Revolution.[18] Given that the Kádár regime was a 'post-1956' regime[19] it is not surprising that in its dynamic of construction, consolidation, decay, and collapse, it embodied many of the ambiguities that were visible during the aftermath of the Revolution.

The paradoxical coexistence of the stability of the Kádár regime with perceptions of its deeper political illegitimacy was enabled, in part, by the fact that the Revolution and its outcome demonstrated definitively to Hungary's anti-communist majority that the country's post-war political order was not going to be dismantled immediately or easily. The collapse of the country's pre-war regime, German occupation and then Soviet occupation at the end of the Second World War, created a deeply divided society. Fear of communist dictatorship among the conservative majority, and a parallel fear of the right among the left-wing minority, polarised Hungarian society during the immediate post-war years, creating the social roots of eventual dictatorship.[20] On the political right, many believed in the inevitably of conflict among the wartime

---

16 The phrase is borrowed from Johanna Granville's 2004 book *The First Domino: International Decision Making during the Hungarian Crisis of 1956*. See also Békés 1993; Ekiert 1996.
17 Rainer 2000, pp. 651–8.
18 There is a growing historical literature in Hungary on those patterns of governance; for two conflicting approaches, which concentrate on different decades and draw different conclusions about the Kádár regime, see Rainer and Baráth 2004; Szerencsés and Simon 2004. For studies and collections that concentrate on aspects of Kádár's rule, see Huszár 2002; Kalmár 1998; Varga 2001.
19 This notion is adapted from the author's introduction to Rainer 2003.
20 This case is made in Pittaway 2004, pp. 453–75.

allies, and that only an effective demonstration of anti-Soviet sentiment in Hungary would bring military intervention from Britain and the United States in the interests of 'liberating' the territory from the clutches of the Red Army. During preparations for the first post-war elections in autumn 1945, in conservative regions – like the north-western county of Győr-Moson – local opinion held that if the country 'votes for the Smallholders' Party [the main party of the centre-right], then the Soviets will leave the country, if they vote for the Communists they'll stay forever'.[21] With the creation of overt socialist dictatorship in the similarly conservative south-west of the country, growing political control led many to believe that the new socialist regime's days were numbered, as it would be removed as the result of an imminent war between the superpowers.[22] As the dictatorship intensified its politics of confrontation and social transformation, especially through agricultural collectivisation campaigns in rural areas, the belief in imminent Western intervention to end socialist rule motivated explicit resistance. In villages on the north-western border in August 1950, smallholders refused to pay taxes or deliver foodstuffs to the authorities on the grounds that 'the English were coming'.[23] These expectations of deliverance through foreign intervention encouraged many to interpret the aggressive propaganda of Western radio stations and other propaganda actions – such as the balloon campaigns, launched by similar bodies – as a promise of 'liberation'.[24]

In this context, the defeat of the Revolution and its failure to spark foreign military intervention against the Soviets produced a feeling of hopelessness and a gradual acceptance of the relative permanence of the socialist regime. Belief in the imminence of foreign intervention was conspicuous by

---

21 Győr-Moson-Sopron Megye Győri Levéltár (Győr branch of the Győr-Moson-Sopron County Archive, hereafter Gy.MSM.Gy.L), Győr-Moson Megye és Győr thj. város főispánja 1945–1950, Általános iratok (Papers of the Lord-Lieutenant of Győr-Moson County and of the City of Győr 1945–1950, General Papers, hereafter XXIf.1b)1d; Győr-Moson Megye és Győr thj. város főispánjától. 75/5.főisp.1945.sz. Tárgy: Szeptember havi tájékoztató jelentés, p. 1.

22 Zala Megyei Levéltár (Zala County Archive, hereafter ZML), Az MDP Zala Megyei Bizottságának iratai (Papers of the Zala County Committee of the Hungarian Workers' Party, hereafter XXXV.57f)1/70ö.e, pp. 26–31.

23 Gy.MSM.Gy.L, Az MDP Győr-Moson-Sopron Megyei Bizottság Mezőgazdasági Osztály iratai (Papers of the Agricultural Department of the Győr-Moson-Sopron County Committee of the Hungarian Workers' Party, hereafter Xf.402/2/Mezőgazdaság)/8ö.e; MDP Járási Bizottság Mosonmagyaróvár, Sallai Imre út 3 sz, Jelentés. Mosonmagyaróvár, 1950 augusztus 9-én, p. 1.

24 For the actions of such radio stations and their interaction with domestic opinion, see Pittaway 2003a, pp. 97–116.

its absence in anti-regime rumours during 1957.[25] The deep-seated climate of resignation was expressed by an engineer in one Fejér county factory in March 1957: 'only a third world war can help us, which will break out sooner or later; in the meantime it will be difficult, but afterwards the system will disappear'.[26] While one immediate popular response to this 'culture of defeat'[27] among anti-communists was to retreat into the domestic sphere, alcoholism or religiosity,[28] it laid the foundations for the tacit acceptance of the reality of Kádárism by many of its opponents – particularly its rural and urban middle-class ones – and thus their integration into the system during the 1960s.[29] While the notion of the 'culture of defeat' explains many of the paradoxes of the post-1956 period among those who always opposed Hungary's post-war socialist order, as well as the behaviour of those left-wing intellectuals who initially supported socialism, but turned to Imre Nagy and notions of a reformed socialism in the mid-1950s, it does not explain dominant working class attitudes and patterns of behaviour. Hungary's industrial workers were not homogeneous politically, to be sure, but as the case of Tatabánya shows, their awareness of the illegitimacy of the Kádár regime coexisted with an extraordinary popularity among many that was gained at a very early date. By 1958, the government's popularity was clearly discernible among workers in a number of different sectors and geographical locations.[30] This is especially surprising given the extensive participation of workers in the events of the Revolution. This, in turn, points

---

25   See the documents in ZML, Az MSZMP Zala Megyei Bizottságának iratai (Papers of the Zala County Committee of the Hungarian Socialist Workers' Party, hereafter XXXV.1f)1957/9ö.e.
26   Fejér Megyei Levéltár (Fejér County Archive, hereafter FML), Az MSZMP Fejér Megyei Bizottságának iratai (Papers of the Fejér County Committee of the Hungarian Socialist Workers' Party, hereafter XXXV.19f)/1957/14ö.e, p. 59.
27   For a discussion of this phenomenon in general terms, which reveals parallels with the climate inside Hungary after 1956, see Schivelbusch 2003.
28   Budapest Főváros Levéltára (Archives of the City of Budapest, hereafter BFL), Az MSZMP Budapesti Bizottságának iratai (Papers of the Budapest Committee of the Hungarian Socialist Workers' Party, hereafter XXXV.1f)/1958/138ö.e, pp. 289–95.
29   For the generation of this settlement in rural areas, see Varga 2001. The issue of the acceptance of the regime among conservative members of the middle-class is best addressed in Rainer 2005, pp. 65–105.
30   Magyar Országos Levéltár (Hungarian National Archive, hereafter MOL), A. Magyar Szocialista Munkáspárt Központi Bizottságának iratai (Papers of the Central Committee of the Hungarian Socialist Workers' Party, hereafter M-KS-288f)21/1958/20ö.e, pp. 252–3; MOL M-KS-288f.21/1958/23ö.e, p. 502; ZML XXXV.1f.1958/12ö.e; Feljegyzés a Zalaegerszegi Ruhagyár pártszervezetének agitációs munkájáról, pp. 25–6; BFL XXXV.1f.1958/42ö.e, pp. 49–52.

to the need to consider the role of workers in the Revolution in greater depth, in order to explain their behaviour afterwards and, thus, to tease out the nature of the relationship between the socialist state and working class in the Hungarian context.

Despite the speedy consolidation of the Kádár regime in working class communities, the party leadership remained deeply shocked at the extent of worker participation in and support for the Revolution. In early 1957, party-officials commented with dismay that among the thousands who left the north-western county of Győr-Moson-Sopron for Austria, there were many 'workers from traditional working class families'.[31] With the regime's consolidation party officials underplayed the role and extent of working class discontent in the Revolution, arguing that the majority simply remained 'passive' in the face of 'counter-revolutionary' mobilisation. This was because 'the working class was primarily disappointed in the party-leadership and did not see the Party as the true representative of their class'.[32] The notion of industrial workers as 'passive' during the Revolution was, however, a myth. But so too was the Party's collective notion of what constituted the 'working class'. In general terms, the Party's use of the term 'working class' tended to subsume all wage workers into an imaginary and homogeneous entity, which universally shared the values of those of the skilled, urban, male elite of the workforce who had supported the labour movement pre-1948. This underpinned notions – prevalent in the discussions among leading party officials after 1956 – of the 'working class' as a social body that would act as the bulwark of the regime.[33] These were underpinned by a hegemonic discourse of the working class outside the party leadership that stressed the pre-eminence of the male skilled elite and subordinated other more peripheral groups – this discourse of the working class had structured hierarchical relationships between workers in workplaces and communities since the end of the nineteenth century. It was embedded in the practice and common sense of the labour movement, and came to represent a pattern of relationships and cultural practices that shaped the contours of working class identity by the mid-twentieth century.

The industrial and labour policies of Hungary's socialist regime after 1948 caused a fundamental breach between industrial workers and the 'new' state. In the workplace, the regime attacked the privileges of the skilled through the

---

31   MOL M-KS-288f.5/23ö.e/1957 április 23, p. 92.
32   MOL M-KS-288f.5/96ö.e, p. 3.
33   For a good example of these cultural assumptions manifesting themselves in internal discussions, see MOL M-KS-288f.21/1958/20ö.e, pp. 1–8.

introduction of labour competition, new wage forms and different management structures. At the same time, they expanded the workforce, aiming to subvert the hierarchies of gender, generation, and those based on distinctions between the urban and the rural. Their economic policies produced endemic income insecurity, widespread penury, and severe shortage, while they responded to the tensions these produced with repression. These policies caused the crumbling of working class support for the regime during the early 1950s, but the patterns of relations in the workplace caused by the chaos produced by the state's industrialisation drive allowed hierarchical relationships to reproduce themselves under new circumstances. Skilled workers, while profoundly alienated from the regime, continued to sit at the apex of modified hierarchical relationships in which greater numbers of working class youth, women, and those from rural areas, were cast to a discontented periphery.[34]

Considerable working class anger alone was not sufficient to provoke widespread mobilisation – between 1953 and 1956, the initiation of the 'New Course' under the government of Imre Nagy, followed by ever more bitter struggles within the Party, led to the fragmentation of the authority of the regime. These were met, in turn, by a greater expression of the considerable working class discontent that persisted in Hungary's factories, mines, and on its construction sites, that were never successfully alleviated by any of the protagonists engaged in the internal Party struggles. The onset of the revolutionary events in October 1956 was met with a social explosion in which many working class Hungarians – particularly those young workers cast to the periphery – provided the most militant sections of the working class crowds which drove forward the Revolution in the country's towns and cities. Different groups within the working class, especially the skilled, the young and rural workers, participated in the Revolution in highly distinctive ways. The reconstruction of the regime's authority was underpinned by different processes within different groups, but given the cultural power employed by older, urban, skilled, male workers within hegemonic discourses of the working class, it was the regime's ability to repair its relations with this group that was fundamental to the consolidation of its authority.

---

34 This argument is outlined in Pittaway 2003b, pp. 71–82, and chapters 3 and 4 of this volume.

The Politics of Gradual Collapse: From Reform to Rebellion, 1953–6

The spring and early summer of 1953 was a period of intense worker protest across Eastern Europe that demonstrated the tensions created by socialist rule. In May, workers in the tobacco plant in Plovdiv in Bulgaria rioted as a result of unfavourable changes made to work norms. In Czechoslovakia, a currency reform was introduced in the same month cutting into wages and eliminating savings, which resulted in generalised revolt in Plzen. In the GDR, decisions to tighten work norms led to a wave of demonstrations and strikes on 17 June 1953 across the country.[35] While the events in the GDR did not lead to open mass protest in Hungary, they had an electrifying effect in workplaces. The notion that a population could express its discontent openly in a socialist state began (albeit slowly) to lift the lid on a well of discontent. Industrial workers in Budapest stated openly that 'the Hungarian party can learn from the German party that it is not correct to apply pressure all the time through the norms'. In a neighbouring factory, one party-member called for the smallholders to be given back land that had been 'donated' to agricultural cooperatives.[36]

Against this background of growing social upheaval, and under instruction from the Kremlin, the Hungarian leadership modified their course. The country's effective dictator Mátyás Rákosi was forced to relinquish his position as prime minister, although crucially not his role as secretary of the ruling party. His successor as head of government, Imre Nagy, launched a policy that suspended collectivisation drives in rural areas and placed the problem of working class material discontent at the centre of government action.[37] The announcement of the 'New Course' led to both the growing public expression of working class discontent[38] and official attempts through the press to address

---

35   For the Plovdiv events, see Crampton 1987, p. 176; on the revolt in Plzen, the best available account is still Ulc 1965, pp. 46–9; for a summary of the 1953 events in the GDR, see Fulbrook 1995, pp. 177–87.

36   BFL, Az MDP Budapesti Bizottságának iratai (Papers of the Budapest Committee of the Hungarian Workers' Party, hereafter XXXV.95f)2/215ö.e, pp. 54–5.

37   For the political background, the best account is provided in Rainer 1996, pp. 489–542.

38   For some examples, see Politikatörténeti és Szakszervezeti Levéltár (Archive of Political History and the Trade Unions, hereafter PtSzL), A Szakszervezetek Országos Tanácsa iratai (Papers of the Central Council of Trade Unions, hereafter XII.2f)7/33d./1953; Feljegyzés a kormányprogrammal kapcsolatos üzemi tapasztalatokról, p. 1; ZML XXXV.57f.2/Agitprop/15ö.e; Jelentés Nagy Imre országgyűlési beszéde utáni megnyilvánulásokról, p. 1.

the neglect of workers' 'legitimate concerns' by the authorities in workplaces across the country.[39] More concretely, it was met through a policy of concessions: the state moved to permit smallholders to leave agricultural cooperatives; fines and criminal penalties for work discipline infringements were revoked; an amnesty was granted to political prisoners; a higher priority was given to the implementation of protective legislation in the workplace; and wages were raised.[40]

In terms of their impact on the working class, 'New Course' policies had two effects. On the one hand, they failed to transform decisively the material conditions of industrial workers, except the skilled elites in some sectors. On the other, they strengthened many of the hierarchies that had reproduced themselves under the circumstances of the shortage economy of the early 1950s. This reinforcing of hierarchy was the product of the effects of different policies of different groups of workers, and these shaped the political attitudes of these groups towards Nagy's reformist project. Among groups on the periphery of the workforce, Nagy's project attained most popularity among anti-communist rural workers. However, this was not due to the programme's effect on industry, but rather on agriculture, as many felt the 'New Course' heralded an end to agricultural collectivisation. Some had greeted its announcement by attempting to quit their jobs and return to agriculture: at Mosonmagyaróvár's aluminium smelter, the 250 workers who owned land tried to quit as soon as the programme was announced. Their attempts were blocked by the plant director. Although this resulted in an explosion of discontent, only one hundred departed illegally.[41] As local party-bodies and state authorities fought a rearguard action to prevent the dissolution of agricultural collectives and implemented more informal policies of administrative restriction against farmers,[42] this illusion dissipated. Despite this, however, the post-1953 period was a relatively good one for many rural workers, especially those who belonged to a household with a farm that could produce for the market, as the incomes of

---

39 For some examples, see 'Forditsunk nagyobb gondot a dolgozók kéréseire', *Futószalag*, 4 July 1953, p. 2; 'Tűrhetetlen körülmények között dolgoznak a vigonyfonoda tépő dolgozói', *Pamutújság*, 9 July 1953, p. 3.

40 Vásárhelyi 1988, pp. 149–205.

41 Open Society Archives (OSA), Records of the Radio Free Europe Research Institute, Hungarian Unit (300–40), Item No. 08699/53, p. 1.

42 For an excellent insight into this 'rear-guard' action in anti-communist western Hungary, see Gy.MSM.Gy.L.X.402f.2/Mezőgazdaság/20ö.e; MDP Sopron Járási Bizottsága, MDP Megyei Pártbizottsága Mezőg. Osztály Bognár Elvtársnak, Sopron, 1953 augusztus 11. For a useful account of official harassment of individual landholders, see OSA 300/40, Item No. 10105/54, pp. 1–7.

individual smallholders rose quicker (albeit from a much lower base) than those of industrial workers.[43] While such workers had never accepted the legitimacy of the socialist regime, favourable policies towards agriculture did allow Nagy to win a degree of personal popularity in the rural milieu in which such workers lived. In one village in western Hungary, Nagy's relaxation of the collectivisation drive was compared to 'the liberation of the serfs in 1848'.[44] Yet the rising incomes of some rural workers, and continuing problems of food shortage in urban areas, exacerbated the unpopularity of such workers, with many urban residents, especially in Budapest, arguing that the 'New Course' was a 'peasants' policy' rather than a 'workers' policy' – a sentiment that legitimised the casting of rural workers to the periphery of the workforce.[45]

The climate of the 'New Course' reinforced the peripheral position of other groups within the workforce that had been generated by the reproduction of hierarchy within the working class during the early 1950s. This was especially the case with women, where Nagy's arrival in office accompanied attempts to implement protective legislation in the workplace, which it reinforced. This tended not to protect women in unhealthy and low-paying jobs in traditionally feminised sectors, but instead acted to remove women from those occupations traditionally regarded as male and high-paying where they had previously gained a foothold as a consequence of the affirmative action campaigns of the early 1950s.[46] Working class youth, including young skilled workers, remained in a relatively marginal position in workplaces across the country. Their peripheral positions and consequent low wages led to considerable discontent that in turn drove many of them to seek better paid employment in neighbouring establishments.[47] Placed in a peripheral position and deeply alienated, and often influenced by propaganda in Western radio broadcasts, many rejected the socialist system absolutely. In the Tatabánya mines, one young miner urged a workmate to 'go to the West where at least you are valued for as long as you

---

43   No reliable figures are available, but for an indication (which is likely to understate the true effects of this phenomenon), see MOL, Az MDP Központi Vezetőségének iratai (Papers of the Central Leadership of the Hungarian Workers' Party, hereafter M-KS-276f)65/251ö.e, p. 147.

44   Gy.MSM.Gy.L.X.402f.2/Mezőgazdaság/24ö.e; A. Győri Textilművek patronálási csoport jelentése a páli 'Sarló Kalapács' TSZCS-ben tett látogatásról, 1953 július 7, p. 1.

45   BFL XXXV.95f.2/215ö.e, p. 139.

46   On the implementation of protective legislation in 1953, see Pittaway 1998, p. 276; MOL M-KS-276f.94/593ö.e, pp. 1–4.

47   MOL M-KS-276f.94/827ö.e, pp. 319–20.

can work, here you are just treated like a dog to whom they occasionally throw a bone so you don't starve'.[48]

The hardening of reproduced hierarchies in the workforce was driven, in part, by Nagy's relaxation of despotic policies in the workplace which had led to an intensification of informal bargaining that favoured the older, male, skilled elite. Often sympathetic party members, union officials and lower-level managers had actively participated in opening the floodgates to a wave of bargaining in late 1953 that enshrined considerable informal control over remuneration by the skilled elite in everyday workplace practice.[49] Despite state intentions and frequent complaints over their 'inadequacy',[50] the wage increases mandated by the Nagy government in late 1953 further boosted the position of experienced skilled workers.[51] In some sectors, especially coalmining, the increases in skilled workers' wages were substantial, as they were linked to a premium system, which ensured that when it was introduced in late 1953 face-workers' wages increased by 22.3 percent in a two-month period when production fell by four percent.[52] Wage increases of this order generated a degree of satisfaction among miners, which went some way towards defusing discontent.[53]

Yet despite the reinforcement of their position within the workforce as a result of the policies of the Nagy government in the workplace, the skilled elite as a whole were far from satisfied – something that was in part a product of economic chaos during 1954, when shortages intensified and power-supply problems forced industry into short-time working during the winter months.[54] But it was also fed by a perception that amid a climate that was relatively permissive to agriculture and to trade, urban workers were losing ground in

---

48 OSA 300/40, Item No. 8083/54, p. 12.
49 PtSzL XII.2f.7/4d/1953; Jelentés a kormányprogram utáni bérhelyzetről, p. 4; PtSzL XII.2f.7/30d/1953; Levél az Élelmiszeripari Minisztérium Munkaügyi- és Bérfőosztály Vezetőjétől a Szakszervezetek Országos Tanácsa Munkabérosztályának, 1953 október 8, p. 4.
50 MOL M-KS-276f.94/743ö.e, pp. 83–9.
51 For some of the specific wage measures aimed at skilled and experienced workers, see PtSzL XII.2f.7/28d/1953; Minisztertanács Bértitkársága. Javaslat az 1954 évben végrehajtandó bérügyi intézkedésekre.
52 MOL M-KS-276f.94/743ö.e. p. 58.
53 PtSzL, Bányaipari Dolgozók Szakszervezetének iratai (Papers of the Mineworkers' Union, hereafter XII.30f)745d/1954; Bányaipari Dolgozók Szakszervezete, Szénbányászati Trösztbizottság, Tatabánya. Jelentés Bányaipari Dolgozók Szakszervezeti szénbányászati trösztbizottságának 1953 évi IV. negyedévi jelentése, p. 4.
54 See the documents in BFL XXXV.95f.4/62ö.e.

income and prestige – a sentiment that led them to eventually welcome Nagy's dismissal in 1955.[55] It would take Imre Nagy's fall, and the policies pursued after his removal, to persuade the skilled elite of his merits. The turn away from reform – fronted by Nagy's successor András Hegedüs, installed by Rákosi, who at the helm of the Party had never accepted the 'New Course' – was prompted by the continuing economic chaos that gripped the country during 1954 and early 1955, and aimed to return to policies of renewed socialist industrialisation and collectivisation. Young workers, whose peripheral position had been barely touched under Nagy, remained profoundly antagonistic to the regime. Rural workers were infuriated by the renewed collectivisation drives in rural areas, although anti-rural sentiment remained strong among their urban colleagues.[56] The skilled elite was confronted with the regime's attempts to hold down the wage bill – their attempts to increase production norms in heavy-industrial sectors and to limit the impact of the premium system in the coalmines, which had guaranteed higher wages, provoked enormous opposition. This opposition was, indeed, greater in many factories than it had been to equivalent measures in the early 1950s – in some heavy-engineering factories, skilled workers were no longer frightened and refused to work until the older abolished norms were reinstated.[57] The tightening of the premium system in the mines provoked a storm of complaints often supported by local unions and party cells.[58]

The pattern of reform followed by clamp-down had antagonised most of the working class and crucially its skilled elite. It also ensured that the experience of restrictive policies in 1955 created a popular hunger for further reform in a context within which the authorities faced a workforce that would not be cowed as easily as it had been in the early 1950s.[59] This provided an explosive

---

55 FML, Az MDP Dunai Vasmű építkezés és Dunapentele/Sztálinváros Városi Bizottságának iratai (Paper of the Danube Steel Works' Construction Site and Dunapentele/Sztálinváros City Committee of the Hungarian Workers' Party, hereafter 17f.)2/PTO/22ö.e; Kivonat II. A K.V. márciusi határozatával kapcsolatos hangulatról beszámoló, pp. 5–7; BFL XXXV.95f.2/215ö.e, p. 139.

56 Gy.MSM.Gy.L, Az MDP Győr Városi Bizottságának iratai (Papers of the Győr City Committee of the Hungarian Workers' Party, hereafter X.405f)5/117ö.e.; Jegyzőkönyv felvétetett 1956 augusztus 21-én az Öntőde és Kovácsológyárban megtartott Párt-Csúcsbizottsági értekezleten, pp. 2–3.

57 MOL M-KS-276f.94/829ö.e, pp. 90–2.

58 PtSzL XII.30f.922d/1955; Jelentés a bérezés egyszerüsitésének és összevonásának levitele, annak eredményei és hibai.

59 This is clear from the article: 'Teljesíthetők-e bányaüzemeinkben a normák?', *Harc a Szénért*, 4 November 1956, p. 3.

social background for the crisis of the socialist regime during 1956. The year of upheaval began in February with Nikita Khrushchev's denunciation of Stalin, the purges, and the cult of personality, given to the Twentieth Congress of the Soviet Communist Party. The speech had an electrifying effect in Hungary,[60] as it fatally weakened the confidence of many working class party members in the regime. When Khrushchev's denunciation of Stalin was revealed to closed party meetings across the country, working class Communists reacted with total incredulity. In Sztálinváros, party members in the factories questioned the local leadership: 'Stalin led the Party for thirty years, how can it be that his mistakes have been discovered now?', and '[w]hat is the current situation in Hungary with the cult of personality? Was Rajk wrong?', alongside more mundane questions: 'I own a copy of Stalin's complete works and have read them all. What do I do with them now?'[61] In Budapest's United Lighting and Electrics Factory, the Khrushchev speech soon became an open topic of conversation. Workers maintained that 'the cult of personality was just as marked here [in Hungary], as in the Soviet Union, especially among the top leadership'.[62]

As the year progressed, the growing militancy of the debates in the Petőfi kör – the intellectual debating forum of the opposition to Rákosi – and especially its debate on press freedom, increased the boldness of workers, particularly those among the skilled elite, in expressing their views. It also underlined growing support for major political change among all sections of the working class. In the United Lighting and Electrics Factory, workers argued openly that 'the leadership is destroying the national economy. The people no longer believe anything they say and they have no role any more'.[63] The news of the riots in Poznan and the mounting political crisis in Poland contributed to the snowballing of politicised discontent among the skilled elite. For many, 'the riots broke out in Poznan, not because of the enemy and foreign spies, but because twelve years after the end of the war living standards remained low'.[64] As Rákosi was removed as party leader and replaced by Ernő Gerő in July, the loss of regime control became more obvious, as did the spread of open popular opposition. Workers complained not about Rákosi's removal from power, but the method by which it was achieved, arguing that it demonstrated Hungary's lack of national sovereignty. Furthermore, there were growing signs of belief in the effectiveness of collective action: in the Ikarus bus plant, it was argued that

---

60 BFL, Az MDP Budapest IV. kerületi Bizottságának iratai (Papers of the Budapest 4th District Committee of the Hungarian Workers' Party, hereafter XXXV.176f).2/1580.e, p. 32.
61 FML XXXV.17f.2/8ö.e; A rendikivüli taggyűlésen felvetett kérdések, pp. 1–10.
62 BFL XXXV.176f.2/154ö.e, p. 275.
63 Ibid., p. 188.
64 Ibid., p. 274.

'under pressure from the masses the leadership has abolished the peace loans, if we exert even stronger pressure we will be able to force new measures to raise our living standards'.[65] The effect of the combination of a loss of confidence within the Party in its ability to govern, and rising discontent, was enormous. By September, there was 'a real feeling of panic' among members of the apparatus in Budapest.[66]

By summer 1956, the crumbling of the regime was met with greater political assertiveness from among the working class, particularly its urban, skilled, male elite. They were often supported by some factory and union committees who joined their rebellion. This climate was fuelled by an obviously worsening economic situation. In Budapest's Duclós Mining Machinery Factory, in August 1956 the factory party committee issued a statement demanding that 'the rights of the workers be secured' in disputes with management; that workers were right 'to demand a just wage system'; and that the overly 'formal monthly production meetings' be replaced with true forums of factory democracy.[67] More locally, within workplaces working class anger was directed at the autocracy and arrogance of management, supported by the official functionaries of the Party, union and youth organisation. In the Chinoin Pharmaceuticals Factory, skilled workers complained in spring 1956 that 'the cult of personality manifests itself inside the factory, particularly among the middle and upper level economic cadres. It has been common for workers not to criticise, or make suggestions just because they were scared of the management'.[68] Generalised rebellion among oil workers at the Lovászi Oil Drilling Plant in July 1956 was provoked by what workers saw as the 'unjustified' payment of large plan fulfilment premiums to management, at a time when workers' wages had fallen. Most complaints concerned low wages and social provision, and the focus of their attack was on management. Károly Papp, the director of the plant, was openly attacked for promoting a 'cult of personality' around himself and for using factory property to lavishly celebrate his birthday.[69]

As part of this wave of criticism, skilled workers demanded greater democracy in the factories. One fitter in the Duclós Mining Machinery Factory complained in August that 'it is useless complaining to the Party and factory

---

65 MOL M-KS-276f.66/23ö.e, pp. 42–3.
66 Ibid., p. 63.
67 BFL XXXV.176f.2/149ö.e, p. 216; BFL XXXV.176f.2/149ö.e, pp. 7–8.
68 BFL XXXV.176f.2/147ö.e., p. 16.
69 ZML, Az MDP Letenye Járási Bizottságának iratai (Papers of the Letenye District Committee of the Hungarian Workers' Party, hereafter XXXV.61f)1/42ö.e; Lovászi üzem helyzetéről feljegyzések és tájékoztató, pp. 1–2; ZML XXXV.61f.1/42ö.e; Nagyaktiva ülésen készült feljegyzések, p. 1.

committee because they can't do anything. What happens here is basically what the director says'. He saw the only remedy as being 'to give the trade union a greater role'.[70] By September, the factory press began publishing similar complaints. One former trade unionist wrote the following in the paper of Budapest's Danube Shoe Factory:

> [I]n the period following the liberation old, committed trade unionists were promoted to become managers. We should say clearly that later these comrades became detached from the workers, they became one sided and didn't speak up sufficiently for their interests ... new people filled the trade union and the beginnings of the co-option, not the elections of the [new] leaders [of the unions] began ... the union leaders regarded anyone who stood up for their interests as the enemy, and dealt with them in this manner.[71]

Yet as the mood for change in workplaces gathered pace, the regime was close to collapse. The growing thaw in relations with Yugoslavia, the re-burial of László Rajk on 6 October, the retention of power by Gerő (discredited by his Stalinist past), and the lack of any clear leadership from the regime, pushed the situation to crisis-point. When the Revolution began on 23 October, with student demonstrations in Budapest, industrial workers would play more radical roles than they had done previously.

The Power of the Working-Class Crowd: October–November 1956

In the prison camp attached to mine number XVIII in the geographically isolated western Hungarian mining town of Oroszlány, many of the prisoners who worked in the mines under sentence concluded in mid-October that 'they wouldn't be shut inside for much longer'. As students prepared to demonstrate in Budapest to secure political change, at noon on 23 October the prisoners attempted to overpower the guards at the mine entrance and break out. The factory guard was only able to restore order by firing on the prisoners, killing three of them as a result. When three days later the local Revolution was launched by a crowd of around five hundred young workers marching through the town shouting 'Work! Bread! Rákosi to the Gallows! [*Munkát! Kenyeret,*

---

70 BFL XXXV.176f.2/149ö.e, p. 4.
71 'Régi harcos szemmel látom', *Futószalag*, 22 September 1956, p. 3.

Rákosinak kötelet!]', they were motivated as much by solidarity with the prisoners as with demonstrators in Budapest. After the leaders of the demonstration delivered their demands to the local radio station, around one hundred and fifty demonstrators proceeded to mine number XVII where they freed the prisoners after the guard refused to fire on the demonstrators.[72]

While much of the historiography of the revolution has tended to see revolutionary mobilisation as being sparked by the events in Budapest on 23 October, the opening of the archives and research into the 'local revolutions' has qualified this Budapest-centred account, unveiling evidence of much unrest – just as in Oroszlány – that took place before or as the events in Budapest began.[73] Student mobilisation in provincial centres such as Debrecen, Miskolc, and Szeged, was marked, while the authorities were made aware of the simmering discontent and strained patience of industrial workers in their cities.[74] Even where the explosion of the Revolution occurred in response to the events in Budapest, as in many of the capital's working class suburbs, or in Tatabánya as was discussed above, the signs of political mobilisation were present prior to 23 October, while local events themselves were driven by dynamics particular to their location.[75]

The Revolution, right across the country, involved a rapid relocation of political power from the Party and regime to the revolutionary crowd, which during the last week of October and the first days of November acted as the locus of political legitimacy. In cities across the country, the crowd – organised through initially peaceful demonstrations – assumed the role as the representative of the 'will of the people', demanding a change in the political order.[76] Crowds played a central role in the 'cleansing' of public space, through the deliberate, and at times almost theatrical, removal of monuments and artefacts associated with either the Red Army or the socialist regime.[77] The frequent incidents

---

72   OSZK 412VIIf.7d – Komárom Megyei Tanács – Titkárság; Városi Tanács VB. Elnökétől, Oroszlány 775/1957. Tárgy: Az ellenforradalmi események leírása, pp. 1–2.
73   For some useful accounts of the Revolution in the east of the country, see Szakolczai and Varga 2003.
74   Filep 2000; Gazdag 1993, pp. 29–49; Szakolczai 2003, pp. 121–35; Farkas 2003, pp. 201–32.
75   For the former, see Rainer 1990, pp. 101–12; for the latter, see KEMÖL XXXV.2f.3/1958/23ö.e, pp. 4–9.
76   For two provincial examples, see Csomor 2001, pp. 25–33; Bana 2002, pp. 5–6.
77   For one example from Nagykanizsa, see ZML, Az 1956-os Magyar Forradalom és Szabadságharc gyűjtemény (The 1956 Revolution and Struggle for Independence Collection, hereafter XXXII.15f)1d; Zalamegyei Ügyészség Zalaegerszeg, 1957. Bül.59/3 szám. Izgatás büntette miatt Gáti József nagykanizsai lakos elleni bünügyben a nyomzati iratokat az alább vádirat benyujtásával teszem át, pp. 1–2.

that followed 23 October, whereby representatives of either the army or state-security services fired on initially non-violent crowds, both radicalised the revolution and underlined the illegitimacy of the regime.[78] Such acts of violence against revolutionary crowds bolstered the latter's claim to act in the name of the people as a whole. Furthermore, they could and frequently did confer their legitimacy on revolutionary organs set up during the Revolution, while they played a role in supervising the actions of other organs that displayed an ambiguous attitude towards the will of the revolutionary crowd.[79]

While the revolutionary crowd appeared as the unified embodiment of the will of the nation, the crowds were far from homogeneous, either politically or socially. In many towns, like Zalaegerszeg, secondary-school students and industrial workers provided the core of the demonstrations that ignited local revolutions, which attracted members of other occupational groups to join vocal demands for change.[80] Workers played a central role in the demonstrations in urban centres right across the country, and they were often over-represented among the dead and injured when crowds were fired on: when the state-security agencies fired on demonstrators in Mosonmagyaróvár on 26 October, of those killed 65.15 percent were workers.[81] Workers were not the only people in the revolutionary crowds, although they played a crucial role in many. Different groups within the workforce played very different roles in these events – either within the crowd, in their relationships to the crowd, or as participants in crowds in different locations from many of their workmates. Working-class youth were the most radical set in that they drove political change, and were most likely to participate in armed groups during the Revolution. The skilled were the most divided politically and participated most actively in the struggles for control of the factories, while rural workers tended to return to spread the Revolution to their villages and largely sought the reversal of agricultural collectivisation.

The role of young workers in providing a group of militants prepared to drive forward the Revolution was fundamental. In Budapest, younger workers

---

78 See Kahler et al. 1993.

79 An excellent example of the confused ways in which revolutionary councils were elected, and the way in which they reflected the preferences of the crowd, is provided by events in Tatabánya, see OSZK Kt 1956-os Gy., Gy.NB.1127/1957, 1d; Győri megyei biróság népbirósági tanácsa. Nb.1122/1957.3.sz. Jegyzőkönyv készült a népi demokratikus államrend megdöntésére irányuló szervezkedés vezetésének büntette miatt Dr Klébert Márton és társa ellen inditott bünügyben a győri megyei biróság népbirósági tanácsa előtt 1957 október 26-napján megtartott nyilvános tárgyalásról, pp. 2–3.

80 Csomor 2001, pp. 25–8.

81 Adapted from 'Halottak ...', reprinted in Kahler et al. 1993, pp. 61–6.

were frequently drawn to the initial demonstrations and played a central role in first radicalising those demonstrations, and then spreading disturbances to the industrial suburbs. One second-year industrial apprentice in the United Lighting and Electrics Factory, I.M., was working on 23 October when he 'heard that there was a demonstration in Budapest in Stalin square'. Immediately catching the tram and trolleybus into central Pest, he was forced to get off some way short of the square, because 'the crowd was so big that the trolleybuses stood in a jam and everyone went on foot'.[82] Often youth participation in the early stages of the Revolution resembled lower-level and less political forms of youth disorder in industrial communities.[83] One group of young working class males, on hearing of demonstrations, decided to go to the hostel for local student nurses, and 'take the girls off to the demonstration' in Budapest. Once they discovered that the director of the hostel had locked in the inhabitants, they began to shout 'Russians go home, Rákosi to the gallows' until the police arrived.[84]

Outside the capital, young workers played a central role in the first demonstrations in many communities. In Tatabánya, while striking local bus drivers provided the catalyst for the local revolution, they joined younger workers in seeking to transform their strike into an occupation of public space, as apprentices from the mining technical school and young miners from the workers' hostels provided the core of initial demonstrations. The spontaneity of the demonstrations was indicated by the confusion of different slogans – some shouted the old socialist slogan of 'Bread! Work!', while others sang the *himnusz* (Hungary's national anthem) as they marched.[85] As the number of participants in the demonstrations increased, young workers took key roles in the 'cleansing' of public space of monuments associated with either the Soviets or the socialist regime: in Nagykanizsa, those who pulled down the Soviet war memorial in the town were led by a twenty-six year old worker whose working

---

82 Az 1956-os Magyar Forradalom Történetének Dokumentációs és Kutatóintézete, Oral History Archivium (Oral History Archives of the 1956 Institute, hereafter 1956-os Intézet, OHA) 449, p. 5.

83 For some of these, see Horváth, 2004 pp. 172–85.

84 OSZK Kt, 1956-os Gy. Budapest Fővárosi Bíróság Népbírósági Tanácsának anyaga, Kósa Pál és társai (Peoples' Court Council of the Budapest City Court, Pál Kása and associates, hereafter Bp.NB. 4491/74), 3d/4; Budapest Rendőrfőkapitányság Politikai Nyomozó Osztály, Vizsgálati Osztály. Jegyzőkönyv Kollár József kihallgatásáról, Budapest, 1957 augusztus 1, p. 1.

85 'Hogyan történt? Az ellenforradalom naplójából', *Komárom Megyei Hírlap*, 26 January 1957, p. 4.

life had been filled by a series of jobs in the mining and construction sectors.[86] The activities of working class youth extended not merely to violence against the symbols of the socialist regime, but also played a direct role in violence against those they perceived to be representatives of the regime. They frequently acted as the 'agents' of the revolutionary crowd in carrying out demands for removing Communists from the head of public institutions. In Újpest's Danube Shoe Factory, the belief of the crowd that 'the workers' council was in the hands of the Communist director' led to four armed young workers, led by the son of one factory employee, deciding that they should storm the factory and 'arrest' the director, as part of a process through which the workers' council would be purged.[87]

The issue of violence raises the question of the process by which working class youths within demonstrations armed themselves and formed themselves into armed groups. The boundaries between these armed groups of young workers and the informally organised 'national guards', which nominally served local revolutionary committees answerable to the crowd, was a fluid one. In Tatabánya, a small section of the official demonstration successfully laid siege to the local police station, freeing prisoners and gaining access to weapons. These were supplemented by those given to them after laying siege to a local army barrack. While some of the radical armed demonstrations went to join the 'fight' in the capital, a core of around thirty remained to form a 'national guard' detachment to guarantee the local revolution.[88] In Budapest, where peaceful demonstrations were fired upon, and with the subsequent intervention of Soviet troops, young workers who had joined the demonstrations moved to arm themselves, by demanding the weapons that were stored in factories for civil defence purposes. During the early hours of 24 October, young workers joined other demonstrators in raiding factories for weapons – not all were undefended. In some, remembered one young worker, 'the porter on the door was already armed with a machine gun'.[89] In some factories, armed

---

86 ZML XXXII.15f.1d./B.322/1957; Zalamegyei ügyészség, Zalaegerszeg, 1957 Bül.59/3 szám. Izgatás büntette miatt Gáti József nagykanizsai lakos elleni bünügyben a nyomozati iratokat az alább vádirat benyujtásával teszem át, p. 1.

87 OSZK Kt, 1956-os Gy. Bp.NB. 4491/74/3d/8; Budapest Fővárosi Birósági Népbirósági Tanácsa NB.II.8017/1958. LXXXVIII Jegyzőkönyv készült a szervezkedés és egyéb büncselekmények miatt Kósa Pál és 32 társa ellen inditott büntetőügyben a Budapesti Fővárosi Biróság Népbirósági Tanácsánál 1959 február 9-én megtartott zárt tárgyalásról, p. 3.

88 1956-os Intézet, OHA 417, p. 17; OSZK Kt, 412.VIIf.1d – Komárom Megyei Biróság – Elnökségi iratok 1958; Az Esztergom Megyei Biróság Elnökétől, Esztergom, Kossuth Lajos u. 5.sz. Tel: 212. 1958. El.IX.B.27.sz. Tárgy: 1958 évi május havi jelentés, pp. 2–3.

89 1956-os Intézet, OHA 449, p. 9.

bands made up of young workers, and factory security-guards engaged in gun battles at factory gates; in some cases, workers reporting for the morning shift were caught and injured in the crossfire, although in the vast majority of cases the authorities were able to repel these attacks.[90]

The attempts of the authorities to retain control over both factories and, more broadly, working class communities foundered on the breadth of support among workers for the overthrow of the regime, even though many workers were less radical than their younger workmates. In factories in Budapest suburbs like Újpest, the student demonstrations provoked considerable sympathy among workers on 23 October. In one meeting in the Chinoin Pharmaceuticals Factory, 'a university student spoke and read out their demands expressed as a series of points ... some of the points were met with enthusiastic applause'.[91] On the morning of the same day, the 'sixteen points' – the demands of the Budapest student demonstrators[92] – were circulated among the workers of the neighbouring United Lighting and Electrics factory, where they had 'a considerable impact'.[93] In the Chinoin, the mood had only been defused by the director urging workers to 'await the view of the party of the demonstration'.[94] The denunciation of the demonstrators as 'counter revolutionaries' by Ernő Gerő in his radio broadcast, the consequent demonstrations in front of the headquarters of the national radio and the firing on crowds by the state-security services there, followed by the news of the intervention of Red Army troops overnight, turned the mood in the capital's industrial suburbs into one of fury. In the United Lighting and Electrics factory the following morning, two-thirds of the workers arrived at work, but during the morning the skilled workers in the tool workshop and in the vacuum plant stopped work to organise a mass meeting of all workers that launched the strike and decided to remove the red star from above the factory gate.[95] With the spread of the strike, a large number of workers took to the streets to demand political change: over the course of the morning, there 'were many people in front of the State

---

90 BFL, Az MSZMP Budapest IV. kerületi Bizottságának iratai (Papers of the Budapest IV District Committee of the Hungarian Socialist Workers' Party, hereafter XXXV.9f)1957/15ö.e, p. 102; OSZK Kt, 1956-os Gy., Bp.NB.4491/74,1d/8; Bp.Főkap.Pol.Nyom. Osztály Vizsg.alo.57. nov 6, Bp., pp. 1–2.

91 OSZK Kt, 1956-os Gy. Bp.NB.4491/74/1d/6; Budapesti Rendőrfőkapitányság Politikai Nyomozó Osztály, Vizsgálati Alosztály. Jegyzőkönyv Lészai/Lothringer/Béla őrizetes kihallgatásáról, Budapest, 1957 augusztus 23, p. 1.

92 These are reprinted as 'The "Sixteen Points" prepared by Hungarian students 22–23 October 1956' in Békés, Byrne and Rainer 2002, pp. 188–90.

93 BFL, XXXV.9f.1957/15ö.e, p. 102.

94 OSZK Kt, 1956-os Gy. Bp.NB.4491/74/1d/6.

95 BFL, XXXV.9f.1957/15ö.e, p. 102.

Department store, and leaflets were distributed from a black car. They shouted and told me that we were all on strike'.[96] The crowd destroyed the Soviet war memorial, and while its more radical wing turned on the local police station, a majority remained at the site of the war memorial and as a result of local activists addressing the crowd they chose a body of people to represent them and take over public administration. Thus, the crowd delegated a local 'revolutionary committee' through chaotic acclamation, rather than election as such.[97]

The dynamic of a strike in support of the Revolution, providing the spark for the creation of the working class crowd through demonstrations, was replicated in other industrial areas across the country. In Nagykanizsa, the work stoppage began in the Transdanubian Oil Mining Machinery Factory, where strikers called for support 'for Budapest University students', on the 'Russians to go home', 'the introduction of a multi-party system', 'the removal of Communist leaders and managers', 'withdrawal from the Warsaw Pact', and 'the removal of the Gerő government'.[98] Joined by workers from other workplaces and carrying national flags, the demonstrators removed the emblems of the people's republic from public buildings as they passed, converging on and demolishing the town's Soviet war memorial.[99] The 'election' of revolutionary organs was conducted under the same kind of chaotic circumstances as with the revolutionary committee in Újpest. Although the election of the revolutionary organ in Tatabánya was to be conducted by a meeting of representatives of the city's factories and mines, it was chosen in confused circumstances and effectively drew its legitimacy from the fact that it represented the crowd that had assembled in the city the previous day.[100]

---

96   OSZK Kt, 1956-os Gy., Bp.NB.4491/74/2d/6; Budapesti Rendőrfőkapitányság Politikai Nyomozó Osztály VI/7 csop. Jegyzőkönyv Bpest, 1957, június 24, Tóth Gábor gyanusitott kihallgatásáról, p. 2.

97   OSZK Kt, 1956-os Gy. Bp.NB. 4491/74/2d/6; Budapest Fővárosi Biróság Népbirósági Tanácsa NB.8017/1958/III. Jegyzőkönyv készült a szervezkedés és egyéb büncselekmények miatt Kósa Pál és 32 társa ellen inditott büntetőügyben a Budapesti Fővárosi Biróság Népbirósági Tanácsánál 1958 április 30-án megtartott zárt tárgyalásról, p. 4.

98   ZML, XXXII.15f.3d/B.695/1958; Zalamegyei ügyészség, Zalaegerszeg. B.10.050/1958/3.sz. Megyei Biróságnak, Zalaegerszeg. A népi demokratikus államrend megdöntésére irányuló szervezkedés büntette miatt Villányi József pilisszentlászlói lakos és társai ellen inditott bünügyben a keletkezett nyomozati iratokat a következő vádirat kiséretében teszem át, pp. 1–2.

99   'Éjszakai jelentések Kanizsáról', reprinted in Csomor and Kapiller, 1996, p. 56.

100 OSZK Kt, 1956-os Gy., Gy.NB.1127/1957/1d; Győr Sopronmegyei ügyészség, Győr, 1957 Bül. 372 sz. Vádirat népi demokratikus államrend megdöntésére irányuló szervezkedés büntette miatt dr. Klébert Márton és társai ellen inditott bünügyben, pp. 1–2.

The confusion in which revolutionary organs were created to oversee local public administration, and their problematic role given that their legitimacy was located in the revolutionary crowd, was replicated inside enterprises. As many striking workers left to take to the streets, new organs inside workplaces – workers' councils – were created. Their ambiguous position was generated not only by the chaos in which they were created – as shown by the example of the machine plant in Tatabánya's Coal Mining Trust – but also by the fact that they could be used by local Communist cells as part of an attempt to maintain control of their enterprises. The election in this plant took a disorganised form: 'they shouted out names, and the workers replied whether they agreed to their election or not. The first to be elected was L.I., the party-secretary, then me, then F., and then the others'.[101] The first workers' council in an enterprise – that of Újpest's United Lighting and Electrics Factory – was organised by the factory party committee, precisely with the intention of ensuring that 'trustworthy people would be elected'. This attempt was unsuccessful.[102] Before the revolution convulsed the whole country, the creation of workers' councils had been endorsed as a strategy by both the Party and the official trade unions as a means of controlling the economy in the circumstances of outright revolution.[103] In the Gheorgiu-Dej Shipyards, the plant's party organisation used its workers' council as cover to prevent local revolutionary activists empowered by the territorial revolutionary committee from gaining access to the site.[104]

Even among the workers' councils where the Party's attempts to influence the elections had foundered, and a coalition of skilled workers and engineers was able to take control, the councils were less radical than those elected on the streets – at least until the very end of October. In the forty-eight hours that followed the election of the United Electrics Workers' Council, it remade the institutions of the factory. The factory's managing director and one production director were removed; the managing director was replaced by the president of the workers' council. It announced that it saw itself as provisional, existing only until full elections could be held. It abolished the Personnel Department,

---

101 OSZK Kt, 412/VIIf.2d – Esztergom Megyei Bíróság – 429/1957 – Kovács Imre és társai; B.429/1957/5.sz. Jegyzőkönyv készült a népi demokratikus államrend megdöntésére irányuló szervezkedés büntette miatt Kovács Imre és társai ellen inditott bűnügyben az Esztergomi Megyei Bíróság Tatabányai bíróságánál, 1957 szeptemberi-hó 2 napján tartott zárt tárgyalásról, p. 3.
102 BFL, XXXV.9f.1957/1ö.e, p. 102.
103 Pittaway 1998, pp. 347–8.
104 PtSzL, Az 1956-os gyűjtemény (The 1956 Collection, hereafter IX.290f)37ö.e, p. 57.

which under Rákosi had been used as the representative of both the Party and the secret police within the management of the factory. It further announced that the strike would be maintained and full wages would be paid, while low-paid workers would be given a 15 percent wage rise and other workers a 10 percent raise. Moreover, it began the process of more fundamental reforms to factory administration, including administrative decentralisation and the elimination of bureaucracy, an overhaul of the payment-by-results wage system in the factory, and a call for the establishment of a 71 member general workers' council and the creation of shop workers' councils under it.[105] The skilled worker majority – whose thinking dominated the changes instituted by the workers' councils – made their philosophy and distrust of centralisation clear at a meeting of all the councils in Újpest on 29 October: 'the mistakes of recent years show that we have to build from below, we have to solve problems using our own strength'. Yet they also underlined their distrust of the radicalism of bodies like the territorial revolutionary committee in Újpest, which drew its legitimacy from the crowd: 'it seems that the power that has been paid in the blood of our young people is falling into the hands of different, fractious elements'.[106]

The skilled elite that dominated the early workers' councils built on the calls for factory democracy that preceded the Revolution, forcing radical transformation of management structures and working conditions. But politically they tended to be more moderate than much of the crowd; in the words of the newspaper of the workers' council of the Ganz Wagon and Machine Factory, 'with the help of Imre Nagy, we have already been able to start out on a road that will bring about the realisation of our other demands ... But ... we aren't going to demand the immediate implementation of demands for which time is needed'.[107] This stance, coupled with the knowledge that many Communists continued to participate in workers' councils, brought them into conflict with the revolutionary crowd and its delegated representatives. Distrust could deteriorate into conflict: on 29 October, an incorrect statement on national radio claiming that fifteen-hundred workers reported for work at the United Lighting and Electrics, provoked demonstrations against the workers' council, who were accused of sabotaging the Revolution, despite the fact that the workers' council stated clearly that it 'will not restart work, until Soviet troops leave the

---

105   For the deeds of the workers' council in its first three days of operation, see Cosic 1989, pp. 80–2; Lomax 1990, pp. 15–17.
106   PtSzL, IX.290f.39ö.e, pp. 1–2.
107   Quoted in Lomax 1990, p. 51.

country'.[108] The failure to pay wages to strikers at the neighbouring Duclós Mining Machinery plant brought about similar demonstrations at the factory gates,[109] provoking complaints from the more radical workers in the crowd that this was because there were many 'who did not represent the workers' interests' on the workers' council, leading to demands that it be purged of Communists.[110] The growing radicalisation of the crowd, and the consolidation of the authority of territorial revolutionary committees, restricted the room for manoeuvre of many of the workers' councils, especially those with weaker leadership. In Újpest, largely against the will of many of the workers' councils, especially that of the United Lighting and Electrics, the local revolutionary committee decided that all the districts' workers' councils were 'provisional', and that 'persons who had been functionaries could not be elected'.[111]

In many of the workers' councils the removal of former Communist functionaries provoked a marked radicalisation of their policies. In the Chinoin Pharmaceuticals Plant, the Újpest revolutionary committee succeeded in reconstituting the workers' council. The Revolution inside the factory was instantly radicalised, moving further politically than earlier workers' councils, by banning Communists from organising, but allowing the newly re-founded Smallholders' Party to set up a work-based cell and forcing the director to resign after he refused to renounce Communism.[112] Workers' councils set up at the end of October, and which were constituted in workplaces where the influence of skilled workers and a labour movement tradition was weaker, tended to be more radical from their foundation. At the Nagylengyel Oil Drilling Plant, a relatively new workplace and located in a rural area, the formation of the workers' council took a very different direction to that in Budapest. On 28 October, the local official union organisation attempted to call workers together to elect a workers' council – when the head of a factory-level union began his speech by addressing the assembled workers as 'Comrades!', he was

---

108   PtSzL, IX.290f.37ö.e, pp. 95, 107.
109   OSZK Kt, 1956-os Gy., Bp.NB.4491/74/3d/8; Budapesti Fővárosi Biróság Népbirósági Tanácsa, NB.II.8017/1958.sz. Jegyzőkönyv készült a szervezkedés és egyéb büncselekmények miatt Kósa Pál és 29 társa ellen inditott büntetőügyben a Budapesti Fővárosi Biróság Népbirósági Tanácsánál 1958 október 13-án megtartott zárt tárgyalásról, p. 11.
110   OSZK Kt, 1956-os Gy., Bp.NB.4491/74/2d/6; B.M. Budapesti Rendőrfőkapitányság Pol.Nyom. Oszt.Vizsg.Alosztálya. Jegyzőkönyv Sohonyai János gyanusított kihallgatásáról, Budapest, 1957 augusztus 15-én, p. 4.
111   OSZK Kt, 1956-os Gy., Bp.NB.4491/74/3d/5; B.M. Budapesti Rendőrfőkapitányság Pol.Nyom. Oszt.Vizsg.Alosztálya. Jegyzőkönyv, Budapest, 1957 június 10-én, p. 3.
112   PtSzL, IX.290f./52ö.e, pp. 5–20.

shouted down by workers who responded with 'Your time is up!' An anticommunist workers' council was elected as a result of the meeting, whose president proclaimed that 'the time of the Stalinists is over; we have to wipe them out'. The mass meeting sacked most of the management, and crucially those responsible for setting norms.[113]

While the democratic socialist vision of the urban, skilled elite that was implicit in the early workers' councils was eclipsed by the growing radicalism of crowds, and was largely absent in workplaces in which this group was less well-represented, worker-peasants instead focused on joining a rural revolution directed against agricultural collectivisation. Among Komló's miners, there were many who 'regularly went home for the weekend. So when the real Revolution came and the work was stopped, most of the people went home and did not return to Komló for several weeks'.[114] While long-distance commuters melted away, returning to their home villages, in areas where there was substantial commuting from villages to industrial establishments on a daily basis, the revolution in urban working class communities ignited revolution in rural areas. In the village of Várgesztes, on the fringes of the Tata coalfield, all but six of the 97 households had members working outside agriculture in 1956, almost all in mining. News of revolutionary events in neighbouring Oroszlány fed growing anger in the village, which in turn led to the overthrow of the local council and its replacement by a national committee elected by the crowd.[115] In rural areas, the largest local industrial enterprise and its worker-peasant workforce played a crucial role in spreading revolution to the villages. In Bázakerretye, after demonstrators destroyed the Soviet war memorial, worker-peasants commandeered the trucks owned by the local oil drilling plant and used them to spread the revolution to their home villages, where they proclaimed that 'there has already been a demonstration in Bázakerretye, it is time to burn the portraits of Stalin and Rákosi, and all red flags too'.[116]

---

113   ZML, XXXII.15f.2d/B.833/1957; A zalaegerszegi megyei biróság B.833/1957.6.sz. Jegyzőkönyv készült a népi demokratikus államrend megdöntésére irányuló szervezkedés és egyéb bűntette miatt Mecséri József ellen inditott bűnügyben a zalaegerszegi megyei biróságnál Zalaegerszegen 1958 január 14-én megtartott nyilvános tárgyalásról, pp. 1–6.
114   Columbia University Libraries, Rare Book and Manuscript Library, Bakhmeteff Archive (hereafter CUL RBML, BAR), Hungarian Refugees Project (hereafter CURPH), Box 16, Interview No. 524, pp. 5–6.
115   OSZK Kt, 412/VIIf.7d – Komárom Megyei Tanács, Titkárság; Várgesztes községi Tanács V.B. Az 1956 évi október 23-utáni események megörökitése, pp. 1–7.
116   ZML, XXXII.15f.2d/B.781/1957; Zalamegyei ügyészség, Zalaegerszeg. 1957 Bül.189.sz. Vádirat. a népi demokratikus államrend megdöntésére irányuló büntette miatt Papp Imre és társai ellen inditott bűnügyben, pp. 3–4.

In rural communities dominated by worker-peasants, issues of agricultural land ownership figured prominently, together with demands for Soviet withdrawal and anti-communism. Worker-peasants were as likely to join the anti-collectivisation revolt as were other village-dwellers: in the mining village of Vértesszöllős, next to Tatabánya, demonstrators demanded the break-up of the local collective farm and the return of land to its previous owners.[117] In Dömeföld, in the far south-west, the degree to which anger, even among rural dwellers, with jobs in industry or mining was directed against those responsible for implementing the regime's agrarian policies was underlined. The first acts of the worker-peasant revolutionaries were to break into the offices of the village council and burn the paperwork connected with the local collective and the taxation of local farmers.[118] In nearby Becsehely, worker-peasants joined with individual landholders in demonstrations against the local collective farm, demanding its dissolution and the distribution of its property, although they failed to achieve their goal in the face of resistance from the members of the collective.[119]

The Fragmentation of Resistance and the Dynamics of Post-Revolutionary Consolidation: November 1956–June 1958

During his trial for 'participation in a movement that aimed at the overthrow of the people's democratic order' in September 1957, Imre Kovács, who had led the anti-communist workers' council in the Tatabánya Mining Enterprise machine plant during the strike that followed Soviet intervention in November 1956, defended himself in part by denying his anti-Soviet stance. Yet he also did so by arguing that the demands of revolutionary bodies in Tatabánya he had supported had 'been largely met by the Kádár government' since the Revolution.[120] In making this rather strange defence, Kovács put his finger on

---

117   OSZK Kt, 412/VIIf.7d – Komárom Megyei Tanács, Titkárság; Vértesszöllős községi tanács V.B. 572/1957.sz. Tárgy: 1956 október 23 és azt követő ellenforradalmi cselekmény leírása, p. 1.
118   ZML, XXXII.15f.2d/B.1003/1957; A zalaegerszegi megyei biróság B.1003/1957-6.sz. A Népköztársaság nevében! A zalaegerszegi megyei biróság Zalaegerszegen, 1958 január 28 és 29 napján nem nyilvánosan megtartott tagyaláson meghozta a következő itéletet, p. 5.
119   ZML, XXXII.15f.2d/B.780/1957; A zalaegerszegi megyei biróság B.780/1957/6.sz. A Népköztársaság nevében! A zalaegerszegi megyei biróság Nagykanizsán, 1957 november 11-19-én nyilvánosan megtartott tagyalás alapján meghozta a következő itéletet, p. 7.
120   OSZK Kt, 412.VIIf.2d – Esztergom megyei biróság – 429/1957 – Kovács Imre és t·rsai B.429/1957/5 sz. Jegyzőkönyv készült a nép.d.áll.rend.megdönt.ir.mozg.való részv.btte miatt Kovács Imre és társai ellen inditott bűnügyben a Esztergomi megyei biróság Tatabányai biróságnál 1957 évi szeptember-hó 2 napján tartott zárt tárgyalásról, p. 3.

the split opinion held by many urban, and especially skilled, workers of the government the Red Army had brought to power: they felt, on the one hand, that many of their material aspirations were met, but they continued to be fearful and mistrustful of the regime that ruled them. In the Domestic Worsted Mill in the capital, most workers in June 1958 spoke of the poor economic situation 'before 1956', and the better one 'after 1956', arguing that 'the counter-revolution played a definite role in the improvement of the situation'.[121] The deep-seated distrust of the regime and perceptions of its illegitimacy were revealed in the working class reactions to the execution of Imre Nagy in the same month. In the Csepel Works, many compared it openly to the show trial conducted against László Rajk in 1949, and wondered how long it would take the Party to 'rehabilitate' him. Others argued that 'Imre Nagy died a freedom fighter', while some maintained that 'had the trial not been held in secret, then Imre Nagy's supporters would have hindered his execution'.[122]

Yet this split opinion did not emerge overnight with Soviet intervention, nor was it shared by all workers. Rather it emerged slowly over the course of the eighteen months that followed the arrival of Soviet tanks in many industrial communities in the days following their attack on Budapest on 4 November 1956. Their overthrow of Imre Nagy and the attempt to replace him with Kádár was initially met with the same kind of explosion of working class anger that had ignited the Revolution twelve days earlier. In Tatabánya's new town, as one local journalist recalled:

> there was a large telegraph pole with a loudspeaker, which carried the news from the miners' radio; one evening – Wednesday 7 November – they announced that the city's Soviet commander was speaking to the city's population. The crowd, with their bare hands brought down the pole, broke it completely, and smashed up the loudspeaker when it crashed to the ground.[123]

One other local miner spoke of the 'blind rage' that greeted Soviet intervention and fuelled the strike: 'Everyone was stunned that their independence, their neutrality was over', he remembered:

> the people were most happy about neutrality ... There was Austria as an example, because they were neutral. The Russians went, they became

---

121   MOL M-KS-288f.21/1958/22ö.e, p. 241.
122   BFL, XXXV.1f.1958/46ö.e. p. 44.
123   1956-os Intézet, OHA 484, p. 44.

neutral, and their living standards just went up . . . Because of that neutrality was very important.[124]

The motivations of working class crowds were complex, but behind the political demands lay deep-seated fury at the material poverty experienced by many workers under Rákosi. The role of penury in fuelling political protest presented the regime with both a problem and an opportunity. It offered the difficulty that without addressing material grievances successfully it would be unable to consolidate its authority. But it also offered them the possibility that if they succeeded in offering material improvement, combined with selective repression, they could encourage enough of the working class to forget their political demands and aspirations, and accommodate themselves to the situation. Yet workers were also far from united about the extent to which they adapted to or, indeed, resisted the new regime.

Armed resistance on the streets, in which working class youth were overrepresented, was effectively quashed within days of the Soviet intervention. The armed guerrilla groups in the capital continued to resist before they were overwhelmed by superior Soviet firepower on 8 November.[125] In Csepel, armed resistance lasted for a further three days, falling to the Soviets on 11 November.[126] It is difficult to estimate the total casualties of the street fighting: official statistics that almost certainly underestimate the number of casualties give an indication. They show that in Budapest some sixteen thousand seven hundred were injured and 2,502 were killed. Of those who were killed a majority were under thirty years old and industrial workers.[127] In the provinces, resistance was more sporadic. In Tatabánya, news of the Soviet intervention was greeted with anger, although many believed that armed resistance would be futile and the revolutionary bodies resisted calls to arm angry youths with petrol bombs to stop the advance into the town.[128] In Sztálinváros, this was not the case. As news of the Soviet intervention spread, 'at least eighty percent of the male residents' prepared to fight Soviet tanks with petrol bombs. Aware of the preparations being made, the Soviets held back until 7 November, attacking the

---

124   1956-os Intézet, OHA 449, p. 21.
125   Eörsi 1993, 1997 and 2001.
126   Drucker 1965, pp. 476–7.
127   Hegedüs 1996, pp. 303–5.
128   OSZK Kt, 1956-os Gy, Gy.NB.1127/1957/2d; B.M. Komárom megyei Rendőrfőkapitányság Politikai Osztály, Vizsgálati Alosztály, Jegyzőkönyv, dr. Klebert Márton kihallgatásáról, Tatabánya, 1957 augusztus 3, pp. 2–3.

town initially by air and then by land. In the ensuing battle, eight were killed and thirty-five wounded before the town was overrun.[129]

In the factories, the immediate reaction to the news of the Soviet intervention was one of furious shock. The result was an immediate and solid strike against the new government and its Soviet patrons. In the capital, this strike remained solid for up to a week. In the United Lighting and Electrics Factory, the moderate workers' council backed the strike, refusing workers entry into the factory until 12 November. Even then work was unable to start due to reduced electricity supplies, while the workforce remained deeply distrustful and fearful.[130] More generally, in Újpest, 'a mood behind the strike' remained,[131] while the radical territorial Revolutionary Committee struggled to master a situation over which, following the Soviet intervention, they had no real control. With the drift back to work, they attempted to seize the initiative. Renaming themselves the Újpest Revolutionary Workers' Council they threw down a challenge to the Kádár government, proclaiming: 'every worker in Budapest wants to see order in the capital. Of course we do not wish to see any sort of order, but revolutionary order, one which is based on the realisation of the demands of the Revolution'. In order to achieve this aim, they invited representatives of all factories in the capital to Újpest's town hall in order to found a Budapest workers' council.[132]

In response to the move, the Kádár government and its Soviet allies adopted a two-track strategy. They issued a decree allowing the workers to elect legal Workers' Councils within three weeks of returning to work.[133] At the same time, they attempted to prevent the Újpest meeting from taking place. Soviet tanks surrounded the town hall and the members of the Újpest Revolutionary Workers' Council were arrested.[134] The meeting was postponed and held the next day under the auspices of the more moderate United Lighting and Electrics Workers' Council, which established the Budapest Central Workers' Council. The new council was split between relative moderates, who argued for a political compromise with the Kádár regime, and members of anti-communist workers' councils, who demanded that the Soviet-imposed

---

129 FML, Az MSZMP Dunaújvárosi Bizottságának iratai (Papers of the Dunaújváros City Committee of the Hungarian Socialist Workers' Party, hereafter XXXV.22f)1957/4a/ö.e, p. 41.
130 PtSzL, IX.290f/38ö.e, pp. 10–12.
131 BFL, XXXV.9f.1957/15ö.e, p. 104.
132 PtSzL, IX.290f/31ö.e, p. 5.
133 Lomax 1990, p. 97.
134 Rainer 1990, p. 107.

government not be recognised. The workers' representatives were much more militant, and it was one of them, Sándor Báli, from the Workers' Council of the Standard factory, who gave the new body a clear strategy: to refrain from recognising the Kádár government, but to negotiate with it.[135] The new council called for the introduction of a multi-party system, the withdrawal of Soviet troops from Hungary, and greater democracy in the Hungarian workplace. It negotiated with the government, although relations between the Workers' Council and the state were tense, and by the beginning of December an agreement seemed to be highly unlikely. Furthermore, it continued to be dogged by splits between moderates and radical anti-communists over strategy and tactics.[136]

At the same time that it became clear there was no basis for agreement between the council and the government, the body was becoming a *de facto* national workers' council and, thus, a focus of opposition to the Kádár government.[137] Taking these factors into consideration, Kádár shifted from a policy of negotiation to one of repression. On 5 December, some two hundred activists in the workers' council movement and the former intellectual opposition were arrested. This combined with the active prevention of plans to call a meeting to found a National Workers' Council, and growing government intransigence, led to a series of stand-offs between the Budapest Central Workers' Council and the state. The Council called for a two-day general strike on the 11th and 12th of December, which was immediately outlawed. Its members were gradually arrested over the next few days, and by the morning of the 11th, with the arrest of the two leaders of the council – Sándor Rácz and Sándor Báli – the government succeeded in effectively eliminating its most dangerous adversary.[138] Following the removal of the Greater Budapest Central Workers' Council, state policy moved to one of explicit repression. Fear of retribution created a situation in which factory-level workers' councils refused to heed the strike call on 11 December, although many in the workforce did. Arrests of workers' council members continued throughout December.[139] On 13 December, the government banned strikes and demonstrations – a position that was

---

135 PtSzL, IX.290f/31ö.e, pp. 5–8; Nagy 1980, pp. 165–81; Lomax and Kemény 1986, pp. 160–89, 217–39.
136 BFL, XXXV.1f.1957/29ö.e, pp. 24–26; PtSzL, IX.290f/31ö.e, pp. 138–43.
137 PtSzL, IX.290f/31ö.e, pp. 172–84.
138 For the final elimination of the Greater Budapest Central Workers' Council, see Lomax 1976, pp. 165–9; BFL, XXXV.1f.1957/29ö.e, pp. 24–85.
139 Kajári 1996, pp. 383–4, 415, 432, 467, 478–9, 505; MOL M-KS-288f.25/1957/7ö.e, p. 135.

to be strengthened in January 1957 when the government decreed that striking or incitement to strike be made a capital offence.[140]

Yet Kádár's turn to repression was informed by a knowledge that by early December industrial workers were becoming ever more weary of strike action, in part because they came to see the eventual victory of Kádár as inevitable, but more so because of the effect of the collapsing economy on their incomes and the food supply situation. The Budapest party-committee noted that 'in the first half of November, at a decision of the Workers' Council, without any sign of resistance the factories would stop', yet 'by the second half of November they [the Workers' Councils] tried to find better justifications for work stoppages: wage demands, solidarity, strike', yet even at this stage 'the desire to work is growing'.[141] On the first day of the 48-hour general strike – 11 December – in Újpest, in most of the factories no work was done. In the Magyar Pamutipar cotton factory, however, work began as normal on the morning shift, and workers walked out only when news arrived of the arrests of the leaders of the Greater Budapest Central Workers' Council. Despite this, on 13 December the Workers' Council in the plant vowed that it would restart production and take greater care over the maintenance of work discipline. By this point, however, it was not merely a recognition of the defeat of the Revolution, or growing fear of police retribution, that was deterring workers from resorting to the strike weapon; it was also the growing fear of unemployment given the crisis-ridden state of the economy and the lack of strike pay.[142]

Despite the gradual breaking of the strike, and the elimination of revolutionary organs in cities and villages alike, the situation in industrial communities remained tense well into 1957. Many younger workers had fled the country, while worker-peasants remained in their villages for months afterwards. Among urban and skilled workers, a culture of protest simmered. During the early part of the year, anti-regime leaflets were still being circulated throughout the United Lighting and Electrics factory. One leaflet stated that 'Kádár still keeps the Rákosite Antal Apró, out with the swindler Marosán, bring Imre Nagy into the government, out with the Soviet Army, declare Hungarian neutrality, why is the Kádár government scared of arming the peasants and workers? Perhaps they are fascists'.[143] On the national holiday of 15 March,

---

140 FML, XXXV.19f.1957/14ö.e, p. 2; MOL M-KS-288f.25/1957/7ö.e, p. 75; MOL M-KS-288f.25/1957/8ö.e, p. 152; Lomax 1976, pp. 168–9.
141 BFL, XXXV.1f.1957/42ö.e, p. 121.
142 BFL, XXXV.1f.1956–7/41ö.e, pp. 23, 160, 170.
143 BFL, XXXV.1f.1957/43ö.e, pp. 16–17.

anti-government leaflets circulated in the Stalin Steel Works.[144] On the first anniversary of the outbreak of the Revolution, 23 October 1957, rumours – such as 'they are striking in Csepel', or 'in Újpest there were demonstrations' – were widespread.[145] In the United Lighting and Electrics factory, some of the workers engaged in a deliberate act of sabotage to commemorate the Revolution by destroying the electrical box that supplied power to light the red star on the front of the building, thus ensuring that during the week following the 23 October, the red star did not light up.[146]

Yet during the first half of 1957, urban workers significantly underlined their distrust of the government through support for cultural practices and institutions associated with anti-communism, even though they had not done so in the Rákosi years. One of the concrete manifestations of this was the growth of popular religious observance following the suppression of the Revolution. In the capital, in 1957 the population was considerably more assertive about its perceived right to celebrate Christmas than it had been in previous years. For midnight mass and for the Christmas Day services, the churches in many 'working class' districts of the capital were full; according to one party official, 'there hasn't been such attendance [at church] for years'.[147] In contrast to the pre-Revolution years when church congregations in the capital had consisted of elderly women, during Christmas 1957, in one industrial district twenty-five to thirty percent of the congregations were aged between eighteen and twenty. In another similar district, some sixty percent of those attending the Christmas morning service were male manual workers. During 1958, it was noticed that a significant minority of manual workers in one district spent ten minutes in their local church before and after work each day. Furthermore, in schools in the same districts, 38 percent of parents of children from worker households opted for religious education.[148]

This was combined with a retreat from the public realm entirely, which was especially marked among the young, as well as worker-peasants. Alienation from official political activity could be seen among younger workers who tended to develop more individualistic and exclusively material aspirations. One young female commuter, who worked in the Zalaegerszeg Clothing

---

144 FML, Az MSZMP Fejér megyei bizottságának iratai (Papers of the Fejér County Committee of the Hungarian Socialist Workers' Party, hereafter XXXV.9f)/1957/14ö.e; B.M. Fejér megyei Rendőrfőkapitányság Politikai Nyomozó Osztálya, p. 2.
145 BFL, XXXV.1f.1957/45ö.e, p. 243.
146 BFL, XXXV.1f.1957/46ö.e, p. 46.
147 BFL, XXXV.1f.1958/41ö.e, pp. 28–9.
148 BFL, XXXV.1f.1958/134ö.e, p. 372.

Factory, illustrated the attitudes of this group. She was described as 'exhibiting passivity' as far as political questions were concerned, and refused to participate in any political organisation established in the factory. Her sole ambition was reportedly to become a skilled worker.[149] These attitudes fed through to the newer skilled workers. Another party brigade that spoke to three newly-trained skilled workers in 1958 found them uninterested in and uninformed about politics. In many cases, interest in material things was strong.[150] Furthermore, another symptom of withdrawal from the public realm after 1956 that was particularly pronounced among male workers was the increase in the already high number of alcoholics and alcohol-related domestic violence.[151]

In this climate dominated by withdrawal and distrust of the government, the Kádár government offered tangible material improvements that met working class hunger for better economic circumstances for their own households – something that had provoked the anger that stimulated working-class mobilisation during the Revolution. By the end of 1957, as a result of wage increases, the average income of a working family in Budapest was 18 percent higher than it had been a year previously.[152] In Újpest, in 1958 there was much greater satisfaction with wage rates than there had been several years earlier, although workers still felt that not all problems with wages had been resolved.[153] In the Zalaegerszeg Clothing Factory, Kádár's policies had a similar effect: in 1952 the average wage of workers in the factory had stood at 703 Forints per month; by 1957 the average wage level had risen to 1,147 Forints per month. The problems of the wage system for the workers on the production line changed little. While the intensity of work was reduced and the supply of raw material improved, as wages were raised many of the problems of the wage systems remained.[154] The visible improvements in living standards had led to the development of a degree of trust between the government and industrial workers by early 1958 in Budapest, as in other working class areas.[155]

---

149   ZML, XXXV.1f.1958/12 ö.e; A tapasztalatok összefoglalása, p. 12.
150   ZML, XXXV.1f.1958/12 ö.e; Feljegyzés a Zalaegerszegi Ruhagyár pártszervezetének agitációs munkájáról, pp. 5–6.
151   BFL, XXXV.1f.1958/134ö.e, p. 29.
152   MOL M-KS-288f.23/1957/34ö.e, p. 34.
153   MOL M-KS-288f.21/1958/20ö.e, pp. 252–3.
154   ZML, XXXV.1f.1958/12 ö.e; Feljegyzés a Zalaegerszegi Ruhagyár pártszervezetének agitációs munkájáról, pp. 25–6.
155   BFL, XXXV.1f.1958/42ö.e, pp. 49–52.

Conclusion

It would be a mistake to overestimate this degree of trust, however. The memory of the 1956 Revolution was never far below the surface in 1958. Many workers attributed their improved financial situation in large part to the 1956 Revolution. Furthermore, workers remained somewhat distrustful, and were uncertain as to what extent the increases in living standards were a temporary phase before the wage increases were withdrawn and the state reverted to Stalinism. In Újpest, 'the influence of old, bad experiences still has a big impact on people, fluctuations in earnings, even the slightest falls in wages that are pretty frequent cause disquiet, discontent and distrust among the workers'.[156] The reconstruction of socialism after 1956, and its limits in Hungary's industrial communities, bore the imprint of both socialism's decay and its outright collapse in those areas before and during the 1956 Revolution. While in the short- and medium-term this reconstruction paved the way for the consolidation of socialist rule in Hungary, its ambiguous nature would come back to haunt the regime during its eventual and final collapse in the 1980s.

---

156   MOL M-KS-288f.21/1958/20ö.e, p. 250.

CHAPTER 7

Accommodation and the Limits of Economic Reform: Industrial Workers during the Making and Unmaking of Kádár's Hungary

Introduction

During the late 1960s, Hungary embarked on a process of economic reform that profoundly changed the nature of the country's economic model. Hungary's New Economic Mechanism (NEM), as the reform was known, emerged out of the long-term discussion of the country's economists and growing concern within the party leadership over poor export performance and the inefficient operation of much state-owned industry during the mid-1960s.[1] Decided upon in 1966 and implemented in 1968, the NEM confronted these problems by dismantling the apparatus of centralised economic planning, and replacing it with indirect state control over more autonomous state enterprises, which were instructed to maximise their profits. Indirect control was established through state setting of prices and the taxation of enterprises, which were shielded from the impact of the world market by administratively determined prices and the maintenance of the state monopoly over foreign trade.[2] The semi-planned, quasi-market nature of the economic system established in 1968 existed to provide an improvement in economic performance that could maintain the social settlement that had allowed the Kádár regime to consolidate its authority in the aftermath of the 1956 Revolution. Its implementation, however, directly challenged many aspects of that social settlement, especially insofar as the skilled, male, urban elite of the working class were concerned. This challenge, the opposition it revealed, and the way it came to be politically articulated, reveal a great deal about the nature of that social settlement, particularly in relation to patterns of working class accommodation and opposition, and the nature of late socialism in Hungary.

---

* Originally published in Mark Pittaway 2005, 'Accommodation and the Limits of Economic Reform: Industrial Workers during the Making and Unmaking of Kádár's Hungary', in *Arbeiter im Staatsozialismus, Ideologischer Anspruch und Soziale Wirklichkeit*, edited by P. Hübner, C. Kleßmann and K. Tenfelde, Köln: Böhlau Verlag, pp. 453–71.
1 Földes 1995, pp. 39–43.
2 For the best summary of the NEM, see Swain 1992, pp. 99–107.

The introduction of the reform was met with a wave of working class protest. The most common form this took was that of labour mobility, as workers made use of the liberalisation of the rules on changing jobs introduced in the 1967 Labour Code to seek higher earnings.[3] Behind the increasing willingness of workers to take up and leave lay deep-seated grievances, as many felt that their status was being eroded by economic reform. Some felt alienated by what they saw as a 'new managerialism' in industry, marked by high premium payments to managers in spring 1969, and rationalisation campaigns in the workplace. According to party-investigators, many workers 'spoke of the leading role of intelligentsia, and some said that management are a "new class"'.[4] In the consumerist climate of the late 1960s, many complained that 'the price of consumer goods can only be paid through overtime, the income earned from a second job or another source'.[5] Much of this discontent took the form of urban working class jealousy over the rural population, who were believed to have access to supplementary incomes not open to their counterparts in the towns. One working class correspondent to the party newspaper complained that 'a family in an agricultural producer cooperative can get together enough money in two or three years to build a very nice house from their own resources. The factory worker, however, can only build if they take on a loan for the rest of their life'.[6]

The history of this discontent has been overshadowed by its widespread political uses during the early 1970s by the managers of large industrial companies and those in the party apparatus who opposed economic reform. As elements of the change of 1968, particularly those that impacted on the labour market, were reversed, further changes were put on ice, and the state moved to curb what it saw as the growth of 'capitalist elements' within the economy, while officials justified such shifts with reference to the presumed need to ensure that 'the core of the workforce of each factory receives better moral and material rewards'.[7] The political uses of working class discontent by factions of

---

3 Fazekas and Köllő 1990, p. 98.
4 'Az MSZMP Központi Bizottsága Politikai Bizottságának Állásfoglalása a Munkásosztály helyzetéről szóló 1958-as KB-határozat végrehajtásáról, a Munkásosztály jelenlegi helyzetéről, 1970 január 10', in Vass 1974, p. 462.
5 Magyar Országos Levéltár (Hungarian National Archive, hereafter MOL) M-KS-288f.21/1969/27ö.e, p. 115.
6 MOL M-KS-288f.21/1969/29ö.e, p. 288.
7 'Közlemény az MSZMP Központi Bizottságának üléséről. 1969. November 26–28', in Vass 1974, p. 448.

the apparatus during the early 1970s have led some to deny, or at least underplay, the existence of this discontent. Instead, it has been argued that it instead constituted little more than 'a politics of complaint' instituted by officials in the trade union and those sections of the Party opposed to reform, designed to ensure the maintenance of ideological orthodoxy in the economic sphere.[8]

While it is impossible to deny the political uses of working class protest by opponents of economic reform, it was not invented by them. The story of the source of worker discontent at the turn of the 1970s, why it was able to have such political impact, and the consequence of the failure of opponents of reform to address the roots of discontent, tells us much about the nature of the relationship between workers and state socialism in post-war Hungary. It also tells us a great deal about the social relationships that allowed socialist rule to be successfully consolidated during the rule of János Kádár, after the disasters of Stalinism and the 1956 Revolution, which all but brought the regime to total collapse. There is a growing body of literature on the nature of socialist rule in Hungary under Kádár, which has highlighted several distinctive features. After 1956, ideological conformity was reasserted as the regime consolidated a political system and set of institutional arrangements that, at the formal level at least, conformed to those that existed elsewhere in the Soviet bloc. Behind this relatively conservative façade, Kádár pursued a politics of social conciliation, which involved considerable informal negotiation at the local level and, in fact, quietly remade the institutions of the state, insofar as they had an impact on daily life. The sharp contradiction between the regime's formal adherence to the institutions of Soviet-type socialism and its local practice of seeking informal compromise was frequently bridged by a political strategy that stressed pragmatism and expertise, and it sought legitimacy by promising and delivering material improvement.[9]

This chapter sets the working class discontent that surrounded the economic reform of 1968 in its context by arguing that it was a product of the dynamics of Kádárist rule, insofar as it impacted on the industrial working class. The regime's political consolidation after 1956 relied on it being able to cast itself as the authentic representative of the working class. In order to do this, it had to construct a social settlement in the factories over the course of the 1960s that accepted a range of informal practices and hierarchies that had emerged during the industrialisation drives of the 1950s. This settlement rhetorically and materially privileged the urban, male, skilled core of the working

---

8   Soós 1988, pp. 89–110; Pető 2001, pp. 18–19.
9   For a sample of the developing literature on the Kádár era and its nature, see Földes 1989; Huszár 2002 and 2003; Rainer 2003; Varga 2001.

class. At the same time, however, it pursued a strategy of increasing living standards through the promotion of socialist consumerism, which it combined with a variety of informal settlements at the local level that increased social differentiation through the creation of a large informal economy to satisfy consumer demand. Workers had to participate in this informal economy to significantly raise their living standards. The spread of an informal economy was interpreted by the skilled urban core as an erosion of their position, just as the regime asserted rhetorically their centrality to socialist society. Economic reform brought the tensions generated by this contradiction to a head, producing a wave of protest among the skilled core of the working class. Because of the importance of its social settlement with this group to preserving the notions that the regime ruled in the interests of the working class, this discontent was effectively blamed on the economic reform and was used to stall the latter. The reversal of reform did not reverse the spread of the informal economy, instead generating a slow eclipse of the bargain between the Kádár regime and the skilled core of the working class that paved the way for the end of socialism in the 1980s.

Shaping the Social Settlement in the Workplace, 1956–65

The events of the 1956 Revolution revealed the depth of discontent among the working class with the socialist regime. The days that followed the outbreak of the Revolution on 23 October were marked by considerable working class mobilisation. The formation of workers' councils in the factories was testament to this mobilisation. Working class youth provided the demonstrators and the members of fighting groups, which effectively turned the demonstrations into a full-blown Revolution.[10] For as much as a year after Soviet intervention in November 1956, which restored the socialist regime – installing János Kádár as leader of the Party and the country – working class resistance remained considerable.[11] While industrial peace was bought with a combination of the carrot of substantial increases in wages and social benefits, and the stick of repression, as far as many functionaries in the post-1956 ruling Party (the MSZMP) were concerned, there was a worrying gap between the regime

---

10   Pittaway 2001.
11   MOL M-Bp.-1f.1957/43ö.e, pp. 16–17; Fejér Megyei Levéltár (Fejér County Archive, hereafter FML) MSZMP FMBA ir.9f.1957/14ö.e: *B.M. Fejérmegyei Rendőrfőkapitányság Politikai Nyomozó osztálya*, p. 2; Kenedi, 1996, pp. 9–68; MOL M-Bp.-1f.1957/45ö.e, p. 243. On the general picture, see MOL M-Bp.-1f.1957/45ö.e, pp. 264–8; MOL M-Bp.-1f.1957/46ö.e, p. 46.

and the industrial working class that constituted its supposed constituency. Statistics on the social composition of the party membership compiled in December 1957 revealed that while 60.8 percent were of 'working class origin', only 29.2 percent were employed as factory workers – a proportion lower than that found in the ruling Party of the Stalinist era (the MDP) on the eve of October 1956.[12] The tenuous relationship between the regime and working class was directly addressed by a survey conducted by functionaries in summer 1958 whose aim was 'to gain a realistic picture of the political, economic and cultural situation of the working class'.[13] The materials collected as part of the survey revealed a regime and a body of functionaries deeply concerned about both the implications of socialist industrialisation for the culture of the working class, and the long-term stability of the regime.

Socialist industrialisation had been initiated during the early 1950s, heralded by a process of transforming production-relations in the country's factories, mines, and on its construction sites. Systems of remuneration had been tied closely to individualised plan targets, while labour competition had been used to drive workers to constantly increase their productivity. The wage cuts brought about by the implementation of these policies were deeply unpopular, while the regime's revolution in production foundered on the chaos wrought by the bottlenecks and shortages generated by an over-ambitious industrialisation drive that in turn forced management to informally negotiate production with the most skilled sections of the workforce. The workforce expanded, but 'new' workers – recruited from the ranks of women, youth or the rural poor – entered socialist industrial production on the periphery of informal networks that privileged the older, urban, skilled core of the working class, allowing presocialist hierarchies to reproduce themselves under socialist conditions.[14] Despite their relative privileges in production, the skilled elite was deeply discontented with the results of the socialist transformation of workplaces – as one skilled worker in the machine industry recalled, 'psychologically the situation was ... that they were happy if they could harm the Communist system'.[15]

It was this discontent that underpinned the extensive participation of older core workers in the workers' councils that sprung up across the country during the 1956 Revolution and which stubbornly opposed the consolidation of the Kádár regime.[16] Consequently, when party functionaries collected materials

12   Szenes 1976, p. 195.
13   MOL M-KS-288f.21/1958/19ö.e, p. 4.
14   See Pittaway, chapter 3 and 4 of this volume, and 2003, pp. 71–82.
15   Open Society Archives (OSA) RFE Magyar Gy.6/Item No. 08794/53, p. 1.
16   Bondy 1990, p. 523.

for their survey of the working class in 1958, they concentrated on the complaints of the skilled, older, urban elite. In the capital, they zeroed in on the complaint that traditionally skilled groups had lost out as a consequence of the revolution in production in the early 1950s. This was felt to have destroyed the relationship between the regime and the workers. For the party secretary of the industrial district of Kőbánya, 'one part of the workforce does not agree with us. It does not accept this system'. This group consisted of 'toolmakers, turners etc.' who had lost their prestige and high wages. Consequently, they took an openly anti-regime stand.[17] In the coalmines of Esztergom-Komárom county, the party-investigators picked out the complaint of older, skilled coal hewers that 'wage categories do not differentiate between older experienced workers and young skilled workers'.[18] In Újpest, the functionaries noted that while many older workers constituted a solid base for the regime given their memories of the interwar years, they bitterly complained at 'the lack of respect for skilled workers'.[19]

In addition to concern with the political consequences of the apparent erosion of the status of the skilled elite, those responsible for the survey identified another central and related process that worried them. The final report of the survey argued:

> as a consequence of forced industrialisation the working class has been considerably diluted. The increase in the workforce has been at the expense of agriculture, furthermore it has come from the urban middle classes, and finally in smaller measure from the former ruling class. The consequence of the dilution of the working class has been a strengthening among it of a petty-bourgeois mentality.[20]

Enterprises produced a mass of statistical evidence to support arguments put forward about the 'dilution' of the working class. In the Tatabánya mines, for example, 39.4 percent of coal hewers employed in 1957 had begun work between 1947 and 1954, outnumbering those with over ten years' experience.[21]

The concentration on policies aimed at countering the apparent 'dilution' of the working class and protecting the skilled urban elite shaped an institutional space, which strengthened those informal compromises that had grown

---

17 MOL M-KS-288f.21/1958/19ö.e, p. 301.
18 MOL M-KS-288f.21/1958/20ö.e. p. 179.
19 Ibid., p. 253.
20 MOL M-KS-288f.5/96ö.e, p. 2.
21 MOL XXIX-F-107-m/54d.

in workplaces and had allowed traditional hierarchies to reproduce themselves. In the climate created after 1958, the male, skilled, urban elite asserted their position at the apex of the hierarchies that underpinned working class culture in the face of continued expansion of the industrial workforce. Between 1960 and 1970, the total numbers employed in industry rose from 1,347,945 to 1,835,556; those in construction increased from 289,056 to 370,044.[22] This expansion had come 'from the ranks of the peasantry, in a large part from working women previously in the household and to a lesser extent from the urban petty-bourgeoisie'.[23] The completion of agricultural collectivisation at the beginning of the decade had created huge demand, particularly among rural women, for industrial work, while the expansion of industry had generated a shortage of male labour.[24] Increasingly, these positions were filled by rural-dwellers: by the end of the 1960s, 19.2 percent of all skilled workers, 45 percent of the semi-skilled, and 58.3 percent of the unskilled, had begun their working lives performing manual labour in agriculture.[25] Members of the skilled male elite greeted what many party officials regarded as further 'dilution' of the working class by asserting their superiority as workers over the new recruits to the labour force. As the country's oil fields expanded to include the east of the country during the 1960s, many of the older skilled workers – trained prior to 1948 – continued to draw a cultural contrast between their 'discipline' and the 'laxness' of many of the new or recently recruited workers.[26]

The party leadership also remained concerned about the consequences of the changing nature of the industrial workforce. By 1970, they had conceded that 'they had not sufficiently taken into account the stratification of the working class'.[27] The sympathy of party and union functionaries in the factories for the values of the skilled elite had generated a space for the further reproduction of hierarchy under conditions in which the workforce had greatly expanded. For all the social change that occurred during the 1960s, the mechanisms by which hierarchy had been reproduced bore traces of striking continuities with the 1950s, even though after 1956 these mechanisms were underpinned and not challenged by party officials concerned over the impact

---

22 *1970 évi népszámlalási adatok. Foglalkozási adatok I* 1973, p. 20.
23 'Az MSZMP Központi Bizottsága Politikai Bizottságának Állásfoglalása . . .', in Vass 1974, p. 462.
24 Fazekas and Köllő 1990, p. 95.
25 Kemény 1990, p. 12.
26 Mocsár 1970, p. 213.
27 'Az MSZMP Központi Bizottság Politikai Bizottságának Állásfoglalása . . .', in Vass 1974, p. 462.

of the 'dilution' of the working class. A study of the automated assembly line in the Csepel Motorcycle factory, conducted at the beginning of the 1970s, revealed stark continuities with the early socialist factory regime established twenty years earlier. Despite the improvements in the economy, shortages of tools and parts hindered continuous production on the assembly line. While the assembly line had been designed to be serviced by semi-skilled workers, in reality the workforce along it was sharply bifurcated. The semi-skilled majority were alienated and low-paid. Consequently, their work was of low quality. A skilled minority kept production moving by employing superior skill and experience, informally bargaining with lower management for greater remuneration achieved through overtime payments.[28]

In the face of the advance of mechanisation during the 1960s, skilled workers through informal compromises on the shop floor, encouraged both by the operation of the economy and by a climate created by party officials anxious to protect their working class, had largely preserved their position in production. This ensured that in 1972 some 71.5 percent of skilled workers were classified as performing handicraft work, rather than that dictated by the pace of a machine.[29] Informal compromises not only represented a formidable constraint to management attempts to subordinate the skilled male elite to their rationalisation drives, but also allowed them to maintain their position at the apex of a hierarchy which was qualitatively similar to that which had existed fifteen years earlier. That hierarchy reflected divisions of gender, generation and social origin. Across the country as a whole in the mid-1960s, 58 percent of those who worked in skilled positions came from the ranks of the industrial working class, while only 36 percent came from agricultural backgrounds. Some sixty percent of the semi-skilled and 68 percent of the unskilled came from rural families.[30] The highest paid skilled positions were monopolised by the urban elite; in the Csepel works in 1969, on the southern fringes of the capital, only 10.6 percent of tool-makers and 18.3 percent of turners came from agrarian backgrounds. For the less well paid, workers of rural origin were better represented, making up, for example, 42.4 percent of crane drivers.[31]

Outside the capital, the impact of the expansion of the working class under the impact of the industrialisation of the 1960s was made clear by the fact that the majority of workers belonged to a rural dwelling periphery. In Borsod-Abaúj-Zemplén county, dominated by heavy industry, 57.2 percent of

---

28   Kemény 1990, pp. 29–73.
29   Benedek 1973.
30   Mód, Ferge, Láng and Kemény 1966, pp. 103, 360–6.
31   Kemény and Kozák 1971a, p. 23.

industrial workers lived in villages in 1970.[32] Of the two hundred and twenty thousand workers who, at the end of the 1960s, lived in Pest county, which surrounded Budapest, one hundred and thirty thousand travelled into the capital to work each day.[33] Hierarchies based on social origin were not the only ones to influence the stratification and culture of the working class. Hierarchies based on generation had not been eroded since the mid-1950s, despite action by the state to increase the wages of those training for skilled work and to create programmes for training 'new' workers. A sociological survey conducted in the early 1970s revealed a pattern of power relations almost identical to that which had existed two decades earlier: '[f]or as long as young workers are in their probationary period, in general they have a guaranteed wage and perform low category work. Later, however, when they become independent, they [the foremen] don't give them complex and better paid work'.[34] Hierarchies based on gender were marked by similar continuities; women had failed to break into male, skilled occupations in heavy-industrial sectors, and remained concentrated in sectors such as textiles where they made up 70.8 percent of the workforce in 1964.[35] Women earned significantly less than men working in the same position in a similar sector throughout the 1960s. This contributed to a national situation in which the average wage of male skilled workers in 1964 was 2,140 Forints per month, while for female skilled workers the figure was only 1,579 Forints. Male semi-skilled workers earned 1,844 Forints per month, while women earned only 1,367 Forints.[36]

The Workplace Politics of Getting and Spending: Socialist Consumerism and the Privatisation of the Working Class

The roots of the explosion of working class discontent that occurred at the end of the 1960s lie in the social consequences of another central plank of Kádár's consolidation. These were the policies of increasing living standards and promoting a socialist consumerism. Throughout the 1960s, working class real incomes rose at a steady rate – albeit at a lower rate than the eight percent per annum by which they rose between 1956 and the end of the decade.[37] Within

---

32 Lehoczky 1974, p. 8.
33 Kemény and Kozák 1971b, p. 21.
34 Balogh and Gál 1973, p. 167.
35 Turgonyi and Ferge 1973, p. 74.
36 Turgonyi and Ferge 1969, p. 42.
37 Monigl 1982, p. 152.

its living standards policy, the regime protected the incomes of those they saw as the 'core' segments of the working class, privileging those who worked in traditional heavy-industrial sectors that contained most of the skilled elite of the working class. While wages in mining, the most privileged of industrial sectors, had been 129.7 percent of the industrial average in 1955, these had risen to 140.3 percent ten years later. Wages in electrical goods production, steel-making and machine manufacture were set above the industrial average throughout the 1960s; those in chemicals, light industry and food processing, where the workforces conformed less to the regime's vision of an urban, male working class lagged behind that average.[38] The preferential position of what the regime perceived to be the 'core' of the working class was bolstered by the increases through the decade in social benefits, which were often explicitly tied to work in the socialist sector and key industrial sectors.[39]

The beginnings of mass house building programmes to address shocking housing shortage in industrial areas during the late 1950s and early 1960s, as well as the state's moves from the late 1950s to encourage a 'socialist consumerism' in the country, had an uneven impact on core working class communities. This was underlined by a 1962 survey of ownership of consumer goods in two very different apartment blocks in the industrial Budapest district of Angyalföld. The newly-built *Tomori* estate was populated by the young working class, and their ownership of consumer goods was higher than the national average: 59.7 percent of families owned a washing machine, 41.7 percent owned a television, and 22.2 percent owned a record player. In the other apartment block, the *Tizenhárom Ház*, built at the end of the nineteenth century, the residents were older; here only 26.8 percent of families owned a television. Investigators noted a difference in mindsets between the residents of the two blocks, which suggested that the gradual modernisation of the housing stock and growing consumerism were leading to an erosion of certain aspects of urban working class culture. In the *Tizenhárom Ház*, relative poverty led to greater community among the residents, with several households sharing the use of a fridge; on the *Tomori* estate, a majority of families did not know their neighbours.[40] This unevenness was eliminated by growing material prosperity and the spread of consumer goods; nine years later, in the provincial town of Salgótarján, 83.9 percent of skilled workers, 77.9 percent of semi-skilled workers, and 64 percent of the unskilled, owned a television.[41] By the end of the

---

38   Központi Statisztikai Hivatal 1971.
39   For an overview of key benefits, see Gál 1969.
40   Szántó 1967, pp. 78–80.
41   Dávid and Kovács 1974, p. 21.

decade, the ownership of washing machines had become general and sewing-machines could be found among certain families, while the fridge was also popular among working class households.[42]

As the ownership of consumer goods spread, this gave considerable impetus to the acceptance of work outside primary employment. Sought-after consumer goods were expensive relative to the wages paid by factories. This led to a situation whereby, in 1969, party-investigators reported that 'a substantial section of the working class uses its free time in order to take on additional work'.[43] Work outside primary employment was not new. During the early 1950s, the management of the state railway company had expressed concern about large numbers of its unskilled labourers taking secondary employment in view of their low wages.[44] The transformation of working class culture outside the factory, under the influence of socialist consumerism during the 1960s, increased its social role and importance. In Győr's MÁVAG plant, by the end of the 1960s, workers invested considerably in socialist consumerism, and in response to the creation of a consumer culture, they had developed a wide range of differentiated needs which drove their demands for more money:

> there were those who were fully absorbed in the acquisition of consumer goods... Others were making an investment in starting a family and were bearing the enormous expense of building or buying some accommodation... At the same time there were also workers who were already busily satisfying their demands for additional consumer durables: they had their TV sets, washing machines, motorcycles, and were now spending money improving their apartments, buying refrigerators or even cars.[45]

Progressive cuts in working time between 1968 and 1972, which included the abolition of Saturday shifts for most workers in industry, reinforced the trend of taking on work beyond primary employment. One survey of supplementary work conducted in the early 1970s concluded that some seventeen percent of employees in industry took secondary employment, about half of whom did

---

42 Szántó 1974, pp. 82–3.
43 'Az MSZMP Központi Bizottság Politikai Bizottságának Állásfoglalása ...', in Vass 1974, p. 468.
44 Politikatörténeti és Szakszervezeti Levéltár (Archive of Political History and Trade Unions, hereafter PtSzL) SZKL SZOT Bér és Munkaügyi Osztálya/21d/1953: *Közlekedés- és Postaügyi Minisztérium Vasúti Főosztálya levél Varga Jánosnak, Szakszervezetek Országos Tanács titkára, 1953 november 21.*
45 Héthy and Makó 1972, p. 144.

so because their income did not cover their needs. Even this figure, according to those conducting the survey, considerably underestimated the extent of the phenomenon.[46]

Additional employment was created outside the state sector by a mushrooming informal economy, which was in part a response to the marked differentiation of consumer demand, but also contributed to that process of social differentiation. As with alternative employment, the existence of shadow economies in which workers participated was nothing new. In the climate of severe shortage that had accompanied the early phase of socialist industrialisation in the 1950s, an informal economy had existed that provided opportunities to many workers to earn substantial sums of money on the side. One skilled worker in the Sopron Gas Factory recalled that in the early 1950s:

> we had plenty of opportunities to do black work, after our work in the plant. Everybody needed some installation work, or pipe-fitting, or anything like that. We were always called to private homes to do different kinds of work. Out of the black work we could make as much money as our regular pay was. All the workers were doing the same, this was the main reason they liked the gas-factory, and tried to stay there. Everybody used the material of the plant for the private works, the material was simply stolen.[47]

The changes of the early part of the Kádár era, however, increased the scope and changed the nature of the informal economy in a way that visibly fuelled social differentiation. This shift had its roots in Hungary's successful final collectivisation drive in 1961, which ensured the integration of small-scale agricultural production and the work of cooperatives.[48] The dramatic improvement in housing conditions during the 1960s gave further impetus to this development. Private family housing and the building of flats through flat-construction cooperatives substantially involved both the legal private sector and the shadow economy; in practice, both played a major role in the maintenance and repair of shoddy state-built housing.[49] This was, however, the tip of the iceberg; the repair of clothing, motor vehicles, electrical goods, telephones,

---

46   Szántó 1974, pp. 50–1.
47   CUL Bakhmeteff Archive, CURPH Box 12, Interview No. 232, pp. 20–1.
48   Juhász 1988, pp. 24–50.
49   Kemény 1992, pp. 222–3.

and personal services, were all areas in which the influence of the shadow economy was marked.[50]

These fed a growing perception among the urban core of the working class that their social position was being eroded by the growth of a semi-legal private sector economy in an atmosphere of growing social differentiation. Miners in the city of Komló complained that '1,200 Forints isn't worth as much as it was a couple of years ago',[51] while across the country party officials in 1969 complained that workers 'spoke about a reduction or a stagnation in real incomes'.[52] While these subjective perceptions were to some extent belied by the reality of gradually increasing living standards throughout the 1960s, they reflected concern among the urban core of the workforce about their loss of status amid increasing social differentiation – a process intensified by economic reform in 1968. These perceptions were fed by the feeling among many of the skilled urban core of the working class that urban workers faced huge disadvantages in gaining access to additional sources of income for participating in 'socialist consumerism'. Furthermore, they felt the struggle for additional income was illegitimate, and many of their attitudes were fed by a view that the state should give a sufficient primary income to allow a worker to acquire sought-after consumer goods.[53]

The clear discontent fuelled by the belief that for an urban worker to participate fully in the emerging consumer society, access to additional income was essential, brought on another dimension of discontent within the core of the working class. The urban, male, skilled elite felt that their position was undermined by the perceived ability of rural-dwellers to command additional sources of income.[54] This jealousy was transferred to those who took factory work and yet maintained their ties to agriculture. According to sociologists Gyula Kozák and István Kemény, 'many believe that the rural working class, that is the semi-peasant *kétlaki* workers, who supplement their factory work with agriculture, are – in terms of earnings and income – in a preferential situation'.[55] Yet this perception was, at best, only partially founded on reality. Party-investigators concluded that 'the working class does not have either an appropriate or

---

50   Gábor and Galasi 1982, p. 201.
51   MOL M-KS-288f.21/1969/26ö.e, p. 171.
52   MOL M-KS-288f.21/1969/27ö.e, p. 56.
53   Ibid., p. 115.
54   MOL M-KS-288f.21/1969/29ö.e, p. 288.
55   Kemény and Kozák 1971b, p. 17.

accurate picture of living and working conditions in agriculture'.[56] The complaint against the *kétlaki* reproduced notions that had existed in working class culture, and rested on the perceived hierarchies within the workforce between urban- and rural-dwellers.[57]

The Weak Strength of the Core of the Working Class: Workers, Functionaries and Recentralisation

The implementation of the NEM had an impact on the skilled urban core of the working class when it felt the privileged position promised by the regime was already being eroded by the social differentiation that socialist consumerism and a burgeoning informal economy brought in train. The implementation of a semi-planned, quasi-market economic system in 1968, however, intensified some of these pre-existing sources of discontent, while it also added new ones, further reinforcing a perception that the skilled urban core of the workforce was under siege. Such new forms of grievance were generated by the impact of the reform at the level of the enterprise.

In establishments producing for export, the introduction of the NEM was met by concerted attempts to further rationalise production and control wage costs in order to maximise enterprise profitability, often building on the rationalisation drives of 1964 and 1965. This process was illustrated by the experience of the MÁVAG plant in Győr – a key producer heavily involved in the state's export drive. The enterprise greeted the introduction of the mechanism by attempting to generalise stricter norms, to dramatically cut back overtime payments, and to remove special production premiums.[58] Rationalisation drives occurred in a climate of labour shortage, and, furthermore, a situation in which both local and national party-leaderships feared unemployment, thus leading them to place controls on the enterprises. They also occurred immediately after the introduction of a new labour code in 1967, which had substantially liberalised rules on changing jobs.[59] Given the focus on profitability and decentralisation entailed by the NEM, its implementation resulted in different

---

56 'Az MSZMP Központi Bizottság Politikai Bizottságának Állásfoglalása . . .', in Vass 1974, p. 460.
57 For the 1950s, see Pittaway, chapter 3 of this volume.
58 Héthy and Makó 1972, pp. 92–3.
59 Fazekas and Köllő 1990, p. 98.

economic situations in different enterprises, differences that had often not been anticipated by planners.[60]

Some enterprises and, indeed, some factory units within enterprises, sought to maximise their bargaining power in the labour market by offering preferential wage rates to their workers. The MÁVAG engine plant in Győr came on stream in 1968. To ensure that in its early years it attracted the best skilled workers, management introduced a range of wage supplements ensuring that it avoided the pitfall of labour shortage and that almost sixty percent of its workers were skilled by 1970.[61] In other parts of the economy, and, indeed, the MÁVAG factory, traditional forms of informal bargaining among 'key' workers of the kind seen since the 1950s could be used to beat back management's rationalisation drives.[62] Across units and factories in which either workers had less countervailing power or profitability was poorer, workers were subject to the full force of management's rationalisation. Poor profitability shaped production relations in Budapest's Red Star Tractor Factory, where the higher-than-average work intensity and poor working conditions were described in Miklós Haraszti's account of shop-floor life shortly after the implementation of economic reform.[63] In certain shops in enterprises, which were more profitable than Red Star, even members of the skilled elite were faced with an uncompromising stance from management. In such circumstances, labour shortage and the managerial offensives that accompanied reform produced job-quitting. In the MÁVAG in 1968 and 1969, labour turnover was most marked among experienced component-fitters who had failed to gain preferential treatment in the informal bargaining process.[64]

The impression of a direct managerial challenge to the predominance of the skilled male elite was reinforced by the enterprise profit-sharing provision of the economic reform, which created the impression of a managerial elite seeking to enrich itself at workers' expense. For the purpose of allocating profit shares, the employees of an enterprise were divided into three categories: the first consisted of senior management; the second middle management; while the third, and most numerous, consisted of all the remaining employees of

---

60   'Az MSZMP Központi Bizottságának Határozata az 1968. évi Gazdasági Fejlődésről, a Gazdasági Reformról és az 1969. évi Gazdasági Munka Fő Irányairól, 1968 december 4', in Vass 1974, p. 265.
61   Fazekas 1982, p. 263.
62   Héthy and Makó 1972, pp. 234–5.
63   The environment in which Haraszti worked is contextualised in Burawoy and Lukács 1992, p. 8. For the account itself, see Haraszti 1977.
64   Héthy and Makó 1989, p. 157.

the enterprise. Those employed in the third category enjoyed almost complete income security, and while those in the first two categories did not enjoy such security, they gained in exchange greater rewards when an enterprise performed well.[65] With the payment of the 1968 profit-sharing premiums in the spring of 1969, payments in some enterprises to senior management were, in some cases, ten times greater that those made to the workforce, sparking a public storm over an apparent devaluation of 'the leading role of the working class'.[66]

The skilled urban core of the workforce believed that its position was not only being eroded by the spread of social differentiation, but was also under attack from an insurgent managerial elite. One worker in 1969 pointed to the 'nastiness and abusive nature of middle and upper management, which in certain cases leads to mass job quitting'.[67] Perceptions of the dictatorial behaviour of management in some workplaces marked the attitudes of the skilled worker elite: 'many managers just don't like honest discussion'.[68] These attitudes fed a belief among the core of the working class that class distinctions between themselves and managers were crystallising. Workers felt increasingly unable to articulate their discontent to managers who had appropriated a technocratic language from which they had been shut out. For one party official, 'the workers are less well informed than the managers. If they speak to a given issue, this shows their rawness and lack of understanding. Instead they choose to keep quiet'.[69]

While the countervailing power of the working class core in the workplace rested on informal bargaining, in the political sphere it rested on the relationship between 'workerist' members of the party apparatus of the skilled, male, urban elite that had been established during the late 1950s. This dimension of Kádár's settlement shaped how working class discontent was articulated politically, and, furthermore, determined the limits of the expression of that discontent. Concerns about the need to protect the skilled core of the working class, which had constituted one of the defining demands of 'workerist' functionaries in the late 1950s, resurfaced in 1969 in official discourse, as many sought to use working class discontent to advance their own anti-reform agenda. In November 1969, the Central Committee of the MSZMP stated that

---

65   Swain 1992, p. 105.
66   Soós 1988, p. 91.
67   MOL M-KS-288f.21/1969/27ö.e, p. 121.
68   MOL M-KS-288f.21/1969/27ö.e, p. 8.
69   MOL M-KS-288f.21/1969/26ö.e, p. 187.

'the achievement of our economic goals demands ... that the core of the workforce of each factory receives better moral and material rewards'.[70]

This kind of 'workerism' on the part of sections of the party apparatus represented a political position that contributed to the recentralising logic, which blunted the impact of economic reform during the first half of the 1970s. 'Workerism' on the part of functionaries that articulated the discontent of the urban core of the working class resulted in modifications to the distribution of profit-share premiums between managers and workers, and measures to centrally regulate wages in order to protect the incomes of 'core' members of the workforce.[71] This was to culminate in the wholesale reintroduction of centralised guidelines for the wage rates to be paid for a given job in 1975.[72] The extent to which 'workerism' drove a recentralising logic should not, however, be overestimated. It was also pushed by interests – such as the interests of the management of large enterprises – which were antagonistic to the concerns of the workforce. This can be seen most clearly in the attempts of recentralisers to target high labour mobility, and to effectively criminalise those whom they termed 'wandering birds' during the early 1970s. At a rhetorical level, those who sought to curb labour mobility deployed the language of the grievances of the urban core of the working class, by arguing for the protection of the 'core' of enterprise workforces, attacking the influence of private trade and the 'irresponsible' behaviour of small industrial units attached to agricultural producer cooperatives, for allowing some to unjustly gain high incomes at the expense of others.[73] The gradual criminalisation of labour mobility that formed a key plank of the recentralisation drive, retreating from the liberal intent of the 1967 Labour Code, removed to some extent the power of labour to use their 'market' position to increase their wages by effectively quitting and moving elsewhere.[74] Despite this, however, the power of the political alignments that had developed between large sections of the party apparatus and the urban skilled elite among the working class, which had developed in the aftermath of the 1956 Revolution, remained considerable. Yet while this weak countervailing power in the political sphere could offer skilled workers rhetorical compensation for the perceived erosion of their status, the 1970s would prove it was incapable of offering much more than this.

---

70 'Közlemény az MSZMP Központi Bizottságának üléséről, 1969 november 26–28', in Vass 1974, p. 448.
71 Soós 1988, pp. 91–9.
72 Swain 1992, p. 119.
73 This is analysed in Soós 1988, pp. 93–7.
74 Kemény 1985, pp. 104–14.

The Bankruptcy of Working class Countervailing Power, 1976–89

The central complaints of many members of the urban skilled elite of the working class had revolved around living standards and the growing feeling that their status was eroded as a result of the growing importance of sources of income beyond their primary employment for participation in the consumer economy. Particularly in this area 'workerist' supporters of recentralisation within the party apparatus had so little to offer their constituency. Throughout the 1970s, while the patterns of hierarchy within the workforce continued to shape patterns of stratification of the workforce within the workplace, much as they had done during the 1960s,[75] the growing importance of additional sources of income for working class households further eroded the status of the skilled elite.

By the end of the decade, official, semi-official and unofficial estimates demonstrated an enormous increase in work supplementary to the main wage, despite the fact that official average monthly wages for those working in industry were 78.9 percent higher in 1979 than they had been in 1970.[76] The extent of overtime within the factory was considerable by the end of the decade: 34.8 percent of workers regularly performed overtime in 1979,[77] while by 1976 between seventy-five and eighty-five percent of all employees across the economy were believed to have some source of additional income to that earned in their main job.[78] This development was pushed by the continued growth of the semi-legal shadow economy. By 1979, around a third of all maintenance of flats and housing was performed by those working in the shadow economy.[79]

The dynamic of reform and recentralisation that had characterised economic policy during the late 1960s and early 1970s contributed to the development of the shadow economy. While the NEM had given formal recognition to a complex economy consisting of enterprises of differing sizes and with different patterns of ownership, the politics of recentralisation had directly targeted small-scale enterprises in either the small private sector or those operated close to agricultural cooperatives.[80] Under the impact of recentralising politics, the numbers employed in legal small-scale private industry hit a post-war

---

75   This is made most clear in Nagy and Sziráczki 1982, pp. 37–59.
76   *A lakosság jövedelme és fogyasztása, 1960–1979* 1983, p. 22.
77   Héthy 1984, pp. 66–7.
78   Kemény 1992, p. 220.
79   Gábor and Galasi 1982, p. 201.
80   Soós 1988, pp. 91–7.

low in 1976, before rising as recentralising policies were relaxed.[81] This drove private sector activity underground, while the tightening of central control over the labour market and wages created an environment in which workers increasingly combined a job in the state sector with income from outside in order to meet material demands for consumer goods or housing that could not easily be met by regular wages.[82] By 1977, estimates suggested that 40 percent of all workers in industry and construction, and over one in five of all skilled workers, worked in the shadow economy.[83]

During the 1970s, the development of earnings within state-run industry witnessed a small narrowing of differentials between high and low earners,[84] while the growth of earnings outside the state sector further eroded hierarchies within the workforce. This erosion disrupted hierarchies of income based on skill, and demonstrated the inroads that more traditionally peripheral workers had been able to make in terms of increasing their relative incomes by extending their working hours (largely outside, but also within, the socialist sector).[85] As hierarchies that had reproduced themselves throughout the socialist era were modified by newer patterns of stratification, official discourse on the working class shifted. As early as 1974, the 'core' of the working class was redefined: no longer did it consist simply of the skilled male elite of the working class, but for the regime, 'the most secure base of the working class consists of the industrial workers concentrated in large factories. The Party believes that the situation of workers concentrated in large factories deserves continued measures and special attention from central organs'.[86] The desire of party functionaries to improve the position of those working in large enterprises was a product of the difficulties faced by those enterprises in recruiting and retaining labour during the endemic labour shortage of the mid-1970s.[87] It also reflected the way in which official rhetoric conflated the interests of large enterprise managements and their lobby with the language of 'workerist' sections of the party apparatus by the mid-1970s. It was also tied, to some extent, to the way in which the discontent of the urban core of the working class turned to

---

81 Valuch 2001, p. 177.
82 For a useful analysis of the connections between the shadow economy and socialist consumerism in the late 1970s, see Róna-Tas 1997, pp. 124–7.
83 Gábor and Galasi 1982, p. 204.
84 Héthy 1984, p. 54.
85 Hunyadi 1984, pp. 108–9.
86 'Az MSZMP Központi Bizottságának Irányelvei a Munkásosztály Társadalmi Szerepének Fejlesztéséről, Helyzetének További Javításáról, 1974 március 19–20', in Vass 1978, p. 666.
87 Fazekas and Köllő 1990, pp. 105–31.

resignation and accommodation, as additional sources of income became more widespread and, thus, more accepted in the eyes of workers throughout the decade.

Party reports compiled in the aftermath of the introduction of the NEM, which recorded the working class discontent it had unleashed, suggested that the wave of discontent was not as serious for the regime as that of the 1950s, and that it was not deep-rooted. Officials reading reports of opinion among the workers in 1969 had concluded that 'the political mood is highly changeable, it responds to very specific factors'.[88] Despite this, complaints about the difficulty of achieving what workers deemed to be a reasonable standard of living and gaining access to consumer goods persisted throughout the 1970s. For one Budapest worker in the early 1970s, a television had been bought from his profit-share premium from his workplace, while new furniture had been purchased through low-interest loans from the state savings bank. Despite being able to participate in socialist consumerism, his discontent remained: 'once I've paid the instalment on my loan, what remains of my wages, is needed for food and the household ... If I didn't have the garden, for growing the vegetables, a few other things, a couple of chickens, and that, then my wages wouldn't be enough to feed us'.[89] Yet as the decade progressed, this feeling did not contribute to open discontent that would be articulated politically, as it had been at the end of the 1960s. Instead, it fed more individualistic attitudes in the workplace, as urban workers concentrated more on increasing household incomes. One skilled worker in an Angyalföld factory noted in the mid-1970s that 'it is interesting that now everyone is turning in on themselves. In this factory everyone is busy with thinking about themselves, and they don't deal with each other'.[90] While discontent with wages perceived as low in relation to consumer needs remained throughout the decade, the spread of the shadow economy and its growing importance for working class incomes led to greater privatisation.

While the social climate of the mid-1970s led to greater working class accommodation with some of the trends that had provoked discontent and complaint at the end of the 1960s, the grievances of the skilled worker core that had been directed at the greater power of management had received little redress. The regime only offered workers rhetorical compensation during the period of recentralisation. Measures directed at social groups to whom the urban

---

88 'Az MSZMP Központi Bizottság Politikai Bizottságának Állásfoglalása . . .', in Vass 1974, p. 463.
89 László-Bencsik 1975, p. 203.
90 Halmos 1978, p. 120.

skilled core of the working class were traditionally antagonistic, to some extent, formed part of this rhetorical compensation. Decrees passed in December 1975, which were designed to reduce the number of white-collar staff in enterprises and the discussion this provoked can be placed under this heading, although it is important to note that they were also motivated by concerns over labour shortage.[91] The economically disastrous restrictions on incomes earned in agriculture from private plots can also be explained partly by the attempts of the party leadership to appease a jealous working class.[92]

The period of recentralising politics marked a transition in terms of the relationship between regime and working class, in which the post-1956 contract between 'workerist' party functionaries and the skilled urban core of the workforce was replaced with a poor bargain based on a combination of state employment, toleration of a shadow economy, and a rhetorical privileging of the working class. Yet the recentralising politics and its balancing of the pressures towards greater social differentiation, coupled with the resentment of the regime's key constituency with that differentiation, proved untenable not only in the social sphere, but also in the economic sphere. Partial market reform proved a flawed instrument for restructuring the economy, particularly when combined with the politics of recentralisation, which blunted its impact on large enterprises. Unwillingness to reduce real incomes, and the mushrooming of a shadow economy under the pressure of more differentiated consumer demand and the impact of the dialectic of reform followed by recentralisation, placed greater demands on the economy. These pressures resulted in spiralling state indebtedness, which continued until the point at which the political leadership was threatened with the spectre of outright bankruptcy in the autumn of 1978.[93]

The threat of insolvency forced the Hungarian state to change gear and shift decisively away from the policies of recentralisation and to modify many key aspects of the settlement on which Kádár's regime had rested since 1956. Policies that placed emphasis on economic growth and rising living standards were replaced by policies of austerity in order to bring the economy back into balance.[94] As retail prices were increased from 1979 and the growth in wages was curbed, the shift in policy produced greater demand among workers for more sources of income as supplementary to their main employment, as workers continued to focus on their own perceived household needs.

---

91   Kovrig 1977, p. 400.
92   For this campaign and its impact, see Swain 1992, p. 131.
93   Földes 1995, pp. 77–142.
94   Swain 1992, p. 134.

This turn towards austerity unsurprisingly produced further pressures towards social privatisation, which were combined with a delegitimation of the discourses of class that helped, to some extent, to bind workers to the regime. By the mid-1980s, quiescence was replaced by outright cynicism. In the Budapest industrial surburb of Csepel, which played a central role in the official labour-movement culture promoted by the regime in view of its past reputation as 'Red Csepel', workers by the mid-1980s were heard to remark: '[t]he only thing that's "red" in Csepel today is the sunset, but even that is darkened by the smog'.[95]

Conclusion

When socialism ended in Hungary in 1989, it ended with the marginalisation of the working class, rather than its mobilisation. Economic reformers, perhaps in view of the effects of working class discontent on the course of earlier economic reform, celebrated rather than mourned the marginalisation of the working class during the events of the year. Attempts at trade-union renewal – either through the formation of new confederations or the renewal of the previously state-dominated ones – demonstrated the lack of working class faith in representative institutions at the workplace. Subordinated to the interests of middle class and intellectual activists in new parties, unions and working class politics found themselves marginalised during the political transition that ended socialist rule.[96]

This marginalisation is partially explained by the fact that socialism in Hungarian working class communities ended with a whimper rather than a bang, as workers concentrated on mitigating the impact of economic crisis on their incomes by working ever longer hours to satisfy material needs, rather than protest. Yet part of the explanation can be found in the way in which the working class was relatively successfully integrated into the political system under Kádár. This chapter has suggested that the story of the fluid relationship between workers and the regime in socialist Hungary is that of an informal social settlement between the regime and the workers that rested on the failure of Stalinist politics under Rákosi. It was constructed in the aftermath of the 1956 Revolution and reached its peak during the mid-1960s. Challenged by economic reform in 1968, this settlement provided a social base for the attack on reform during the early 1970s.

---

95 Quoted in Kürti 1990, p. 448.
96 Tóth 2000, pp. 308–43.

While the reshaping of the relationship between regime and working class after 1968 represented the decay of that original settlement, the reshaping also demonstrated its durability. Despite the considerable discontent with the low level of wages relative to the differentiated needs generated by socialist consumerism, the settlement was modified by the generation of a poor bargain based on the toleration of a large shadow economy, and a continuous desire on the part of many in the Party to address working class grievances. The degree to which the regime was able to maintain any kind of tacit social settlement with the workforce was undoubtedly eroded during the 1970s, while the ground was cut from beneath the Party's feet by the economic crisis of the 1980s. The outright delegitimation of the regime occurred only in the mid-1980s, as the gap between official rhetoric and the reality of daily life became painfully obvious. Yet even then, working class passivity rather than mobilisation characterised the events of 1989, while the memory of the Kádár era provided one basis for the recovery of the successor Party of the MSZMP, the MSZP, in many industrial working class communities during the mid-1990s.[97]

---

[97] The individual constituency seats won by the MSZP in all three of the 1994, 1998 and 2002 elections reads like a roll-call of industrial working class areas. In Budapest, it includes the working class districts of Újpest, Rákospalota, Kőbánya, Kispest, Pestszentlőrinc, Pesterzsébet and Csepel. In the provinces, towns like Tatabánya, Komló, Dunaújváros, Salgótarján, Ózd and Tiszaújváros all fall into this category.

CHAPTER 8

Research in Hungarian Archives on Post-1945 History

Introduction

Since 1989, research on the post-1945 period has been transformed. Access for all scholars has greatly improved over the past decade. The collapse of state socialism and growing distance even from the Kádár era means that the post-1945 period can be investigated as history. A large number of historians – both Hungarian and international – have taken advantage of the new climate to reshape our understanding of the period. Research into the politics of the Rákosi and early Kádár years have proved popular, as have investigations into the 1956 Revolution, and cultural policy. Much less work has been done that takes advantage of newly available materials to produce much-needed studies in the fields of social history, economic history, or the history of policy making by the party-state. Although there are incredible opportunities for the historian seeking to work in Hungarian archives to consult materials generated in the post-1945 period, there are a number of pitfalls and problems. I aim to provide a brief survey of some of the most important obstacles confronting the researcher based on my own experience – gathered during the last five years – of research in Hungarian public collections.

A Brief Description of the Kinds of Holdings

The most important public collections dealing with the post-1945 period are now open to research, with some restrictions. National level materials of the MDP and MSZP are held by the National Archives of Hungary (*Magyar Országos Levéltár*, MOL), as are most of the materials generated by state bodies. The Ministry of the Interior has a separate archive – most recent information suggests that it is possible to gain access. The records of the post-1945 trade unions are held by the small Central Archives of Trade Unions (*Szakszervezetek*

---

* Originally published in Mark Pittaway 2000, 'Research in Hungarian Archives on Post-1945 History', *Austrian Studies Newsletter*, 12, 1: 18–20.

Központi Levéltára, SZKL), which is currently maintained by the major post-Communist trade-union confederation, the National Confederation of Hungarian Trade Unions (*Magyar Szakszervezetek Országos Szövetsége*, MSZOSZ). The situation with the records of former state enterprises is more complicated. Some holdings, most from the late 1940s and early 1950s, are deposited in public archives at both national and county levels. The majority of the holdings are still in the possession of the enterprises themselves. Some of the wealthier companies, like MOL (the former state oil company), fund archives and make some of their records available to researchers; in others, access is much more difficult. As companies go bankrupt, the law states that the local public archive has to take the records. State-funded archives do not always have the resources to do this, and there is serious cause for concern about what will happen to these records. The records of local public administration and local party organisations are held at county level, and in the case of some local government records they are held at city level. Some museums – most notably the former National Museum of Labour Movement History, now the Contemporary History Department of the Hungarian National Museum – have important holdings of interest to the historian.

Legal Issues Relating to Access

The 1995 Archive Act regulates access to public collections. It stipulates that materials are to be made freely available to Hungarian and non-Hungarian researchers alike. With reference to the socialist period, government and party documents generated prior to 1990 are subject to a fifteen-year embargo. A researcher wishing to work on documents still subject to the embargo has the right to petition a supervisory body for archival research (*Levéltári Kutatások Kuratóriuma*, LKK) for privileged access to such sources. Private archives can impose similar conditions – the former Communist trade unions place their documents under a ten-year embargo. There are, however, two other acts that further regulate access. The first are state secrecy provisions. Although most Communist-era documents were declassified in a process designed to liberalise access that was completed in 1996, some information remains classified. The second provision is the 1992 Privacy Act. This directly contradicts the 1995 Archive Act, in that it subjects all documents that contain the personal data of a given individual – including party-political or religious affiliation – to a sixty-year embargo. To the extent that it fails to make any distinction between private citizens and those who held public positions, the Act can cause serious problems for a researcher if the document (s)he wishes to consult contains the name of a local party secretary, for example, or the party-affiliation of a given diplomat or public servant. The situation was further confused in February 1997 by a ruling from the Data Protection Ombudsman. He ruled that only researchers affiliated with Hungarian academic institutions, or those affiliated with academic institutions from countries with a bilateral treaty with Hungary relating to the protection of personal data, could be granted access to documents containing personal data. Researchers affiliated with institutions from other countries can only consult photocopies of the said documents with the names redacted. The foreign researcher is by law obliged to pay the costs of copying. While this ruling is not always rigorously applied by archives if they believe that the goal of the research is academic, it can cause serious delays for the researcher.

Non-Legal Issues Relating to Access

Archives and public collections in Hungary face a hostile financial and economic climate. All state collections, whether at national or local level, have been severely affected by reductions in public expenditure during the last decade. At one and the same time, state-run archives have had to cope with a number of demands. Their ability to cope with these demands can affect archive access.

The first is that changes in the ownership of certain collections have forced public archives to house documents for which they do not have space. This is of particular interest to historians of the socialist era because the collections most affected have been the records of the MDP and the MSZMP. In the Kádár era, the Party and its county committees each had their own archives. In 1989, the Institute of Party History, later renamed the Institute for Political History [*Politikatörténeti Intézet*], attempted to centralise the holdings in one archive in Budapest. The county party archives were dissolved, and in most cases the materials went to the capital. In a small number of counties, mostly in the west of the country, local archivists succeeded in preventing the removal of the documents, insisting that they were state documents of public importance. In 1993, the Antall government resolved the dispute by nationalising all party documents created after the merger of the Communist and Social Democratic parties in 1948. The Institute of Political History retained the pre-1948 labour movement records, as well as the records of social organisations like the official youth and women's organisations. The national party organs' records, the papers of the Party's Budapest and Pest County Committees,[1] went to the Hungarian National Archive. Between 1993 and 1995, county party records were given to the relevant county archives. Both the National Archives and the county archives had serious problems accommodating this new material. The National Archive rented half of the building of the Institute of Political History to hold the post-1948 materials until they were removed to the castle district of Buda in early 1999. County archives have had similar problems, and in most cases the materials are stored in rented warehouses. Due to a lack of manpower on the part of county party archives, the county level party materials remain very disorganised. In some counties, there are no inventories or catalogues at all; in all counties, archivists are still reliant on catalogues compiled in the 1970s, which frequently no longer conform to reality. In such counties, some of the materials catalogued in the Kádár era have subsequently gone missing.

The second of the pressures relates to a growth in public, non-academic use of archives, especially at the county or local level during the past decade. Much of the evidence for this is anecdotal, but it was a trend noticed by the author in several counties. The land restitution schemes of Hungary's first post-Communist government relied on archive holdings and seem to have stimulated interest in archival research. Family history is becoming more popular. More autonomous local government and the growth of representative institutions for Hungary's national minorities, combined with the growth of city- and regionally-based foundations, have sparked off an interest in and generated sources of financial support for community history. Secondary-school pupils have increasingly been encouraged to use local archives as part of project work. This explosion in interest has increased the workload of archivists, especially given that no commensurate increase in funding for archives has been forthcoming.

Low levels of funding have had an uneven impact on archives. The lack of space for increased holdings seems to be a problem common to all Hungarian public archives. Not all county archives have a reading room service, and while all allow the photocopying of documents for what, by Western standards, are modest fees, a researcher can expect to wait several weeks for their copies due to staff shortages. Only one county archive of those visited by the author offers overnight accommodation for visitors (Zala County Archive in Zalaegerszeg rents guest rooms on the ground floor of the county hall to visitors, but there is normally a waiting list of several weeks). Furthermore, like all pub-

---

[1] On a research trip in 1999, the author was told that the Pest County Archive had requested the Pest County Committee materials from the National Archives.

lic employees in contemporary Hungary, archivists' pay is lamentably low – a gross monthly salary of HUF 40,000 is not uncommon. Archivists are, therefore, under considerable pressure to seek additional sources of income. In the case of employees of the National Archive and the better organised county archives, additional income is gained through research grants, book contracts, or periodical publication. Not all county archives are so fortunate – this author has met archivists who work for their local newspaper, teach part-time in local schools, or stay on past retirement simply to supplement their pensions. The kinds of pressures that the low incomes of archive staff generate affect the overall level of service.

The most worrying aspect of the pressures that have been brought to bear on archives relate to the possibility of the disappearance of collections altogether. If a company with records goes bankrupt, or a private archive containing records of public importance closes, the law places an obligation on a relevant public archive to take the collection over. Because of the severe material constraints under which public archives operate in contemporary Hungary, it is less than certain that public archives will be able to perform this function.

Some private archives containing materials of public importance have faced closure in recent years because of the financial crises of their parent institutions. In this context, the Central Archive of the Trade Unions is worth mentioning. The archive contains the materials of the national union confederation (SZOT) for the whole of the socialist period, as well as the materials of all branch unions from 1945 onwards. Because of the central role played by the socialist-era unions in the management of production, social policy, culture and sport, the collection is of national importance. The collection stretches to almost twenty kilometres of shelf space, and could not be realistically accommodated by a public institution. It is maintained by the MSZOSZ – the largest of Hungary's trade union federations. As the membership of the MSZOSZ has evaporated, the federation has been hit by financial crisis. In 1994, the archive was threatened with closure. It was only kept going as the result of donations by trade unions outside of the MSZOSZ federation and a small subsidy from the government. The archive has attempted to gain sufficient sources of finance to form a private foundation and thus regularise its legal situation. At the time of writing, however, it did not have enough income to do this.

The confused legal situation with regard to access is a serious cause for concern. It is, however, not as serious as the funding situation, which represents a major threat to some collections. Archives have to date coped well in extremely difficult circumstances. There is no guarantee that this will continue in future. While there is no serious threat to the public archives, either at national and county level, there are serious threats to a number of nationally significant collections – like that of the trade unions – held by private bodies. These archives lack access to the press or concerned academics who can publicise their plight.

Differences in the Culture of Archives

The original call for contributions, to which this brief survey is a response, asked: 'What is a given archive's "culture of accessibility"?' Here it is worth underlining some of the differences between various archives. There are marked differences between the styles and levels of service in different archives and in different kinds of archives. The author's experience is not comprehensive – it is based on five years' work (and three and a half years' continuous work) in six Budapest-based archives and four provincial ones. One might divide the various archives into several different types.

The first would be that of the major Budapest-based national collections, of which perhaps the most significant is the Hungarian National Archive. The Budapest City Archive would fall into this category. These are bureaucratic but relatively efficient in their operation. The researcher has limited contact with the archivists themselves, and generally deals with the reading room staff.

The provincial county archives are very different. They have a large number of non-academic researchers, or the academic researchers they do attract tend to make short trips. The academic researcher who spends considerable time in a provincial archive is seen by the archivists as exceptional, in some cases unusual. County archives tend to be divided into those that are researcher-friendly and those that are researcher-unfriendly. The category into which a given archive can be placed can only be ascertained through extensive pre-research. This kind of pre-research is essential; a researcher-friendly archive can help enormously – one can be bogged down with bureaucratic obstacles in a researcher-unfriendly institution. The best county archives are extremely helpful and informal. The archivists are a mine of information about the collections for which they are responsible and often they have good links to librarians, other local archives and the local community. If, for example, a given research project requires the use of oral history methods, the local archive is a good place to go to identify potential interviewees.

The private collections are very different again. Because of their small staffs they are much more informal, and research here can entail a considerable amount of negotiation. It is something of a generalisation, but it can be said that such archives are friendly and helpful, but inefficient.

Conclusion

While this survey has been brief and impressionistic, it does shed light on some of the key issues that relate to doing archival research in Hungary on the post-1945 period. The issues of access should be of tremendous concern for those who believe (like me) that the writing of the history of socialist Hungary in the light of the archives is a serious task. Nevertheless, the brief comments here are designed to provide a starting point to any researcher seeking information on the issues that need to be confronted when planning research on Hungary in the post-1945 period.

CHAPTER 9

Making Peace in the Shadow of War: The Austrian-Hungarian Borderlands, 1945–56

Introduction

During spring 1946, Hungary's popular front regime – created as a consequence of the Red Army's occupation of the country that had ended the Second World War – proceeded with the deportation of an ethnic German minority that it held partly responsible for the country's tragic entanglement in that conflict. In the far north-west of the country, the deportation and broader process of expulsion of substantial numbers of Germans, and their replacement with agrarian settlers from Hungary's interior, was motivated by a desire both to secure the country's border with Austria and to build a reliable social basis for left-wing parties within the anti-fascist ruling coalition – especially the MKP – in a region that was politically hostile to the left.[1] The selective nature of the 1946 deportation and settlement programme shattered village communities. In Sopronbánfalva, on the fringes of the city of Sopron, approximately seven hundred of the 3,304 pre-1945 residents had been allowed to remain.[2] They were mostly ethnic German miners who worked in the nearby pit at Brennbergbánya, who escaped deportation because of the dire shortages of skilled labour available for mining, and the importance of scarce coal to post-war reconstruction. Over the course of 1946, village society became polarised between the 'old' residents and almost three hundred new settlers who arrived with the support of the authorities to occupy the houses and property of the deportees. Tensions came to a head in February 1947, when the local authorities confiscated all the property of 89 'old' Sopronbánfalva residents whom they accused of being members of the *Volksbund* – the pre-1945,

---

* Originally published in Mark Pittaway 2008, 'Making Peace in the Shadow of War: The Austrian-Hungarian Borderlands, 1945–1956', *Contemporary European History*, 17, 3: 345–64.
1 Tóth 2001; Kirsch 2006.
2 Győr-Moson-Sopron Megye Soproni Levéltára (Sopron Archives of Győr-Moson-Sopron county, hereafter GyMSM.SL), Soproni járás főjegyzőjének iratai, 1945–1950 (Papers of the Chief Notary of Sopron District, 1945–1950, hereafter XXI/21)/b, 1d, Kimutatás a soproni járás községeinek lakosságáról az 1941.I.31-i népszámlálás adatai, továbba az 1945.I./1-i állapot szerint.

pro-Berlin association of the German minority. 'Old' residents mobilised against the state, attacking its weakest point. Left-wing parties were the most enthusiastic advocates of deportation, but they also claimed to rule in the interests of the working class. As many ethnic Germans worked at the Brennbergbánya mine, they forced the local trade union to threaten a solidarity strike with the 89 Sopronbánfalva residents, forcing local left-wing parties to successfully demand that confiscated property be returned.[3]

While acts of state despotism in polarised local communities weakened the authority of the state on the Hungarian side of the border, eight kilometres from Sopronbánfalva, in Austria, the local state acted to protect an established local community from the consequences of upheaval brought about by deportation and the broader process of expulsion from Hungary. The village of Baumgarten lay only a few hundred metres from the Hungarian border, and had a population of predominantly Croatian ethnicity who worked as agricultural labourers on a large local farm. In 1946, it employed as the farm manager A.S., an ethnic German refugee from Hungary who had fled to Austria to avoid deportation. His relations with the workforce were poor almost from the beginning,[4] but they worsened dramatically when he began sacking Croatian workers and evicting them from tied cottages in order to replace them with ethnic German refugees like himself.[5] This generated ethnic tensions in the village, which intensified during the late 1940s, culminating in protest by Baumgarten residents in 1949. A.S. dismissed the protestors by referring to their ethnicity: 'You are no Austrians, you are Croatians; we [ethnic Germans] are better and truer Austrians than you'.[6] This statement provoked a spectacular retaliation from the local Austrian Socialist Party (*Sozialistische Partei Österreichs*, SPÖ), the dominant party in Baumgarten. Arguing that A.S. was unable to prove his status as an Austrian citizen, and was a threat to the local community, it interceded, using its influence over security issues in the provincial government to ban him permanently from residence in Burgenland – the easternmost Austrian

---

3 GyMSM.SL, XXI/21/b/14d, Sopronbánfalva község nemzeti bizottsága. Emlékirat, 1947 február 26.
4 Burgenländisches Landesarchiv (Burgenland Provincial Archive, hereafter BgLA), Bezirkshauptmannschaft Mattersburg (Office of the Mattersburg District Governor, hereafter BH Mattersburg), XI-Polizei, Abschrift, Draßburg, am 15 Jänner 1949, pp. 1–2.
5 BgLA, BH Mattersburg, XI-Polizei, Niederschrift, Draßburg, am 12 Jänner 1949, p. 1.
6 BgLA, BH Mattersburg, XI-Polizei, Niederschrift, Gendarmeriepostenkommando Draßburg, 31 Jänner 1949, p. 1.

province which lay along the international border with Hungary – using a law passed by the Nazis in August 1938 to remove 'undesirables'.[7]

These two incidents reveal the different ways in which the Austrian and Hungarian state approached the creation of the post-war peace, and the process of state (re)construction on which it rested. The experience of the war and its end in the Austrian-Hungarian borderland focused residents on the immediate needs of their local communities, especially for material security. This focusing of political aspiration on the local generated demands for a politics that concentrated less on national, or ideological, mobilisation than had been the case in the pre-war years. Residents demanded that would-be state-builders combat the insecurity generated by the military and economic impact of war by shaping protective institutions and practices that focused on these local-community needs. The post-war Austrian and Hungarian state-building projects differed profoundly in the way they confronted this political environment. The emergent Hungarian state utterly failed to address popular aspirations adequately, and thus proved unable to build for itself a legitimate state authority that would have enabled it to overcome generalised political polarisation, which its practices instead exacerbated. Furthermore, its despotism generated real fear outside its borders, which further increased demands for protection in those Austrian communities that were Hungary's most immediate neighbours. Austrian state-builders, on the other hand, proved relatively successful in constructing legitimate state authority in the post-war climate, because they built institutions and practices that served to protect local communities in the borderland from a variety of external threats, both real and imagined.

A focus on processes of pacification and state (re)construction in the Austrian-Hungarian borderland sheds light on the social history of the Early Cold War and trajectories of post-war state formation more generally. This is not to deny the importance of international and high politics in determining eventual political outcomes. The Moscow Declaration in 1943, the existence of a unified Austrian government from 1945 and four-power (rather than simply Soviet) occupation played a decisive role in Austria's integration into Western economic and political structures, while Hungary found itself part of the Soviet bloc. In Austria, the unity between the dominant political traditions – political Catholicism represented by the Austrian People's Party (*Österreichische Volkspartei*, ÖVP), and social democracy represented by the SPÖ – against the tiny Austrian Communist Party (*Kommunistische Partei Österreichs*, KPÖ) contrasted with the bitter polarisation across the border in Hungary between a left led by the MKP (supported by the Soviet occupation forces), and the

---

7 BgLA, BH Mattersburg, XI-Polizei, Bezirkshauptmannschaft Mattersburg, Zahl: XI-57/3-1949.

centre-right majority.⁸ An exclusive focus on high and international politics suggests that local communities and their residents played an essentially passive role in the shaping of the post-war peace. This article, by contrast, seeks to show that the reception of the projects of national and international actors at the local level played a central role in their success or failure in constructing legitimate state authority. The post-war Hungarian state's failure to do so helped to determine the local dynamics of the country's slide into dictatorship, and the consequent intensification of despotism in the late 1940s and early 1950s. The Austrian state's relative success aided its consolidation and the population's pacification. They also textured the local experience of the Early Cold War in the borderland.

The Politics of Protection

At the turn of 1945, despite the considerable violence perpetrated by both the German and Hungarian states against tens of thousands of Jewish forced labourers building border defences for Germany, and the penury brought about by the end of the conflict, populations on both sides of the border were deeply fearful of what the end of the war might bring. In north-western Hungary, this fear provoked the flight of much of the local population – especially in those villages with substantial ethnic German populations – in the face of the advance of the Red Army. In the Mosonmagyaróvár district – next to the border with the collapsing German Reich – around forty percent of the population had gone before the new occupiers arrived.⁹ Across the border, the pattern of flight was similar. In Nickelsdorf, 70 percent of the total population left.¹⁰ As was the case in Hungary, the regime demanded that the population flee with them. In Gols, Nazi officials threatened to shoot those who insisted on staying, asking 'if they wished to be communists'. The village's party leadership attempted to remove most of the cattle, taking them from their owners and

---

8   For Austria, see Rathkolb 2005; Berger 2007, pp. 232–70. For Hungary, see Borhi 2004; Kenez 2006; Pittaway 2004, pp. 453–75.

9   Győr-Moson-Sopron Megye Győri Levéltára (Győr Archives of Győr-Moson-Sopron County, hereafter GyMSM.Gy.L), Győr-Moson-Sopron Megye és Győr thj. város főispánja (The Prefect of Győr-Moson-Sopron County and the City of Győr, hereafter XXIf.1)a.1d, Jelentés Győr, Moson és Pozsony k.e.e. vármegyék alispánjától.

10   BgLA, Landeshauptmannschaft Burgenland (Burgenland Governor's Office, hereafter A/VIII-11)/V, Nickelsdorf, Berichte der Gemeinden über die Ereignisse 1945–1956.

letting them free. The behaviour of Nazi activists – who had internalised their leaders' demands that they 'fight until the end' – generated considerable fear.[11]

Those who remained faced the Red Army. In western Hungary, attitudes toward the Soviet troops were defined by the wave of lawlessness that accompanied their arrival. In April 1945, in the Mosonmagyaróvár district:

> occupying forces... during their searches for enemy soldiers became interested in wine, and spirits, as well as pocket-, and wrist-watches. In those villages where they got hold of drink, they did not refrain from raping the women either. In the places where they rested, or where they were stationed, they took food and clothing from the population.[12]

In Csorna, Red Army troops stationed in the small town stripped the population of its property: 'in general they took clothes and food, in many houses they removed the furniture and in others emptied the yards. A few days after the occupation they began to search for the warehouses, and from those they took all the corn and food stored'.[13] The extent of rape in the city of Sopron provoked panic among midwives and doctors, who at the end of April 1945 petitioned the county authorities to relax restrictions immediately on the performance of abortions.[14]

The actions of Soviet troops produced widespread fear. When local schools reopened in Győr in May 1945, inaccurate rumours spread that the local Soviet command had sent 'two trucks' to a local school in order 'to take away the pupils'. Within a short space of time, 'the greater mass of pupils and parents shouted out that others "should flee to their homes, because the Russians are taking away the children"', a situation that resulted in panic.[15] The behaviour of Soviet troops created serious problems for Hungary's new civil authorities that represented the provisional government (a popular front coalition that had been constituted under Soviet auspices, in which the MKP was the first among equals). Many in conservative regions, such as the counties of Győr-Moson

---

11 BgLA, Bezirkshauptmannschaft Neusiedl am See (Office of the Neusiedl am See District Governor, hereafter BH Neusiedl), Verschiedenes-XI-1945, Abschrift: Gendarmerieposten Gols, Gols, 11 Oktober 1945.
12 GyMSM.Gy.L, XXIf.1b.1d, A magyaróvári járás főszolgabirójától, ad 1132/1943.sz. Tárgy: 1945 évi április helyzetjelentés, p. 1.
13 GyMSM.SL, Sopron Megye és Sopron Város főispánjának iratai (Papers of the Lord-Lieutenant of the County and City of Sopron, hereafter XXI/11f), 2d, Csorna község jegyzőségtől, 1485/1945.sz. Tárgy: Jelentéstétel Csorna község általános helyzetéről, p. 1.
14 GyMSM.SL, XXI/11f/2d, Levél dr. Hám Tibor urnak, Sopron, 1945 április 30.
15 GyMSM.Gy.L, XXIf.1a.1d, Jegyzőkönyv készült 1945 május 17-én, p. 1.

and Sopron that were adjacent to the border of the newly restored Austria, expected the new authorities to intercede to protect their communities from the occupying forces, and believed that because of their political stance they were able to do so effectively. In late April, a lorry carrying an armed Soviet officer and eight soldiers turned up in the village of Ménfőcsanák. After searching the village they rounded up eleven pigs from the residents at gunpoint, driving off with them and refusing to pay the owners. The irregular village police force, which was unarmed, was powerless to defend the villagers, leaving village authorities to demand that the county government intervene to secure the return of the 'stolen' pigs.[16] In Hegyeshalom, when Soviet troops confiscated the only cow owned by one agricultural labourer, village authorities demanded that the county authorities intercede to secure the return of all locally-owned cattle, given that many of their owners had 'large families and young children to feed'.[17] This perception was encouraged by the pro-Soviet rhetoric of communist leaders, for they argued that they represented a promise of 'liberation' from 'the German/Arrow Cross fascists'[18] that had been brought by the Red Army.[19] Consequently, the experience of Soviet occupation seriously undermined support for the post-war state in western Hungary.

On the other side of the border, the population did not perceive the emergent Austrian state in the Soviet zone of occupation to have any privileged relationship with the Red Army. The wave of widespread violence, theft, rape and murder committed by Soviet troops endured by western Hungarian communities was repeated across Burgenland. It did not, however, have the same political consequences.[20] The trauma of rape played a fundamental role in generating fear and insecurity.[21] Soviet troops were not the only 'outsiders' who fuelled the disorder during spring and summer 1945. The arrival of the Red Army led to the freeing of substantial numbers of prisoners of war, who worked as forced labourers on the land during the war years.[22] Once freed they

---

16   GyMSM.Gy.L, XXIf.1b.1d, Ménfőcsanak jegyzőségtől. Tárgy: Sértesigénybevétel, Ménfőcsanák, 1945 április 25.
17   GyMSM.Gy.L, XXIf.1b.1d, Hegyeshalom község elöljáróságtól, Jegyzőkönyv készült Hegyeshalom községben, 1945 április 26-án.
18   Hungary's national socialist party, brought to power by a German-backed *coup d'état* in October 1944.
19   Komárom-Esztergom Megyei Önkormányzat Levéltára (Local Government Archive of Komárom-Esztergom County, hereafter KEMÖL), Az MKP Tata Járási Bizottságának iratai (Papers of the Tata District Committee of the MKP, hereafter XXXV.24f)1ö.e, p. 2.
20   Wagner 2005, p. 497.
21   Bayer 2005, pp. 139–50.
22   Hornung, Langthaler, and Schweitzer 2004.

joined the wave of terror against the local population – in one incident in July 1945, four thousand Greek former prisoners-of-war, who had been freed from a camp in Wiener Neustadt, descended on the village of Pöttsching and forced their way into the homes and gardens of the population, stealing what they could. When local police irregulars intervened, a hail of stones confronted them and they beat a hasty retreat.[23] Around the town of Mattersburg, local authorities believed that Soviet troops and bands of freed Ukrainian prisoners of war worked in concert to pillage the area's vineyards.[24] The crime wave and food shortages focused local residents on the needs of local communities. Residents in Drassburg demanded greater protection against 'outsiders' and 'foreigners', who threatened 'the property and security of residents' in August 1945.[25]

The perception of the state as a credible protector of the security of local communities was shaped not only by their perceived relationship with the Red Army, but also by their concrete policies towards policing and crime. As in Hungary, the authorities at both provincial and federal level in Austria asked villages to organise their own unarmed, irregular, volunteer police forces to keep the peace.[26] In Hungary, the popular front government – suspicious of an organisation that had enthusiastically supported the wartime and then the Arrow Cross regimes, and which had played a central role in the organisation of the deportation of Jews in 1944 – disbanded the gendarmerie outright.[27] In Austria, while the KPÖ was suspicious of the gendarmerie, it was marginalised within the federal government in Vienna (dominated by the ÖVP and SPÖ), which strongly supported the institution.[28] While the gendarmerie survived, communist suspicion of it meant that in the Soviet zone its powers and its right to carry arms were severely curbed by the occupation authorities.[29] Tension between local gendarmerie commanders and communists could explode into protest, especially in the small number of communities where

---

23   BgLA, BH Mattersburg, XI-Polizei-Besondere Vorfälle, Gendarmerieposten Pöttsching, E.Nro.18, Vorkomisse in Pöttsching durch Ausländer.
24   BgLA, BH Mattersburg, XI-Situationsberichte, Gendarmeriepostenkommando Mattersburg, E.Nr.183, Situationsbericht vom 15–31 August 1945, p. 1.
25   BgLA, BH Mattersburg, XI-Situationsberichte, Gendarmeriepostenkommando Drassburg, Er.Nr.34, Situationsbericht vom 4–8 August 1945.
26   BgLA, A/VIII-11/VI, Gemeindeamt Deutsch-Jahrndorf, 12 Juli 1960, Zl:207/1960., Betr.: Ereignisse 1945–1956.
27   Kovács 2001, pp. 103–40.
28   Mugrauer 2006.
29   BgLA, BH Mattersburg, XI-Situationsberichte, Gendarmeriepostenkommando Wiesen, Er.Nr.251, Situationsbericht für die Zeit vom 14–21 Jänner 1946, p. 3.

the KPÖ enjoyed significant support.[30] Given the demands of communities for protection in the climate of crime and insecurity, majorities supported strengthening the police and the routine arming of gendarmes as part of a drive to bolster institutions capable of protecting local communities. This was especially the case since police irregulars often had few means and little power to protect the population.[31] This popular pressure was in turn used by provincial and federal authorities to secure Soviet consent for the routine arming of the gendarmerie.[32]

If the politics of law and order in eastern Austria demonstrated the ways in which legitimate state authority was reconstructed around a desire for the protection of local communities, then in western Hungary they moved in an entirely different direction. While Hungary's population demanded the protection of their communities from crime, black-marketeering, and the occupation authorities, civil government proved unable to offer this to them. The 'new' police force established in spring 1945 barely existed outside the towns for most of the year. Furthermore, the Mosonmagyaróvár police admitted that they were unable to stem the tide of theft, rape, and cross-border smuggling, given gross understaffing and a dire material situation in which the police had to work without food or pay.[33] Furthermore, they were seen as a Party police force in the hands of the occupying authorities and the MKP. This was illustrated dramatically by an incident in the village of Alszopor. On the afternoon of 24 June 1945, a group of Red Army troops arrived in the village, stealing a horse from one resident. The villagers resolved to take the stolen horse back by force, and in the melee that ensued one of the troops was killed. The same evening, the Red Army returned, backed by the Sopron police who arrested twelve locals, including the village judge. While the police took away those arrested, the Soviet troops raided houses in search of weapons and stole a number of 'valuable items'. Incidents like this confirmed for many that the

---

30   BgLA, BH Neusiedl, Verschiedenes-XI-1945, Landesgendarmeriekommando f.d. Burgenland, Nr.160, Frauenkirchen, 20 Oktober 1945.

31   BgLA, BH Mattersburg, XI-Situationsberichte, Gendarmeriepostenkommando Drassburg, Er.Nr.34, Situationsbericht vom 4–8 August 1945.

32   BgLA, Sicherheitsdirektion für das Burgenland (Burgenland Security Directorate, hereafter A/VIII-14)/V-1, Zahl: SD891/46, Eisenstadt, 13 June 1946, Betrifft: Waffengebrauchsrecht für die Sicherheitsorgane erbeten.

33   GyMSM.GyL, Győr-Moson Megyei Rendőrkapitányság (Győr-Moson County Police Captaincy, hereafter XXIVf.3)/1d, Magyar Államrendőrség Mosonmagyaróvári Járási Kapitánysága, sz: 1014/1945, Tárgy: A rendőrség müködéséről készitendő jelentés, p. 1.

'new' police, rather than offering them protection from threats, was instead only interested in defending those threatening powers.[34]

These incidents were symptomatic of the fact that the Hungarian state and the left-wing parties that played a central role in state-building during 1945 conceived the purpose of the police and other security agencies as being primarily to defend the state-building process against sections of society they believed opposed it. Their priority was not to protect local communities from either the occupying forces or the post-war crime wave fed by hyperinflation and generalised penury. In September 1945, a border police station was established at Hegyeshalom as large numbers of refugees from Germany returned home, for the state realised that among them there could be 'a large number of leading fascists, who are attempting to return to Hungary in secret'.[35] Rather than focus on smuggling and organised violent crime, which generated real misery in borderland communities, the border police concentrated on screening those returnees they suspected of 'political unreliability', who were sent to a camp where their cases were investigated.[36] Furthermore, the police and their political commanders were most interested in the implementation of anti-fascist retributive legislation,[37] which served to strengthen the impression of many that they were more interested in protecting the regime in Budapest than in safeguarding the security of the population. The police in Mosonmagyaróvár were prepared to write off as 'hopeless' the process of fighting crime committed by Soviet troops or organised criminal gangs, while it measured its 'success' by the number of 'fascists' it interned – among whose number it included not merely members of the Arrow Cross, nor those who had collaborated with the German occupiers after March 1944, but many who had served the conservative interwar and wartime regime prior to that date.[38]

This happened against a backdrop of deep-seated political antagonism between the state and the population. Győr-Moson and Sopron counties were

---

34   GyMSM.SL, Csepregi járás főjegyzőjének iratai (Papers of the Chief Notary of Csepreg District, hereafter XX1/12a)5d, Újkéri körjegyzőség, 234/1945. Jelentés az Alszoporon történt őrizetbevételekről.

35   ' Új határrendészeti csoportot állitottak fel a Nyugatról hazatérők ellenőrzésére', *Dunántúli Szabad Nép*, 8 September 1945, p. 3.

36   Magyar Országos Levéltár (Hungarian National Archive, hereafter MOL), Belügyminisztérium iratai (Papers of the Ministry of the Interior, hereafter XIX-B-1)v/4d, Hazahozatali Kormánybizottság, 690/1945. V.F.P. Kh, Budapest, 1945 október 8.

37   'Kétszeresére emelik a győrmegyei rendőrség létszámát', *Dunántúli Szabad Nép*, 12 September 1945, p. 1.

38   GyMSM.GyL, XXIVf.3/1d, Magyar Államrendőrség Mosonmagyaróvári Járási Kapitánysága, sz: 1014/1945, Tárgy: A rendőrség müködéséről készitendő jelentés.

characterised by a hegemonic Catholic and conservative political culture that had allowed the dominant political actors of the conservative interwar regime to win considerable support. Prior to the outbreak of war, anti-communism proved an especially potent part of the construction of the regime's local appeal, given the memory of the Soviet Republic in 1919, and the way in which it was successfully blamed for Hungary's territorial losses after the First World War. Even during the 1930s, this had turned to anti-Soviet sentiment; the local pro-government press in Sopron, for example, had argued that the state that had arisen in Russia after the Revolution of 1917 was a 'regime of command that had created a new form of capitalism – state capitalism – in which all the country's energy was drained into maintaining its rule', and which was marked by 'the most terrible oppression and misery of the Russian people'.[39] However, its railing against communism in Hungary, especially against the tyranny of the *kolkhoz* over the peasantry, and the immorality of godless communism, did not have merely an abstract meaning for many, given the region's experience of the Soviet Republic and the subsequent trauma of border disputes with Austria in the Sopron region. Throughout the 1930s, local elites linked anti-communist propaganda to local memories of 1919.[40]

Anti-communism had been a potent theme of wartime propaganda[41] and shaped attitudes that were reinforced by the behaviour of the Red Army and the 'new' Hungarian state in local communities. While the outcome of the war discredited the authoritarian conservatism of the interwar years, many of the cultural values it rested on allowed a democratic conservatism – represented largely by the FKGP – to become dominant in western border regions. This was despite the fact that while opposing the left and the MKP's vision of a socially radical post-war state, it was simultaneously resolutely anti-fascist and a partner in the popular front coalition government in Budapest.[42] In Csorna, the Party's activists proclaimed their goal as creating an 'independent country, a clean, Christian democracy'.[43] Such rhetoric allowed them to claim support as the Party that could oppose the Soviet occupation successfully. In Győr-Moson, in advance of the 1945 elections, many believed that if the country 'votes for

---

39 'Felelősséggel biró magyar ember nem támogahatja a demagóg jelszavakkal dobálózodó szélsőségeket', *Soproni Hírlap*, 10 May 1938, p. 1.
40 'Moszkvában agyonlőtték az egykori soproni kommunista városparancsnok hugát', *Soproni Hírlap*, 8 January 1938, p. 1.
41 'Komoly idők intelmei', *Mosonvármegye Magyaróvári Hírlap*, 27 January 1944, p. 1.
42 Pittaway 2004, pp. 466–8.
43 'Ujjongó lelkesedéssel fogadták szónokainkat a csornai járásban', *Soproni Újság*, 18 October 1945, p. 3.

the Smallholders' Party, then the Soviets will be forced to leave the country, if they vote for the communists, they'll stay forever'.[44] As elections approached, the FKGP, backed by public opinion in the borderland, attacked the police focus on anti-fascist retribution. They concentrated their fire on the Sopron internment camp, where many former gendarmes, because of their role in the deportations of local Jews in 1944, and other supporters of the interwar regime locally, for reasons that were less clear, had been interned as 'fascists'. Sopron residents did not believe that the detention of many of the camps' inmates was legitimate. The local police were compared both to officials of the 1919 Soviet Republic and the Gestapo. While persistent anti-Semitism fed these protests, so too did a sense that the police stood against the majority of the people and spent too much time interfering in politics and little on fighting crime.[45]

In November 1945, the FKGP won a landslide victory over the MKP and its allies.[46] Although the occupying authorities demanded that a popular-front coalition of all anti-fascist parties continue, the elections intensified political polarisation, as many working class voters demanded greater assertiveness from the left. The MKP leadership responded, attacking the FKGP as enemies of democracy. Within days of the election, the MKP warned that 'it seems that the reaction has drawn the conclusion from the election results that the coming months will see the elimination of democracy'. It accused the FKGP of protecting 'provocateurs' who 'victimised' communists.[47] While the MKP and the police under its control enforced a tough line against those Smallholders it accused of supporting 'reaction', it intensified class-based rhetoric to mobilise industrial workers and other supportive groups who had become disillusioned as a consequence of the hyperinflation that had gripped the country since summer 1945. At Brennbergbánya, the MKP accused the mine management of using transportation to fetch for themselves 'fatted geese and ducks', but not to bring 'oil and margarine' for miners.[48] The focus of the MKP's anti-fascism had shifted – as internment camps were run down, the MKP welcomed working class former-members of the Arrow Cross, who had held no leadership

---

44   GyMSM.Gy.L, XXIf.1b/1d, Győr-Moson Megye és Győr thj. város főispánjától, 75/5, főisp. 1945.sz. Tárgy: Szeptember havi tájékoztató jelentés, p. 1.

45   'Komoly munka folyik a városházán', *Soproni Újság*, 14 October 1945, p. 4.

46   The FKGP won 57.03 percent of the national vote; the Social Democratic Party 17.41 percent; the MKP 16.95 percent; and the National Peasants' Party 6.87 percent. No other party won more than two percent of the votes cast. Information adapted from Balogh 1984, pp. 147, 161.

47   'Kommunista ellenes merényletek Sopron- és Győr megyében', *Dunántúli Szabad Nép*, 14 November 1945, p. 1.

48   'Így élnek a brennbergi bányászok', *Új Sopron*, 21 February 1946, p. 3.

roles, into its ranks, for they were 'workers' who had been 'cheated into joining fascist organisations'.⁴⁹ This represented no let-up in retribution, however, against those who had served Hungary's pre-1945 regime, but rather its refocusing on apparent 'reactionaries' who staffed public administration and private business, and whom it accused the FKGP of protecting.⁵⁰

While the MKP sought to put political retribution in Hungary to work in its attempts to mobilise its base of support and to smash the FKGP following its electoral victory in late 1945, on the Austrian side of the border it was used to bolster the authority of the emergent protective state. While Hungary's practice of anti-fascist retribution gave licence to its police forces to attack all those they perceived to be enemies of the 'new' state, and allowed open wounds from the war years to fester, the implementation of Austria's de-Nazification laws was not to the letter and, being more limited, offered the potential of a closure to conflict. While the 1945 de-Nazification Law mandated the registration of all former Nazis, it contained an implicit bargain, in that it allowed them to petition for 'clemency' if they had never 'misused' their membership of the Party or one of its front organisations.⁵¹ Some of the petitions the authorities received revealed popular understandings of this bargain – that those who professed loyalty to the state would receive from the latter protection from the consequences of prior political affiliations. A former party member in the border town of Mörbisch am See framed his claim for clemency in 1945 on the grounds that he had been deceived by National Socialist promises to 'turn around the situation in agriculture'. He had 'always regarded himself as an Austrian', and promised that 'in future he would act positively towards the state'.⁵²

Processes of Separation

While the local practice of de-Nazification in Burgenland bolstered the inclusive features of post-war 'Austrianness', it was deeply exclusive in other respects as a result of the state's desire to define the new Austria against the Germany of which it had been part for the seven years prior to 1945. When officials in the

---

49   'Kisnyilasokat bocsáttotak szabadon', *Új Sopron*, 29 September 1945, p. 3.
50   'Módot kell találni az antidemokratikus közalkalmazottak eltávolítására', *Dunántúli Szabad Nép*, 4 January 1946, p. 3.
51   Knight 2007, p. 596.
52   BgLA, Bezirkshauptmannschaft Eisenstadt (Papers of the Eisenstadt District Governor, hereafter BH Eisenstadt), NS-Angelegenheiten, Karton 4, H.A., Brief an die provisorische Staatsregierung, Mörbisch am See, 20 Juli 1945.

borderland were asked in 1946 to document 'National Socialist' oppression locally, in order to provide material for the 'Red-White-Red' book that was to record Austrian 'victimhood' at the hands of the Nazis, many returns concentrated on the dismissal of local officials and their replacement by those brought in from Germany proper.[53] The state's definition of itself against Germany was more than simply a matter of rhetoric. In spring 1945, the provisional government in Vienna instructed districts to separate their residents into 'Austrians' and those it termed 'Germans who came from the Reich' [*Reichsdeutsche*], as a prelude to their removal from Austrian soil.[54] In 1946, local authorities faced a steady stream of appeals from Austrian women married to German citizens, who discovered that they were denied Austrian citizenship as a result of their marital status and as a result faced deportation to Germany.[55]

Post-war constructions of 'Austrianness' did not just seek to demarcate Austria and Germany; they also celebrated provincial identities.[56] In the case of the borderland, this meant that the reconstruction of 'Austrianness' was tied to the rebuilding of Burgenland identity. Burgenland had been carved out of Hungary at the end of the First World War, as a consequence of the demands of its German minority that it be ruled by Vienna rather than Budapest. Owing its origin in part to a political project of ethnic Germans within the pre-war Kingdom of Hungary, dominant constructions of its provincial identity during the interwar years had argued for its fundamental kinship to those western Hungarian counties populated by German speakers.[57] Pan-German nationalists dreamed of the territorial extension of the province. While the province was divided, after Austria's incorporation into Germany, between the *Gaue*[58] of Niederdonau and Styria, Burgenland's own Nazis had argued against Berlin that their province should become a *Gau* in its own right within the expanded Reich, in view of its distinctive 'mission' as a 'borderland' [*Grenzland*] that

---

53   Dokumentationsarchiv des Österreichischen Widerstandes (Documentary Archive of the Austrian Resistance, hereafter DÖW), 8339.
54   Niederösterreichisches Landesarchiv, St. Pölten (Lower Austrian Provincial Archive, St. Pölten, hereafter NÖLA, St.P), Landeshauptmannschaft Niederösterreich (Lower Austrian Governor's Office, hereafter Ia-10)/B.nm.208/Stammzahl 29/bis ONv.74/1945, Bezirkshauptmannschaft Scheibbs. Zl.XI-55: Behandlung der Flüchtlinge und Ausländer, Scheibbs, 20 Juni 1945.
55   BgLA, BH Eisenstadt, II-1946, Bezirkshauptmannschaft Eisenstadt, Zl. II-86-46, Eisenstadt, 24 Jänner 1946.
56   Kreichbaumer 1998, pp. 7–13.
57   Barb 2004, pp. 83–9.
58   Sub-national administrative units in Nazi Germany.

could serve as a bridge between Germany and German speakers in Hungary.[59] Berlin's only concession to pro-Burgenland sentiment was to establish a National Groups Office [*Volkstumstelle*] in the former Burgenland capital, Eisenstadt, which supervised the region's ethnic minorities and maintained close contact with pro-Berlin ethnic German activists in the neighbouring Hungarian city of Sopron.[60]

These notions of Burgenland identity were revived in an unfavourable post-war context at the same moment when the Hungarian state engaged in its campaigns of expulsion against the German minority. The waves of expulsion between 1945 and 1946 generally, but especially deportation in 1946, played a fundamental role in the construction of Burgenlander, and by extension Austrian, identities in the region, and shaped perceptions of the Hungarian neighbour that strengthened the authority and legitimacy of the Austrian state as a protector. In border villages, where ties of kin often spread into villages on the Hungarian side, expulsion provoked particular outrage. When ethnic Germans returned home in late 1945 to north-western Hungarian villages, such as Magyarkimle, to find that their homes and land had been redistributed to settlers, they launched an armed uprising with the goal of reclaiming their property, using flight over the border and networks of solidarity with kin on the Austrian side to sustain their fight. While they were beaten back as the Hungarian state flooded the border region with armed police, both the central government and its local representatives remained worried at their lack of control over the border.[61]

Public opinion, the political parties, opinion-makers and even officials in the Burgenland government responded to Hungarian violence against borderland Germans by claiming them as 'Austrians', and arguing – in an adaptation of pan-German arguments from the interwar years to post-war circumstances – that the lands they inhabited were, in fact, eastern Burgenland. These arguments sought to differentiate Hungary's German speakers from Germans proper, and underline their kinship to 'Austrians' living on the Burgenland side of the border. 'Hungary's German speakers refer to themselves as *Donauschwaben* and *Heidebauern*, and are so known by the Hungarians; they know nothing of Germany', according to one opponent of expulsion used by officials in the Burgenland government to make their case against Hungary.

---

59   DÖW, 11498.
60   Österreichisches Staatsarchiv, Archiv der Republik (hereafter ÖStA/AdR), Reichskommisar für die Wiedervereinigung Österreichs mit dem Deutschen Reich (hereafter 'Bürckel'/ Materie), Zl.2770, Kt.83, p. 37.
61   GyMSM.Gy.L, XXIf.1b.5d, Kedves Medei képviselő elvtárs!

These officials in the Burgenland government lobbied Vienna to intervene with the occupying powers, especially the Soviet Army, against expulsion on the grounds that ethnic Germans 'settled right on the border can be seen as good Austrians'.[62] Others argued for a solution that allowed for the Moson and Sopron districts closest to the border to be removed from Hungary and incorporated into Burgenland.[63]

When the Hungarian government drew up regulations to intern German citizens on its territory in spring 1945, it had been aware that some would claim exemption on the grounds of their 'Austrianness'. While it argued that Austrian citizens could not be regarded automatically as 'German citizens', the authorities had to 'pay attention to' Austria's 'true relationship to the German Reich, which had existed over several years'.[64] Neither the Hungarian state, nor the left-wing parties who most enthusiastically supported expulsion, were prepared to make any concession to claims that borderland German speakers should be exempted on grounds of their 'Austrianness'. Aware of calls in the Burgenland press for a redrawing of the border, the Hungarian police rounded up five ethnic Germans for spreading pro-Austrian propaganda in Sopron during early 1946. In a political trial designed to serve as a warning to authorities across the border, prosecutors accused them of conspiring with leading Burgenland politicians to launch an armed uprising in Hungary to secure territorial changes.[65] Mindful of the likely Soviet reaction were it to show any willingness to openly lobby for territorial change or a halt to deportation, Vienna remained silent and urged restraint on Burgenland's government.[66] By early 1946, the Hungarian state prepared for the organised deportation to Germany of most of those it identified as Hungary's ethnic Germans. The MKP press in western Hungary celebrated what it believed would bring an end to tensions generated by the more generalised expulsion efforts it had organised from spring 1945: '[t]he time is coming fast, when we will be able to start deporting the Hungarian Swabians'.[67]

---

62   ÖStA/AdR, Bundesministerium für auswärtige Angelegenheiten, 2 Republik (hereafter BMfAA), II-Pol, Ungarn 9, Gz.110.054-pol/46, Z.110.394-pol/46.
63   ÖStA/AdR, BMfAA, II-Pol, Gz.110.054-pol./46, Z.42.072-pol/46.
64   GyMSM.SL, XXI/21/b, 4d., 1066/1945, KEOKH, sz: 25/162.VII.e.1945.eln., másolat.
65   DÖW, 20000/j5, Vom Volksgericht in Győr, zahl: Nb.859/1946/13; ÖStA/AdR, BMfAA, II-Pol/ Ungarn 9, Gz.105.319-pol/47, Z.108.721-pol/1947.
66   ÖStA/AdR, BMfAA, II-Pol, Ungarn 9, Gz.110.353-Pol/46, Z. 110.353-Pol/46, 247-Pr/46.
67   'A mosoni svábok milliós értékeket lopnak ki a határon túlra', *Dunántúli Szabad Nép*, 11 January 1946, p. 3.

The expulsion drives, which culminated in the deportations during spring 1946, confronted several problems. The first was the fluid and problematic nature of ethnic identities in the borderlands. The published results of the 1941 census recorded 719,762 people (or 4.9 percent of Hungary's population) identifying themselves as German-speakers, although it bears mention that these figures were themselves strongly contested by political representatives of the German minority itself.[68] In many western border districts, the proportions were higher. In the Mosonmagyaróvár district, 37.2 percent of the population declared themselves German-speakers, and in the Sopron district the figure was 39.3 percent, while 12.7 and 29.9 percent, respectively, identified themselves as such in the cities of Mosonmagyaróvár and Sopron.[69] Many ethnic Germans had a 'dual identity' that was both Magyar and German, for German often functioned as a local language rarely used beyond the boundaries of home villages, while ties of kin and friendship often transcended the ambiguous ethnic divide.[70] Furthermore, ethnic German identity did not imply political sympathy for Germany's political goals during the war; *Volksbund* organisations only ever operated in twenty-five villages in Győr-Moson and Sopron counties, and they never mobilised anything like all ethnic German residents in these villages.[71]

This contributed to bureaucratic confusion and arbitrariness as to who was to be marked out for either expulsion or, later, deportation. The process of selection was mired in confusion over goals, for the Hungarian state was never consistent in applying the principle of collective guilt to all ethnic Germans, and argued that those who could demonstrate 'loyalty' to Hungary should be exempted.[72] When asked to draw up lists for eventual expulsion in 1945, they faced an absolute lack of documentary evidence; in Ágfalva the notary commented that his list rested on no independent evidence and contained the names of some he believed to be patriotic Hungarians.[73] These local lists were scrapped when organised deportation began in spring 1946, as the compilation of deportation lists was placed in the hands of national civil servants and the authorities went to considerable lengths to exclude local actors from the process. This was combined with heavy-handed implementation.

---

68   Schödl 1995, p. 520.
69   *Az 1941 évi népszámlalás községek szerint* 1947, pp. 536–8, 602–3.
70   This point is made for another part of Hungary by the ethnographer Györgyi Bindorffer; see Bindorffer 2001.
71   Zielbauer 1989, p. 16.
72   Tóth 2001, pp. 35–70.
73   GyMSM.SL, XXI/21/a/1d., Ágfalvai jegyzőtől., Hiv.sz, 2/1945, Eln., Ágfalva, 1945 május 28-én.

Three hundred policemen were imported into Sopron from outside the region in order to ensure that order was kept during the process.⁷⁴ As the lists were prepared over the Easter weekend, the city was sealed from the outside world, the serving of alcohol was banned in local restaurants, and a night-time curfew enforced.⁷⁵ The police hunted down those on the list who went into hiding. During one night-time raid in early May 1946, almost eighty percent of the city's houses were searched.⁷⁶

The 1946 deportations allowed the impression of a despotic state to crystallise in western Hungarian communities, as the demonstration of arbitrary state power against a group that it argued was its enemy created real fear that transcended the ethnic divide. The sight of deportees being rounded up and placed on cattle trucks awakened fears that reached back to popular memories of the deportation of local Jews in 1944. In Mosonmagyaróvár, the local organ of the left-wing MSZDP, normally supportive of the MKP, reflected commonly held opinion when it equated the removal of Germans with the events of two years earlier: '[e]xpulsion⁷⁷ ... two years ago it was called deportation'.⁷⁸ Reactions to deportation were a product of the way in which it demonstrated the power and will of the state to act against the civilian population. This apparent despotism weakened the state's legitimacy, and its institutions found that the willingness of the population to cooperate with them was weakened as a consequence. The MKP mayor of Mosonmagyaróvár complained in April 1946 of the deportations' corrosive effect on the political authority of the organs of the new state.⁷⁹

Faced with the threat of removal through deportation from Moson or Sopron to Freilassing in southern Bavaria in 1946, many fled over the border with the intention of returning at a later date.⁸⁰ Some took their property with

---

74 'A hét végéig 420 kitelepitési tisztviselő és alkalmazott számára kell helyet biztositani magánlakásokban', *Soproni Újság*, 12 April 1946, p. 3.
75 'A polgármesterhelyettes nyilatkozata a kitelepitésre kerülők névsoráról', *Soproni Újság*, 25 April 1946, p. 3.
76 'Razzián a "mozgási korlátozás" ideje alatt', *Soproni Újság*, 5 May 1946, p. 3.
77 It bears mentioning that the Hungarian state referred even to formal deportation using the more neutral term 'expulsion' [*kitelepités*]. This was precisely because the term 'deportation' evoked direct comparison with the deportation of Hungary's Jews in 1944.
78 'Akiket elvittek, és akik itt maradtak', *Mosonmagyaróvári Barátság*, 2 June 1946, p. 2.
79 GyMSM.Gy.L, XXIf.1b.5.d, Mosonmagyaróvár megyei város polgármesterétől. Jelentés, 1946 áprilís hóról.
80 Ibid.

them to prevent its confiscation.[81] Ethnic German refugees from Hungary met with sympathy from the population on the Austrian side of the border. Furthermore, the 'settlers' who had taken their homes and property were unpopular and were blamed for cross-border crime in border villages such as Nickelsdorf and Zurndorf.[82] Minor officials showed similar sympathy for the plight of refugees, granting border passes in contravention of the regulations so that they could return to Hungary to visit relatives, to explosions of fury from the Hungarian authorities.[83] This sympathy, and the belief that expelled populations from the western border regions were of 'Austrian character', provoked a loosening of both work-permit and citizenship regulations that made it easier for them to claim Austrian citizenship.[84]

The 1946 deportations created a dynamic of mutual suspicion on both sides of the border, which drove a process of separation. While they led many in Austria to see the state over the border as threatening, and generated considerable local sympathy for Hungarian refugees, in Hungary these reactions helped drive a climate of suspicion. Both the local and national state saw the relatively open border as an active threat to the country's security. This was reinforced by apparent attempts by deportees to return home. In Fertőrákos, in one of several such incidents along the border, police were called in March 1947 after five former residents returned from Austria in order to resettle and take back the property that had been confiscated from them and redistributed to new settlers.[85] The border played a central role in the Hungarian left's politics of economic security. During 1947, the MKP smashed the FKGP through the use of the police in order to cement its control over the popular-front coalition and prepare the ground for the construction of dictatorship. A vital accompaniment to this campaign was the mobilisation of industrial workers and the poor, by blaming their poor material situation, persistent high prices, and food shortages, on 'speculators' and the 'reaction'.[86] Ethnic Germans who had escaped deportation were often blamed for 'smuggling' and

---

81   BgLA, BH Mattersburg, XI-Situationsberichte, Grenzgendarmeriekommandos Schattendorf, April 1946.
82   BgLA, A/VII-II/II-1, Zahl: Präs. 2/27-1947, Neusiedl am See, 30 März 1947, Situationsbericht für März 1947.
83   ÖStA/AdR, BMfAA, III-Wpol/Grenzen 2 Ungarn, Gz.120.025-W/Pol/47, Z.121.000-W/Pol/47.
84   BgLA, BH Mattersburg, XI-Polizei, Arbeitsamt Burgenland, Eisenstadt, 15 Juni 1948.
85   'Több visszaszökött ss-legényt fogott el az Államvédelmi rendőrség', Soproni Újság, 28 March 1947, p. 2.
86   Pittaway 2004, pp. 468–73.

'speculation' – accusations that were used to justify the further confiscation of property and expulsion in 1948.[87]

The deterioration of cross-border relations and the politicisation of smuggling continued with the construction of overt dictatorship in Hungary during 1948 and 1949. With opponents of the emergent dictatorship fleeing in large numbers, and Hungary gripped by Cold War paranoia, ethnic Germans returning to Hungary and Austrian smugglers were labelled as 'spies' and 'enemies' against which Hungary's western border needed to be secured. According to one piece of propaganda in March 1949, 'the cells in the Mosonmagyaróvár police station were full yesterday of illegal border crossers. Horse and livestock traders, ethnic Germans [svábok] seeking to return, German and Austrian citizens after food, and escaping fascists, waited out the afternoon'.[88]

Budapest implemented a scheme that involved the physical closure of the border, the creation of barbed-wire fences separating the two countries, the construction of a network of watchtowers, and the clearing of all land of vegetation within 500 metres of the border.[89] When it demanded that Austria create a similar zone on its side of the border, and Vienna refused, Hungary retaliated by closing the border to all Austrian farmers with properties on their side, to the fury of the border villages in Burgenland.[90]

Two States in a Divided Borderland

On the morning of 9 April 1950, in Schattendorf, twelve residents left Sunday mass and walked through the cemetery that lay adjacent to the barbed-wire fence that marked the border with Hungary. As they did so they were fired on by the Hungarian border guard. One shot went right over their heads, hitting a bush that lay just behind them. Panic ensued as the men left the cemetery as quickly as they could, as more shots were fired by the Hungarians.[91] Between the closure of the border in 1949 and the temporary thaw along it in summer 1956, the Austrian authorities recorded a string of incidents, which included

---

87   ÖStA/AdR, BMfAA, III-Wpol/Grenzen 2 Ungarn, Gz.102.793-WPol/49, Z.102.793-WPol/49.
88   'Megszünt a határon való átsétálgatás', *Mosonmagyaróvár*, 30 March 1949, p. 3.
89   MOL, Határőrség Országos Parancsnokság iratai (Papers of the Border Guard National Command, hereafter XIX-B-10)16d, A nyugati határ megerősítésével kapcsolatos műszaki munkálatok.
90   ÖStA/AdR, BMfAA, III-Wpol/Grenzen 2 Ungarn, Gz.103.828-WPol/49, Z.103.828-WPol/49.
91   ÖStA/AdR, BMfAA, II-Pol/Ungarn 9, GZ.120.292-Pol/50, Z.122.836-Pol./50, Grenzzwischenfall an der ungarischen Grenze bei Schattendorf am 9 April 1950.

attempts by Hungarian border guards to kidnap Austrian citizens, one shooting of an Austrian gendarme, and numerous instances of people being fired on; a string of injuries due to the accidental explosion of mines by people walking close to the border; fires; and even an instance of Hungarian border guards protecting agricultural workers trespassing on Austrian territory to steal the crops of local farmers.[92] The Austrian authorities lodged diplomatic protests when confronted with each incident. The Hungarians rejected their protests, arguing that the fault lay with the Austrian side, and that they had a duty to defend their borders.[93]

Despite the unpleasant and abnormal everyday reality of living next to a contested border, it constituted one aspect of the background that enabled the emergent Austrian state to construct its legitimate authority as a protector of local residents. This had begun in 1945 when it protected borderland residents from disorder generated by the Soviet-occupation authorities. In 1950, although the end of the occupation lay five years in the future, the state had restored law and order, while the Red Army, although still present, was by no means as oppressive a presence as it had been during the late 1940s.[94] With the expulsion of ethnic Germans from Hungary and the subsequent rise in tension along the border, an anti-communist consensus, shaped by events in Hungary, bolstered the legitimacy of the Austrian state in northern Burgenland. Fraudulent elections and the repression directed against the Catholic Church in Hungary offended public opinion,[95] as did the material hardship inflicted on Austrian property owners by their inability to cross the border to work their land after 1949.[96] The way in which this consensus strengthened the state was demonstrated during a crisis in the wake of the Fourth Wage and Price Agreement during September and October 1950, the latest of a round of agreements that cemented Austria's post-war 'social partnership' between capital and labour, through which the national trade-union leadership had agreed to a process of managed real-wage reductions as part of a generalised economic stabilisation package. The resulting rebellion in factories was backed by the KPÖ, enabling

---

92   ÖStA/AdR, BMfAA, II-Pol/Ungarn 9, GZ.519.073-Pol./56, Z.511.037-Pol/56, Bundesministerium für Inneres, Abteilung 2, 511.909-Pol/56.
93   For an example, see ÖStA/AdR, BMfAA, II-Pol/Ungarn 9, GZ.120.292-Pol/50, Z.126.694-Pol/50, 021519/1950, szóbeli jegyzék.
94   BgLA, A/VIII-14/II-2, Bezirkshauptmannschaft Oberpullendorf, Zl: Pr.26-1950, Oberpullendorf, 30 Jänner 1950, Situationsbericht für den Monat Jänner 1950.
95   BgLA, A/VIII-14/I-2, Bezirkshauptmannschaft Oberpullendorf, Zl: Pr.-244/19, Oberpullendorf, 30 September 1947, Lagebericht für September 1947.
96   ÖStA/AdR, BMfAA, III-WPol/Grenzen 2 Ungarn, GZ.103.828-WPol/49, Z.144.476-WPol/49.

the federal government, union establishment and the SPÖ to break the strike movement by denouncing it as a Communist plot.[97] Despite the unpopularity of government economic policies caused by the real material hardship for those living on fixed incomes in Burgenland as a consequence of almost constant pressure on real wages, the anti-communist consensus ensured that there was little industrial protest, even in many industrial communities in the region.[98]

On the other side of the border, despite its deployment of considerable violence the Hungarian state was weakened by its failure to generate real legitimacy for itself. While it used repression to secure its rule against the majority of the population that opposed it, which included religious believers and much of the rural population – which it attempted to force into agricultural cooperatives – it had built some conditional legitimacy through mobilising the industrial working class and rural poor by promising material improvement. By 1950, as forced industrialisation began to bite, and the regime's attempts to feed the urban centres and collectivisation led to severe cuts in living standards, even this conditional legitimacy was gone.[99] In the western borderlands, its position was far weaker. When it nationalised church schools in 1948, one of the few places in the country where it provoked open protest was in Sopron, where local priests, teachers and pupils marched against the measure. To assert its authority, the local regime was forced to bus in fifteen thousand activists from the rest of the country to stage a counter-protest against the machinations of the 'clerical reaction'.[100] The fury generated in villages by collectivisation, high taxation, and the government's attacks on organised religion, meant that in many borderland villages, while a semblance of order was maintained through a heavy police presence, the local regime lacked any positive authority at all.[101] Even in Sopron's factories, local party activists were forced to concede that the regime had no real support among the working class, for even most of the Stakhanovites – its exceptional workers – were ethnic Germans, alien-

---

97   Lewis 2000, pp. 533–52.
98   BgLA, A/VIII-14/II-2, Bezirkshauptmannschaft Mattersburg. Mattersburg, 27 September 1950, Bezirkshauptmannschaft Mattersburg, Mattersburg, 30 Oktober 1950.
99   Pittaway 1998; Lampland 1995, pp. 131–60.
100 GyMSM.SL, XX1/11/13d … /1948.
101 GyMSM.Gy.L, Az MDP Győr-Moson-Sopron Megyei Bizottság (the Győr-Moson-Sopron County Committee of the Hungarian Workers' Party, hereafter Xf.402)/2/Mezőgazdaság/8ö.e; MDP Járási Bizottság Mosonmagyaróvár, Sallai Imre u.3.sz, Jelentés: Mosonmagyaróvár, 1950 augusztus 9-én, p. 1.

ated from the regime by its policies of ethnic exclusion during the period of its construction.[102]

Nationally, the Hungarian state compensated for its lack of legitimacy by a reliance on repression, which made the regime dangerously unstable and prepared the ground for its rapid collapse during the 1956 Revolution.[103] It discriminated against the borderlands, whose urban centres, especially Sopron, were starved of new investment and lost industrial establishments and cultural institutions. It also severely restricted the freedom of border-region residents, creating a border zone in order to cut residents off from the rest of the country, and deported those it regarded as 'class enemies' to other parts of Hungary.[104] This combination of retribution and control did not strengthen the regime; instead, it generated complaints. When the regime crumbled during 1956 as a result of splits within the Party, coupled with a chronic lack of legitimacy and support among the population, these complaints shaped local political demands. In summer 1956, residents demanded the lifting of restrictions of travel between the border zone and the rest of Hungary, as well as the legalisation of small-scale cross-border traffic with Austria.[105] While such hopes were dashed after the suppression of the 1956 Revolution, border-region residents accommodated themselves reluctantly to the regime under which they were forced to live. With the post-1956 regime more aware than its immediate predecessor that its survival depended on tacit compromise with those it ruled, the authorities in the border region constantly pressured Budapest to make the lives of its residents more tolerable.[106]

The terms of the peace established after 1945 in the borderlands were unequal, inasmuch as those who lived in Austria found the peace they were offered easier to accept than those on the Hungarian side of the border. The state established in Hungary was weaker, even though, seemingly paradoxically, it was more repressive. This was because of its relative failure in establishing legitimate state authority, which rendered the regime in Budapest vulnerable to outright collapse in 1956, and left its leaders profoundly insecure between 1957 and 1989.

---

102 GyMSM.GyL, Az MDP Sopron Városi Bizottsága (the Sopron City Committee of the Hungarian Workers' Party, hereafter Xf.412)/1/9ö.e, Jegyzőkönyv: felvéve 1952. július 16-án, pp. 1–4.
103 Pittaway 2007, pp. 49–71.
104 MOL, XIX-B-1-j/45d, Kimutatás a déli és a nyugati határövezetbe tartozó városokról és községekről.
105 Pittaway 2006.
106 MOL, XIX-B-1-z, 14d, Szigorúan Titkos! Előterjesztés a határsáv csökkentésére vonatkozóan.

If the events of the mid-1950s in Hungary confirmed that for as long as the post-war settlement was in place its socialist regime could not be replaced, they also underlined the fragility of that regime. In Austria, the mid-1950s underlined the strength of legitimate authority possessed by the state that had been built since 1945. A year before the outbreak of the 1956 Revolution, Austria's leaders had signed a State Treaty with the allies that restored their sovereignty on condition of neutrality. The treaty allowed for the withdrawal of the Red Army from Burgenland. During the Hungarian Revolution and its suppression, neutrality was tested as a consequence of the upheaval on its eastern border and the temporary housing in the country of tens of thousands of refugees.[107] The way in which this revealed the strength of the formula of the protective state, through which the new Austrian state constructed its legitimacy after 1945, was indicated by the changing attitude to the army, established by the State Treaty a year previously. At the time of its establishment, many had argued against its creation on the grounds that in the war years 'enough fathers and sons of this land died for nothing',[108] and that money to be spent on the new military 'should be better put to more productive uses'.[109] By early 1957, the army could make its case credibly to the Burgenland population by arguing that 'the events in Hungary threatened military action on our eastern border. Does anyone now doubt that we need an army to defend our homeland?'[110]

---

107   Murer and Fónagy 2006.
108   BgLA, A/VIII-14-I-5, Sicherheitsdirektion für das Burgenland, Zahl: SD res.27/55, Eisenstadt, 1 Mai 1955, Lagebericht für den Monat April 1955.
109   BgLA, A/VIII-14-I-5, Sicherheitsdirektion für das Burgenland, Zahl: SD res.30/55, Eisenstadt, 2 Juni 1955, Lagebericht für den Monat Mai 1955.
110   BgLA, BH Eisenstadt, I-1957: 'Offizier. Ein Beruf für Mich?'

CHAPTER 10

Workers and the Change of System

Introduction

At least in the Hungarian context, much established opinion has regarded industrial workers – still more the working class – as all but irrelevant to consideration of the events of 1989, and certainly not relevant to the political system that was constructed between 1988 and 1990. While the same could not so easily be said of events leading up to the fall of state-socialist regimes in Romania, the GDR, and still less in Poland, even in these contexts workers seemed to have been marginalised, at least in the public sphere, within a few years of the launch of political transition. What was being built in Hungary, and the rest of the region, was very markedly 'bourgeois democracy' – sometimes mistranslated into English as 'civic democracy'. The attempt to bury a century of class politics, and especially working class politics, always formed part of the underlying script. It was accompanied across the region with the introduction of variants of neoliberal economic policies pioneered in Chile after the military *coup d'état* in 1973 to bolster political repression with a set of economic policies that would emasculate the social forces that sustained the Salvador Allende government, and which spread from the Latin American periphery to the western European core with the election of Margaret Thatcher's government in the United Kingdom in 1979.[1] These policies relied on maintaining tight control of the money supply through high interest rates, combined with sharp reductions in public expenditure to induce a 'transformational recession' that would break the power of labour through generating mass unemployment. Private capital would then be freed to transform the economy as state enterprises were transferred to the private sector. Despite the evidence of the United Kingdom in the 1980s, where the application of such policies brought nothing more than sluggish growth punctuated by two large recessions (1979–82, 1990–92), rising inequality, and widespread mass unemployment, these policies were sold in CEE as the elixir that would make the region's populations rich. The results of the Hungarian version of such policies, pursued by successive governments, were predictable, and hardly differed in kind from those in the UK a decade

---

* Originally published as Mark Pittaway 2011, 'A magyar munkásság és a rendszerváltás' *Múltunk*, 23, 1: 4–18.
1   Harvey 2007.

earlier. The main difference was that the negative social consequences of such policies were starker in Hungary, given its lower overall standard of living, and the higher expectations that were attached to them.

For those, like myself, involved in the writing of the history of workers, work and labour, 1989 was held to have rendered our own labour virtually redundant. In the words of Gareth Steadman Jones – himself originally a leading practitioner of neo-Marxist social history in the United Kingdom during the 1970s – '[t]he fall of communism in 1989 confirmed what had been increasingly apparent in the preceding twenty years: that there was no self-sustaining form of economy beyond commercial society, only centralised and authoritarian regimes in which bureaucratic direction substituted for the processes of commercial exchange'.[2] In short, history – and not just that of CEE – was to be written from a perspective which accepted the inevitability of an economic order based upon the market, and which regarded any critique of the relations of economic power – hence the neutral and empty term 'commercial society', rather than the more critical 'capitalism' – as undesirable and potentially dangerous. Looking back from the standpoint of twenty years later, this view of a historical discipline trapped within a liberal capitalist 'end of history' seems scarcely tenable – 'commercial society' after all has wrought carnage on the social fabric of CEE: it eliminated 27.2 percent of all of the jobs that existed in Hungary in the eight years after 1989; these jobs were never recovered – in 2008, there were 23.2 percent fewer jobs than nineteen years previously – feeding a problem of persistently low labour-market participation and severe poverty.[3] It left a situation in which the real median income of the population stood at only 108.9 percent of their level in the early 1990s at the peak of the boom in the middle of the following decade.[4] While GDP at the onset of the economic crisis in early 2008 was notably but not substantially higher than in 1989, rather than having 'caught up', Hungary had barely held its 1991 economic position relative to the western European core – when compared to 1989, its relative position had deteriorated slightly.[5] Furthermore, not only had Hungary failed to escape from the public debt trap of the 1980s, the country also saw a spectacular increase in private household debt, as the volume of private sector

---

2 Steadman Jones 1996, p. 36.
3 International Labour Organisation (ILO), Labour Statistics. Available on: <http://data.un.org/Data.aspx?q=Employment&d=LABORSTA&f=tableCode%3A2B>.
4 Organisation for Economic Cooperation and Development (OECD), Country Statistical Profiles: Hungary, 2009. Available on: <http://stats.oecd.org/Index.aspx?DataSetCode=CSP2009>.
5 OECD, Country Statistical Profiles 2009, Gross Domestic Product (GDP), US$, current prices, current PPPs, millions. Available on: <http://stats.oecd.org/Index.aspx?DataSetCode=CSP2009>.

domestic credit expanded by 339.4 percent between January 2000 and the end of the third quarter of 2007.[6]

With Hungary and much of the CEE region moving from a 'post-socialist' era, characterised by neoliberal certainties, to a dangerous and uncertain 'post-liberal' era, it seems time to re-examine the class dynamics of the transition out of state socialism, and to start examining the 'post-socialist' period not just in the light of state socialism, but as history in its own right. This chapter is a sketch of the issues involved and is largely an attempt to think theoretically through some of the issues. It sits between two separate pieces of empirical research: the first piece of research is into the history of workers during state socialism, especially the period of early socialism; and in the second unofficial piece of research I have been undertaking to trace the economic history of Hungary in the post-socialist period, stimulated by a sense that the explosion of the economic crisis in 2008 represents both an ending of one period and the opening of a new one. The chapter seeks to explain the markedly anti-socialist nature of mainstream actors in the 'bourgeois democratic' political system, and thus the marginalisation of the labour movement, as well as the effective destruction of the industrial workforce – at the cost of catastrophically low levels of labour market participation, which have acted as a severe constraint on Hungary's economic development – in terms of the position that workers occupied within the state-socialist political system and the dynamics of its collapse.

Workers and State-Socialism

There have been a multitude of attempts to theorise state-socialist societies, and it would be unfeasible here to give a summary of the key theories and to position the argument of this paper in relation to them. Nevertheless, it seems worth beginning this section by offering a rough overview of the key social relations that together constituted the social realm during the state-socialist period:

- Property was, theoretically, owned by the collective of all workers (this form is modified in agriculture by the agricultural producer cooperative), and was managed on their behalf by state organs in the control of the vanguard Party operating according to democratic centralist principles.
- The performance of labour to contribute to the generation of the social product was a basic obligation of all citizens. This labour was alienated,

---

6 Turner 2008, p. 133.

commodified, and fragmented, and was subject to a high degree of managerial supervision.
- The means of subsistence were guaranteed to all who worked. This was covered through a nationally provided social wage, an enterprise-based social wage, and money wages (this could also include the right to participate, to a limited extent, in marginal private sector activity).
- Economic activity was coordinated bureaucratically by the state, and within that framework in the enterprise apparatus. Markets played a subordinate and marginal role within the economy, even in the more reformist variants of the system.
- The state controlled by the vanguard Party was part of the international system – it was dependent politically on other socialist states. Its role within the international system was determined by the conflict between socialist and capitalist states, but at times of thaw the state became more dependent on the capitalist world economy.
- The state managed by the vanguard Party was a 'civil war' state. This was because many did not accept its rule, and many did not accept its programme of social transformation and the nature of state-socialist social-property relations. The attempts of the state to protect itself against its enemies (real or assumed), something also related to its international position, was a central aspect of the social-property relations of the system.

The first of these relationships – that which rested on the state ruling in the name of 'workers' – lies at the heart of what I term the 'politics of legitimacy' of socialist states. What do I mean by this? All states exist in a dual sense: firstly, as a collection of separate institutions that work in complementary and contradictory ways; and secondly, these institutions clothe themselves in the myth of being a singular coherent institution that is the legitimate source of primary authority over society. This myth of state unity and legitimacy is central to its acquisition of infrastructural power, in other words, the ability to operate across the territory it governs and secure its authority at the everyday level. This is because to rule on a day-to-day basis a state requires the active cooperation of those who staff its police, military institutions, tax collection authorities, and other bureaucracies. And for these institutions to operate, those who populate them require that a sufficient number of the ruled – by no means always a majority – are prepared to cooperate with them, on the grounds that they represent a legitimate authority. Therefore, a state needs to construct sufficient legitimacy for itself. It needs to be able to tell enough of the population a credible story as to why it should rule. In order, therefore, to approach the question of 'the politics of legitimacy' in the state-socialist context, one needs to take their ideology seriously, rather than seeing them – as has so often been the case – as simply a cloak for their leaders' unbridled accumulation of their own power. Regimes of the Bolshevik left – and Hungary's was no exception – rested on the revolutionary transformation of pre-existing states into political communities based upon the collective identities of those who worked. The party-states brought to power were, in terms of their own self-presentation, the vanguard of 'the Communist working class', which was the collective subject of the socialist society that they would build.

Maintaining the credibility of this claim, and thus the necessary degree of legitimacy to rule, required the state to maintain the outward support, or at least the quiescence, of the working class – especially those male skilled workers who were deemed the most class conscious of all workers, and as such those most likely to support the regime. And this was often a problem, for the social relations described above allowed class to reproduce itself, often antagonistically toward state authority, within the everyday experience of state-socialist social relations in the factory. Moreover, the community sharply contradicted many of the claims made by the regime. At the same time, the community generated a political language of working class opposition that directly undercut the state's legitimacy. During the very early period of state-socialist rule in the late 1940s, these contradictions were bridged through a politics of informal compromise on the job, in which the conditional legitimacy the regime had constructed was maintained, as was the necessary degree of compromise to maintain production, but at the price of escalating wage costs, as workers demanded material improvement, informal control over remuneration, and a consequent problem for central planners of inadequate productivity growth.

The regime sought to smash the micro-politics of compromise on the job, as the response of the Soviet Union to a deteriorating international climate led the Party and regime in Budapest to prioritise armaments-based industrialisation over the need to maintain the consent of most workers – a decision that destroyed its legitimacy. The cumulative effect of these processes was that by 1953 industrial communities were on the verge of a social explosion; an explosion that was defused temporarily by the wage increases and social measures introduced by Imre Nagy's first government appointed that June. The situation remained serious for the regime, for the discontent and lack of legitimacy it encountered among industrial workers represented the root of a serious crisis of socialist state-building, simply because it sharply contradicted the claims of Hungary's rulers to govern in the name of the 'working class'. During the mounting disputes within the Party and between intellectuals over the future of socialism that took place between 1953 and 1956, workers and the state of the regime's legitimacy in industrial communities were all but invisible. Consequently, industrial communities came to constitute an 'evental site' within the regime's construction of its own legitimacy – namely, a place where central contradictions normally hidden to those outside were laid bare to insiders. Yet the reality of workers' relations with the regime at the everyday level was invisible within the broader public realm beyond the factories and the industrial districts, especially to policymakers, intellectuals and students. However, when the socialist state crumbled during 1956, the reality of the relationship between workers and the state became progressively more visible within the broader public realm, thereby feeding the process of collapse. During the Revolution in October, the very presence of large numbers of workers taking to the streets, while none were prepared to defend the state, led to the collapse of its authority, as the credibility of its claim to legitimacy evaporated.[7]

While the intervention of the Soviet Union enabled a restored socialist state to crush the political institutions of the Revolution and thus occupy power, and while its control over security forces was sufficient to detain revolutionary activists, it could not depend upon repressive means alone to generate stability, simply because the Revolution had completely transformed the situation by revealing the socialist state's lack of legitimacy among workers. Therefore, in order to survive the state was forced to repair its relationship with workers – especially those urban skilled workers who, within the Hungarian social imaginary, spoke for the 'working class'. This was made especially difficult because the regime had to mask the fact that most workers had supported the central political goals of the Revolution, especially the withdrawal of Soviet troops, democratisation of the state, and Hungarian neutrality. Given that the state could not even begin to address these political demands, and was unwilling to do so, it constructed a brittle legitimacy through which it repaired its relationship with workers – at least relatively left-wing urban workers – through formalising tacit bargains in the workplace created through the informal micro-politics of production of the previous eight years, and the raising of living standards. This fragile legitimacy was conditional on the state meeting the material demands of at least the 'core' of the industrial workforce. It also necessitated the *de facto* abandonment of attempts to create a 'new Communist working class'. While the regime paid lip service to the goals of improving cultural and educational provision for workers, and creating a new attitude among workers towards work, in practice it accommodated itself to established working class cultures, especially those of older, skilled, male, urban workers. This 'workerist' settlement that had emerged by summer 1958

---

7 This case is made by Pittaway in chapters 3 and 4 of this volume, and in Pittaway 2007.

was fundamental to the consolidation of the regime, allowing it to weather the storm of renewed agricultural collectivisation in the late 1950s, and acted as a cornerstone of the regime's construction of its legitimacy throughout the 1960s and 1970s.[8]

This tacit political settlement, which was always characterised by tension, enabled the regime to consolidate its authority and to carry through its project of remoulding rural communities through collectivisation in the 1960s. As a consequence, state socialism as a system and workers as a social group were locked together – in this respect, Hungary resembled some of its immediate neighbours, most notably Czechoslovakia and the GDR, where similar 'workerist' settlements developed during the late 1950s and early 1960s. It differed from Poland where the effective failure to develop such a settlement over the course of the 1960s led to the explosions of working class protest across the country in 1970 and 1976, culminating in the eventual crisis of 1980–1.[9]

The Erosion of the State-Socialist Settlement

By the mid-1960s, however, there were signs that Hungary was reaching the limits of its socialist growth model. The pattern of growth underpinned by the social relations of state socialism was characterised by several key features, which were crucial in ensuring that Hungary, along with the rest of CEE, failed to keep up with those states on the southern periphery of western Europe, with which it had been most comparable prior to the onset of socialism.[10] While the development was not visible in official published statistics, independent statistics demonstrate that during the 1960s, according to most independent estimates, Hungary's GDP fell behind first Spain, then Greece, and at the end of the decade Portugal.[11] What were these characteristics of growth? Why did they function as they did, and how did this shape divergence and relative economic underdevelopment?

- State-socialist growth was characterised by a stagnation or decline of labour productivity/output per worker in industry, but there was an expansion of

---

8   Pittaway, chapter 7 of this volume.
9   For these comparative points, see Pittaway 2005b, pp. 1–8.
10 Maddison 1995.
11 Maddison 2010, 'Historical Statistics of the World Economy, 1-2008 AD'. Available on: <www.ggdc.net/maddison/Historical_Statistics/horizontal-file_02-2010.xls>.

labour productivity in agriculture as small private plots were replaced with large agricultural units.
- Growth was driven by expanding industrial employment at the expense of agriculture and economic inactivity.
- Investment for growth was financed at the expense of domestic consumption. This was applied in the sense of current or deferred sacrifice by the population; the latter manifested itself through indebtedness.
- Development was characterised by a lack of balanced growth between individual sectors of the economy determined by the differential bargaining power of enterprises – normally heavy industry expanded at a faster rate than those producing consumer goods, while industrial production expanded faster than general infrastructure.
- Imbalances in growth produced a private sector – whether illegal, grey or permitted – that was dependent upon exploiting the effects of this unbalanced growth, experienced by economic actors as 'shortages'. During the 1970s, this was encouraged by economic reform measures, and in the 1980s it was celebrated as 'the second economy'.
- Living standards rose to a point, but the quality of life for producers was stymied by the relative underdevelopment of infrastructure, while the consequence of the imbalances that characterised growth forced workers to participate in the shadow 'private sector', thus increasing overall working hours, but encouraged workers to redirect their efforts toward high-profit private activities.
- Production was characterised by few incentives to conserve scarce resources – including labour – and to innovate, either through the introduction of new production techniques, or new lines. The lack of market relations, the relative political power of workers to preserve jobs, and the power of managers within bargaining structures, made the identification, let alone the elimination of redundant capacity, close to impossible.
- Because of its extensive rather than intensive nature, and the structural obstacles to intensive growth presented by state-socialist social-property relations, growth ran up against limits imposed by the availability of resources – most notably, labour. After an initial period of high growth there followed a period of stagnation relative to countries at a comparable level of development when state-socialist regimes came to power, and this seems to have happened in the Hungarian case during the 1960s.

Political constraints closed the way to any reconstruction of the basic social relations on which state socialism and its political system rested – something that became obvious as political reform was attempted and crushed in

Hungary. Instead, what survived was a programme, championed by technocrats who stressed economic expertise, which called for the introduction of market relations into the economic sphere. This led to the introduction of the New Economic Mechanism on 1 January 1968, which aimed to loosen plan targets in the interests of using the profit motive to stimulate enterprises to boost productivity. At the same time, the service sector underwent price liberalisation, and a series of measures in agriculture, which gave cooperatives greater commercial independence – building on tacit experiments visible in the mid-1960s, when cooperatives faced with the migration of all their labour of working age to industry had been forced to innovate to survive.

The effects of the reform led initially to a wave of working class protest. But instead of driving a broader political shift and a transformation of state-socialist social relations to resolve the impasse of the state-socialist model, the way in which this protest was politicised as a result of the investment of the leaders in the state in their post-1956 settlement of buying working class quiescence, in order to conserve political structures, paradoxically strengthened the logic of technocratic marketisation. Workers protested profit-share premiums for managers that brought visible social differentiation, leading to complaints about the creation of a 'new class' or 'new rich'. In industry, this came on the back of management drives to cut wages and increase work intensity in order to make their firms more profitable, leading to increased conflict. Similar developments in the service sector led to the greater visibility of luxury goods, which were often out of reach for those who worked for one 'wage or salary' alone. Furthermore, the commercialisation of agriculture brought about high prices for food and visible wealth in villages, which urban workers resented, as many cooperative members worked in industry. This group felt itself to be losing out from social differentiation. With the proportion of working class members of the Party declining, and with the latter becoming a managerial/white-collar organisation, political structures were increasingly called into question openly at the turn of the 1970s. In the aftermath of events in Czechoslovakia, this was dangerous politically, and the Party made concessions, launching a highly limited version of normalisation that stalled rather than derailed the economic reforms, in order to temporarily defuse working class discontent.[12]

Stalled reform brought little improved economic performance during the 1970s, but it did erode Hungary's social settlement. In a kind of Eastern European version of Western European trends, reform led to a fragmentation of the working class and a weakening of the positive value of working class identity in the public sphere. Inequality rose, as did consumption and latent

---

12   Pittaway, chapter 7 of this volume.

demand for luxury goods. Personal credit was expanded through the State Savings Bank (*Országos Takarék Pénztár*, OTP), which extended the home loans scheme it operated since 1955 with personal loans – leading to greater household indebtedness. Wages in the first job were deemed insufficient to support consumer demand, which fed a growth in overtime and supplementary work: 34.8 percent of workers regularly performed overtime in 1979, while by 1976 between seventy-five and eighty-five percent of all employees across the economy were believed to have some source of additional income.[13] This development was pushed by the development of a substantial, semi-legal, shadow economy alongside that of the state sector. Its development was connected both to growing and more differentiated consumer demands on the one hand, and economic reform on the other. The creation of a shadow economy of the size and importance of that which existed by the mid-1970s had its roots in Hungary's successful final collectivisation drive in 1961, which ensured the integration of small-scale agricultural production and the work of cooperatives. The dramatic improvement in housing conditions during the 1960s and early 1970s gave further impetus to this development. Private family housing, and the construction of flats through flat-construction cooperatives, substantially involved both the legal private sector and the shadow economy. In practice, both played a major role in the maintenance and repair of shoddy state-built housing. By 1979, around a third of all maintenance of flats and housing was performed by those working in the shadow economy. This was, however, the tip of the iceberg: the repair of clothing, motor vehicles, electrical goods, telephones and personal services were all areas in which the influence of the shadow economy was marked.[14]

This further intensified as the state attacked living standards through large price hikes in July 1979, and renewed economic problems generated further reform in 1982 and 1985. While many accommodated to these trends, by the turn of the 1980s this paradoxical form of marketisation was eroding the legitimacy of the regime, as many felt that they worked more and more, for less and less, while others profited. In a meeting of senior party members in the capital in 1981, 'Emil Péjak, a major figure in the workers' movement ... really felt the terrible situation which existed in workers' circles ... the party had to understand that people were increasingly dissatisfied ... and felt that they just worked and worked and never got anywhere, and they had no opportunities'.[15]

---

13   Héthy 1984, pp. 66–7; Kemény 1992, p. 220.
14   Gábor and Galasi 1982, p. 201.
15   Quoted in Seleny 1994, p. 458.

Workers and the Change of System

When socialism ended in Hungary during 1989, it ended with the marginalisation rather than mobilisation of the working class. Economic reformers, perhaps in view of the effects of working class discontent on the course of earlier economic reform, celebrated rather than mourned the marginalisation of the working class during the events of that year. Attempts at trade-union renewal – either through the formation of new confederations or the renewal of the previously state-dominated ones – demonstrated the lack of working class faith in representative institutions at the workplace. Subordinated to the interests of middle-class and intellectual activists in new parties, unions and working class politics found themselves marginalised during the political transition that ended socialist rule.

This marginalisation is partially explained by the fact that socialism ended in Hungarian factories and working class communities with a whimper rather than a bang, as workers concentrated on mitigating the impact of economic crisis on their incomes by working ever longer hours to satisfy material needs, rather than opting to protest. Yet part of the explanation can be found in the way in which the working class was relatively successfully integrated into the political system under Kádár. This chapter has suggested that the story of the fluid relationship between workers and regime in socialist Hungary is that of an informal social settlement between the regime and the workers that rested on the failure of Stalinist politics under Rákosi. It was constructed in the aftermath of the 1956 Revolution and reached its peak during the mid-1960s. Challenged by economic reform in 1968, this settlement provided a social base for the attack on reform during the early 1970s.

While the reshaping of the relationship between regime and working class after 1968 represented the decay of that original settlement, it also demonstrated its durability. Despite the considerable discontent with the low level of wages relative to the differentiated needs generated by socialist consumerism, the settlement was modified by the generation of a poor bargain based on the toleration of a large shadow economy, and a continuous desire on the part of many in the Party to address working class grievances. The degree to which the regime was able to maintain any kind of tacit social settlement with the workforce was undoubtedly eroded during the 1970s, while the ground was cut from beneath the Party's feet by the economic crisis of the 1980s, leading to the outright delegitimation of discourses of class and socialism by the end of the 1980s.[16]

---

16 On this outright deligitimation see Bartha 2009, pp. 123–44.

The road was opened to a model of democracy that was not merely 'post-socialist', but was actively 'anti-socialist', largely because it came out of a process in which discourses of socialism and class were jointly discredited. While the events of 1989 opened the road to freedom of speech, assembly, and formal political participation, as well as removing the real barriers to travel across Hungary's western and southern border and forms of political unfreedom that had characterised dictatorship, the flaw was that they banished from the public sphere discussion of socio-economic alternatives, and thus masked the creation and crystallisation of new forms of class domination. This rested on a political culture that resisted participation by anyone other than members of an intellectual elite, or a form of political participation that raised social and economic demands as 'populism'. This political culture in turn masked a fusion between oligarchical political parties and business elites that was revealed in a strikingly open form in the second decade following 1989. Because of the destruction of class as a collective identity, Hungary was denied the labour movement that could have served as the basis for a politics of class compromise and a more social-democratic transition, let alone the kind of democracy that could rest on the broader questioning of social, political and economic inequalities.

CHAPTER 11

Fascism in Hungary

Historical interpretation of Hungarian fascism[1] has been shaped by the political divisions that followed the fall of Fascism in 1945. Almost from the moment of the war's end, Hungary's left-wing political parties used their anti-fascist credentials to legitimise their political project for Hungary's future. They sought to emphasise not only how they distinguished themselves from the country's national socialist parties – especially the Arrow Cross Party (*Nyilaskeresztes Párt*, NP), which briefly held office during the last tragic months of the war – but also attempted to tar Hungary's authoritarian interwar regime with the brush of fascism. From the end of the Second World War, through most of the socialist era, politics in the era of Admiral Miklós Horthy, from 1919 until 1944, was described as 'Horthy fascism' – its pursuit of territorial revision and institutionalised anti-Semitism was held responsible for the tragedies of Hungary's painful entanglement in the Second World War and the murder of the majority of the country's Jewish population. Since the 1970s, and more overtly since 1989, the historiography of the interwar period has emphasised the distance between fascism and the authoritarian and conservative practice of politics during the Horthy era – based as the latter was on an oligarchic parliamentarianism, which harked back to the political system of the dualist era as much as it looked forward to the political practices of Fascist Italy or Nazi Germany.

While Hungary's radical national socialist parties defined themselves as radical-nationalist opponents of the country's interwar political system, it is impossible to explore Hungarian fascism without considering its relationship to the dominant conservatism of the interwar years. This is so principally because Hungarian fascist movements in the 1930s existed in a symbiotic relationship with the structures and patterns of social support for the dominant interwar regime. In many respects the national socialism that emerged during the decade was a radical variant of the conservatism to which most of Hungary's ruling elite subscribed. The boundaries between the conservative governing elite and the radical right had been fluid from the beginnings of the

---

* Originally published as Mark Pittaway 2009, 'Hungary', in *The Oxford Handbook of Fascism*, edited by R.J.B. Bosworth, Oxford: Oxford University Press, pp. 380–97.
1 Editor's note: I have capitalised 'Fascism' and 'National Socialism' when the article refers to the Italian or German movement, party and regime. I leave the terms in lowercase when referring to the phenomena in Hungary.

Horthy era in 1919. Counter-revolutionary governments of the early 1920s had drawn considerable support from the radical right within both the military and the country as a whole. The consolidation of their political authority relied on the development of a symbiotic relationship between the aristocratic governing elite and counter-revolutionary paramilitarism. During Prime Minister István Bethlen's period of office between 1921 and 1931, the influence of the radical right on the political system was contained, and governing practice instead resembled the authoritarian liberalism of the pre-war years. But the depression radicalised political opinion. During the early 1930s, public opinion moved sharply to the right, increasingly associating not only democratic ideas with a 'foreign' and 'liberal' spirit, but also the political practices of the Bethlen era.

Explicit fascism and national socialism were the most radical manifestations of this shift, and this process goes some way towards explaining some of its peculiarities in the Hungarian context. By the turn of the 1940s, national socialism had achieved a considerable popularity, resting on a cross-class coalition that stretched from army officers, public officials, small businessmen, the poorer segments of the agrarian population, and even sections of the industrial working class. However, it was kept out of power at that point only by a combination of the selective use of state power against the movement, and the appeasement of anti-Semitic and irredentist opinion by governments. Its medium- and long-term fortunes were tied to the prestige and popularity of German National Socialism within Hungary. For this reason, hampered by its own political mistakes, the Hungarian far right found that the unpopularity of the Second World War led to an evaporation of support. When it finally came to power as a result of a German-backed coup in October 1944, Hungarian national socialism was considerably weaker than four years previously in terms of the backing it received. Its association with the period in late 1944 and April 1945 – when Hungary was the theatre of bloody military conflict between the Soviet Union and retreating Axis forces – and its own violence and extremism in power, left it profoundly discredited. While the early post-war years were marked by isolated acts of anti-Semitic violence, Hungary's various post-war regimes closed off the political space into which neo-fascist organisations might have emerged. During the years of socialist dictatorship from 1948, 'the struggle against fascism' became a central aspect of the regime's ideological armoury. While the re-emergence of political pluralism since 1989 has seen the appearance of some radical right-wing movements and parties, and, indeed, acts of protest, these hark back more to the broader radical right of the interwar years than solely to those movements that can be unproblematically characterised as fascist.

The roots of both Hungarian fascism and the dominant conservative ideology of the interwar years lie in a polarisation of politics that began in the 1890s, when conservative intellectuals responded to the growing mobilisation of the left in the country's industrial centres and a greater assertiveness from non-Magyar speakers (who composed half of pre-war Hungary's population). They argued that the dominant liberal oligarchy, which ruled Hungary throughout the pre-war years, had allowed society to become dominated by an 'alien spirit', which they associated with the country's Jews, who they asserted had become powerful beneficiaries of the development of capitalism during the last third of the nineteenth century. Their apparent 'power', an emergent labour movement, and the growing influence of democratic ideas based on notions of individual rights, were, according to this view, threatening the territorial integrity and character of a 'Christian', 'historic' Hungary. 'National Christian' conservative ideas were strengthened during the First World War and combined with other and more explicitly racist intellectual currents. With the onset of the crisis of Hungary's variant of authoritarian, oligarchic, liberal nationalism, the ideas of this late nineteenth-century new right came to dominate hegemonic discourses of national identity, thus shaping both interwar Hungarian conservatism and later fascism.

The political crisis of liberalism, to which 'National Christian' conservatism was a response, culminated in the collapse of the Austro-Hungarian monarchy. Mobilisation among the kingdom's minorities, especially on the country's geographical periphery, among Romanians in Transylvania, southern Slav groups along the southern border, Slovaks in northern Hungary, and Germans in western Transdanubia, shattered Hungary geographically. The designs of neighbouring states, such as Romania and newly created Austria, the alternative Yugoslav and Czechoslovak national projects, as well as the interests of the victorious powers, interacted to shape a post-war settlement, which dismantled the kingdom of Hungary. Because of the centrality of notions of the 'permanent' and 'God-given' nature of statehood to notions of 'National Christian' conservatism, such a settlement – institutionalised through the Treaty of Trianon in 1920 – was utterly unacceptable to Hungarian conservatives and, more generally, to the bulk of Hungarian opinion. As the state fragmented, society and politics became polarised along class lines. The strains of the war economy stimulated increasing protest in industrial areas, which generated the social revolutionary pressure leading to bourgeois revolution in the autumn of 1918, and then the creation of a brief Soviet Republic in 1919. Revolution produced counter-revolutionary reaction, aided by neighbouring states that emerged victorious to shape the contours of Hungary's interwar regime. Consolidated by the early 1920s, this regime, institutionally, was far from fascist; instead, it reproduced many of the practices of the pre-war liberal polity. Hungary remained a monarchy, albeit one presided over by a regent, Admiral Miklós Horthy, and one which rejected the attempts of Károly IV, King until 1918, to reclaim his throne in 1921. Interwar Hungary retained a parliamentary system, but from 1922 with an ever more restricted franchise. It also remained a multi-party system and, while elections were competitive, they were far from free or fair. The ruling Party, which existed in several incarnations until 1944, acted as an arm of the administration, and for this reason its power was never seriously threatened. Communist parties were banned and organisations considered subversive – like the legal MSZDP and its unions – were subject to official harassment and police supervision.

Hungary's interwar regime broke more radically with the practice of the pre-war years in several important respects of central relevance to the later development of fascism. The first was the role of paramilitarism within both the political system and culture of interwar Hungary. With defeat in autumn 1918, the Austro-Hungarian military collapsed. The fragmentation of the army was exacerbated by the deep-seated political polarisation of which the revolutionary moment was a part. Those who refused to accept either the democratic or later the Soviet Revolution formed themselves into a number of paramilitary societies, most of which adopted radical nationalist, anti-socialist and anti-Semitic political programmes. Many of these offered their support to the counter-revolutionary forces that crystallised around the Anti-Bolshevik Committee in Vienna and later the anti-communist government based in the south-eastern city of Szeged. The military defeat of the Soviet Republic and the consolidation of the power of the counter-revolutionary government in 1919 countrywide were accompanied by a wave of paramilitary violence. Paramilitary groups murdered those whom they accused of supporting and serving the Soviet Republic, but often targeted anyone they believed to be sympathetic to the aims of the labour movement. Motivated by a clearly anti-Semitic ideology, many of the groups extended this violence to Jews, especially in provincial western Hungary in the immediate aftermath of the Soviet Republic's collapse. Right-wing paramilitary actions in late 1919 are believed to have claimed as many as two thousand lives.

While the wave of paramilitary bloodshed abated, it was often selectively condoned by the emergent regime as it consolidated its authority. In 1921, Hungarian paramilitary violence erupted in those parts of western Hungary awarded to Austria, when the Austrian gendarmerie occupied them in August. This carnage, dubbed officially in Hungary the 'Western Hungarian Uprising', was backed by the Hungarian authorities who used it to force a referendum on the drawing of the border around the city of Sopron. Often there existed a fluid boundary between paramilitaries and the regular army, since the former could be used to shore up the regime when the latter proved unreliable, as during Károly IV's final attempt to reclaim the Hungarian throne in October 1921. His march on Budapest to remove Horthy, supported by legitimist sections of the army, was repelled on the outskirts of the capital at Budaörs by a force organised by the prominent paramilitary and later radical-right politician Gyula Gömbös, who ensured that the ranks of pro-Horthy soldiers were bolstered by paramilitaries and armed members of radical-right student organisations. Even when the interwar regime was consolidated during the 1920s, when István Bethlen sought to place distance between his government and the radical right, forcing some like Gömbös into opposition, paramilitarism preserved a presence within Hungarian society and political culture. Prominent political organisations with their origins in the counter-revolutionary paramilitarism of 1919 – like the Hungarian National Defence Association (*Magyar Országos Véderő Egylet*, or MOVE) – retained a presence in local society and politics, in some areas compensating for the fact that the governing party lacked its own mass-membership organisation in much of the country prior to 1932.

If paramilitarism was one element of the interwar Hungarian political scene relevant to the later emergence of fascism, then anti-liberalism and the hegemony of national Christian ideas within the political culture of interwar Hungary constituted another. Cultural and political commentators during the 1920s defined the regime in opposition to the 'liberalism' of the dualist era, which, it was maintained, had led to the incursion of 'alien elements' that had led the country to catastrophe in the aftermath of the First World War. Such attitudes generated forms of political discourse that stressed the unified and eternal nature of the Hungarian nation, its fundamentally 'Christian' character, and emphasised that political leaders had a duty to 'defend' Magyars from their 'alien' enemies. In turn, such opinions led to a growing interest in *völkisch* ideas of 'race' and 'racial defence' and their translation into a Hungarian context during the 1920s, inspiring political movements that stressed the apparent Turanian origins of Magyars, which embedded themselves in radical right-wing rhetoric. The most disturbing aspect of anti-liberal, national Christian conservatism was its political anti-Semitism, which prompted legislation limiting the proportion of Jews admitted to universities from 1921. During the 1920s, this law was unevenly implemented, but despite this anti-Semitism played a central role in public discourse. It was often married to an anti-capitalism in which 'Jewish international capitalism' was asserted to be undermining the position of Hungary's 'Christian' population, especially at moments of economic dislocation, such as during the hyperinflation between 1922 and 1924, and the period of economic restriction that brought it to an end. Right-wing radicals argued that measures to destroy the economic influence of Jews provided the key to integrating marginal groups – like the working class – into their proposed 'national community'. While they maintained that they were not opposed to capitalism as such, many like Gyula Gömbös maintained that a 'capitalism which is not national, which is not Christian, which does not take into account higher national considerations, but which is simply selfish, I hate and see as dangerous'.[2]

The notion of the creation of a 'Christian Hungary' was allied to the Hungarian regime's core policy goal of reversing the territorial losses institutionalised by the Treaty of Trianon and regaining as much of the territory of pre-1918 Hungary as possible. Irredentism was an article of faith across most of the political spectrum, including the far right, and infused official and popular political culture. Belief in Christianity and irredentism became equated, as anti-Trianon propaganda invited Magyars to 'believe in one God, to believe in one homeland'. Given the circumstances in which 'historic Hungary' had been dismantled, the dominant ideology of the interwar era was characterised by an aggressive anti-socialism, which not only blamed communism for the 'tragedy' that was said to have befallen the nation in 1919, but also attacked Hungary's legal Social Democratic Party. Official rhetoric condemned the labour movement in all its manifestations, maintaining that it had played a role in delivering Hungary into the arms of 'foreigners', because it had concentrated on a politics of class to the exclusion of nation; it should 'not have forgotten, that a Hungarian worker is not just a worker, but a Hungarian too'.[3]

While these notions were hegemonic, political actors committed to radical right-wing policies were successfully marginalised under István Bethlen during the second half of the 1920s. This position changed as a result of the depression, which brought severe economic dislocation that affected social attitudes and the nature of the political system. The political change brought about by the depression occurred simultaneously at both elite and popular levels. The first element was a crisis at governmental level causing the fall of Bethlen in 1931, and then, following a brief interregnum under Gyula Károlyi, Horthy appointed Gyula Gömbös – paramilitary-turned-politician, admirer of Mussolini, and Hungary's most prominent advocate of radical-right politics – as Prime Minister in 1932. His term of office, which ended with his death in October 1936, proved to be a disappointment to supporters of his policies. His attempts to transform the political system within the constraints of the

---

2 'Beszéd a Nemzetgyűlés Indemintási Vitájában Kül- és Belpolitikai Kérdésekről, a Külföldi Kölcsönről', in Vonyó et al. 2004, p. 225.
3 'Munkásvédelem: politika nélkül', *Soproni Hírlap*, 18 May 1939, p. 1.

interwar settlement to create a 'purposeful national state', underpinned by an attack on the autonomy of the labour movement, a more protectionist, dirigiste economic policy and social reform, were frustrated by those members of the governing elite who were suspicious of his intentions. While disappointment in his government generated the space for explicitly fascist mobilisation, some of the reforms he did implement bolstered the later radicalisation of the political system. Among his first acts was to transform the governing party into a mass-membership organisation – the National Unity Party (*Nemzeti Egység Pártja*, or NEP). In organising the party, Gömbös's radical-right supporters were given key positions. Furthermore, in part because of the opportunities for political protection in a clientelist political system, the NEP quickly became a mass party, attracting members from sections of the population who had previously not been politically active and permitting transitions of power at a local level, where the membership was able to restrict the ability of local elites to secure influence over the political system. Within the army, Gömbös also conducted a purge of senior officers, which removed many who were supportive of conservative positions, replacing them with radical-right sympathisers. This step would prove especially fateful during the Second World War.

The depression not only led to a shift in the balance of forces within the ruling elite of the interwar regime, but also brought about considerable social dislocation. The international crash led to severe falls in the world market prices of agricultural goods, which in an economy so dependent upon agriculture caused a serious crisis. Given the enormous inequalities of land ownership, and the numbers dependent upon casual seasonal employment on the country's *latifundia*, the social crisis of Hungary's agrarian poor – both propertied and landless – sharpened considerably. Industrial dislocation led to widespread urban unemployment, while budgetary restriction caused job losses among the state bureaucracy, severely affecting the middle classes. This social crisis placed social reform firmly on the political agenda. While some who advocated radical change could be identified as being on the left, they were in a minority. The impact of the depression radicalised right-wing opinion, both among backers of the radical right and conservative camps within the governing elite, and among intellectuals, in a way that undercut the attempts of those supportive of the regime, such as Bethlen, who wished to pursue a more conservative-liberal course.

Furthermore, Hungary looked to the countries to its west, particularly Germany, for political models. While Italian Fascism had been widely admired among radical right-wing politicians like Gömbös, the rise to power of the National Socialists in Germany interacted with domestic pressures within Hungary to precipitate a number of explicitly fascist formations during the first half of the 1930s. These early movements – like the Scythe Cross Movement, founded by Zoltán Böszörmény in 1931 – demanded social transformation underpinned by radical anti-Semitic measures aiming at removing Jews from economic life. However, Hungarian national socialism was far from a homogenous movement. Böszörmény's attempts to build a mass movement among the seasonally-employed agrarian proletariat on Hungary's Great Plain were quickly eclipsed by other parties that sought to organise in conservative western Hungary. Analysis of the votes cast for national socialist candidates in the 1935 parliamentary elections revealed considerable support for their combination of land reform, radical anti-Semitism and ultra-nationalism that was concentrated among poorer smallholders in western Hungary, whose incomes and, therefore, economic independence had been threatened by the downturn and the slow process of recovery in agriculture.

The coalition of ultra-nationalism, demands for social transformation in the interests of poorer Magyars, combined with the radical anti-Semitism that emerged in Hungary's earliest phase of national socialist mobilisation, characterised the Hungarist or Arrow Cross movement. As a consequence of at times uneven mobilisation and official harassment, the movement existed as a series of different parties. Yet after 1935 it quickly emerged as the dominant national-socialist movement in the country. The movement was closely associated with its founder, Ferenc Szálasi, an army officer who, in view of his exceptional abilities, had been promoted to the Hungarian General Staff on completion of his studies in 1925. Despite the connections he established to leading officers within the army and to certain politicians, including Gyula Gömbös, Szálasi became increasingly active politically, openly advocating a restructuring of the Hungarian state along fascist lines. As a consequence of this political activism, he was pensioned out of the General Staff in 1935 to emerge as leader of a new party, the Party of National Will (*Nemzet Akaratának Pártja*, or NAP). This body was the first of several institutional incarnations of Hungarism, while it rapidly grew to reach its peak of support between 1938 and 1940.

In terms of its own self-presentation, Hungarism was no straightforward copy of German National Socialism, but rather was its adaptation to specifically Hungarian conditions and concerns. As far as Szálasi was concerned, 'Hungarism is the Hungarian practice of the National Socialist world view and *Zeitgeist*'.[4] The party presented itself as the most enthusiastic advocate of 'national Christian' ideas and concepts of the nation, sharing with the conservatism of the ruling elite a desire to overthrow the 'unjust' Treaty of Trianon and

---

4   Szálasi 2004, p. 104.

to 'restore' the borders of Hungary to those of the 'lands of the Holy Crown'.[5] Hungarism expressed itself as being in agreement with the dominant Christian nationalism of the interwar ruling elite. In the words of the 1938 programme of its second institutional incarnation, the National Socialist Hungarian Party-Hungarist Movement (*Nemzeti Szocialista Magyar Párt-Hungarista Mozgalom*, or NSZMP), it rested on 'the moral and religious views of Christianity and the fundamentals of the thousand years of Hungarian constitutionalism'.[6] Its commitment to Christian politics was closely tied to its nationalism. For Szálasi, 'true love of God and true love of Christ leads only to true love of the nation and love of the homeland'. Yet at the same time this stance was combined, paradoxically, with an anti-clerical streak, as it strongly condemned the role of the established Christian Churches as political partners of the conservative regime.[7] Its commitment to radical Christian nationalism fused with national-socialist influence from abroad to shape Hungarism's radical anti-Semitism. While its belief in a 'Christian' Hungary was deployed to justify its belief in the necessity of solving 'the Jewish question', the movement's definition of Jewishness was racial and not religious: 'Jewry is a race, not a religious group. We regard someone as of Jewish race, if they have more than one Jewish grandparent'. They argued that 'a person who is of Jewish race may not exercise the full rights of a Hungarian citizen', and sought the separation of Jews and Christians and active, radical, economic discrimination.[8]

Radical anti-Semitism operated as a consequence of Hungarism's commitment to radical Christian nationalism but also formed a means through which the movement sought to realise its goal of an organic national community based around peasant and worker. Within Hungarist conceptions of the national community, 'the peasant is the sustainer of the nation...the worker is the builder of the nation'.[9] This conclusion provided the ideological foundation of a radical social programme, which promised to free subordinate social groups from the 'service of Jewish big capital' through the creation of what it termed 'a Hungarian work-based state' that would 'secure the greatest earnings possibilities for... those who want to work and are capable of

---

5   Ibid., p. 105.
6   'A Nemzeti Szocialista Magyar Párt: Hungarista Mozgalom Programja', reprinted in Gergely, Glatz and Pölöskei 2003, p. 372.
7   Szálasi 2004, pp. 110–11.
8   'A Nemzeti Szocialista Magyar Párt: Hungarista Mozgalom Programja', reprinted in Gergely, Glatz and Pölöskei 2003, p. 375.
9   Szálasi 2004, p. 140.

work ... workers, tillers of the land, farmers, and artisans alike'.[10] Its concentration on an egalitarian Magyar national community purged of 'Jewish' influence would, as far as Hungarism was concerned, allow Magyars to recover their role as 'a leading people' within the 'living space of the Carpathians and the Danube'.[11] Yet Hungarism recognised the ethnic pluralism of the territory of the pre-Trianon Hungary it sought to restore, arguing that all non-Jewish and non-Roma ethnic groups could be united behind one national border under Hungarian leadership, while at the same time being given cultural autonomy. For Szálasi, 'according to our Hungarist view the maintenance of the mother tongue and a particular folk culture is not in contradiction with loyalty to the homeland'.[12]

During the second half of the 1930s, Hungarism grew in influence, and by the end of the decade it had sufficient public support to mount a serious challenge to the hegemony of the country's ruling elite. Its growth was closely tied to the way pent up desire within Hungary for social reform, especially agrarian reform, interacted with the increasing prestige of Nazi Germany. Germany's armaments-based economic boom came to be seen as a positive model for Hungary given its slower process of recovery. Large sections of Hungarian opinion drew the conclusion that a similar economic programme, combined with more radical anti-Semitic measures, held the key to national economic recovery. While many within the governing elite held these opinions – indeed, Prime Minister Kálmán Dáranyi increasingly moved in this direction during 1937 and 1938 – its effect on subordinate social groups was to produce an upsurge in support for Hungarism. In 1937 and 1938, many Hungarian agricultural labourers worked on seasonal employment contracts in Germany to plug labour shortages. Their experiences of wages that were substantially higher than in Hungary served to enhance the prestige of Nazi Germany and national socialist ideas at home. The incorporation of Austria into National Socialist Germany further increased this prestige because it raised the possibility that an alliance with Germany would allow Hungary to achieve its own territorial goals. More immediately, however, the impact of incorporation on the former Austrian province of Burgenland, lying immediately adjacent to Hungary, into the Third Reich, where the new rulers forcibly expelled most of the region's Jews in spring 1938 and immediately introduced discriminatory measures against the Roma population, was marked. Combined with the rapid elimination of unemployment there, these actions represented a further demon-

---

10   'A Nyilaskeresztes Párt Programja', reprinted in Gergely, Glatz, and Pölöskei 2003, p. 426.
11   Szálasi 2004, pp. 230–2.
12   Szálasi 2004, p. 156.

stration for many in western Hungary that racist measures combined with an assertive programme of social reform could solve the economic problems of subordinate social groups. The high tide for national socialist and Hungarist positions coincided with parliamentary elections in May 1939 when such parties polled almost a quarter of the vote. Due to the restricted franchise and the considerable obstacles the pro-government public administration placed in the way of these parties, their actual level was almost certainly higher.

There is little more than fragmentary evidence as to the social base of Hungarist and national socialist movements. In November 1938, the NSZMP, Hungarism's second institutional manifestation, claimed a public membership of 240,000. Because of bans on public servants and army officers – among whom it maintained it had considerable backing – joining the party, it claimed a further 300,000 secret members.[13] Its successor, the NP, founded in March 1939 after its predecessor was banned, claimed 400,000 open members and a further 100,000 who belonged in secret.[14] In the absence of archival sources it is very difficult to check the reliability of such figures. It is similarly impossible to properly reconstruct the social composition of the membership. From the fragmentary evidence available on the state of the movement at a local level, the figures given above do not seem unrealistic: in the north-western town of Magyaróvár in 1938, the local police estimated a membership of around one thousand – just short of 10 percent of the local population – concentrated among its artisans and skilled workers.[15]

The 1939 election results provide a better, if still partial, guide to the extent of national-socialist support. Analysis of these results is suggestive of the broad movement's strength in those parts of rural western Transdanubia, where national socialism had made substantial inroads among the propertied smallholder population in 1935. Yet it performed especially well in all those areas where a poor smallholder population was an especially significant element of local society, not merely in the far west of the country. A second significant trend was its success in industrial areas, among working-class voters. In the industrial towns adjacent to Budapest, regarded as strongholds of the labour movement, it outpolled the Social Democrats in 1939. While the election results themselves were an imperfect guide, on account of the shortcomings of the election process, a number of conclusions can be drawn from these results. To begin with, national socialist support was frequently a reaction to

---

13   ÖStA/ADR, 'Bürckel' Materie, Zl. 1575/2, Kt.12, Die Hungaristische Bewegung in Ungarn, p. 1.
14   Szöllösi-Janze 1989, p. 128.
15   Gy.MS.GyL, IVf.B.451a, A m.kir.rendőrség magyaróvári kapitánysága.

ethnic tension and it attracted considerable backing from Magyars in regions characterised by diversity. In regions with large ethnic German populations in the 1939 elections, the key to defeating Arrow Cross challengers was to persuade German populations to support pro-government candidates. Where this was not done successfully, in areas like Mosonmagyarvár along the German border, where many German voters spoilt their ballots by drawing swastikas across them, the far right's mobilisation of the local Magyar minority led to the victory of a national-socialist candidate.[16] Likewise, the movement profited from increased anti-Semitism during the late 1930s: in much of rural western Hungary, the organisation of the Arrow Cross was accompanied by violence against the property of Jewish businessmen and a growing willingness to denounce local Jews, for offences both real and imagined, to the local gendarmerie.

While the national-socialist movement profited from increased ethnic conflict – even when its cause, paradoxically, was the politicisation of the German minority as a result of the increased prestige of Nazi Germany, from which Hungarists themselves gained – the most notable aspect of its social base was its plebeian nature. The movement owed most of its support to its credibility as an agent of radical social change and, at the turn of the 1940s, its successfully articulated popular desire for reform. Its open advocacy of radical land reform allowed it not merely to expand the support it had won among poorer smallholders during the mid-1930s, but to extend this support to manorial servants and other agricultural labourers, attracted by the movement's promises of creating 'a peasant state' and breaking the power of large landowners. Perhaps the most notable elements of this plebeian social base were reflected in the movement's success in securing votes among the industrial working class – winning, in 1939, relative majorities in working-class districts, especially those surrounding Budapest and among sections of the labour movement not well integrated into the left-wing political structures of social democracy: in Greater Budapest's machine plants, for example, Arrow Cross support was concentrated among the young, who had become adults amid the right-wing climate of the 1930s, while their elders remained loyal to the political left. Most significant was the poll Hungarism picked up among coal miners as a consequence of the unpopularity of the moderate left-wing mineworkers' union and its weakness in the face of employers. During 1940, the NP built upon the base they had won in mining areas the previous year to organise mineworkers and lead a national miners' strike in 1940, where they sought to arrest the declining living standards that had set in as a consequence of accel-

---

16   BA, R1501/3332, p. 78.

erating inflation. After an initial and unsuccessful recourse to repression, the strike was bought off through a generalised wage settlement. Nevertheless, it represented the peak of Hungarist organisation of the industrial working class.

The ruling elite responded to the challenge of Hungarism in a way that transformed their rule. Publicly, representatives of the governing parties presented their national-socialist rivals as 'extremists', akin to Bolshevik revolutionaries in 1919, with their demands to overturn the existing order. Yet the challenge of Hungarism, combined with the changing international context within which Hungary operated, served to transform the practices of the governing elite. Thus, fascism played a central role in reshaping the governing practice of the ruling party. This was not an uncontested process within the governing elite. One faction wished to closely emulate the radical right, associated with the Prime Minister between 1938 and 1939, Béla Imrédy. Imrédy and his allies sought to reconstitute the ruling party as a 'movement' that would serve as the basis for an explicitly dictatorial form of rule, while driving forward anti-Semitic measures designed to curtail 'Jewish economic influence'. Imrédy's politics generated distrust from more conservative segments of the ruling elite who had the ear of Horthy, and they succeeded in removing him from power by revealing his alleged 'Jewish origins'. While Imrédy left the ruling party, forming his own radical right-wing party in 1940, conservatives within the elite failed to prevent its drift rightward.

The most marked sign of the shift in the practice of Hungary's ruling elite under the influence of the challenge of fascism was the country's transformation at the turn of the 1940s into an explicitly racist state. The most striking marker of this change was the passage of a series of anti-Jewish laws between 1938 and 1942. Initially, the Hungarian state sought to remove those it defined as Jews from intellectual occupations, by first employing a religious definition, which shifted in 1941 to an explicitly racial one based on ancestry. In 1939, it then moved to restrict the political rights of Jews and their rights to engage in commercial and business activities. During the early 1940s, mixed marriages were banned. Jews were to serve in the military as members of 'labour service battalions', while any agricultural land they owned was progressively confiscated. The demotion of Jews to the status of second-class citizens was accompanied by the dominance of anti-Semitism within public discourse and a further layer of discrimination introduced by those local authorities that fell under the influence of radical-right ideas. They also intensified their stigmatisation of and discrimination against the Roma population. Although this policy was far less obvious and more uneven than the measures directed against Jews, it also represented one way in which the governing elite sought to restrict the rights of social groups it saw as being outside the boundaries of the 'nation'.

The second major consequence of this rightward shift was the Hungarian state's growing, if uneven, willingness to work with Nazi Germany in terms of the achievement of its territorial goals against neighbouring states. While Hungary refused to support Germany's invasion of Poland in 1939, it increasingly moved closer to Berlin, regaining southern Slovakia in November 1938, Carpathian Ruthenia in March 1939, and northern Transylvania in September 1940. Hungary's support for Germany's invasion of Yugoslavia in April 1941, which prompted the suicide of the Prime Minister Pál Teleki, led to the reannexation of a substantial part of former Yugoslav territory, including the Vojvodina and the Mura region of Slovenia. While these territorial changes were celebrated as the winning of Hungarian national goals, they came at the cost of a growing militarisation of Hungarian society. Furthermore, frequently motivated by nationalist and racist ideas the Hungarian army in the new territories killed civilians. The reoccupation of northern Transylvania was accompanied by violence on the part of Hungarian troops against Romanian civilians. In Vojvodina, Hungarian forces were embroiled in a brutal guerrilla war against local partisans and they responded with a series of raids in January 1942, in which several thousand civilians, including a substantial number of Serbs and Jews, were murdered by Hungarian forces. This step set the stage for Hungary's entanglement in Hitler's war against the Soviet Union from late June 1941, and the further complicity of the Hungarian military and political authorities in a number of atrocities, the most serious of which was the deportation of 16,000 stateless Jews from Hungary, who were subsequently murdered by German and Ukrainian troops at Kamjanec-Podilskij in 1941.

While Hungarism and national socialism had helped drive the regime to the right, and thereby assisted in entangling the country in Nazism's racist war of conquest against the Soviet Union, the unpopularity of the conflict at home undermined support for the movement. The NP in parliament had been damaged by individual political errors, most notably when two of its members of parliament, Kálmán Hubay and Pál Vágó, proposed a bill to realise the party's programme of cultural autonomy for ethnic minorities within Hungary in 1940, and were accused of 'treason' by the government. More fundamentally, Arrow Cross support had rested on the prestige of National Socialist Germany and their credibility as a party that could improve the position of the poor, both of which were eroded by the impact of the war on the home front. Among poorer smallholders, the spread of conscription was highly unpopular given the lack of adequate material compensation for absent family members who would have worked on their farms. The impact of the introduction of war economy, which brought more despotic practice in industry, compulsory deliveries and high taxation in agriculture, and cuts in real incomes, intensified this unpopularity.

The mounting human costs of the conflict, especially after the destruction of the Second Hungarian Army on the Don in early 1943, further undermined support for the war effort. As the likelihood that the Soviet Union would overrun Hungary increased, and the Hungarian government sought a way out of the war, society became more fearful and polarised. By the time the Germans occupied Hungary in March 1944 out of concern that the latter would switch sides and join the Allies, the NP was a shadow of the organisation it had been four years before. In western Hungary, police reports suggested that in spring 1944 the party's membership was only a quarter of the level it had been in 1940.[17]

Thus, when the party finally took power as the result of a coup supported by the German occupation authorities in October 1944, in response to Horthy's attempt to take Hungary out of the war, the party was effectively well past its peak. The pro-German government of Prime Minister Döme Sztójay, in power between March and August 1944, had already implemented much of the programme of the radical right. The labour movement had been disbanded, while, most significantly, 430,000 Jews from all over the country, save Budapest, were deported. The overwhelming majority of those deported were murdered at Auschwitz. Horthy dismissed Sztójay in August and began to negotiate Hungary's exit from the war. Soviet troops crossed Hungary's border in the following month and the country became a direct theatre of military conflict. When the NP was brought to power, with Szálasi combining the roles of head of government and head of state, proclaiming himself Leader of the Nation [*Nemzetvezető*], his support rested on the most militant sections of the army, state bureaucracy, and those among the population who believed that the very survival of 'Christian Hungary' was threatened by the 'Bolshevik menace'. Szálasi's control over the country quickly ebbed: by Christmas 1944, Budapest was surrounded and Soviet troops were advancing across western Hungary. Szálasi, however, was determined that Hungary should fight until the end, and despite the weakness of his regime, it was actively terroristic. In order to guarantee its power in Budapest and other cities that remained under its control, it armed party activists, giving them powers equivalent to the police. This was done in order to bypass regular police forces and a public administration that the NP regarded as too compromised by the previous system to provide effective support to the German and Hungarian armies in reversing the war situation. In urban centres, these militants became the face of the regime and gained a reputation for arbitrary violence, torture and murder, directed especially against any Jews who remained, political opponents, and even those they suspected of avoiding the call-up into the army as the Soviets approached. Budapest's Jews,

---

17 GyMSMGy.L, IVf.451.B.35d, A m.kir.rendőrség mosonmagyaróvári kapitánysága.

who had avoided deportation earlier in the year, were the primary focus of the wave of terror launched by the Arrow Cross regime. In order to meet German demands for forced labour to construct defences on the German border and prevent Soviet troops from crossing into the Reich, some tens of thousands of Budapest Jews – most estimates suggest 76,000 of them – of working age were rounded up and force-marched the 220 kilometres from the capital to the western border. Following the encirclement of Budapest, NP activists determined to kill all Jews who remained in the city, by whatever means were available. Despite the attempts of diplomats from those neutral states who continued to operate in Budapest to save Jewish lives, an estimated fifteen thousand Jews were murdered in the Hungarian capital between October 1944 and February 1945. While Hungary's remaining Jews were the primary targets of the Arrow Cross's attentions, the country's Roma were also targeted, albeit sporadically, by the regime's policies of extermination.

Terrorism and racist murder were tied to Szálasi's policies of the total mobilisation of the population in the interests of the war effort, and the enforced evacuation to Germany of those who could not be mobilised in the face of the Soviet advance. As the regime was restricted during early 1945 to a narrow portion of western Transdanubia, the population became ever more difficult to mobilise. The attempts of many among the population to avoid conscription, believing further participation in the war to be senseless, were met with arbitrary violence and even murder by militant local NP activists determined to 'fight to the end'. Few among the civilian population were enthusiastic about evacuation to Germany, even though war had brought near-starvation conditions to many communities. In Mosonmagyaróvár, locals expressed their opposition to evacuation, maintaining that 'here we are starving and freezing, and if we have to starve and freeze, at least we are at home'.[18] Much of the population was terrified by the prospect of eventual Soviet occupation. Popular anti-communism interacted with news of atrocities committed against civilians by Soviet troops further east, which served to intensify this climate of fear. This situation was exacerbated by the presence of substantial numbers of refugees from parts of Hungary that had already fallen to the Red Army. Some western cities reported that their populations had swollen to three times that of their peacetime level, placing severe strain on food supplies.

With Hungary's 'liberation' complete in April 1945, the new Soviet-backed regime – a popular front coalition of anti-fascist parties in which the Communist Party was first among equals – defined itself by its anti-fascism. 'Fascism' was

---

18   GyMSMGy.L, IVf.451a, 2d, A m.kir.rendőrség politikai rendészeti osztálya szombathelyi kirendeltsége. 7/1945 pol.rend.biz., p. 5.

blamed for the war and the consequent devastation that had overtaken the country. The 'new' state set out on a course of anti-fascist retribution. Those it identified as war criminals, who had fled west, were arraigned by specially constituted People's Courts. Many who had played leading roles on the radical right, including Szálasi and Imrédy, were brought to trial and executed. Many others, including registered members of the NP, were interned. Others still were prevented from returning to their pre-war jobs, while institutions, like the gendarmerie, that were seen to have supported the occupation and anti-Jewish measures were simply disbanded. Left-wing anti-fascism was shaped to define the 'new' state against the practice of the entire interwar regime, which was blamed for the Second World War and the material destruction that resulted. The whole of the Hungarian people were said to be the victims of this system, subsuming the Holocaust within a generalised narrative of national victimhood. This set the pattern for the whole of the period until 1989. Yet at the same time, the post-war state and especially the Hungarian Communist Party sought to appease those whom it regarded as 'little Arrow Crossists', who had sympathised with Hungarism because of its promise of social reform. With the relaxation of regulations concerning internment in 1946, many 'little Arrow Crossists' were freed from the camps. During the late 1940s, large numbers of those who supported Hungarism's radical programme of reform joined or supported the Communist Party. Indeed, one Communist journalist admitted that Communist-voting poor peasants in Fejér County had transferred their allegiances because in the 1930s, 'the far right represented a revolutionary promise'. Often the Communists' class-based rhetoric directed against 'speculators' and 'reactionaries', in the climate of post-war penury, fused with anti-Semitism. As far as the same peasants were concerned, 'the Jews are reactionaries, who squeeze the poor'.[19]

In the hyperinflation of the immediate post-war years, heightened social tension fed popular anti-Semitism that occasionally erupted into open violence, as it did with two pogroms in Miskolc and Kunmadaras in 1946. This wave of popular anti-Semitism subsided as socialist dictatorship was built. While fragmented opposition to the dictatorship during its early Stalinist phase in the early 1950s betrayed traces of the dominant political attitudes of the Horthy era, the expression of right-wing opinion was firmly suppressed throughout the early part of the decade. During the 1956 Revolution, there were a small number of serious, albeit isolated, incidences of anti-Semitic violence. For the rest of the socialist era, opinions incompatible with the official 'anti-fascist' stance of the regime were driven underground. After Hungary's 'change of system'

---

19   Sándor 1948, pp. 55–8.

in 1989, radical right-wing movements began to re-emerge. While Hungarist movements have only won a negligible following, a significant radical right has emerged displaying notable continuities with that of the interwar years. The first free elections were won in 1990 by a coalition of centre-right parties, led by the Hungarian Democratic Forum (*Magyar Demokrata Fórum*, MDF), who formed a government led by József Antall. His politics were based on a synthesis of post-war Western European centre-right ideals and some springing from the liberal-conservative wing of the governing elite of interwar years. All three of the parties who supported his government were, however, loose coalitions, and some of their component parts supported more radical-right positions. The coalition fractured under the pressure of political disputes over the degree to which the new Hungarian state would be based on radical anti-communism and issues of the restitution of property. The latter issue led to the takeover of one of the junior partners in the coalition, the FKGP, by the right-wing populist demagogue József Torgyán. Antall's government was forced to deal with economic crisis that led to high inflation, a difficult fiscal position, a deep recession, and tremendous social polarisation. The consequence of economic difficulties, combined with considerable government unpopularity, led to a split within the MDF. Right-wing radicals were led by István Csurka, a senior member of the party, who advocated an explicitly anti-Semitic course reminiscent of the right-wing radicalism of the interwar years. Thrown out of the MDF, Csurka founded the Hungarian Justice and Life Party (*Magyar Igazság és Élet Pártja*, MIÉP) in 1993 – until recently Hungary's most successful party to sit openly on the radical right since the 'change of system'.[20] While it has only entered parliament once – in 1998 with 5.47 percent of the vote – its social base differed substantially from that of the interwar far right, attracting disproportionate support from elderly, middle-class, urban voters, especially those living in the wealthy Buda districts of the Hungarian capital. Ideologically, the party harked back more to the political positions of the radical right of the interwar governing elite than to Hungarists; indeed, its name contains echoes of the Hungarian Life Party (*Magyar Élet Pártja*, MÉP), the ruling party between 1939 and 1944. Its self-identification as 'a Christian and Hungarian party', its desire to overthrow the Treaty of Trianon, and its anti-Semitism, made it a focal point for the far right throughout the 1990s.

While Csurka and his party have had to compete with other groups for leadership on the radical right – most notably, during the 1990s with Torgyán's

---

20   Editor's note: This article was written before the 2010 general elections, when the far right Jobbik party became the third largest party in parliament with 16.67 percent of the votes (obtaining 47 of 385 seats in parliament).

Smallholders, and since 2000, with a range of far right groups composed of younger activists more prepared to engage in direct action, sometimes violent direct action, than in formal electoral politics – one notable feature of the post-socialist radical right has been its symbiotic relationship with the mainstream right, a reproduction under post-socialist conditions of similar links during the interwar years. This process began with the return to power in 1994 of the ruling party of the state-socialist years, reconstituted as the MSZP, in coalition with the liberal wing of the former opposition. This act began a process of polarisation between right and left, since many right-wingers refused to accept that a party they regarded as 'Communist' had any legitimate role in the political system. The result was a realignment on the mainstream right, under the leadership of the Alliance of Young Democrats (*Fiatal Demokraták Szövetsége*, or FIDESZ), originally a liberal youth group that adopted increasingly conservative positions. Through its period in office under Prime Minister Viktor Orbán between 1998 and 2002, it sought the unification of the whole right under its banner. Following its narrow defeat in the 2002 elections at the hands of the Socialists, FIDESZ moved to integrate the radical right into its electoral coalition and became rhetorically more radical, casting itself as the sole legitimate representative of the nation, thus denying legitimacy to its political opponents. This process was consolidated following its second consecutive electoral defeat in 2006, when violent protest erupted following revelations that Prime Minister Ferenc Gyurcsány lied to voters about the state of the economy in order to win the elections. Radical right-wing activists stormed and briefly occupied the headquarters of state television in September 2006 before being evicted by police. The following month – on the fiftieth anniversary of the 1956 Revolution – serious violence again erupted in the capital, initiated by radical-right protestors, who demanded the overthrow of the government and a change of system. While FIDESZ as the official opposition did not openly back the radical right-wing protesters, they did not distance themselves from the protesters either, blaming the October violence, to which a rally they had called contributed, on excessive police brutality and arguing that the government, which they described as 'legal, but not legitimate', should resign. In a climate of intense political polarisation between right and left, and a situation in which the mainstream right has been unprepared to distance itself from the more radical of the demonstrators, the radical right has grown in confidence. Its past may be complicated, but, at the time of writing, the radical right seems likely to have a future.

CHAPTER 12

Towards a Social History of the 1956 Revolution in Hungary

What follows is a sketch of possible ways of approaching the social history of the Hungarian Revolution. As I will say at the end, it is not in itself that social history – that would be way beyond the scope of this event. I present here a set of arguments, try to suggest how the Hungarian Revolution fits into what came before, and what came after it, and then I will make a few remarks about participation in demonstrations between 23 October and 4 November 1956, and then will aim to draw some conclusions from my analysis.

Beyond Budapest: The Local Dimensions of the 1956 Revolution in Hungary

I choose to begin this lecture with a picture of the local events of the 1956 Revolution in Bázakerretye, in the Letenye district of Zala county, in the far southwest of Hungary. Around two hundred and fifty kilometres from Budapest, along the border with then Yugoslavia, now closest to the Mura region of Slovenia, it is about as far as one can get from Budapest and still remain within the borders of Trianon Hungary. It shows the destruction of the village's Soviet war memorial after the opening local demonstration of the revolution on 26 October 1956.

At first sight, the local Revolution in Bázakerettye – incidentally, the location of the country's single largest oil-drilling plant at that time – seems to have been one of the localised ripples of the larger Revolution, driven by the dramatic upheaval in Budapest. After the mass demonstrations and the violent clashes between demonstrators, Soviet troops and Hungarian security forces, which convulsed the capital from 23 October, the Zala county party newspaper was able to state a little complacently on 25 October that 'our county is far from the capital, not only in the sense of distance, but also in attitude'.

---

* This is the edited version of a keynote lecture given by Mark Pittaway at 'The 1956 Revolution – 50 Years Later' conference, held at the University of Ottawa, Canada, 12–14 October 2006. The titles of the subheadings are those of the editor.

However, on the same day, demonstrations began in the local industrial town of Nagykanizsa, started by oil-industry workers. They marched peacefully, carrying national flags through the town, protesting against the Soviet intervention, when a group of younger workers broke away destroying the monument to the Red Army troops in the centre. As evening set in, the protest grew larger and they were joined by workers in the town's other factories who gathered around the statue of Petőfi in the town centre to demand the withdrawal of Soviet troops, an amnesty for the armed groups, and that the Stalinist party leadership be brought to justice.

26 October was the day on which the Revolution finally broke out across the county. In Nagykanizsa, a demonstration of secondary-school pupils and students was supported by workers and the police. After taking the town council building, demonstrators moved to the army barracks where they demanded weapons – a demand that was refused. Meanwhile, one middle-aged woman was shot dead in the centre by an unknown attacker, which pushed the situation to breaking-point. Demonstrators once again attacked the barracks demanding weapons. The army fired on them, killing one and injuring fourteen. The army only managed to calm the situation by imposing martial law on the town. Demonstrations had by now spread across the county: in Zalaegerszeg, student-led demonstrations occurred. Demonstrators attacked the county party headquarters; the guards fired back and three were killed. The Revolution spread also to the oil-drilling plants, beginning at Lovászi on 26 October. Workers downed tools in the morning and began to demonstrate. Supported by the local ÁVH – mainly border guard troops who policed the border with Yugoslavia – and, copying the events in Nagykanizsa the previous day, demonstrators destroyed the Soviet war memorial in the centre of the village, returning to the drilling plant where they occupied the personnel office, destroying the cadre files. They then returned to the plant and elected a worker's council to run the plant whose first decision was to remove the plant's managing director. Similar events also occurred at other oil-drilling plants.

While the events across Zala and the oil fields were triggered by the events in Budapest, the spread of the Revolution to Hungary's south-western corner cannot be adequately explained by them. Among the rural population, the decisions of the revolutionary crowds to destroy local council records connected with compulsory deliveries of agricultural produce, punitive taxation of local smallholders, and the property of collective farms, was testimony to utter fury over collectivisation drives that had been renewed in 1955 (following their suspension in 1953). Nagykanizsa's oil workers had agitated for the removal of the piece-rate system of payment and its replacement with one based on hourly wages with a premium, which would have given them greater security of income throughout 1956. There had been generalised rebellion among oil workers at the Lovászi Oil Drilling Plant in July 1956, provoked by what workers saw as the 'unjustified' payment of large plan-fulfilment premiums to management, at a time when workers' wages had fallen. Most complaints concerned low wages and social provision; the focus of their attack was on management. Echoing the language of Khruschev's 'secret speech', the director of the plant was attacked openly for promoting a 'cult of personality' around himself and using factory property to lavishly celebrate his birthday.

Although there has been much work undertaken by historians on the local dimensions of 1956 that has attempted to discover what happened beyond Budapest, there has been very little real social history of the Revolution that would aim to explain the extraordinary ferment in Hungarian society during the autumn of 1956. This is partly because it can be credibly argued that this ferment can be explained by the conduct of the regime associated with Mátyás Rákosi, which ruled the country from the 'year of change' in 1948 until 1956. Indeed, as we shall see, this is true to a point: the policies of the Rákosi regime really do explain much of the discontent. But we need to look in much greater depth at the interactions of the state and social groups in order to examine their participation in the Revolution.

Often our focus on Hungarian society has been distracted by those who have argued – pointing to the fact of the country's 'limited sovereignty' in the period between 1945 and the end of the 1980s – that Hungary's geopolitical position, as occupied by the Red Army, and then incorporated into the Soviet bloc, determined political developments in the country. Again, this is a partial truth. Without Soviet occupation of Hungary between 1945 and the Peace Treaty of 1947, and without the presence of Red Army troops thereafter – justified between 1947 and 1955 by continued Soviet occupation of eastern Austria, and then by Hungary's membership of the Warsaw Pact – Hungary's socialist state would never have been established and maintained. Furthermore, without Soviet intervention that same socialist state would not have been rescued from a condition of outright collapse in November 1956. But as I have argued elsewhere, the history of Hungary's first decade and a half of state socialism cannot be reduced to that of Soviet occupation, nor to the interests of Moscow. Instead, they interacted with a number of other local considerations. Hungary's own Communist leaders and its apparatus enjoyed more autonomy than was often supposed, and those like Rákosi and Ernő Gerő were at numerous points more radical than Moscow in the pursuit of socialist transformation. Secondly, the political divisions within Hungarian society, which manifested themselves in elections in 1945 as a virtual sixty-forty split between the centre-right and the left, was also crucial. Certainly, in the rigged elections of August 1947, these divisions became ever more unclear, and with the effective consolidation of a one-party system in 1947–49, the divisions seemed to disappear completely from view. But they endured. While those who made up the relatively conservative majority never accepted the dictatorship during the 1950s, whatever conditional political support it endured during the late 1940s had entirely crumbled by the mid-1950s. This was important, for it implied the crumbling of support among those whose cooperation on a day-to-day basis – like Lovászi's border guard – was necessary for the continued functioning of the regime, without which the unrest would not have turned into outright political revolution.

Furthermore, – and this is the reason why I started with events in Zala county – the geographical breadth of the Revolution clearly points to the fact that it was not just a Budapest affair. The capital was important, both as centre of political power and the location for the events that sparked outright state collapse and political revolution. But even before 23 October, Hungary was undergoing a political and social revolution. To see the signs of this one must look beyond Budapest.

Rethinking the 1956 Revolution in the Light of What Came After

Interrogating the social history and the experience of the Revolution means setting it in the context of what came after it, namely, the era associated with the rule of János Kádár, and, indeed, placing it in a longer context. The 1956 Revolution has often been seen – especially in the last sixteen years – as a precursor of the final fall of Eastern Europe's state-socialist regimes in 1989–90. This view is in many ways an accurate one. It undoubtedly underlined for the western-European left the dictatorial and despotic nature of the socialist regimes on the eastern half of the continent. Furthermore, it provided a beacon for many anti-Communists across the region during the final agony of socialist regimes in the late 1980s. Indeed, more concretely and locally, in Hungary it symbolised the fundamental illegitimacy of the regime – as a form of political authority that had owed its survival to the military intervention of a foreign power – and was a potent weapon during the events of 1989.

Almost immediately after the military suppression of the Revolution, the Kádár regime began to project its own 'myth' about what had occurred in 1956. As it moved to arrest and detain those it regarded as responsible for the Revolution, it constructed a fiction, which suggested that no 'honest' worker had anything to fear from repression: only groups of 'counter-revolutionary' agitators need be concerned. The myth the Kádár regime projected was of the events of late 1956 as a 'counter-revolution', in which anti-socialist agitators, 'reactionaries', and 'agents of imperialism', had stirred up discontent in order to overthrow socialism. Increasingly, as the Revolution was beaten back during 1957 and 1958, the wave of political trials launched by the restored regime became less about defusing discontent, or even intimidating opponents, than affirming and supporting this myth. My own work across several Hungarian counties suggests this: in the western mining town of Tatabánya, for example, the most significant political trials underpinned a 'local myth' of counter-revolution, in which the state attributed the events to anti-communist activists in the factories and more significantly to local professionals, who despite holding key positions in the city's revolutionary committee were, in reality, either marginal or had been unable to control the consequences of the explosion of working-class anger that had, in reality, driven the local Revolution.

Behind the official promotion of the 'myth' of 'counter-revolution' lay the surprisingly speedy consolidation of the regime during the late 1950s. The defeat of the Revolution produced an enforced peace within Hungarian society – among opponents of socialist dictatorship, defeat and the lack of western intervention led to a climate of resignation and acceptance, a 'culture of defeat' that assured their selective incorporation into the political system during the 1960s. Yet among other groups – especially among the industrial working class and to some extent the rural poor – Kádár's consolidation rested on a different social base. While an awareness that the regime was a government imposed by the armies of foreign power remained, it was able to generate a degree of popularity and acceptance in the late 1950s on the basis that it distanced itself from the practice of the early 1950s by seeking improvement in the standards of living of its constituency, and through a greater rhetorical privileging of the working class. Thus, the Revolution's defeat presented an ambiguous picture of an event defeated through the highly selective rather than very widespread use of force. Moral and economic coercion played a larger role, upon which were laid substantial concessions in the workplace and the community. While this produced a degree of popularity and support for the Kádár regime by the end of 1957, this coexisted with profound awareness of its deeper illegitimacy, as a regime imposed through force of arms by the armies of a foreign power.

This outcome points to the need to look at the 1956 Revolution in a new and different way. It was certainly not, unproblematically, 'the first domino', which led irreversibly to the decay, decline and collapse of state socialism 33 years later, as many have suggested. While the revival of the memory of the 1956 Revolution played a fundamental role in the events of 1989 in Hungary – on account of the way it symbolised the illegitimacy of the regime – in the short and medium term it led to its consolidation. Yet this consolidation occurred on the basis of a very different pattern of socialist governance to that which had characterised its rule during the early 1950s, and which drew lessons from the outbreak of the 1956 Revolution. Thus, the Revolution, paradoxically, both challenged and confirmed Hungary's dictatorial post-war settlement. In the short and medium term, this paradox created a socialism obsessed with working-class living standards, which was not scared to challenge the rural population – as it did during collectivisation between 1958 and 1961 – nor the intelligentsia. However, it did so within more restricted parameters than before.

The 'Socialist' State and Society in Hungary Before 1956

Setting the Revolution in the context of what came after it therefore implies that we also need to ask about the dynamic of relations between the socialist state and social groups that emerged before it. As it challenged, confirmed and modified the direction of socialist state formation in the post-war period, we need to try to sketch the relations upon which it rested.

As we have seen, according to many observers the history of the socialist state in Hungary during the immediate post-war period is one in which the social has little role to play at all, for it is a story of the brutal imposition of a Soviet model of political, economic and social development, as a direct consequence of military occupation. According to this argument, the genesis of the socialist regime in Hungary forms a small part of a larger story of the 'Sovietisation' of CEE. While this account accurately describes the international backdrop against which socialist rule was imposed on different states across the region, it fails to account for the marked differences in the patterns of conflict and consent between those states as dictatorship was built. It does not explain, and sometimes even denies, the different natures of many of the socialist regimes as they were constructed and then consolidated. Furthermore, it obscures our understanding of how socialist regimes were experienced by those under their rule, and leaves unexamined the social bases on which socialist regimes rested.

The contradictory policies pursued by Hungary's Soviet occupiers suggest that they had little in the way of a coherent plan for the country's future in early 1945. While the country's smashed economy and devastated agricultural sector were bled dry to support the material demands of continued conflict and the troops stationed in the country, the Soviets pursued policies of retribution through an insistence on reparation, radically anti-fascist political justice, the semi-legal deportation of thousands of male civilians, and the expulsion of ethnic German minorities. Formal retribution was bolstered by semi-official violence against people and property by the occupying forces who often instituted waves of terror – characterised by rape, looting, and random murder. The cumulative effect of such policies on a population – one that had been warned that the Soviets were mortal enemies in a war of national survival – ran counter to the policies pursued by the country's new occupiers that aimed at the creation of a legitimate yet pliant political order.

That pliant political order was not, at least at the turn of 1945, an overt socialist dictatorship. Soviet intervention in Hungarian politics was limited, and the post-war government rested on a multi-party system based on the principles of a 'popular front', whose rule would be legitimised through free elections. While the Communists were first among equals in the post-war multi-party coalition government, and enjoyed a key role in the security services of the new state, the 'dictatorship of the proletariat' was firmly off the agenda. This policy of limited Soviet intervention clashed, however, with the more radical goals of the Communists themselves who dreamed of revolutionary transformation. Its leaders built their organisation and base of support in preparation for an eventual 'dictatorship of the proletariat', and saw initial Soviet moderation as a tactical and above all temporary step – so much so that at times they had to be restrained by the Soviets. The radicalism of the Communists was even greater at its grassroots. Many Communists recruited in late 1944 and early 1945 were motivated by the memory of the Soviet Republic of 1919 and expectations of wholesale revolution, and as a result they found the moderation of the party leadership and the Soviet occupying forces difficult to understand. Although such voices could be cowed by the employment of the mechanisms of Party discipline, the Communists were driven by the radicalism of much of its natural working-class constituency – a radicalism often fuelled by frustration that the Party and the unions they often dominated in 1945 failed 'to defend the interests of the workers'.

This constellation of forces was partially the product of, but also coexisted with, the political dynamics of a deeply polarised society – one sharply divided and traumatised by the human tragedy of the Second World War. The combination of the actions of Soviet troops, the radicalism of the social base of the Communists and the left more generally, the legacy of polarisation and fear left by Hungary's experience of war, genocide, multiple occupation, and the parlous state of the shattered economy, generated a climate deeply unfavourable to the consolidation of 'popular front' rule in 1945. The creation of the 'popular front' regime was accompanied by a widespread popular belief that the end of the war was only temporary and that renewed military conflict between the victors would bring further political upheaval. Post-war Hungary was not only deeply tense; it was also a state in which there was no majority for the Communists' nor the Red Army's state-building project. The MKP and its left-wing allies proved unable to win support beyond the substantial but restricted ranks of industrial workers, the rural poor and the smaller group of left-wing intellectuals. Most of the rural majority, those who attended church, and the urban middle class, rallied behind a more conservative vision of a parliamentary state that protected private property, defended the family, and asserted Hungary's national independence from the Soviet occupier. In the first post-war national elections in November 1945, the Independent Smallholders' Party appealed successfully to this political constituency in order to win a substantial majority of votes, thus ensuring that the Communists' vision of the post-war state could not be legitimated through democratic means. Trapped by the rejection of its vision by a conservative majority, and its own desire for outright social transformation, the fear among many of its activists and supporters of a return of the pre-war regime, and their frustration with the Party's moderation, the Communists responded by intensifying political polarisation. Defining its enemies as 'reactionaries', mobilising its supporters, using its control over the police and emergent security forces, and drawing in Soviet support, it progressively destroyed the Smallholders Party as an organisation capable of realising the aspirations of the majority during 1946 and 1947, as part of its bid to reverse the results of the 1945 elections and assert its vision of the post-war state.

The Communists' success in imposing their vision of the post-war state, cemented by the rigged parliamentary elections of August 1947, was one that occurred in a society characterised by considerable political polarisation and where its legitimacy was deeply contested. Supporters of a more conservative vision of the country's future, despite their numerical weight in society, were excluded from any political influence. The state depended for its legitimacy on social groups like the working class and rural poor, who were socially excluded yet politically central. This dependence created a dynamic of radicalisation that interacted with the international pressures created by the onset of the Cold War to shape the social bases of an emerging dictatorship. The debt of the emergent dictatorship to the practice of Soviet Stalinism was quickly made visible in its institutions and its practice: the last years of the 1940s witnessed a substantial expansion of the state-security apparatus and its scope for repression and surveillance. At the same time, the state divided Hungarian society into 'allies' and 'enemies of socialism', as social tensions and everyday protest were attributed by the state to political malcontents, and 'western, imperialist agitation' in the climate of the Cold War was blamed for domestic political conflict. Yet when 'enemies' were identified outside of the ranks of the Party, it was clear that the practices of the emergent dictatorship represented an adaptation of Stalinist techniques to the polarised climate of post-war Hungary. Individuals, organisations and social groups that had sustained political cultures, and which had been antagonistic to the Communists in the 'popular front' years, were targeted. Those with close personal connections to the political institutions or security services of Hungary's interwar regime faced particularly intense persecution. The churches, especially the Catholic Church, were subjected to outright attack, as their leaders, clergy and believers were stigmatised as part of what the regime termed the 'clerical reaction'. This was tied to an 'intensification of the class struggle' as the regime implemented policies of radical nationalisation and a redistribution of wealth towards working-class wage earners. In agriculture, it entailed the spread of methods of class-based taxation that underpinned the attempts of the state to organise the rural poor into agricultural collectives.

The emergent socialist dictatorship attempted to construct its legitimacy by asserting its identity as a 'dictatorship of the proletariat' in a climate of extreme social and political polarisation. Large sections of society saw the dictatorship as not merely a threat to, but an attack on, their very way of life. This was particularly marked in conservative, rural Hungary, where attacks on both religious belief and land ownership through the collectivisation drive placed the state and its representatives on a direct collision course with the moral economies of village communities. Yet the regime's relationship with those in whose name it claimed to rule was also tense. Representatives of the regime claimed, as did Mátyás Rákosi in 1949, that they were the political representatives of the 'worker-peasant alliance', and that as a consequence of their actions 'the vast majority of the proletariat, exploited by the capitalists has turned into the working class serving the construction of socialism'. This required that the industrial working class and rural poor outwardly demonstrate their support for the goals of the regime. These goals, however, clashed sharply with both the cultures and aspirations of the rural poor in agriculture, and the expectations rooted in working class cultures in industrial communities across the country. This contradiction was brought to the fore by the forced industrialisation drives mandated by the regime in the first five-year plan begun in 1950, and the ever more intense collectivisation drives combined with the compulsory requisitioning of agricultural produce to feed the industrial centres. These measures created a climate of material penury that left the regime bereft of any real legitimacy among those it claimed as its supporters by 1952. The regime fell back on the repressive apparatus it had established in the late 1940s to ensure compliance with its goals – a strategy that risked the explosion of the social tensions into an open crisis for the socialist regime.

Revolutionary Overtures

The catalyst for the open crisis was the decision of the MDP's Soviet patrons to rein in Rákosi following the death of Stalin in 1953, through the appointment in June of Imre Nagy, a reformer, as Prime Minister. Relaxation in the cultural, industrial and agricultural spheres followed. The power of the repressive apparatus was curtailed as political prisoners were freed. Yet the attempts at reform were botched. The economy continued its slide into shortage-induced chaos that combined with tensions between urban workers and those in agriculture – exacerbated by Nagy's relaxation of pressure on rural dwellers – to produce discontent. This was used by opponents of reform who rallied around Rákosi, who retained his power base as secretary of the MDP, initiating a power struggle within the elite, which finally removed Nagy in 1955.

The turn away from reform fronted by Nagy's successor András Hegedüs (installed by Rákosi) aimed to return to policies of renewed socialist industrialisation and collectivisation. While many have argued that it was Khruschev's secret speech that unleashed the dynamic of collapse that led to the Revolution in early 1956, the outright collapse of the regime can be traced to 1955 – indeed, this turn set in train a 'long Revolution' in factories and on farms across the country. Industrial workers were confronted with the regime's attempts to hold down the wage bill – their attempts to increase production norms in heavy-industrial sectors and to cut production premiums in the mines provoked enormous opposition. This opposition was, indeed, greater in many factories than it had been to equivalent measures in the early 1950s – in some heavy-engineering factories, workers were no longer frightened and refused to work until the older abolished norms were reinstated. The tightening of the premium system in the mines provoked a storm of complaints. But what was new here was the fact that these were often supported by local unions and party cells. In rural areas, attempts to renew collectivisation produced a state of virtual local civil war between the community and the village party cells. Ferment among intellectuals and students has been relatively well-documented. Even among those who were supposed to support the regime, and among those who served in the armed forces, the signs of a loss of authority for the regime were clear. My own recent work on the history of the border guard demonstrates growing 'indiscipline', and real problems recruiting informers to assist in border protection by early 1956.

Indeed, the 'secret speech' seems to have poured fuel on the fire. These comments from March 1956 are revealing. In Sztálinváros, party members in the factories questioned the local leadership, asking them: 'Stalin led the Party for thirty years, how can it be that his mistakes have been discovered now?'; and: 'What is the current situation in Hungary with the cult of personality?'; alongside more mundane questions: 'I own a copy of Stalin's complete works and have read them all. What do I do with them now?' In Budapest's United Lighting and Electrics Factory, the Khruschev speech soon became an open topic of conversation. Workers maintained that 'the cult of personality was just as marked here [in Hungary] as in the Soviet Union, especially among the top leadership'. Yet events in Poland, especially the riots in Poznan, also probably contributed to the growing revolutionary wave: 'the riots broke out in Poznan not because of the enemy and foreign spies, but because 12 years after the end of the war living standards remained low'.

Especially in the factories, political demands were articulated far more openly than they had been before. One fitter in the Duclós Mining Machinery Factory complained in August that 'it is useless complaining to the Party and factory committee because they can't do anything. What happens here is basically what the director says'. He saw the only remedy as giving 'the trade union a greater role'. By September, the factory press began publishing similar complaints. In the paper of Budapest's Danube Shoe Factory, one former trade unionist wrote:

> [I]n the period following the liberation old, committed trade unionists were promoted to become managers. We should say clearly that later these comrades became detached from the workers, they became one sided and didn't speak up sufficiently for their interests... new people filled the trade union and the beginnings of the co-option, not the elections of the [new] leaders [of the unions] began... the union leaders regarded anyone who stood up for their interests as the enemy, and dealt with them in this manner'.

'A World Turned Upside Down': Hungary, 23 October–10 November 1956

Thus, a 'long Revolution' of sorts was well advanced by 23 October 1956, and the beginnings of outright political revolution involved a rapid relocation of political power from the Party and regime to the revolutionary crowd, which during the last week of October and the first days of November acted as the locus of political legitimacy. In cities across the country, the crowd – organised through initially peaceful demonstrations – assumed the role as the representative of the 'will of the people', demanding a change in the political order. Crowds played a central role in the 'cleansing' of public space, through the deliberate and at times almost theatrical removal of monuments and artefacts associated with either the Red Army or the socialist regime. The frequent incidents whereby representatives of either the army or state-security services fired on initially non-violent crowds after 23 October both radicalised the revolution and underlined the illegitimacy of the regime. Such acts of violence against revolutionary crowds bolstered their claim to act in the name of the people as a whole. Furthermore, they could and frequently did confer their legitimacy on revolutionary organs set up during the Revolution, while they played a role in supervising the actions of other organs that displayed an ambiguous attitude towards the will of the revolutionary crowd.

While the revolutionary crowd appeared as the unified embodiment of the will of the nation, the crowds were far from homogenous either politically or socially. In many towns, like Zalaegerszeg, secondary-school students and industrial workers provided the core of the demonstrations that ignited local revolutions, which attracted members of other occupational groups to join in vocal demands for change. In the capital and university towns, demonstrations were made up of a coalition of students and workers. Workers played a central role in the demonstrations in urban centres right across the country, and often were over-represented among the dead and injured when crowds were fired upon: of those killed when the state-security agencies fired on demonstrators in Mosonmagyaróvár on 26 October, workers made up 65.15 percent. Workers were not the only people in the revolutionary crowds, although they played a crucial role in many. But different groups within the workforce played very different roles – either within the crowd, or in having very different relationships to the crowd, or in participating in crowds in various locations. Working-class youth were the most radical group, inasmuch as they drove political change and were most likely to participate in armed groups during the Revolution.

The role of young workers in providing a group of militants who were prepared to drive forward the Revolution was fundamental. In Budapest, younger workers were frequently drawn to the initial demonstrations, and played a central role in radicalising those demonstrations, before spreading the disturbances back to the industrial suburbs. One second-year industrial apprentice in the United Lighting and Electrics Factory, I.M., was working on 23 October, when, as he reports: 'I heard that there was a demonstration in Budapest in Stalin square'. Immediately catching the tram and trolleybus into central Pest, he was forced to get off some way short of the square because 'the crowd was so big that the trolleybuses stood in a jam and everyone went on foot'. Often youth participation in the early stages of the Revolution resembled lower-level and less political forms of youth disorder in industrial communities. Upon hearing of a demonstration, one group of young working-class males determined to go to the hostel for local student nurses to 'take the girls off to the demonstration' in Budapest. Once they discovered that the director of the hostel had locked the inhabitants in, the men began to shout 'Russians go home, Rákosi to the gallows' until the police arrived.

Young workers took key roles in the 'cleansing' of public space of monuments associated with either the Soviets or the socialist regime. In Nagykanizsa, those who pulled down the Soviet war memorial in the town were led by a 26-year-old worker, whose working life had been filled with a series of jobs in the mining and construction sectors. The activities of working-class youth extended not merely to violence against the symbols of the socialist regime; they also played a direct role in violence against those they perceived to be representatives of the regime. They frequently acted as the 'agents' of the revolutionary crowd in carrying out demands for removing Communists from the head of public institutions. In Újpest's Danube Shoe Factory, the belief of the crowd that 'the workers' council was in the hands of the Communist director', led to four armed young workers – led by the son of one factory employee – deciding that they would storm the factory and 'arrest' the director, as part of a process through which the workers' council would be purged.

The issue of violence raises the question of the process by which working-class youths within demonstrations armed themselves and formed themselves into armed groups. In Budapest, where peaceful demonstrations were fired upon, and with the subsequent intervention of Soviet troops, young workers who had joined the demonstrations moved to arm themselves by demanding the weapons that were stored in factories for civil defence purposes. During the early hours of 24 October, young workers joined other demonstrators in raiding factories for weapons – not all were undefended. In some, as one young worker recalled, 'the porter on the door was already armed with a machine gun'. In some factories, armed bands made up of young workers and factory security guards engaged in gun battles at factory gates. In some cases, workers reporting for the morning shift were caught and injured in the crossfire, although in the vast majority of cases the authorities were able to repel these attacks.

The demands of crowds depended upon the settlements where they were formed. In rural communities, issues of agricultural land-ownership and collectivisation dominated, together with demands for Soviet withdrawal and anti-communism. In the village of Vértesszöllős, demonstrators demanded the break up of the local collective farm and the return of land to its previous owners. In Dömeföld, the first act of the revolutionaries was to break into the offices of the village council and burn the paperwork connected with the local collective and the taxation of local farmers. In nearby Becsehely, protesters demonstrated against the local collective farm, demanding its dissolution and the distribution of its property.

In urban centres, the crowd rallied around less place-specific political demands. In Nagykanizsa, the demands of demonstrators were: support 'for Budapest University students', 'Russians to go home', 'the introduction of a multi-party system', 'the removal of Communist leaders and managers', 'withdrawal from the Warsaw Pact', and 'the removal of the Gerő government'. These crowds also sought to choose revolutionary organs – in effect, these were selected more through chaotic acclamation than election. In factories within Budapest suburbs like Újpest, the events of 23 October sparked revolution. In the United Lighting and Electrics factory on the following morning, two-thirds of the workers arrived at work, but during the morning the skilled workers in the tool workshop and the vacuum plant stopped work to organise a mass meeting of all workers that launched the strike and decided to remove the red star from above the factory gate. With the spread of the strike a large number of workers took to the streets to demand political change. Over the course of the morning there 'were many people in front of the State Department store, and leaflets were distributed from a black car. They shouted and told me that we were all on strike'. The crowd destroyed the Soviet war memorial. Its more radical wing turned on the local police station, yet a majority remained at the site of the war memorial, and as a result of local activists addressing the crowd they chose a body of people to represent them and take over public administration. Thus, the crowd delegated a local 'revolutionary committee' through chaotic acclamation rather than election as such.

The confusion in which revolutionary organs were created to oversee local public administration, and their problematic role given that their legitimacy was located in the revolutionary crowd, was replicated inside enterprises. As many striking workers left to take to the streets, new organs inside workplaces – the workers' councils – were created. Their ambiguous position was not only generated by the chaos in which they were created – as the example of the machine plant of Tatabánya's Coal Mining Trust shows – but also by the fact that they could be used by local Communist cells as part of an attempt to maintain control of their enterprises. The election in this plant took a disorganised form: 'they shouted out names, and the workers replied whether they agreed to their election or not. The first to be elected was L.I., the party secretary, then me, then F., and then the others'. The first workers' council in an enterprise – that of Újpest's United Lighting and Electrics Factory – was organised by the factory party committee, precisely with the intention of ensuring that 'trustworthy people would be elected'. This attempt was unsuccessful. In the forty-eight hours that followed the election of the United Electrics Workers' Council, it remade the institutions of the factory. The factory's managing director and one production director were removed. The managing director was replaced with the president of the workers' council. It announced that it saw itself as provisional, existing only until full elections could be held. It abolished the Personnel Department, which under Rákosi had been used as the representative of both the Party and the secret police within the management of the factory. It further announced that the strike would be maintained and full wages would be paid, while low paid workers would be given a 15 percent wage increase and other workers would receive a raise of 10 percent.

Moreover, it began the process of more fundamental reforms to factory administration, commencing administrative decentralisation and the elimination of bureaucracy, an overhaul of the payment-by-results wage system in the factory, and called for the establishment of a 71 member general workers' council and the creation of shop workers' councils under it. The skilled worker majority, whose thinking dominated the changes instituted by the workers' councils, made their philosophy and distrust of centralisation clear at a meeting of all the councils in Újpest on 29 October: 'the mistakes of recent years show that we have to build from below, we have to solve problems using our own strength'. Yet they also underlined their distrust of the radicalism of bodies like the territorial revolutionary committee in Újpest that drew their legitimacy from the crowd: 'it seems that the power that has been paid in the blood of our young people is falling into the hands of different, fractious elements'.

Themes for Future Research on the 1956 Revolution

I have not presented anything like a coherent sketch of the social history of the 1956 Revolution – that would be a book rather than a lecture, and one that I do not yet feel qualified to write (and – as politicians say when asked whether they intend to raise taxes – I do not yet have any plans to do so!) But I think there are some important themes from the information presented here that I think a social history of 1956 will have to address:

- The importance of *domestic social conflict* – in other words, let us move the focus of work away from international relations/international history, and instead consider the 'geopolitical' as part of a dynamic with the domestic-political and the social.

- The importance of looking *beyond Budapest*, and not just at the period of October–November 1956, for revolution. Socialism's crisis in Hungary was far longer.
- Then I think there is *the centrality of industrial workers*. The fact that they were central to the legitimacy of the socialist regime, the extent of their role in the revolutionary crowd, and the fact that Kádár's consolidation rested to such a degree on buying them off, suggests that understanding their participation is essential to grasping the dynamics of the Revolution.

Epilogue

By Nigel Swain

Mark Pittaway was my graduate student from 1993 to 1998, and over the course of these years we became good friends. It was not difficult to like Mark. As all those who knew him can attest, Mark was a *'mensch'*, as one contributor to the website in his memory put it. He was generous, open, approachable and friendly, never pompous, and with an impish sense of humour and the absurd, which generally triggered a characteristic, mischievous giggle. He was a serious scholar, politically engaged, but always ready to laugh at the political and academic establishments. We all have fond memories of him as a person, but my focus here will be on his intellectual biography, namely, his contribution to history.

I first met Mark on the afternoon of Wednesday 26 August 1992. He had contacted me the previous June, at the suggestion of Bill Lomax,[1] enquiring about the possibility of beginning a research degree at the University of Liverpool the following year. He had then just completed his second year as an undergraduate at the University of Warwick. We shared two interests: Hungary, and the position of labour in socialist economies. My own dissertation had the rather cumbersome title *Collectivisation and the Development of 'Socialist Wage Labour' in Hungarian Agriculture 1946–77*. We spent the Spring of 1993 putting together a proposal for a studentship to the Economic and Social Research Council (ESRC), considering how to organise language training and tentatively identifying sources and archives in Hungary. After he graduated, Mark attended the summer school in Debrecen, where many academics who work on Hungary learn their first smattering of Hungarian, and in August we learned that his ESRC application had been successful. But things did not continue so smoothly. The ESRC did not like the package of language training we had organised, nor the fact that we both felt that Mark should go immediately to Hungary: he had to master the language as soon as possible, and he had already read almost everything that was of use to his dissertation in English. In the end, helped by an extremely stern letter that Mark himself wrote to the ESRC in November 1993 while I was on research visits in Eastern Europe, they relented, and Mark was in Budapest by early 1994.

---

1 In his seminal 1976 work entitled *Hungary 1956*, Bill Lomax argued the now unfashionable case that 1956 was primarily a workers' uprising.

I had put Mark in contact with a number of my friends who helped him find his feet in the very early days, but over the first months of 1994 he developed his own contacts, and by the summer he had located all of the archives that he needed and was up and running; he scarcely needed me. In January 1996, I helped him chose between three possible chapter structures, and that was the sum total of my input into the thesis.

Mark's dissertation was pathbreaking. It demolished completely the idea put forward by theorists of totalitarianism that society under totalitarian regimes was atomised and impotent. In the introduction, he insisted Stalinism was not just a political process, but also a social one, and one with unintended consequences. In fact, he claimed, it was surprisingly vulnerable. While rejecting 'atomisation', he did not romanticise, referring rather to the 'particularisation' of the working class: elements within a differentiated working class pursued separate but not individualised strategies. In demolishing totalitarianism, he also convincingly demonstrated that the sorts of informal labour behaviour that Hungarian sociologists had discovered in the 1970s (a literature that I had used for my undergraduate dissertation) were present in the 1950s as well, at the height of Stalinism. That is to say, he demonstrated that they were intrinsic to socialist labour itself, not to the particular reform relations of late socialism, as these writers had assumed.

This rejection of the idea that any elements of society might be an undifferentiated, impotent mass, the plaything of omnipotent politicians, is, I think, the common thread in Mark's writing. Indeed, in the very first draft of his proposed research project that he sent me in August 1992, he talked of 'putting the "totalitarian" view of workers as passive and atomised under scrutiny'. For Mark, society, not just the working class, was never undifferentiated and impotent. Politics was important for Mark, but what interested him was how political actors – especially those engaged in large-scale social change – negotiate with the social world. Politicians do not act on a *tabula rasa*. Karl Marx famously said: 'Men make their own history, but they do not make it as they please; they do not make it under self-selected circumstances, but under circumstances existing already, given and transmitted from the past'.[2] Hungary's Stalinist rulers in the 1950s also had to deal with 'circumstances transmitted from the past', including, as Mark's research demonstrated, workers, and different generations of workers, who rejected their remoulding into a 'new communist working class' that was forced upon them in Hungary's socialist project to create a society based on productive labour.

---

2 Marx 1968 [1852], p. 93.

The process of turning his thesis into a book has been a protracted one, partly because Mark had so many other projects with which to occupy himself, and partly because his perspective was too radical for a generation of historians still influential in American academic circles that remained committed to the idea that Moscow controlled everything. The 'book of the thesis' (*The Workers' State: Industrial Labour and the Making of Socialist Hungary, 1944–58*), which was published by Pittsburgh University Press in October 2012, has broadened and matured the original arguments of the dissertation. In the interim, Mark had introduced a new concept – 'legitimacy' – into his arsenal, which allowed him to bring out the links between the political and the social more clearly.

In the book, the failure of the project to create a 'new communist working class' and a society based on productive labour, the persistence of working class differentiation and the ability of these groups to win concessions through informal bargaining, were recast as dimensions of a more general failed legitimacy. Building on work by Phillip Abrams, Michael Mann and others,[3] he argues for the dual nature of the state – on the one hand, as a concert of institutions that are social actors in their own right, populated by different groups and pursuing political agendas, and on the other, projecting an appearance of both unity and being above society, that is, the myth of the state as a unified whole, which gives it the ability to enforce its will at the everyday level. Successful regimes are able to persuade their populations at this everyday level that this power is legitimate. Thus, legitimacy is historically contingent:

> [a]ccording to this historically contingent re-conceptualization of the concept, legitimacy has always been a fluid and contested state, defined by the relationship between a given regime's construction of its own claim to legitimacy, and the constellation of values, cultural and political identities among those it attempted to rule. The legitimacy of a given regime was thus often claimed, established, contested and undermined... the achievement of a sufficient degree of legitimacy among enough of the ruled, has been a central aspect of state formation.[4]

Mark is aware of the dangers of arguing that socialist regimes in post-war CEE were in any sense 'legitimate'. Measured by the most common criteria for judging the legitimacy of a political regime – that a regime conformed to given legal and social rules, if those rules could be justified in terms of the belief-

---

3 The works he cites are: Abrams 1988, pp. 58–89; Blom Hansen and Stepputat 2001, pp. 1–38; Krohn-Hansen and Nustad 2005, pp. 3–26; Mitchell 1999, pp. 76–97; Mann 1988, pp. 5–9.
4 Pittaway 2012, p. 4.

systems of both the dominant and subordinate, and then, if the subordinate consented to the exercise of power[5] – socialist regimes could not be regarded as legitimate. But Mark sees political regimes with the eyes of a social historian, not merely as entities and institutions, but as entities 'populated by different groups and pursuing agendas that can be both complementary and contradictory'. 'Legitimate' is not a synonym for 'democratic'. Democratic and undemocratic regimes alike have to establish some form of legitimacy in the eyes of the peoples over whom they rule, otherwise the population realises that 'the emperor has no clothes', as happened in 1956 (in Mark's account) and 1989 (my argument perhaps more so than Mark's). Legitimacy is historically contingent, fragile, and thus vulnerable.

In the light of this new engagement with legitimacy, in Mark's conception the socialist government not only failed to create its 'new communist working class', in so failing it was also unsuccessful in establishing the legitimacy of the regime in the eyes of the workers. His concern with legitimacy led Mark to have the book's area of focus begin some years earlier than the thesis, namely, in 1944 rather than 1948. The thesis took a socialist economy as a given: the book also considers how it was created. That political regimes need legitimacy is hardly new as a general statement of political principles. But Mark's originality was in engaging with society and social history, and ferreting out materials to reveal the how and the why. The task that faced Hungary's political leaders, as revealed by Mark, was not the creation of some non-specific compromise with the population in order to gain their acquiescence; instead, it was a 'workerist' compromise, because the working class was its biggest obstacle in creating a society based on productive labour, and that was what early socialism required – 'from each according to his ability, to each according to his labour'.

In the clash between the vision of a 'new communist working class' based on productive labour and the everyday concerns of a differentiated working class, a conditional legitimacy emerged in the politics of informal compromise on the job, which both threatened managerial (and Party) control and increased differentiations based on gender, generation, skill, and social origin. The more it imposed the 'new communist working class' model and policies associated with it – as it did so between 1950 and 1953 – the less legitimate it became. What little legitimacy remained derived rather from the informal concessions that workers could win from their power in the workplace. When the working class not only failed to defend the regime in 1956, but took to the streets in large numbers to challenge it, the regime's legitimacy evaporated,

---

5   He adapts these criteria from Beetham 1991, p. 16.

and the government strived to repair it by abandoning the project to create a 'new Communist working class' and accommodated itself to the established working class cultures, particularly that of older, skilled, male, urban workers – a 'workerist' settlement that had parallels elsewhere in the socialist world and remained unchallenged until the early 1970s when elements of the NEM were reversed to satisfy the complaints of this section of the working class. Many of these themes recur in his journal articles published between the completion of his PhD and his final submission of the *Working-class* manuscript. These articles are contained in this volume.

In 2004, Mark published his *Eastern Europe 1939–2000* in Arnold's *Brief Histories* series, selections of which have been reproduced in this volume. Although the book is brief, it is also pathbreaking. He reinterprets late twentieth-century Eastern European history through a social-historical lens: how regimes won and consolidated support; what 'workerist' (although he does not use the term) compromises meant for the world of work; the private sphere; gender; youth; and so on. As he says in the preface, he sketches out the contours of a huge and inclusive vision for a new history of Eastern Europe, which is sensitive to the social, but in a politicised context.[6]

By starting the volume in 1939 rather than the more conventional 1945, Mark was able to introduce three very important themes of relevance to legitimacy, although he was only grappling with the significance of the concept at this stage. One of these was the rottenness of the regimes that went before, and therefore the attractiveness of a socialist alternative for large sections of the population, even if it was a socialist alternative with Stalinist question marks. The second was unresolved ethnic tensions. The history of Eastern Europe in the twentieth century cannot be told without reference to ethnic tensions, but if the narrative begins in 1945 with a brand new socialist/Stalinist world, ethnic questions can easily be displaced. Their salience was lower in the socialist years, although they continued below the surface, and they returned in the post-socialist period with a vengeance. The third theme was emphasising the origins of the socialist regimes in the immediate post-war settlement, when wartime goals were paramount and democratic practices less so. In Mark's account, the Communist Party, with Red Army assistance, established a parallel police state alongside the democratic one, but it is important to understand that its origins lay in wartime concerns – the hunt for fascists, collaborators, individuals and groups – and this rather than ethnic hatred (or perhaps compounded by ethnic hatred) resulted in the mass expulsion of Germans. As Mark says, the Popular Front era was neither the 'prelude to Stalinism' nor a

---

6   Pittaway 2004a.

'democratic interlude'. It was an era whose outcome was uncertain. It was an era of mass mobilisation in multi-party politics, but one in which questionable democratic practices that had been tolerated in the war years 'for the greater good' persisted and became the monopoly of only one political party.

An early attempt to flesh out this new history was a conference that Mark and I (but mainly Mark) organised in April 2003 on *Everyday Socialism: States and Social Transformation in Eastern Europe 1945–65*. Eighteen papers over three days covered Czechoslovakia, the GDR, Hungary, Romania, Bulgaria, Poland, and Yugoslavia, and topics as diverse as the activities of voluntary police assistants, post-war expulsion and resettlement, consumer policy, socialist architecture, life in the new socialist city, collectivisation, heroes of socialist labour, the position and role of the artist under socialism, women factory workers, Catholic priests and everyday resistance, cross-border shopping tourism, remembering Red Army rape, socialist and non-socialist memorialisation. Our plan to publish a conference volume was unsuccessful, but contributions or works derived from them were published in the following places: a special issue of *International Labor and Working-class History*, the *Journal of Contemporary History*, the *Journal of Consumer Culture*, the *Journal of Modern History, Social History*, two contributions to edited collections, and two monographs.[7]

In Mark's intellectual biography, legitimacy takes on a much wider significance in his later works. From the specific case of the model of the 'new communist working class' as an inadequate and illegitimate model for the real desires of Hungary's particularised working class, we move towards a more general sense of legitimacy rooted in the ability of regimes to satisfy the basic material requirements of European populations who experienced war-time privations. 'Legitimacy' might appear in places to act as a pretext for retelling political history, but it is crucially different. In standard accounts of political history, political actors decide and act. For the historian concerned with legitimacy, however, there is constant dialogue between citizens and the economic and social conditions of their existence. This approach was also central to the final project in which Mark was engaged before his untimely death, namely, his study of the Austro-Hungarian borderlands. At its very crudest, the argument put forward in this huge study, which covers the period 1938–60, was

---

7 Special issue from 2005 on 'Workers and Socialist States in Post-war Central and Eastern Europe', *International Labor and Working-Class History*, 68; Luthar 2006, pp. 229–59; Glassheim 2006, pp. 65–92; Thelen 2005, pp. 25–44; Schultz 2004, pp. 67–86; Boyer 2005, pp. 151–73; Zarecor 2011; Mark 2011. I am grateful to Kimberly E. Zarecor for helping me compile this information.

that Austria eventually created a form of government that gained legitimacy, whereas Hungary did not. But there is much more to it than that. Austria achieves political stability not because of the innate superiority of liberal democracy, but rather because its regime is considered legitimate by its citizens because it creates an economic and social environment in which basic material requirements are met and living standards gradually but appreciably improve. Hungary, by contrast, despite the 'total' controls that its communist government enjoys over its population, remains illegitimate because such mundane demands are not met. As a result, its government is insecure and severely challenged, most notably in 1956. These considerations are addressed at a fairly general level in a contribution published with Hans Fredrik Dahl in 2008.[8] More concrete illustrations of Hungary's comparative failure to establish legitimacy in areas other than the workplace are presented in his 2004 publication, which is not included in this volume.[9] The Communist Party was dependent on the industrial working class and the rural poor, whose material conditions they improved or promised to improve, but the Smallholders – aided by the Allied Control Commission, which did not permit the creation of any other right-of-centre parties – built up a more powerful alliance from nearly all other social groupings, not just the smallholding peasantry in whose interests the Party was created. In the end, the Communist Party had to resort to extra-parliamentary techniques to overcome its disadvantage. In his consideration of these themes, but with a much fuller elaboration than in the *Brief Histories* book, Mark emphasises that the period between 1944 and 1948 was neither a prelude in an ineluctable progression to Stalinism, nor a 'democratic interlude'. The post-war coalition governments in Hungary scarcely conformed to a democratic norm, yet the outcome – until 1947 at least – was not predetermined.

The differing successes of regimes either side of the Austro-Hungarian border at establishing legitimate rule over their populations was the general topic of the comparative article published in 2008 that constitutes chapter 9 of this volume. This article gives equal treatment to the Austrian side of the border, fleshing out the Austrian successes in establishing a government that not only provided material rewards, but also created a strong Austrian identity defined against a German one, as well as a specific Burgenland identity. The new police in Hungary focused on political reliability and ignored issues of crime and smuggling; the Austrian police established law and order. Retribution and political reliability dominated administrative life in Hungary; in Austria, all

---

8 Pittaway and Dahl 2008, pp. 177–209.
9 Pittaway 2004b, pp. 453–57.

sides connived to minimise the extent to which local political and administrative actors might have been compromised while they were citizens of the German Reich.

Ethnic issues are also central to an article Mark submitted to the journal *Past and Present* just before he died, and which was published posthumously in May 2012.[10] Again, the theme is how local identities of ordinary ethnic citizens obstructed the totalising ambitions of governments, which sought to reproduce border space. In the slightly earlier period that the article considers – the eve of the Second World War following Austria's annexation by Germany – these ambitions were complex. For some Germans, the answer to the minority question was population exchange: swap the Hungarians in what confusingly was now no longer a coherent entity called the Burgenland for the Germans living in western Hungary. That would not get rid of the large Croatian minority, of course, but it had a logic to it, and there were much bleaker logics at work with regard to the Jewish and Roma minorities. But the Germans in the Burgenland had a different vision of themselves, and in some respects maintained a Burgenland identity despite the disappearance of the region from the Nazi political map. They saw themselves as a bridgehead to all of the Germans resident in western Hungary – a bridgehead that might permit the eventual inclusion of regions as far east as the Danube at Budapest into the Reich. If the population-exchange policy were implemented, the Reich's borders would become fixed at the Danube opposite Bratislava with no prospect of eastward expansion. Himmler, somewhat inconsistently, came down against population exchange. The Hungarian government, concerned by attacks on Hungarians in what was now Germany, and also by the increased militancy of Germans in western Hungary, was tempted. In the build up to and beginnings of war, Germany pursued an 'aggressive' brand of nationalism beyond its border, that is to say, in Hungary. Within its borders, however, nationalism was more 'defensive', inasmuch as it did not expel the Hungarian minority. Hungary's nationalism, by contrast, was necessarily more 'defensive' in the face of the German attack. 'Aggressive nationalism' is explored particularly via the activities of the *Volksbund der Deutschen in Ungarn* – the official body sanctioned by Germany to represent German interests in Western Hungary – which ultimately adopted a form of 'regional imperialism', but also in terms of its anti-Jewish and anti-Roma measures and its pressure for the assimilation of Croats as well as Hungarians. Hungary's 'defensive nationalism' is reflected in its crackdowns on German nationalist activities, so increasing their alienation and ultimately eroding Hungarian authority in the region.

10   Pittaway 2012, pp. 143–80.

Mark's borderland work inevitably brought him into contact with local archives on both sides of the Austro-Hungarian border, and with the local dimension to anti-Jewish and anti-Roma measures. His work in local archives led him to suspect that there were more materials on the Hungarian Holocaust in that county's and district's archives than was generally accepted – all the more important because of the gaps in the national archives, their overall lack of transparency, not to mention the petty restrictions imposed by their administrators on foreign researchers. He discussed the idea of pursuing research into these archives further with representatives of the Holocaust Museum in Washington, but was unable to write anything up in a publishable form before he died.

Mark's book in the *Brief Histories* series took Eastern European history in general up to the year 2000, but he addressed the impact of 1989 on the Hungarian working class in particular in a later work that was only published in Hungarian.[11] He began with a sweep of history until 1989, which reprised themes present in the concluding sections of the working class book: loss of legitimacy and 1956, the abandonment of the 'new working class' project thereafter, and a workerist compromise. Slightly more is said about the NEM and its encounter with the interests of the skilled, urban, male working class. But this, as he notes, was the last time any organised working class action was of political significance in Hungary. The 'paradoxical marketisation' of the 1980s further detracted from the regime's legitimacy. Yet despite the role of independent trade unions in prompting system change, working class influence on its subsequent course was insignificant, as neoliberal policies were imposed unquestioned and unopposed.

An English draft of the article contains a brief but nuanced statement on how Mark interpreted the political economy of Eastern European socialism. For him, the 'key social relations that acting together constituted the social realm during the state socialist period' were:

- Property was theoretically owned by the collective of all workers (this form is modified in agriculture by the agricultural producer cooperative), and was managed on their behalf by state organs in the control of the vanguard party operating according to democratic centralist principles.
- The performance of labour to contribute to the generation of the social product was a basic obligation of all citizens. This labour was alienated, commodified and fragmented, and subject to a high degree of managerial supervision.

---

11   Chapter 10 of this volume.

- The means of subsistence were guaranteed to all of those who worked. This was covered through a nationally-provided social wage, an enterprise-based social wage, and through money wages (this could also include the right to participate, to a limited extent, in marginal private sector activity).
- Economic activity was coordinated bureaucratically by the state, and within that framework by enterprise apparatuses. Markets played a subordinate and marginal role within the economy, even in the more reformist variants of the system.
- The state controlled by the vanguard party was part of the international system – it was dependent politically on other socialist states; its role within the international system was determined by the conflict between socialist and capitalist states, but at times of thaw became more dependent on the capitalist world economy.
- The state managed by the vanguard party was a 'civil war' state. This was because many did not accept its rule, and many did not accept its programme of social transformation and the nature of state-socialist social-property relations. The attempts of the state to protect itself against its enemies (real or assumed) – something also related to its international position – was a central aspect of the social-property relations of the system.

As this characterisation suggests, Mark's work was clearly informed by a critical reading of Marx, and his sympathies were unambiguously with the working class and the downtrodden, but his analysis was far from simplistic. Moreover, he was never 'soft' on the Communist Party, or any other party that claimed knowledge of the needs of the working class abstractly conceived over and above their everyday empirically expressed requirements. Mark was a socialist, 'of the left', although he was increasingly attracted to the Green Party. But he adhered to none of the standard revolutionary socialist positions on Eastern Europe. His view of the state as a concert of institutions populated by different groups and pursuing political agendas permits a class analysis, but does not claim that the state is necessarily the agent of the 'bourgeoisie' or the 'revolutionary working class'.

Mark was not an empiricist, but his work was driven by the data that his forensic archival research uncovered. His insights come from what he discovered in archives about Hungarian industrial relations in the 1950s, or Austrian (German) ethnic policy in the late 1930s. His published works invariably begin with a little vignette taken from these archives: the trial of Pál Kósa, President of the Újpest [1956] Revolutionary Committee; the frustration of Sándor Hajósi, an experienced miner in pit XII of the Tatbánya coal trust, at quotas which were impossible to achieve; worker discontent in the Ikarus bus plant in Budapest in 1951 at the postponement of the payment of wages until after the Christmas holiday; the introduction of individualist work targets at the Budapest factory of the Magyar Pamutipar; the mural above the main gate at the Danube Steel works in Dunaújváros (formerly Dunapentele and Sztálinváros); deportation of ethnic Germans from Sopronbánfalva in 1946; ethnic composition of Petržalka when it was incorporated into the expanded Germany in 1938.

Mark was a historian by temperament. He had an insatiable appetite to know 'stuff', and one of the things that distinguish historians from practitioners of other academic disciplines is the need simply to be aware of what is available 'out there'. Searchers after the truth in other disciplines can design their research to reflect their research goals. Natural scientists and psychologists set up experiments designed to test a particular hypothesis; social scientists conduct social surveys or carry out interviews with a research tool that they have designed to elicit certain information from individuals who can respond to those tools. But historians deal with the past, and the past is immutable. Historians have to deal with what there is, with the traces that have been left behind; they cannot design elegant research from scratch. They have to ferret around from what has been left and work out what use can be made of it. This means knowing what has been left – the more you know, the more you might hit upon something that might be useful. With the exception of the rather few archives that have digitised their whole content, finding things in primary sources requires hard work and often intuition. For the historian, the more you know about what archives or other resources exist, and their contents, the more effective you are. And Mark knew a lot. He was the master of the obscure archive. Never satisfied just with national archives, from his PhD onwards he investigated the contents of local archives and the less well-known Budapest-based archives, such as that of the trade-union movement.

Mark carried that knowledge of 'stuff' through to the secondary literature. He was a voracious reader and buyer. The reader of his books and articles is struck immediately by the number and length of the footnotes used. His knowledge of the secondary literature on Eastern Europe generally, but in particular on Hungary (and written in Hungarian), was truly encyclopaedic. Readers will be relieved to learn that much of his huge library (in particular the Hungarian books) has not been dispersed and lost, but is now housed in a special collection in Glasgow University library.

Mark was a historian who crossed borders.[12] He collaborated with scholars in the German-speaking world and has published in Germany. More

---

12   'Crossing Borders' was the English version of the title of the memorial conference held in Mark's memory in Budapest on 24 March 2011.

significant, of course, was his relationship with Hungary. He was as respected in Hungary by Hungarian historians as he was by British and American historians in the Anglo-Saxon world. He was accepted as a complete equal by his Hungarian colleagues, not just as a curious westerner who happened to dabble in Hungarian history. He published articles drawn from both the working class project and the borderlands project in *Eszmélet* – a journal of critical scholars similar to *Debatte* in the UK – and contributed to a volume of the latest research on 1956 by the prestigious 1956 Institute in Budapest.[13]

Mark's contribution to scholarship was tragically cut short. The working class dimension to his oeuvre is more or less complete, certainly with the publication of the *Workers' State* monograph. His *Brief History* of Eastern Europe opened up tantalising vistas to which others can and will contribute. The outlines of what his borderlands project promised are visible from the few publications that have made it into press, but it will remain unfinished. At the time of his death, he had completed his research and had two slightly different chapter plans for a future book. He had hoped to have written the first three chapters by the end of 2011 and have the full manuscript completed by the end of 2012. From the two plans it is clear that none of the existing papers would constitute book chapters. It would be a wholly original manuscript. His research materials are housed at the University of Glasgow. Nobody can write the book that Mark would have written, and no one should try. But perhaps some future scholar can stand on the shoulders of this giant and produce their own story of the Austro-Hungarian borderland from the documentation that he so meticulously collected and has gifted to the academic community.

---

13   Pittaway 2005a, pp. 97–110 and 2007, pp. 49–71.

References

Archival Sources

Az 1956-os Magyar Forradalom Történetének Dokumentációs és Kutatóintézete, Oral History Archivium (Oral History Archives of the 1956 Institute, hereafter 1956-os Intézet, OHA), Budapest.
Budapest Főváros Levéltára (Archive of the City of Budapest, BFL), Budapest.
Burgenländisches Landesarchiv (Burgenland Provincial Archive, hereafter BgLA), Eisenstadt.
Columbia University Libraries, Rare Book and Manuscript Library, Bakhmeteff Archive (hereafter CUL RBML, BAR), New York, NY.
Dokumentationsarchiv des Österreichischen Widerstandes (Documentary Archive of the Austrian Resistance, hereafter DÖW), Wien.
Fejér Megyei Levéltár (Fejér County Archive, hereafter FML), Székesfehérvár.
Győr-Moson-Sopron Megye Győri Levéltára (Győr Branch of the Győr-Moson-Sopron County Archive, hereafter Gy.MSM.Gy.L.), Győr.
Győr-Moson-Sopron Megye Soproni Levéltára (Sopron Branch of the Győr-Moson-Sopron County Archive, hereafter Gy.MSM.S.L.), Sopron.
Komárom-Esztergom Megyei Levéltár (Komárom-Esztergom County Archive, hereafter KEML), Esztergom.
Komárom-Esztergom Megyei Önkormányzat Levéltára (Archive of the Local Government of Komárom-Esztergom County, hereafter KEMÖL), Esztergom.
Magyar Országos Levéltár (Hungarian National Archive, hereafter MOL), Budapest.
Niederösterreichisches Landesarchiv (Lower Austrian Provincial Archive, hereafter NÖLA, St.P), St. Pölten.
Open Society Archives (OSA), Budapest.
Országos Szechényi Könyvtár (National Széchényi Library, hereafter OSZK), Budapest.
Österreichisches Staatsarchiv, Archiv der Republik (hereafter ÖStA/AdR), Wien.
Politikatörténeti és Szakszervezeti Levéltár (Archive of Political History and Trade Unions, hereafter PtSzL), Budapest.
Politikatörténeti Intézet Levéltára (Archive of the Institute of Political History, hereafter PIL), Budapest.
Public Records Office (PRO) Foreign Office (FO), British Embassy: Bratislava and Prague.
Szakszervezetek Központi Levéltára (Central Archive of the Trade Unions, hereafter SZKL), Budapest.
Tatabánya Városi Levéltára (Archive of the City of Tatabánya, hereafter TVL), Tatabánya.
Zala Megyei Levéltár (Zala County Archive, hereafter ZML), Zalaegerszeg.

Internet Databases

International Labour Organisation (ILO), 'Labour Statistics'. Available at: <http://data.un.org/Data.aspx?q=Employment&d=LABORSTA&f=tableCode%3A2B>

Magyar Nemzeti Bank (Hungarian National Bank, or MNB), 'Statistical Releases and Notes, Household and Non-Financial Corporate Sector Interest Rates'. Available at: <http://english.mnb.hu/engine.aspx?page=mnben_vallakozozi_kamatok>

Organisation for Economic Co-operation and Development (OECD), 'Country Statistical Profiles 2009, Gross domestic product (GDP), US$, current prices, current PPPs, millions'. Available at: <http://stats.oecd.org/Index.aspx?DataSetCode=CSP2009>

—— 'Country Statistical Profiles: Hungary, 2009'. Available at: <http://stats.oecd.org/Index.aspx?DataSetCode=CSP2009>

Interviews

B.P.-né, Dunaújváros, 8 February 1995
Gille, Zsuzsa, July 1998
T.J-né, Dunaújváros, 6 May 1996

Newspapers and Periodicals

Duna Híradó 1950, Budapest
Dunántúli Szabad Nép 1945–46, Győr
Futószalag 1952–56, Budapest
Harc a Szénért 1951–56, Tatabánya
Komárom Megyei Hírlap 1956–57, Tatabánya
Mosonmagyaróvári Barátság 1946–49, Mosonmagyaróvár
Mosonvármegye Magyaróvári Hírlap 1944, Mosonmagyaróvár
Munkaerőtartalék 1951, Budapest
News from Behind the Iron Curtain 1952–53, New York, NY

Pamutipari Értesítő 1948, Budapest
Pamutújság 1950–53, Budapest
Soproni Hírlap 1938, Sopron
Soproni Újság 1945–47, Sopron
Szabad Nép 1950, Budapest
Sztálin Vasmű Építője 1952–54, [Sztálinváros]/Dunaújváros
Társadalmi Szemle 1948–53, Budapest
Tungsram Híradó 1949, Budapest
Új Sopron 1945–46, Sopron

Published Primary Sources

1970 évi népszámlalási adatok. Foglalkozási adatok I 1973, Budapest: Központi Statisztikai Hivatal.

A dolgozó nép alkotmánya: a Magyar Népköztársaság alkotmánya 1949, Budapest: Szikra.

Aladárné Mód, Sándorné Ferge, Györgyné Láng and István Kemény (eds.) 1966, *Társadalmi rétegződés Magyarországon*, Budapest: Központi Statisztikai Hivatal.

A lakosság jövedelme és fogyasztása, 1960–1979 1983, Budapest: Központi Statisztikai Hivatal.

'A magyar munkásosztály fejlődése' 1954, Budapest: Központi Statisztikai Hivatal Könyvtára (unpublished manuscript).

A szocializmus építésének útján: a Magyar Dolgozók Pártja II. kongresszusának anyagából 1956, 2nd edition, Budapest: Szikra.

Az 1941 évi népszámlalás községek szerint 1947, Budapest: Stephaneum Nyomda.

Az ellenforradalom Komárom megyei eseményeiből 1957, Tatabánya: MSZMP Komárom Megyei Intézőbizottsága.

Balogh, Sándor 1984, *Választások Magyarországon 1945. A fővárosi törvényhatósági és nemzetgyűlési választások*, Budapest: Kossuth Könyvkiadó.

Belényi, Gyula and Lajos Sz. Varga (eds.) 2001, *Munkások Magyarországon 1948–1956: dokumentumok*, Budapest: Napvilág Kiadó.

Benedek, Sándor 1973, *Változások a munkásosztály struktúrájában*, Budapest: MSZMP KB Társadalomtudományi Intézete.

Birta, István 1970, 'A szocialista iparositási politika néhány kérdése az első ötéves terv időszakában', *Párttörténeti Közlemények*, 16, 3: 113–51.

Budai, Ernő, Ferenc Györő and József Kovács (eds.) 1987, *Ötven éves a magyar kőolaj- és földgázbányászat: KFV, 1937–1987*, Nagykanizsa: Kőolaj- és Földgázbányászati Vállalat.

Cosic, Dobricia 1989, *7 nap Budapesten: 1956 október 23–30*, Budapest: Bethlen Gábor Könyvkiadó.

Csomor, Erzsébet 2001, *1956 Zalaegerszegen*, Zalaegerszeg: Millecentenárium Közalapítvány.

Csomor, Erzsébet and Imre Kapiller (eds.) 1996, *1956 Zalában: a forradalom eseményeinek Zala megyei dokumentumai, 1956–1958*, Zalaegerszeg: Zala Megyei Levéltár.

Dávid, János and Ferenc Kovács (eds.) 1974, *A Salgótarjáni munkások műveltsége és művelődése: az 1971-es művelődésszociológiai vizsgálat válogatott táblaanyaga. Második kötet*, Budapest: MSZMP KB Társadalomtudományi Intézete.

Dékán, Sándor 1950, *Darrabérrendzerrel a szocialista bérezés megvalósitása felé*, Budapest: Népszava Kiadó.

Déri, Károly 1952, *Hogyan teljesitette Pióker Ignác ötéves tervét 23 hónap alatt?*, Budapest: Népszava Kiadó.

Ellenforradalmi erők a magyar októberi eseményekben, I–V kötet 1957, Budapest: A Magyar Népköztársaság Minisztertanácsa Tájékoztatási Hivatala, Zrinyi Nyomda.

Fekete, Margit 1951, 'Szünjék meg a szakmunkások belső munkanélkülisége', *Sztálin Vasmű Épitője*, 14 December 1951.

Gál, László (ed.) 1969, *Szociálpolitikánk két évtizede*, Budapest: Táncsics Könyvkiadó.

Garai, Tibor 1948, *A kultúrtényező jelentősége a versenyszellem kialakításában*, Budapest: Munkatudományi és Racionalizálási Intézet.

Gazdag, István (ed.) 1993, *1956 dokumentumai Hajdú-Biharban: az 1956-os forradalom Hajdú-Bihar megyei történetének válogatott dokumentumai*, Debrecen: 1956-os Intézet Hajdú-Bihar Megyei Kutató Csoportja.

Gereblyés, László 1959, *Így volt: szociográfiai jegyzetek a 30-as évekből*, Budapest: Magvető Kiadó.

Gergely, Jenő, Ferenc Glatz and Ferenc Pölöskei (eds.) 2003, *Magyarországi pártprogramok (1919–1944)*, Budapest: Eötvös Kiadó.

Gerő, Ernő 1952, *A vas, az acél, a gépek országáért*, Budapest: Szikra.

Harc a másodpercekért: kézikönyv az országos termelési versenyhez 1948, Budapest: Szakszervezeti Ifjúmunkás és Tanoncmozgalom.

Hevesi, Gyula 1949, *Sztahanov útján: a Magyar Újítómozgalom fejlődése és feladatai*, Budapest: Atheneum Könyvkiadó.

—— 1950, 'A magyar sztahanovista mozgalom sajátosságai és feladatai ipari tartalékaink mozgósításában', *Társadalmi Szemle*, 5, 1: 1.

International Monetary Fund (IMF) 2010, 'IMF Mission to Hungary Reaches Staff-Level Agreement on Fifth Review under Stand-by Arrangement', Press Release 10/38, 15 February 2010. Available at: <http://www.imf.org/external/np/sec/pr/2010/pr1038.htm>

Kahler, Frigyes et al. (eds.) 1993, *Sortűzek 1956*, 2nd edition, Budapest: Igazságügyi Minisztérium, Antológia Kiadó.

Kajári, Erzsébet (ed.) 1996, *Rendőrségi napi jelentések: 1956. október 23-december 12*, Budapest: Belügyminisztérium 1956-os Magyar Forradalom Történetének Dokumentum és Kutató Intézete Közalapítványa.

Kemény, István and Gyula Kozák 1971a, *A Csepel Vas- és Fémművek munkásai*, Budapest: MSZMP KB Társadalomtudományi Intézete.

—— 1971b, *Pest megye munkásai*, Budapest: MSZMP KB Társadalomtudományi Intézete.

Kétlakiság 1952, Budapest: Szakszervezeti Ismeretterjesztő Előadások, Népszava/ Révai Nyomda.

Központi Statisztikai Hivatal Statisztikai Évkönyv 1950 1951, Budapest: Központi Statisztikai Hivatal.

Központi Statisztikai Hivatal Statisztikai Évkönyv 1953 1954, Budapest: Központi Statisztikai Hivatal.

Központi Statisztikai Hivatal Statisztikai Évkönyv 1970 1971, Budapest: Központi Statisztikai Hivatal.

Lehoczky, Alfréd (ed.) 1974, *Az ipari dolgozók helyzete Borsod megyében. Szociológiai vizsgálat. Második kötet: lakóhelyi és lakásviszonyok*, Budapest: Kossuth Könyvkiadó.

Lomax, Bill (ed.) 1990, *Hungarian Workers' Councils in 1956*, translated by B. Lomax and J. Schöpflin, New York, NY: Columbia University Press.

Lomax, Bill and István Kemény (eds.) 1986, *Magyar munkástanácsok 1956-ban*, Paris: Magyar Füzetek.

Maddison, Angus 1995, *Monitoring the World Economy, 1820–1992*, Paris: OECD Press.

—— 2010, 'Historical Statistics of the World Economy, 1–2008 AD'. Available at: <http://www.ggdc.net/maddison/Historical_Statistics/horizontal-file_02-2010.xls>

Magyary, Zoltán and István Kiss 1939, *A közigazgatás és az emberek: ténymegállapító tanulmány a Tatai Járás közigazgatásáról*, Budapest: Dunántúli Nyomda.

Márkus, István 1991, *Az ismeretlen főszereplő: tanulmányok*, Budapest: Szépirodalmi Könyvkiadó.

Miskolczi, Miklós and András Rózsa 1969, 'A húszéves Dunai Vasmű', Dunaújváros (unpublished manuscript).

Mit adott a népi demokrácia a dolgozóknak? 1953, Budapest: Magyar Dolgozók Pártja Központi Vezetősége Agitációs és Propaganda Osztály.

Mód, Aladár 1945, 'Az üzemi bizottságok és az újjáépités', *Szakszervezeti Közlöny*, 1 June 1945.

Nagy Imre és bűntársai ellenforradalmi összesküvése 1958, Budapest: A Magyar Népköztársaság Minisztertanácsa Tájékoztatási Hivatala, Zrinyi Nyomda.

Pew Research Center 2010, 'Hungary Dissatisfied with Democracy but Not its Ideals', in *The Pulse of Europe 2009: 20 Years After the Fall of the Berlin Wall. Pew Global Attitudes Report 2009*. Available at: <http://pewresearch.org/pubs/1554/hungary-economic-discontent>

Rákosi, Mátyás 1950, 'Mi a Magyar demokrácia?', in *Válogatott beszédek és cikkek*, Budapest: Szikra.

—— 1997, *Visszaemlékezések. Második kötet, 1940–1956*, Budapest: Napvilág Kiadó.

Rézler, Gyula (ed.) 1940, *Magyar gyári munkásság: szociális helyzetkép*, Budapest: Magyar Közgazdasági Társaság.

—— 1943, *Egy magyar textilgyár munkástársadalma*, Budapest: Magyar Ipari Munkatudományi Intézet.

Sándor, András 1948, *Övék a föld*, Budapest: Szikra.

Srágli, Lajos 1985, 'Adatok az olajipari munkásság szociális helyzetének alakulásához, 1937–1944 (A MAORT munkás jóléleti intézkedés)', in *Közlemények Zala megye közgyűjteményeinek kutatásaiból 1984–1985*, edited by Alajos Degré and Imre Halász, Zalaegerszeg: Zala Megyei Levéltár.

—— 1986, 'A dunántúli olajbányászat hároméves terve: adatok a MAORT történetéhez, 1947–1949', in *Közlemények Zala megye közgyűjteményeinek*

kutatásaiból, edited by Endre Gyimesi, Zalaegerszeg: Zala Megyei Levéltár.

Szabó, Zoltán 1938, *Cifra nyomorúság: a Cserhát, Mátra, Bükk földje és népe*, Budapest: Cserépfalvi Könyvkiadó.

Szálasi, Ferenc 2004, *Hungarizmus: a cél*, Budapest: Gede Testvérek Bt.

Varga, Domokos 1951, *Kiszlinger József sztahanovista esztergályos élete és munkamódszere*, Budapest: Szikra.

Vass, Henrik (ed.) 1974, *A Magyar Szocialista Munkáspárt határozatai és dokumentumai, 1967–1970*, Budapest: Kossuth Könyvkiadó.

—— (ed.) 1978, *A Magyar Szocialista Munkáspárt határozatai és dokumentumai, 1971–1975*, Budapest: Kossuth Könyvkiadó.

Vass, Henrik and Ágnes Ságvári (eds.) 1973, *A Magyar Szocialista Munkáspárt határozatai és dokumentumai, 1956–1962*, 2nd edition, Budapest: Kossuth Könyvkiadó.

Vidos, Dénes 1990, *Zalai olajos történetek*, Zalaegerszeg: Magyar Olajipari Múzeum.

Vonyó, József et al. (ed.) 2004, *Gömbös Gyula: válogatott politikai beszédek és írások*, Budapest: Osiris Kiadó.

Published Secondary Sources

Abrams, Bradley F. 1996, 'The Politics of Retribution: The Trial of Jozef Tiso', *East European Politics and Societies*, 10, 2: 255–92.

—— 2002, 'The Second World War and the East European Revolution', *East European Politics and Societies*, 16, 3: 623–64.

Abrams, Philip 1988, 'Notes on the Difficulty of Studying the State (1977)', *Journal of Historical Sociology*, 1, 1: 58–89.

Alexander, Stella 1979, *Church and State in Yugoslavia since 1945*, Cambridge: Cambridge University Press.

Aly, Götz 1999, *Final Solution: Nazi Population Policy and the Murder of the European Jews*, translated by B. Cooper and A. Brown, London: Hodder Education.

Aly, Götz and Susanne Heim 2002, *Architects of Annihilation: Auschwitz and the Logic of Destruction*, translated by A.G. Blunden, London: Weidenfeld and Nicolson.

Andrle, Vladimir 1988, *Workers in Stalin's Russia: Industrialisation and Social Change in a Planned Economy*, Brighton: Harvester Books.

Apor, Péter 1998, 'A népi demokrácia építése: Kunmadaras, 1946', *Századok*, 132, 3: 601–32.

Ballinger, Pamela 2002, *History in Exile: Memory and Identity at the Borders of the Balkans*, Princeton, NJ: Princeton University Press.

Balogh, István and Róbert Gál 1973, 'A munkásifjúság' in *Tanulmányok a munkásosztályról*, edited by Tibor Halay, Budapest: Kossuth Könyvkiadó.

Barb, Alfons 2004, 'Der Burgenländer', in *'Die Geburt des Burgenländers': Ein Lesebuch zur Historischen Volkskultur im Burgenland*, edited by Elisabeth Bockhorn, Olaf Bockhorn and Veronika Plöckinger, Eisenstadt: Wissenschaftliche Arbeiten aus dem Burgenland.

Barbu, Zeev 1980, 'Psycho-historical and Sociological Perspectives on the Iron Guard, the Fascist Movement of Romania', in *Who Were the Fascists? Social Roots of European Fascism*, edited by Stein U. Larsen, Bernt Hagtvet and Jan P. Myklebust, Bergen: Universitetsforlaget.

Bartha, Eszter 2009, 'Would You Call Back the Capitalists? Workers and the Beginnings of Market Socialism in Hungary', *Social History*, 34, 2: 123–44.

—— 2011, 'Mark David Pittaway: 1971–2010', *Eszmélet*, 91: 130–1.

Bayer, Pia 2005, 'Die Rolle der Frau in der burgenländischen Besatzungszeit, 1945–1955', in *Befreien – besetzen – bestehen: das Burgenland von 1945–1955*, edited by Felix Tobler, Eisenstadt: Burgenländisches Landesarchive.

Beetham, David 1991, *The Legitimation of Power*, Basingstoke: Macmillan.

Békés, Csaba (ed.) 1993, *Az 1956-os magyar forradalom helye a szovjet kommunista rendszer összeomlásában*, Budapest: 1956-os Intézet.

Békés, Csaba, Malcolm Byrne and János M. Rainer (eds.) 2004, *The 1956 Hungarian Revolution: A History in Documents*, Budapest and New York, NY: Central European University Press.

Belényi, Gyula 1993, *A Sztálini iparosítás emberi ára: foglalkozási átrétegződés és belső vándorlás Magyarországon, 1948–1956*, Szeged: JATE Press.

Bencze, Géza 1980, *Zala megye iparának története a felszabadulás után, 1945–1970*, Zalaegerszeg: Zala Megyei Tanács.

Berend, Iván T. 1964, *Gazdaságpolitika az első ötéves terv megindulásakor, 1948–1950*, Budapest: Közgazdasági és Jogi Könyvkiadó.

―― 1974, *A szocialista gazdaság fejlődése Magyarországon 1945–1968*, Budapest: Kossuth Könyvkiadó.

―― 1986, *The Crisis Zone of Europe: An Interpretation of East-Central European History in the First Half of the Twentieth Century*, Cambridge: Cambridge University Press.

―― 1988, *Decades of Crisis: Central and Eastern Europe before World War II*, Berkeley, CA: University of California Press.

―― 1993, 'The Composition and Position of the Working Class during the War', in *Hungarian Economy and Society during World War II*, edited by György Lengyel, translated by J. Pokoly, Boulder, CO: Social Science Monographs.

―― 1996, *Central and Eastern Europe 1944–1993: Detour from the Periphery to the Periphery*, Cambridge: Cambridge University Press.

Berend, Iván T. and György Ránki 1958, *Magyarország gyáripara a második világháború előtt és a háború időszakában, 1933–1944*, Budapest: Akadémiai Kiadó.

―― 1985, *The Hungarian Economy in the Twentieth Century*, London: Croom Helm.

Berger, Peter 2007, *Kurze Geschichte Österreichs im 20. Jahrhundert*, Vienna: WUV Universitaets Verlag.

Berry, Burton Y. 2000, *Romanian Diaries 1944–1947*, edited by Cornelia Bodea, Iași: Center for Romanian Studies.

Bessel, Richard and Ralph Jessen (eds.) 1996, *Die Grenzen der Diktatur: Staat und Gesellschaft in der DDR*, Göttingen: Vandenhoeck und Ruprecht.

Biddiscombe, Perry 1993, 'Prodding the Russian Bear: Pro-German Resistance in Romania, 1944–1945', *European History Quarterly*, 23, 2: 193–232.

Bindorffer, Györgyi 2001, *Kettős identitás: etnikai és nemzeti azonosságtudat Dunabogdányban*, Budapest: Új Mandátum Könyvkiadó-MTA Kisebbségkutató Intézet.

Blom Hansen, Thomas and Finn Stepputat (eds.) 2001, *States of Imagination: Ethnographic Explorations of the Postcolonial State*, Durham, NC: Duke University Press.

Bloomfield, Jon 1979, *Passive Revolution: Politics and the Czechoslovak Working Class, 1945–1948*, London: Allison & Busby.

Blumi, Isa 1997, 'The Politics of Culture and Power: the Roots of Hoxha's Postwar State', *East European Quarterly*, 31, 3: 409–28.

Bohle, Dorothee and Béla Greskovits 2012, *Capitalist Diversity on Europe's Periphery*, Ithaca, NY: Cornell University Press.

Bokovoy, Melissa K. 1998, *Peasants and Communists: Politics and Ideology in the Yugoslav Countryside 1941–1953*, Pittsburgh, PA: University of Pittsburgh Press.

Bondy, François 1990, 'The Government vs. the Workers', in *Hungarian Workers' Councils in 1956*, edited by Bill Lomax, translated by B. Lomax and J. Schöpflin, New York, NY: Columbia University Press.

Borhi, László 2004, *Hungary in the Cold War 1945–1956: Between the United States and the Soviet Union*, Budapest and New York, NY: Central European University Press.

Boyer, Christoph 2005, 'Verflechtung und Abgrenzung: sozial- und konsumpolitische Beziehungen im RGW', in *Sozialstaatlichkeit in der DDR: Sozialpolitische Entwicklungen im Spannungsfeld von Diktatur und Gesellschaft 1945/49–1989*, edited by Dierk Hoffmann and Michael Schwarz, München: Oldenbourg Verlag.

Braham, Randolph L. 2000, *The Politics of Genocide: The Holocaust in Hungary*, Detroit, MI: Wayne State University Press.

Brown, Keith 2003, *The Past in Question: Modern Macedonia and the Uncertainties of Nation*, Princeton, NJ: Princeton University Press.

Brus, Wlodzimierz 1986, '1950 to 1953: The Peak of Stalinism', in *The Economic History of Eastern Europe 1919–1975, Volume 3: Institutional Change within a Planned Economy*, edited by Michael C. Kaser and Edward A. Radice, Oxford: Oxford University Press.

Bryant, Chad 2002, 'Either Czech or German: Fixing Nationality in Bohemia and Moravia, 1939–1946', *Slavic Review*, 61, 4: 683–706.

Brzezinski, Zbigniew 1967, *The Soviet Bloc: Unity and Conflict*, Cambridge, MA: Harvard University Press.

Burawoy, Michael 1985, *The Politics of Production: Factory Regimes under Capitalism and Socialism*, London: Verso.

Burawoy, Michael and János Lukács 1992, *The Radiant Past: Ideology and Reality in Hungary's Road to Capitalism*, Chicago, IL: University of Chicago Press.

Burleigh, Michael 2001, *The Third Reich: A New History*, London: Pan Books.

Cartwright, Andrew L. 2001, *The Return of the Peasant: Land Reform in Post-communist Romania*, Aldershot: Ashgate.

Connelly, John 1999, 'Nazis and Slavs: From Racial Theory to Racist Practice', *Central European History*, 32, 1: 1–33.

—— 2000, *Captive University: The Sovietization of East German, Czech and Polish Higher Education, 1945–1956*, Chapel Hill, NC: University of North Carolina Press.

Coutovidis, John and Jamie Reynolds 1986, *Poland 1939–1947*, Leicester: Leicester University Press.

Crampton, Richard J. 1987, *A Short History of Modern Bulgaria*, Cambridge: Cambridge University Press.

Dale, Gareth 2005, *Popular Protest in East Germany, 1945–1989*, London: Routledge.

—— (ed.) 2011, *First the Transition, Then the Crash: Eastern Europe in the 2000s*, London: Pluto Press.

Darvas, Péter 1983, 'Oktatás és tervgazdálkodás', *Medvetánc*, 4: 59–75.

Daskalov, Rumen and Holm Sundhaussen 1999, 'Modernisierungsansätze', in *Südosteuropa: Gesellschaft, Politik, Wirtschaft, Kultur: Ein Handbuch*, edited by Magarditsch A. Hatschikjan and Stefan Troebst, München: Beck.

Deletant, Dennis 1999, *Communist Terror in Romania: Gheorghiu-Dej and the Police State, 1948–1965*, London: C. Hurst.

Dessewffy, Tibor and András Szántó 1989, *'Kitörő éberséggel' – A budapesti kitelepítések hiteles története*, Budapest: Háttér Kiadó.

Djilas, Aleksa 1991, *The Contested Country: Yugoslav Unity and Communist Revolution, 1919-1953*, Cambridge, MA: Harvard University Press.

Dobos, Ilona S. 1958, *Szegény ember vízzel főz: életrajzi vallomások, igaz történetek*, Budapest: Magvető Kiadó.

Don, Yehuda 1997, 'Economic Implications of Anti-Jewish Legislation in Hungary', in *Genocide and Rescue: The Holocaust in Hungary 1944*, edited by David Cesarani, Oxford: Berg Publishers.

Donáth, Ferenc 1977, *Reform és forradalom: a magyar mezőgazdaság strukturális átalakulása, 1945-1975*, Budapest: Akadémiai Kiadó.

Dreisziger, Nándor F. 1985, 'The Dimensions of Total War in East Central Europe', in *East Central European Society in World War I*, edited by Béla K. Király and Nándor F. Dreisziger, Boulder, CO: Social Science Monographs.

Drucker, Tibor 1965, 'A felszabadult Csepel', in *Csepel története*, edited by Jenő Adamovits et al., Budapest: Csepel Vas- és Fémművek Pártbizottsága.

Eby, Cecil D. 1998, *Hungary at War: Citizens and Soldiers in World War II*, University Park, PA: Penn State University Press.

Ekiert, Gregorz 1996, *The State Against Society: Political Crises and their Aftermath in East Central Europe*, Princeton, NJ: Princeton University Press.

Eörsi, László 1993, *A Tűzoltó utcai fegyveres csoport a forradalomban*, Budapest: Századvég Kiadó.

—— 1997, *Ferencváros 1956: a kerület fegyveres csoportjai*, Budapest: 1956-os Intézet.

—— 2001, *Corvinisták 1956: A VIII kerület fegyveres csoportjai*, Budapest: 1956-os Intézet.

Erdei, Ferenc 1977, *Futóhomok*, Budapest: Akadémiai Kiadó.

Erdmann, Gyula 1992, *Begyűjtés, beszolgáltatás Magyarországon 1945-1956*, Békéscsaba: Tevan Kiadó.

Erdős, Ferenc 2000, 'Dunapentelétől Sztálinvárosig', in *Dunaújváros története*, edited by Ferenc Erdős and Zsuzsanna Pongrácz, Dunaújváros: Dunaújváros Önkormányzata.

Farkas, Csaba 2003, 'Csongrád megye', in *A vidék forradalma, 1956: Első kötet*, edited by Attila Szakolczai and László A. Varga, Budapest: 1956-os Intézet.

Fazekas, Károly 1982, 'Bér-teljesítmény-alku a belső munkaerőpiacon', in *A munkaerőpiac szerkezete és működése Magyarországon*, edited by Péter Galasi, Budapest: Közgazdasági és Jogi Könyvkiadó.

Fazekas, Károly and János Köllő 1990, *Munkaerő piac tőkepiac nélkül*, Budapest: Közgazdasági és Jogi Könyvkiadó.

Filep, Tibor 2000, *Debrecen, 1956: forradalom, nemzeti ellenállás, megtorlás*, Debrecen: Csokonai Kiadó.

Filzer, Donald 1986, *Soviet Workers and Stalinist Industrialization: The Formation of Modern Soviet Production Relations, 1928-1941*, London: Pluto Press.

Fitzpatrick, Sheila 1999, *Everyday Stalinism - Ordinary Life in Extraordinary Times: Soviet Russia in the 1930s*, New York, NY: Oxford University Press.

—— (ed.) 2000, *Stalinism: New Directions*, London: Routledge.

Földes, György 1980, 'Az újpesti munkásság életviszonyai az 1930-as években', *Történelmi Szemle*, 20, 2: 309–18.

—— 1989, *Hatalom és mozgalom 1956–1989: társadalmi-politikai erő viszonyok Magyarországon*, Budapest: Reform Könyvkiadó.

—— 1993, 'A Kádár rendszer és a munkásság', *Eszmélet*, 18–19: 57–73.

—— 1995, *Az eladósodás politikatörténete, 1957–1986*, Budapest: Maecenas Kiadó.

Földes, László 1994, 'A város peremén: Leírás Nagy-Budapest szeméttelepéről, 1954-ben', *Mozgó Világ*, 20, 5: 22–9.

Frommer, Benjamin R. 1999, *Retribution against Nazi Collaborators in Postwar Czechoslovakia*, DPhil Thesis, Harvard University.

—— 2001, 'To Prosecute or to Expel? Czechoslovak Retribution and the "Transfer" of Sudeten Germans', in *Redrawing Nations: Ethnic Cleansing in East Central Europe, 1944–1949*, edited by Philipp Ther and Ana Siljak, Lanham: Rowman & Littlefield.

Fulbrook, Mary 1995, *Anatomy of a Dictatorship: Inside the GDR, 1949–1989*, Oxford: Oxford University Press.

Gábor, István R. and Péter Galasi 1982, 'A "kiegészítő tevékenységek" társadalmi összefüggései', in *Válság és megújulás: gazdaság, társadalom és politika Magyarországon. Az MSZMP 25 éve*, edited by Henrik Vass, Budapest: Kossuth Könyvkiadó.

Galasi, Péter and György Sziráczki (eds.) 1985, *Labour Market and Second Economy in Hungary*, Frankfurt: Campus.

Gati, Charles 1986, *Hungary and the Soviet Bloc*, Durham, NC: Duke University Press.

Gergely, Jenő 1977, *A politikai katolicizmus Magyarországon, 1890–1950*, Budapest: Kossuth Kiadó.

Gerlach, Christian and Götz Aly 2004, *Das letzte Kapitel: Der Mord an den ungarischen Juden, 1944–1945*, Frankfurt: Fischer Taschenbuch Verlag.

Glassheim, Eagle 2000, 'National Mythologies and Ethnic Cleansing: The Expulsion of Czechoslovak Germans in 1945', *Central European History*, 34, 4: 463–86.

—— 2006, 'Ethnic Cleansing, Communism, and Environmental Devastation in Czechoslovakia's Borderlands, 1945–1989', *Journal of Modern History*, 78, 1: 65–92.

Glenny, Misha 1999, *The Balkans, 1804–1999: Nationalism, War and the Great Powers*, London: Granta Books.

Goven, Joanna 1993, *The Gendered Foundations of Hungarian Socialism: State, Society and the Anti-politics of Anti-feminism, 1948–1990*, DPhil Thesis, University of California, Berkeley.

Granville, Johanna 2004, *The First Domino: International Decision Making during the Hungarian Crisis of 1956*, College Station, TX: Texas A&M University Press.

Gross, Jan 1979, *Polish Society under German Occupation: The Generalgouvernement, 1939–1944*, Princeton, NJ: Princeton University Press.

—— 1988, *Revolution from Abroad: The Soviet Conquest of Poland's Western Ukraine and Western Belorussia*, Princeton, NJ: Princeton University Press.

—— 1997, 'War as Revolution', in *The Establishment of Communist Regimes in Eastern Europe, 1944–1949*, edited by Norman Naimark and Leonid Gibianski, Boulder, CO: Westview Press.

Gyarmati, György, János Botos, Tibor Zinner and Mihály Korom 1988, *Magyar hétköznapok Rákosi Mátyás két emigrációja között, 1945–1956*, Budapest: Minerva Kiadó.

Gyekiczky, Tamás 1989, *A fegyelem csapdájában: munkafegyelmi kampányok társadalmi hatásának elemzése*, Budapest: MTA Szociólógiai Intézet.

Habuda, Miklós 1986, *A magyar szakszervezetek a népi demokratikus forradalomban 1944–1948*, Budapest: Népszava.

Halmos, Ferenc 1978, *Illő alázattal*, Budapest: Szépirodalmi Könyvkiadó.

Hamm, Harry 1963, *Albania: China's Beachhead in Europe*, London: Weidenfeld & Nicholson.

Hámor, István 1951, 'Lakóháztipusok fejlődése a Sztálin Vasmű tükrében', *Épités-Épitészet*, 3: 11–12.

Hanák, Péter and Katalin Hanák 1964, *A magyar pamutipar története, 1887–1962*, Budapest: Magyar Pamutipar 1. sz. Gyáregysége.

Hanebrink, Paul A. 2006, *In Defense of Christian Hungary: Religion, Nationalism and Antisemitism, 1890–1944*, Ithaca, NY: Cornell University Press.

Hankiss, Elemer 1990, *East European Alternatives*, Oxford: Clarendon.

Hanson, Stephen E. 1997, *Time and Revolution: Marxism and the Design of Soviet Institutions*, Chapel Hill, NC: University of North Carolina Press.

Haraszti, Miklós 1977, *A Worker in a Worker's State: Piece Rates in Hungary*, translated by M. Wright, Harmondsworth: Penguin Books.

Harvey, David 2007, *A Brief History of Neoliberalism*, Oxford: Oxford University Press.

Hauner, Milan 1986, 'Military Budgets and the Armaments Industry', in *The Economic History of Eastern Europe 1919–1975: Volume 2: Interwar Policy, the War and Reconstruction*, edited by Michael C. Kaser and Edward A. Radice, Oxford: Oxford University Press.

Haynes, Mike 1992, 'Class and Crisis: The Transition in Eastern Europe', *International Socialism*, 54: 45–104.

Hegedűs, András B. et al. (eds.) 1996, *1956 kézikönyve: Megtorlás és emlékezés*, Budapest: 1956-os Intézet.

Héthy, Lajos 1984, 'A bér és az anyagi boldogúlás perspektívája', in *A munkásság helyzete az üzemben: jogok, tények, távlatok*, edited by Lajos Héthy, Budapest: Kossuth Könyvkiadó.

Héthy, Lajos and Csaba Makó 1972, *Munkásmagatartasok és gazdasági szervezet*, Budapest: Akadémiai Kiadó.

—— 1978, *Munkások, érdekek, érdekegyeztetés*, Budapest: Gondolat Kiadó.

—— 1989, *Patterns of Workers' Behavior and the Business Enterprise*, Budapest: Hungarian Academy of Sciences and Hungarian Ministry of Labour.

Heumos, Peter 1999, 'Normalisierung und soziale Beschwichtigungsstrategien in der ČSSR: KPTsch-Politik, Gewerkschaften und Arbeiterbewußtsein', in *Repression und Wohlstandsversprechen: Zur Stabilisierung von Parteiherrschaft in der DDR und der ČSSR*, edited by Christoph Boyer and Peter Skyba, Dresden: Hannah Arendt Institut.

—— 2001, 'Aspekte des sozialen Milieus der Industriearbeiterschaft in der Tschechoslowakei vom Ende des Zweiten Weltkrieges bis zur Reformbewegung der Sechziger Jahre', *Bohemia*, 42, 2: 323–62.

Hitchins, Keith 1994, *Romania 1866–1947*, Oxford: Oxford University Press.

Hodos, George H. 1988, *Schauprozesse: Stalinistische Säuberungen in Osteuropa 1948–1954*, Frankfurt: Campus.

Hornung, Ela, Ernst Langthaler and Sabine Schweitzer 2004, *Zwangsarbeit in der Landwirtschaft in Niederösterreich und dem nördlichen Burgenland*, München: Oldenbourg Verlag.

Horváth, István et al. 2000, *Dunaferr Dunai vasmű krónika*, Dunaújváros: Dunatáj Kiadó.

Horváth, Sándor 2004, *A kapu és a határ: mindennapi Sztálinváros*, Budapest: MTA Történettudományi Intézete.

Hübner, Peter 1995, *Konsens, Konflikt und Kompromiss: Soziale Arbeiterinteressen und Sozialpolitik in der SBZ/DDR 1945–1970*, Berlin: Akademie Verlag.

Hunt, Pauline 1995, 'Gender and the Construction of Home Life', in *The Politics of Domestic Consumption: Critical Readings*, edited by Stevi Jackson and Shaun Moores, London: Prentice Hall & Harvester Wheatsheaf.

Hunyadi, Zsuzsa 1984, 'A munkások rétegződéséről', in *Gazdaság és rétegződés: műhelytanulmányok*, edited by Imre Kovách, Budapest: MSZMP KB Társadalomtudományi Intézete.

Huszár, Tibor (ed.) 2002, *Kedves jó Kádár elvtárs! Válogatás Kádár János levelezéséből, 1954–1989*, Budapest: Osiris Kiadó.

—— 2003, *Kádár János politikai életrajza. 2 kötet: 1957 november-1989 június*, Budapest: Kossuth Kiadó.

Jankowiak, Stanislaw 2001, '"Cleansing" Poland of Germans: The Province of Pomerania, 1945–1949', in *Redrawing Nations: Ethnic Cleansing in East Central Europe, 1944–1949*, edited by Philipp Ther and Ana Siljak, Lanham: Rowman & Littlefield.

Jarosz, Dariusz 1999, 'Polish Peasants versus Stalinism', in *Stalinism in Poland, 1944–1956: Selected Papers from the Fifth World Congress of Central and Eastern European Studies, Warsaw, 1995*, edited by Anthony Kemp-Welch, Basingstoke: Macmillan.

Jelinek, Yeshayahu 1976, *The Parish Republic: Hlinka's Slovak People's Party 1939–1945*, Boulder, CO: Social Science Monographs.

Juhász, Pál 1988, 'Agrárpiac, kisüzem, nagyüzem', in *Medvetánc: Magyar gazdaság és szociológia a 80-as években*, edited by Tamás Miklós, Budapest: Minerva Könyvkiadó.

Kádár, Zsuzsanna B. 1999, 'A szociáldemokraták üldözése és diszkriminálása', in *A magyar szociáldemokrácia kézikönyve*, edited by Lajos Varga, Budapest: Napvilág Kiadó.

Kaiser, David E. 1980, *Economic Diplomacy and the Origins of the Second World War: Germany, Britain, France and Eastern Europe, 1930–1939*, Princeton, NJ: Princeton University Press.

Kalmár, Melinda 1998, *Ennivaló és hozomány: a kora kádárizmus ideológiája*, Budapest: Magvető Kiadó.

Kaplan, Karel 1987, *The Short March: The Communist Takeover in Czechoslovakia 1945–1948*, London: Hurst.

Karsai, László 2000, 'The People's Courts and Revolutionary Justice in Hungary, 1945–46', in *The Politics of Retribution in Europe: World War II and its Aftermath*, edited by István Deák, Jan T. Gross and Tony Judt, Princeton, NJ: Princeton University Press.

Katzburg, Nathaniel 1981, *Hungary and the Jews: Policy and Legislation, 1920–1943*, Ramat-Gan: Bar-Ilan University Press.

Keane, John 2000, *Václav Havel: A Political Tragedy in Six Acts*, London: Basic Books.

Kemény, István 1985, *Ouvriers hongrois, 1956–1985*, Paris: L'Harmattan.

—— 1990, *Velük nevelkedett a gép: magyar munkások a hetvenes évek elején*, Budapest: VITA.

—— 1992 [1978], 'Kompromisszumok egyezség nélkül', in *Szociológiai írások*, edited by István Kemény, Szeged: Replika Könyvek.

—— 1992, 'A nem regisztrált gazdaság Magyarországon', in *Szociológiai írások*, edited by István Kemény, Szeged: Replika Könyvek.

Kenedi, János (ed.) 1996, *Kis állambiztonsági olvasókönyv: október 23, március 15, június 16 a Kádár-korszakban. Első kötet*, Budapest: Magvető Könyvkiadó.

Kenez, Peter 2006, *Hungary from the Nazis to the Soviets: The Establishment of the Communist Regime in Hungary, 1944–1948*, Cambridge: Cambridge University Press.

Kenney, Padraic 1997, *Rebuilding Poland: Workers and Communists, 1945–1950*, Ithaca, NY: Cornell University Press.

—— 1999, 'The Gender of Resistance in Communist Poland', *American Historical Review*, 104, 2: 399–425.

Kershaw, Ian 2000, *Hitler 1936–1945: Nemesis*, Harmondsworth: Penguin Press.

Kersten, Krystyna 1999, 'The Terror, 1949–1954', in *Stalinism in Poland, 1944–1956: Selected Papers from the Fifth World Congress of Central and Eastern European Studies, Warsaw, 1995*, edited by Anthony Kemp-Welch, Basingstoke: Macmillan.

King, Jeremy 2002, *Budweisers into Czechs and Germans: A Local History of Bohemian Politics, 1848–1948*, Princeton, NJ: Princeton University Press.

King, Robert R. 1980, *The History of the Romanian Communist Party*, Stanford, CA: Hoover Institution Press.

Király, Béla K. 1983, 'Red Wave in Central Europe: A Repercussion of a Total War', in *The Effects of World War I: The Class War after the Great War: The Rise of Communist Parties in East Central Europe, 1918–1921*, edited by Ivo Banac, Boulder, CO: Social Science Monographs.

Kirsch, András 2006, *A Soproni németek kitelepítése, 1946*, Sopron: Escort Kiadó.

Knight, Robert 2007, 'De-nazification and Integration in the Austrian Province of

Carinthia', *Journal of Modern History*, 79, 3: 572–612.

Kok, Jan (ed.) 2002, *Rebellious Families: Household Strategies and Collective Action in the Nineteenth and Twentieth Centuries*, Oxford: Berghahn Books.

Kopstein, Jeffrey 1997, *The Politics of Economic Decline in East Germany, 1945–1989*, Chapel Hill, NC: University of North Carolina Press.

Kornai, János 1992, *The Socialist System: The Political Economy of Communism*, Princeton, NJ: Princeton University Press.

—— 1994 [1959], *Overcentralisation in Economic Administration: A Critical Analysis Based on Experience in Hungarian Light Industry*, translated by J. Knapp, Oxford: Oxford University Press.

Kotkin, Stephen 1995, *Magnetic Mountain: Stalinism as a Civilization*, Berkeley, CA: University of California Press.

Kovács, András Z. 2001, 'Csendőrsors Magyarországon 1945 után', in *Katonai perek a kommunista diktatúra időszakában, 1945–1958*, edited by Imre Okváth, Budapest: Történeti Hivatal.

Kovrig, Bennett 1977, *Communism in Hungary: From Kun to Kádár*, Stanford, CA: Hoover Institution Press.

Kozák, Gyula and Molnár Adrienné (eds.) 1994, *'Szuronyok hegyén nem lehet dolgozni': válogatás 1956-os munkástanácsvezetők visszaemlékezéseiből*, Budapest: Századvég Kiadó.

Krausz, Tamás and Péter Szigeti (eds.) 2007, *Államszocializmus. Értelmezések, viták, tanulságok*, Budapest: L'Harmattan Kiadó-Eszmélet Alapítvány.

Kreichbaumer, Robert (ed.) 1998, *Liebe auf den zweiten blick: Landes- und Österreichbewusstsein nach 1945*, Vienna: Böhlau Verlag.

Krohn-Hansen, Christian and Knut G. Nustad (eds.) 2005, *State Formation: Anthropological Perspectives*, London: Pluto Press.

Kuromiya, Hiroaki 1988, *Stalin's Industrial Revolution: Politics and Workers, 1928–1932*, Cambridge: Cambridge University Press.

Kürti, András 1953, 'A bányászok közötti politikai munka néhány időszerű kérdése', *Társadalmi Szemle* 8, 10–11: 1020–35.

Kürti, László 1990, '"Red Csepel": Working Youth in a Socialist Firm', *East European Quarterly*, 23, 4: 445–68.

—— 2001, *The Remote Borderland: Transylvania in the Hungarian Imagination*, Albany, NY: SUNY Press.

Lackó, Miklós 1966, *Nyilasok, Nemzetiszocialisták 1935–1944*, Budapest: Kossuth Kiadó.

—— 1969, *Arrow Cross Men, National Socialists, 1935–1944*, Budapest: Akadémiai Kiadó.

—— 1980, 'The Social Roots of Hungarian Fascism: the Arrow Cross', in *Who Were the Fascists? Social Roots of European Fascism*, edited by Stein U. Larsen, Bernt Hagtvet and Jan P. Myklebust, Bergen: Universitetsforlaget.

—— 1989, 'Gépgyári munkások az 1930-as években', *Századok*, 123, 1–2: 3–44.

Lampe, John R. 1986, *The Bulgarian Economy in the Twentieth Century*, London: Croom Helm.

—— 1996, *Yugoslavia as History: Twice There was a Country*, Cambridge: Cambridge University Press.

Lampland, Martha 1989, 'Biographies of Liberation: Testimonials to Labor in Socialist Hungary', in *Promissory Notes: Women in the Transition to Socialism*, edited by Sonia Kruks, Rayna Rapp and Marilyn B. Young, New York, NY: Monthly Review Press.

—— 1995, *The Object of Labor: Commodification in Socialist Hungary*, Chicago, IL: University of Chicago Press.

Landau, Zbigniew and Jerzy Tomaszewski 1985, *The Polish Economy in the Twentieth Century*, translated by W. Roszkowski, London: Routledge.

László-Bencsik, Sándor 1975, *Történelem alulnézetben*, Budapest: Szépirodalmi Könyvkiadó.

Lebowitz, Michael A. 2012, *The Contradictions of 'Real Socialism': The Conductor and the Conducted*, New York, NY: Monthly Review Press.

Lewis, Jill 2000, 'Austria 1950: Strikes, "Putsch" and their Political Context', *European History Quarterly*, 30, 4: 533–52.

Lilly, Carol S. 2001, *Power and Persuasion: Ideology and Rhetoric in Communist Yugoslavia, 1944–1953*, Boulder, CO: Westview Press.

Linden, Marcel van der 2007, *Western Marxism and the Soviet Union: A Survey of Critical Theories and Debates since 1917*, Leiden: BRILL.

Livezeanu, Irina 1995, *Cultural Politics in Greater Romania: Regionalism, Nation Building and Ethnic Struggle*, Ithaca, NY: Cornell University Press.

Lomax, Bill 1976, *Hungary 1956*, London: Allison & Busby.

—— 1981, 'The Working Class in the Hungarian Revolution of 1956', *Critique*, 13, 32: 27–54.

Lukes, Igor 1997, 'The Czech Road to Communism', in *The Establishment of Communist Regimes in Eastern Europe, 1944–1949*, edited by Norman Naimark and Leonid Gibianski, Boulder, CO: Westview Press.

Luthar, Breda 2006, 'Remembering Socialism: On Desire, Consumption and Surveillance', *Journal of Consumer Culture*, 6, 2: 229–59.

Macartney, Carlyle A. 1961, *October Fifteenth: A History of Modern Hungary, 1929–1945*, Edinburgh: Edinburgh University Press.

Malcolm, Noel 1994, *Bosnia: A Short History*, London: Macmillan.

Mann, Michael 1988, *States, War and Capitalism: Studies in Political Sociology*, Oxford and New York, NY: Basil Blackwell.

Mark, James 2003, 'Prospering through Discrimination and Manufacturing New Identities: How the Middle Class Survived the Stalinist State in Hungary', Paper presented at BASEES Annual Conference, Cambridge, 2003.

—— 2011, *The Unfinished Revolution: Making Sense of the Communist Party in Central-Eastern Europe*, New Haven, CT: Yale University Press.

Márkus, István 1946, 'A demokrácia két éve Martonvásáron: Szociográfiai vázlat', *Fórum*, 251–261.

Marx, Karl 1968 [1852], 'The Eighteenth Brumaire of Louis Bonaparte', in *Karl*

Marx and Friedrich Engels: Selected Works, Volume 1, Moscow: Progress Publishers.

——— 1969 [1850], 'The Class Struggle in France, 1848 to 1850', in *Karl Marx and Friedrich Engels: Selected Works*, Volume 1, Moscow: Progress Publishers.

Mastny, Vojtech 1971, *The Czechs under Nazi Rule: The Failure of National Resistance, 1939–1942*, New York, NY: Columbia University Press.

Melvius, Martin 2002, *Agents of Moscow: The Hungarian Communist Party and the Origins of Socialist Patriotism, 1941–1953*, DPhil Thesis, University of Oxford.

Melvius, Martin and Thomas Escritt 2010, 'Mark Pittaway: Obituary', *The Guardian*, 22 November 2010.

Micgiel, John 1997, '"Bandits and Reactionaries": The Suppression of the Opposition in Poland, 1944–1946', in *The Establishment of Communist Regimes in Eastern Europe, 1944–1949*, edited by Norman Naimark and Leonid Gibianski, Boulder, CO: Westview Press.

Mitchell, Timothy 1999, 'Society, Economy and the State Effect', in *State/Culture: State-formation after the Cultural Turn*, edited by George Steinmetz, Ithaca, NY: Cornell University Press.

Mocsár, Gábor 1970, *Égő arany*, Budapest: Szépirodalmi Könyvkiadó.

Monigl, István 1982, 'Életmódváltozás és életkörülmények', in *Válság és megújulás: gazdaság, társadalom és politika Magyarországon. Az MSZMP 25 éve*, edited by Henrik Vass, Budapest: Kossuth Könyvkiadó.

Montias, John M. 1981, 'Observations on Strikes, Riots and Other Disturbances', in *Blue Collar Workers in Eastern Europe*, edited by Jan F. Triska and Charles Gati, London: George Allen & Unwin.

Mugrauer, Manfred 2006, *Die Politik der KPÖ in der Provisorischen Regierung Renner*, Innsbruck: Studien Verlag.

Murer, Ibolya and Zoltán Főnagy (eds.) 2006, *Die Ungarische Revolution und Österreich 1956*, Vienna: Czernin Verlag.

Myant, Martin R. 1981, *Socialism and Democracy in Czechoslovakia 1945–1948*, Cambridge: Cambridge University Press.

Nagy, Anna and György Sziráczki 1982, 'Munkaerőpiaci szegmentáció Magyarországon a hetvenes évek közepén', in *A munkaerőpiac szerkezete és működése Magyarországon*, edited by Péter Galasi, Budapest: Közgazdasági és Jogi Könyvkiadó.

Nagy, Balázs 1980, 'Budapest 1956: The Central Workers' Council', in *Eyewitness in Hungary*, edited by Bill Lomax, Nottingham: Spokesman.

Naimark, Norman M. 2001, *Fires of Hatred: Ethnic Cleansing in Twentieth-Century Europe*, Cambridge, MA: Harvard University Press.

Ormos, Mária et al. 1991, *Törvénytelen szocializmus: a tényfeltáró bizottság jelentése*, Budapest: Zrinyi Kiadó.

Őrszigethy, Erzsébet 1986, *Asszonyok férfisorban*, Budapest: Szépirodalmi Könyvkiadó.

Paczkowski, Andrzej 1997, *Fél évszázad Lengyelország történetéből, 1939–1989*, translated by L. Pálfalvi, Budapest: 1956-os Intézet.

Pahl, Raymond E. 1984, *Divisions of Labour*, Oxford: Blackwell.

Paládi-Kovács, Attila 2000, 'Az ipari munkásság', in *Magyar néprajz VIII: társadalom*, edited by Attila Paládi-Kovács, Budapest: Akadémiai Kiadó.

Pavlowitch, Stevan K. 1971, *Yugoslavia*, London: Praeger.

Pálfalvi, Nándor 1958, *Mint fához az ág*, Budapest: Kossuth Könyvkiadó.

Pelikán, Jiri (ed.) 1971, *The Czechoslovak Political Trials, 1950–1954: The Suppressed Report of the Dubček Government's Commission of Inquiry*, Stanford, CA: Stanford University Press.

Pelle, János 2004, *Sowing the Seeds of Hatred: Anti-Jewish Laws and Hungarian Public Opinion, 1938–1944*, Boulder, CO: East European Monographs.

Pető, Andrea 1999, 'Stimmen des Schweigens: Erinnerungen an Vergewaltigungen in den Hauptstädten des "ersten Opfers" (Wien) und des "letzten Verbündeten" Hitlers (Budapest) 1945', *Zeitschrift für Geschictswissenschaft*, 47, 10: 892–913.

Pető, Iván 2001, 'Változások a változatlanságért: a gazdasági rendszer átalakulása a Kádár-korszakban', in *Ki volt Kádár? Harag és részrehajlás nélkül a Kádár-életútról*, edited by Árpád Rácz, Budapest: Rubicon Kiadó.

Pető, Iván and Sándor Szakács 1985, *A hazai gazdaság négy évtizedének története, 1945–1985: I. Az újjáépítés és a tervutasításos irányítás időszaka*, Budapest: Közgazdasági és Jogi Könyvkiadó.

Pintér, István 1999, 'A Kényszerpályára Szavazó Ország – 1939', in *Parlamenti Választászok Magyarországon 1920–1998*, edited by György Földes and László Hubai, Budapest: Napvilág Kiadó.

Pittaway, Mark 1998, *Industrial Workers, Socialist Industrialisation and the State in Hungary, 1948–1958*, PhD Thesis, University of Liverpool.

——— 1999, 'The Victory of Production Over Consumption: Reform, Workers and the Possibilities of a New Course', Southport (unpublished manuscript).

——— 2000, 'Stalinism, Working Class Housing and Individual Autonomy: The Encouragement of Private House Building in Hungary's Mining Areas, 1950–1954', in *Style and Socialism: Modernity and Material Culture in Post-war Eastern Europe*, edited by Susan E. Reid and David Crowley, Oxford: Berg Publishers.

——— 2001, 'Reconstructing Socialism in the Aftermath of Revolution: Industrial Workers and the Making of the Kádár regime in Hungary', paper presented at the *Core Seminar in Modern European History*, Faculty of Modern History, University of Oxford, 25 October 2001.

——— 2002, 'The Politics of Legitimacy and Hungary's Postwar Transition', (unpublished manuscript).

——— 2003a, 'The Education of Dissent: the Reception of the Voice of Free Hungary, 1951–1956', *Cold War History*, 4, 1: 97–116.

——— 2003b, 'Az állami ellenőrzés társadalmi korlátainak újraértékelése:

az ipari dolgozók és a szocialista diktatúra Magyarországon, 1948-1953', in *Munkástörténet - Munkásantropológia*, edited by Sándor Horváth, László Pethő and Eszter Zs. Tóth, Budapest: Napvilág Kiadó.

—— 2004a, *Eastern Europe, 1939-2000*, London: Arnold Hodder.

—— 2004b, 'The Politics of Legitimacy and Hungary's Postwar Transition', *Contemporary European History*, 13, 4: 453-75.

—— 2005a, 'A múlt lezárása a háború utáni Ausztriában: emlékezet, nemzetiszocializmus és 1945 értlemezése Észak-Burgenlandban', *Eszmélet*, 65: 97-110.

—— 2005b, 'Introduction: Workers and Socialist States in Post-war Central and Eastern Europe', *International Labor and Working Class History*, 68: 1-8.

—— 2006, 'Challenging and Confirming Europe's Cold War Divide: The 1956 Revolution and the Austrian-Hungarian Borderland', Paper presented in the series *Revolution in the Soviet Empire: New Perspectives on 1956*, Department of History, University of British Columbia, 10 October 2006.

—— 2007, 'A magyar forradalom új megközelítésben: az ipari munkásság, a szocializmus széthullása és rekonstrukciója, 1953-1958', in *Ezerkilencszázötvenhat az újabb történeti irodalomban*, edited by Gábor Gyáni and János M. Rainer, Budapest: 1956-os Intézet.

—— 2012a, 'National Socialism and the Production of German-Hungarian Borderland Space on the Eve of the Second World War', *Past and Present*, 216, 1: 143-80.

—— 2012b, *The Workers' State: Industrial Labour and the Making of Socialist Hungary, 1944-1958*, Pittsburgh, PA: University of Pittsburgh Press.

Pittaway, Mark and Hans Fredrik Dahl 2008, 'Legitimacy and the Making of the Post-war Order', in *The War for Legitimacy in Politics and Culture 1936-1946*, edited by Martin Conway and Peter Romijn, Oxford and New York, NY: Berg Publishers.

Port, Andrew 1998, 'When Workers Rumbled: The Wismut Upheaval of August 1951 in East Germany', *Social History*, 22, 2: 145-73.

Prakfalvi, Endre 1994, 'A budapesti ős-metró, 1949-1956', *Budapesti Negyed*, 5, 3: 25-47.

Radice, Edward A. 1985, 'General Characteristics of the Region between the Wars', in *The Economic History of Eastern Europe 1919-1975, Volume 1: Economic Structure and Performance between the Two Wars*, edited by Michael C. Kaser and Edward A. Radice, Oxford: Oxford University Press.

—— 1986a, 'Agriculture and Food', in *The Economic History of Eastern Europe 1919-1975, Volume 2: Interwar Policy, the War and Reconstruction*, edited by Michael C. Kaser and Edward A. Radice, Oxford: Oxford University Press.

—— 1986b, 'Territorial Changes, Population Movements and Labour Supplies', in *The Economic History of Eastern Europe 1919-1975, Volume 2:*

Interwar Policy, the War and Reconstruction, edited by Michael C. Kaser and Edward A. Radice, Oxford: Oxford University Press.

—— 1986c, 'The Collapse of German Hegemony and its Economic Consequences', in *The Economic History of Eastern Europe 1919–1975, Volume 2: Interwar Policy, the War and Reconstruction*, edited by Michael C. Kaser and Edward A. Radice, Oxford: Oxford University Press.

—— 1986d, 'The Development of Industry', in *The Economic History of Eastern Europe 1919–1975, Volume 2: Interwar Policy, the War and Reconstruction*, edited by Michael C. Kaser and Edward A. Radice, Oxford: Oxford University Press.

Radvanovský, Zdeněk 2001, 'The Social and Economic Consequences of Resettling Czechs into Northwestern Bohemia, 1945–1947', in *Redrawing Nations: Ethnic Cleansing in East Central Europe, 1944–1949*, edited by Philipp Ther and Ana Siljak, Lanham: Rowman & Littlefield.

Rainer, János M. 1990, 'Helyi politikai szerveződés 1956-ban: az Újpesti példa', in *Az ostromtól a forradalomig: adalékok Budapest múltjáról*, edited by Zsuzsanna Bencsik and Gábor Kresalek, Budapest: Budapest Főváros Levéltára.

—— 1996, *Nagy Imre: politikai életrajz. Első kötet, 1896–1953*, Budapest: 1956-os Intézet.

—— 2000, 'A rendszerváltás és ötvenhat', in *A rendszerváltás forgatókönyve: kerekasztal-tárgyalások 1989-ben*, edited by András Bozóki, Budapest: Új Mandátum.

—— (ed.) 2003, *Ötvenhat útán*, Budapest: 1956-os Intézet.

—— 2005, 'Submerging or Clinging On Again? József Antall, Father and Son in Hungary after 1956', *Contemporary European History*, 14, 1: 65–105.

Rainer, János and Magdolna Baráth (eds.) 2004, *'Hatvanas évek' Magyarországon: tanulmányok*, Budapest: 1956-os Intézet.

Rákosi, Sándor 1985, 'Normarendezések 1948–1950-ben', in *Tanulmányok a magyar népi demokrácia negyven évéről*, edited by János Molnár, Sándor Orbán, and Károly Urbán, Budapest: Kossuth Könyvkiadó.

Rathkolb, Oliver 2005, *Die paradoxe Republik: Österreich 1945 bis 2005*, Vienna: Zsolnay Verlag.

Rév, István 1987, 'The Advantages of Being Atomized: How Hungarian Peasants Coped with Collectivization', *Dissent*, 34, 3: 335–50.

Rogel, Carole 1997, 'In the Beginning: The Slovenes from the Seventh Century to 1945', in *Independent Slovenia: Origins, Movements, Prospects*, edited by Jill Benderly and Evan Kraft, Basingstoke: Palgrave Macmillan.

Roksandic, Drago 1995, 'Shifting References: Celebrations of Uprisings in Croatia, 1945–1991', *East European Politics and Societies*, 9, 2: 256–71.

Romsics, Ignác 1999, *Magyarország története a XX. században*, Budapest: Osiris Kiadó.

Róna-Tas, Ákos 1997, *The Great Surprise of the Small Transformation: The Demise of Communism and the Rise of the Private Sector in Hungary*, Ann Arbor, MI: University of Michigan Press.

Rosenberg, William G. and Lewis H. Siegelbaum 1993, *Social Dimensions of Soviet Industrialisation*, Indianapolis, IN: Indiana University Press.

Rozsnyoi, Sándor 1972, 'A város nagyüzemei', in *Tatabánya története. Helytörténeti tanulmányok, II. kötet*, edited by Gábor Gombkötő et al., Tatabánya: Tatabánya Városi Tanácsa.

Rusinow, Dennison 1977, *The Yugoslav Experiment, 1948–1974*, London: C. Hurst.

Satjukow, Silke and Rainer Gries (eds.) 2002, *Sozialistische Helden: Eine Kulturgeschichte von Propagandafiguren in Osteuropa und der DDR*, Berlin: Ch. Links Verlag.

Sayer, Derek 1998, *The Coasts of Bohemia: A Czech History*, Princeton, NJ: Princeton University Press.

Schivelbusch, Wolfgang 2003, *The Culture of Defeat: On National Trauma, Mourning, and Recovery*, translated by J. Chase, London: Granta Books.

Schödl, Günter (ed.) 1995, *Deutsche Geschichte im Osten Europas: Land an der Donau*, Berlin: Siedler Verlag.

Schultz, Deborah 2004, 'Forced Migration and Involuntary Memory: The Work of Arnold Daghani', in *Cultures of Exile: Visual Dimensions of Displacement*, edited by Peter Wagstaff and Wendy Everett, Oxford: Berghahn Books.

Scott, James C. 1990, *Domination and the Arts of Resistance: Hidden Transcripts*, New Haven, CT: Yale University Press.

Seleny, Anna 1994, 'Constructing the Discourse of Transformation: Hungary, 1979–1982', *East European Politics and Societies*, 8, 3: 439–66.

Seton-Watson, Hugh 1961, *The East European Revolution*, London: Methuen.

Shiomi, Haruhito and Kazuo Wada (eds.) 1995, *Fordism Transformed: The Development of Production Methods in the Automobile Industry*, Oxford: Oxford University Press.

Siebel-Achenbach, Sebastian 1994, *Lower Silesia from Nazi Germany to Communist Poland, 1942–1949*, Basingstoke: Macmillan.

Siegelbaum, Lewis H. 1988, *Stakhanovism and the Politics of Productivity in the USSR, 1935–1941*, Cambridge: Cambridge University Press.

Siegelbaum, Lewis H. and Ronald Grigor Suny (eds.) 1994, *Making Workers Soviet: Power, Class, and Identity*, Ithaca, NY: Cornell University Press.

Sipos, Péter 1988, *Legális és illegális munkásmozgalom 1919–1944*, Budapest: Gondolat Kiadó.

Skendi, Stavro (ed.) 1956, *Albania*, London: Atlantic Press.

Soós A. Károly 1988, 'Béralku és "sérelmi politika": adalékok a mechanizmusreform 1969. évi első megtorpanásának magyarázatához', in *Medvetánc: Magyar gazdaság és szociológia a 80-as években*, edited by Tamás Miklós, Budapest: Minerva Könyvkiadó.

Spulber, Nicolas 1957, *The Economics of Communist Eastern Europe*, London: Chapman & Hall.

Standeisky, Éva, Gyula Kozák, Gábor Pataki and János M. Rainer (eds.) 1998, *A fordulat évei: 1947–1949. Politika, képzőművészet, építészet*, Budapest: 1956-os Intézet.

Stark, David 1985, 'The Micropolitics of the Firm and the Macropolitics of Reform: New Forms of Workplace Bargaining in Hungarian Enterprises', in *States Versus Markets in the World-System*, edited by Peter Evans, Dietrich Rueschmeyer, and Evelyn H. Stephens, Beverly Hills, CA: SAGE.

—— 1986, 'Rethinking Internal Labor Markets: New Insights from a Comparative Perspective', *American Sociological Review*, 51, 4: 492–504.

—— 1989, 'Coexisting Organizational Forms in Hungary's Emerging Mixed Economy', in *Remaking the Economic Institutions of Socialism: China and Eastern Europe*, edited by Victor Nee, David Stark and Mark Selden, Stanford, CA: Stanford University Press.

Steadman Jones, Gareth 1996, 'The Determinist Fix: Some Obstacles to the Further Development of the Linguistic Approach to History in the 1990s', *History Workshop Journal*, 42: 19–35.

Straus, Kenneth M. 1997, *Factory and Community in Stalin's Russia: The Making of an Industrial Working Class*, Pittsburgh, PA: University of Pittsburgh Press.

Szabó, Lajos 1955, 'A társadalmi tulajdon védelme', *Futószalag*, 9 April 1955.

Szakács, Sándor 1998, 'From Land Reform to Collectivization', in *Hungarian Agrarian Society from the Emancipation of Serfs (1848) to the Reprivatization of Land (1998)*, edited by Péter Gunst, translated by T. Bodnár, Boulder, CO: Social Science Monographs.

Szakács, Sándor and Tibor Zinner 1997, *A háború "megváltozott természete" – Adatok, adalékok, tények és összefüggések, 1944–1948*, Budapest: Batthány Társaság.

Szakolczai, Attila 2003, 'Borsod-Abaúj-Zemplén megye', in *A vidék forradalma, 1956. Első kötet*, edited by Attila Szakolczai and László A. Varga, Budapest: 1956-os Intézet.

Szakolczai, Attila and László A. Varga (eds.) 2003, *A vidék forradalma, 1956. Első kötet*, Budapest: 1956-os Intézet.

Szántó, Miklós 1967, *Életmód, művelődés, szabadidő*, Budapest: Akadémiai Kiadó.

—— 1974, *Munkaidő-csökkentés és életmód*, Budapest: Akadémiai Kiadó.

Szekeres, József and Árpád Tóth 1962, *A Klement Gottwald (Ganz) villámossági gyár története*, Budapest: Közgazdasági és Jogi Könyvkiadó.

Szenes, Iván 1976, *A kommunista párt újjászervezése Magyarországon, 1956–1957*, Budapest: Kossuth Könyvkiadó.

Szerencsés, Károly and István Simon (eds.) 2004, *Azok a Kádári 'szép' napok: dokumentumok a hetvenes évek történetéből*, Budapest: Kairosz Kiadó.

Szöllösi-Janze, Margit (ed.) 1989, *Die Pfeilkreuzlerbewegung in Ungarn: Historischer Kontext, Entwicklung und Herrschaft*, München: Oldenbourg Verlag.

Swain, Nigel 1992, *Hungary: The Rise and Fall of Feasible Socialism*, London: Verso.

Tamás, Gáspár M. 2007, 'Counter-Revolution Against a Counter-Revolution: Eastern Europe Today', in *Global Flashpoints, Socialist Register 2008*, Pontypool: Merlin Press.

—— 2008, 'A Capitalism Pure and Simple', *Left Curve*, 32: 66–75.

—— 2011, 'Marx on 1989', in *First the Transition, Then the Crash: Eastern Europe in the 2000s*, edited by Gareth Dale, London: Pluto Press.

Tanner, Marcus 1997, *Croatia: A Nation Forged in War*, New Haven, CT: Yale University Press.

Teichova, Alice 1988, *The Czechoslovak Economy 1918–1980*, London: Routledge.

Thelen, Tatiana 2005, 'Violence and Social (Dis)continuity: Comparing Collectivization in Two East European Villages', *Social History*, 30, 1: 25–44.

Ther, Philipp 1998, *Deutsche und polnische Vertriebene: Gesellschaft und Vertriebenenpolitik in der SBZ und in Polen 1945–1956*, Göttingen: Vandenhoeck & Ruprecht.

Thompson, Edward P. 1993 [1967], 'Time, Work-Discipline and Industrial Capitalism', in *Customs in Common: Studies in Traditional Popular Culture*, London: Penguin Books.

Tismaneanu, Vladimir and Dan Pavel 1994, 'Romania's Mystical Revolutionaries: The Generation of Angst and Adventure Revisited', *East European Politics and Societies*, 8, 3: 402–38.

Tóth, Ágnes 2001, *Migrationen in Ungarn 1945–1948: Vertreibung der Ungarndeutschen, Binnenwanderungen und Slowakisch-Ungarischer Bevölkerungsaustausch*, translated by Rita Fejér, München: Oldenbourg.

Tóth, András 1994, *Civiltársadalom és szakszervezetek*, PhD Thesis, Budapest.

Tóth, Attila 1992, 'A pokol tornácán', in *Tatabánya 45 éve város. Tatabánya várossá nyilvánításának 45. évfordulója alkalmából rendezett tudományos konferencia előadásainak anyaga (Tatabánya 1992. október 1–2)*, edited by József Somorjai, Tata: Komárom megyei Múzeumi Szervezet.

Troebst, Stefan 1997, 'Yugoslav Macedonia, 1943–1953: Building the Party, the State, and the Nation', in *State-Society Relations in Yugoslavia, 1945–1992*, edited by Melissa K. Bokovoy, Jill A. Irvine and Carol S. Lilly, New York, NY: Palgrave Macmillan.

Turgonyi, Júlia and Zsuzsa Ferge 1969, *Az ipari munkásnők munka- és életkörülményei*, Budapest: Kossuth Könyvkiadó.

—— 1973, 'Az ipari munkásnők munka- és életkörülményei', in *Tanulmányok a munkásosztályról*, edited by Tibor Halay, Budapest: Kossuth Könyvkiadó.

Turner, Graham 2008, *The Credit Crunch: Housing Bubbles, Globalization and the Worldwide Economic Crisis*, London: Pluto Press.

Turnock, David 1986, *The Romanian Economy in the Twentieth Century*, London: Palgrave Macmillan.

Ulc, Otto 1965, 'Pilsen: The Unknown Revolt', *Problems of Communism*, 14, 3: 46–9.

Valuch, Tibor 2001, *Magyarország társadalomtörténete a XX. század második felében*, Budapes: Osiris Kiadó.

Várdy, Steven B. 1998, 'The Impact of Trianon upon the Hungarian Mind: Irredentism and Hungary's Path to War' in *Hungary in the Age of Total War, 1938–1948*, edited by Nándor F. Dreisziger, Boulder, CO: Social Science Monographs.

Varga, Lajos Sz. 1995, *Szakszervezetek a diktatúrában: a Magyar Dolgozók Pártja és a szakszervezetek, 1948–1953*, Pécs: Pannónia Könyvek.

Varga, László 1984, *Pató Pálok vagy sztahanovisták?*, Budapest: Magvető Kiadó.

Varga, Zsuzsanna 2001, *Politika, paraszti érdekérvényesítés és szövetkezetek Magyarországon, 1956–1967*, Budapest: Napvilág Kiadó.

Vásárhelyi, Miklós 1988, 'Az első meghiúsitott reformkisérlet: az 1953-as kormányprogram', *Medvetánc*, 2–3: 149–205.

Vaska, Miklós 1979, *Paraszti gazdálkodás Nován a két világháború között*, Zalaegerszeg: Zala Megyei Levéltár.

Verdery, Katherine 1996, *What Was Socialism and What Comes Next?*, Princeton, NJ: Princeton University Press.

Vickers, Miranda 1999, *The Albanians: A Modern History*, London: I.B. Tauris.

Völkl, Ekkehard 1991, 'Abrechnungsfuror in Kroatien', in *Politische Säuberung in Europa: Die Abrechnung mit Faschismus und Kollaboration nach dem Zweiten Weltkrieg*, edited by Klaus-Dietmar Henke and Hans Woller, München: Deutsche Taschenbuch Verlag.

Vrzgulová, Monika 2000, 'Jewish Tradesmen and Craftsmen during the Slovak Republic Period, 1939–1945', in *Identity of Ethnic Groups and Communities: The Results of Slovak Ethnological Research*, edited by Gabriela Kiliánová and Eva Riečanská, Bratislava: Institute of Ethnology of Slovak Academy of Sciences.

Wachtel, Andrew B. 1998, *Making a Nation, Breaking a Nation: Literature and Cultural Politics in Yugoslavia*, Stanford, CA: Stanford University Press.

Wagner, Sonja 2005, '"Der Sowjetstern auf dem Schlossberg". Besatzungserfahrungen im Burgenland', in *Die Rote Armee in Österreich: Sowjetische Besatzung 1945–1955*, edited by Stefan Karner and Barbara Stelzl-Marx, München: Oldenbourg Verlag.

Walston, James 1997, 'History and Memory of the Italian Concentration Camps', *The Historical Journal*, 40, 1: 169–83.

Weiner, Tibor 1959, 'Sztálinváros', in *Sztálinváros, Miskolc, Tatabánya: városépitésünk fejlődése*, edited by Aladár Sós, Budapest: Műszaki Könyvkiadó.

Winner, Irene 1971, *A Slovenian Village: Žerovnica*, Providence, RI: Brown University Press.

'Workers and Socialist States in Post-war Central and Eastern Europe' 2005, *International Labor and Working Class History*, 68.

Zarecor, Kimberly E. 2011, *Manufacturing a Socialist Modernity: Housing in Czechoslovakia, 1945–1960*, Pittsburgh, PA: University of Pittsburgh Press.

Zielbauer, György 1989, *Adatok és tények a Magyarországi németség történetéből, 1945–1949*, Budapest: Akadémiai Kiadó.

―― 1992, 'Magyar polgári lakosok deportálása és hadifogsága, 1945–1948', *Történelmi Szemle*, 3–4: 270–91.

Zinner, Tibor 1988, *Adalékok a magyarországi koncepciós perekhez*, Székesfehérvár: József Attila Művelődési Ház és Könyvtár.

Index

Albania   15–16, 23, 30, 34–35, 38, 43–44, 46–47, 49–50, 52
Alliance of Young Democrats (FIDESZ)   275
Antall, József   217, 274
anti-communism   231
   in Hungary   53, 183, 189, 231, 274, 288
   in Poland   53
   in Slovenia   52
anti-fascism   232, 272
   policies of Communist parties in Central and Eastern Europe   34–36, 39, 47, 49, 281
   policies of MKP   222, 230–233, 272–273
anti-Semitism   232
   as a central feature of Hungarism   264–265
   fusion with class-based rhetoric of the MKP   273
   in Central and Eastern Europe   17, 19, 24, 32
   influence on paramilitary movements in interwar Hungary   260
   in post-1989 Hungary   274
   institutionalised during Horthy regime   257–258, 261
   popular support for anti-Semitic measures   266, 268–269
   See also Arrow Cross Party; fascism; Hungarism
Arrow Cross Party (*Nyilaskeresztes Párt*, Hungary)   17, 30, 40, 227–228, 230, 232, 257
   'little Arrow Crossists' joining MKP   273
   massacre of Jews and Roma in Hungary   29–30, 272–273
   social base of   258, 264, 268, 270
   See also anti-Semitism; fascism; Hungarism;
Austria/Austrians   14, 17–18, 31, 163, 184, 222–225, 227–229, 231, 233–236, 239–241, 243–244, 259–260, 266, 278
Austrian Communist Party (*Kommunistische Partei Österreichs*, KPÖ)   224, 228–229, 241

Austrian People's Party (*Österreichische Volkspartei*, ÖVP)   224, 228
Austrian Socialist Party (*Sozialistische Partei Österreichs*, SPÖ)   223–224, 242
ÁVH. *See* State Security Agency (*Államvédelmi Hatóság*, ÁVH)

Báli, Sándor   187
borders/borderlands   29, 31, 46, 56, 256, 271–272, 276–277
   deportation of ethnic Germans after World War II   41–42, 222, 236–238
   opposition to Rákosi regime in north-western Hungary   161
   opposition to post-World War I of Hungary   16, 18, 259–260, 265–266
   politics of state-building in Austria and Hungary after World War II   225, 227, 229–236, 239–244
   territorial expansion of Nazi Germany   19
Budapest   32, 56, 61, 65, 76, 81, 108, 126, 140, 148, 167, 200, 261
   factories in   75, 92, 94, 116–117, 121, 129, 134, 165, 170–172, 206, 276, 289
   industrial districts of   86, 90, 141, 184, 190, 201, 213–214(n97), 267–268
   massacre of Jews during World War II   30, 271–272
   research in archives in   217–218, 220
   revolution of 1956 in   156, 172–178, 185–189, 287–288
   revolution of 1956 outside   276–279
Bulgaria   15, 18, 24, 27–29, 31, 33, 35–37, 39, 44, 46, 49–51, 55, 59, 165

Catholic Church   224, 231, 241
   anti-Communism of   52–53
   influence on fascist regimes   17, 24–25
   influence on rural communities   45, 51–52
   repression of   51–53, 284
Csurka, István   274
Czechoslovakia   14–19, 30–32, 35–37, 40–47, 49–50, 53, 56, 58–59, 64, 69, 74, 92, 122(n2), 165, 251, 253

Dunaújváros (formerly known as
    Sztálinváros)   139, 141–142, 214(n97)
  gender division of labour in   81, 83–84
  informal labour market in   148
  revolution of 1956 in   170, 185, 285–286
  Soviet-style industrialisation in   108, 114, 138

fascism   16
  in Horthy era   257–258, 263, 269
  in interwar Central and Eastern Europe
    16–17
  social and ideological origins of in
    Hungary   259–261
  See also anti-Semitism; Arrow Cross Party;
    Hungarism
FIDESZ. See Alliance of Young Democrats
  (Fiatal Demokraták Szövetsége, FIDESZ)
FKGP. See Independent Smallholders' Party
  (Független Kisgazdapárt, FKGP)

gender   121
  and state's attempt to build a 'new
    working class'   66–67, 93, 164
  in workplace hierarchies   65, 68, 75–76,
    80–85, 90–91, 118, 142, 151–152, 199–200
  resistance and protest based on   123–124,
    136, 139, 155
  roles in Hungary   124–127, 132–133
German Democratic Republic (GDR)   64, 92,
  122(n2), 165, 245, 251
Germany   14, 28, 32, 37, 225, 230
  efforts to relocate industry and workers to
    20
  expansion in Eastern Europe   16–17, 19,
    23, 27, 234–235
  Hungarian political elite pursuing closer
    links with   18, 257, 263, 266, 270
  Stalin's policy towards   34
  See also borders/borderlands
Gerő, Ernő   121, 126(n16), 170, 172, 177–178,
  278, 289
Gömbös, Gyula   261–264
Győr   226
  factories in   104, 202, 205–206
  programme (for developing military
    industry)   18
  support for FKGP in county of Győr-
    Moson   161, 226–227, 230–232

workers leaving from county of Győr-
  Moson after revolution of 1956   163

Hegedüs, András   169, 285
Hitler, Adolf   15–20, 22–23, 25, 27–28, 34, 47,
  270
  See also national socialism
Horthy, Miklós   29, 269, 271
Horthy regime   15–16, 40, 257–258, 260–262,
  273
  See also anti-Semitism; Jews; Hungarian
    Social Democratic Party (MSZDP)
Hungarian Communist Party (Magyar
  Kommunista Párt, MKP)   30, 222, 224, 226
  electoral support for   45, 232(n46)
  in Brennbergbánya   232
  in Mosonmagyaróvár   229
  merger with MSZDP   48, 50, 124(n8)
  relationship to FKGP   231–233, 239
  policy towards German minority in
    Hungary   236, 238
  industrial workers' support for   283
Hungarian Democratic Forum (Magyar
  Demokrata Fórum, MDF)   274
Hungarian Justice and Life Party (Magyar
  Igazság és Élet Pártja, MIÉP)   274
Hungarian Life Party (Magyar Élet Pártja,
  MÉP)   274
Hungarian National Defence Association
  (Magyar Országos Véderő Egylet,
  MOVE)   261
Hungarian Social Democratic Party
  (Magyarországi Szociáldemokrata Párt,
  MSZDP)   28, 238, 260, 267
  electoral support   232(n46)
  MKP's liquidation of   48, 50, 124(n8)
  MKP's view of   78–79
  Horthy regime's repression of   262
Hungarian Socialist Party (Magyar Szocialista
  Párt, MSZP)   214–215, 275
Hungarian Socialist Workers' Party (Magyar
  Szocialista Munkáspárt, MSZMP)   195,
  207, 214
  foundation of   124(n8)
  research in Hungarian archives on   217
  social composition of   196
  See also János Kádár; Kádár regime;
    New Economic Mechanism

Hungarian Workers' Party (*Magyar Dolgozók Pártja*, MDP)
  merger of MKP and MSZDP forming 48, 124(n8)
  polarisation in 164, 285–286
  research in Hungarian archives on 215, 217
  See also Imre Nagy, New Course; Mátyás Rákosi
Hungarism 264
  ideological origins of 264–265
  MKP seeking to appease symphatisers of 273
  support for Hungarist movements during Horthy regime 258, 266–270
  support for Hungarist movements in post-1989 Hungary 274

Independent Smallholders' Party (*Független Kisgazdapárt*, FKGP) 28, 45, 231–232, 274–275, 283
  electoral support for 45, 232(n46)
  MKP destroying 45, 232–233, 239, 283
intellectuals 20, 56, 213, 249–250, 255–256, 269
  in revolution of 1956 170, 187, 285
  support for national-conservative ideas 259, 263
  support for socialism 162, 283

Jews
  deportation from Hungary 270–272
  legislation against by the Horthy regime 261, 266, 269
  persecution of in Central and Eastern Europe 19–22, 24, 27, 29–30
  See also anti-Semitism

Kádár, János 91, 194, 279
Kádár regime 91–92, 156, 183, 194–195, 203
  consolidation of 92, 162–163, 190, 192, 200–202, 279–280
  defeat of 1956 revolution 157–160, 186–188
  relationship with the working-class 184, 196, 207, 212–213, 255, 291
  research in Hungarian archives on 215, 217–218

See also socialism; socialist consumerism; working-class
kétlaki. *See* worker-peasants
Khrushchev, Nikita 170
KPÖ. *See* Austrian Communist Party

labour 32, 40
  and the change of system (1989) 245–247, 255–256
  conflict 45, 65–66
  effects of Soviet-style industrialisation on 57–58, 63–64, 67, 73, 84, 89, 97, 106–113, 135, 141–142, 148, 151–153
  policies of Horthy regime 259–260, 262–263, 269, 271
  policies of Nazi Germany 20, 27, 225, 271
  policies of Soviet-style regimes 56–57, 64, 66, 69–70, 75, 80–82, 87–88, 95–96, 100–105, 118–119, 123–127, 208, 210, 212
  research on labour movement in Hungary 216, 218
  support for labour movement in Hungary 28, 163, 181
  See also gender; New Economic Mechanism (NEM); women; working-class, worker-peasants (*kétlaki*)
labour competition 57, 164
  as method for individualisation of production 103–106, 119
  attempts to speed up production through 64, 69–70, 124, 196
  in Magyar Pamutipar cotton plant 102–103
  in United Lighting and Electrics Factory 100
  opposition to 65, 67, 128–129
legitimacy 34
  free markets suffering from problem of 139
  of Eastern bloc regimes 34, 39, 45, 52, 248–249
  of Kádár regime 92, 160, 162, 184, 194, 250–251, 254, 279–280
  of post-World War I settlement 14
  of post-World War II Austrian state 235, 241, 244
  of post-World War II Hungarian state 238, 242–243

of Rákosi regime   44, 129, 137, 167, 250, 283–284
of revolutionary committees   173–174, 178–180, 286–287, 289–291
See also Alliance of Young Democrats (FIDESZ)

Magyars   14, 42, 261–262, 264, 266, 268
MDF. *See* Hungarian Democratic Forum (*Magyar Demokrata Fórum*, MDF)
MDP. *See* Hungarian Workers' Party (*Magyar Dolgozók Pártja*, MDP)
MÉP. *See* Hungarian Life Party (*Magyar Élet Pártja*, MÉP)
MIÉP. *See* Hungarian Justice and Life Party (*Magyar Igazság és Élet Pártja*, MIÉP)
MKP. *See* Hungarian Communist Party (*Magyar Kommunista Párt*, MKP)
MOVE. *See* Hungarian National Defence Association (*Magyar Országos Véderő Egylet*, MOVE)
MSZDP. *See* Hungarian Social Democratic Party (*Magyarországi Szociáldemokrata Párt*, MSZDP)
MSZMP. *See* Hungarian Socialist Workers' Party (*Magyar Szocialista Munkáspárt*, MSZMP)
MSZOSZ. *See* National Confederation of Hungarian Trade Unions (*Magyar Szakszervezetek Országos Szövetsége*, MSZOSZ)
MSZP. *See* Hungarian Socialist Party (*Magyar Szocialista Párt*, MSZP)

Nagy, Imre   131, 285
blamed for 'counter-revolution' of 1956   156
overthrow of government of   184
reforms under government of   165, 166–169, 249, 285
support for   162, 166–169, 180, 184, 188
See also New Course
NAP. *See* Party of National Will (*Nemzet Akaratának Pártja*, Hungary)
National Confederation of Hungarian Trade Unions (*Magyar Szakszervezetek Országos Szövetsége*, MSZOSZ)   216, 219
National Planning Office (*Országos Tervhivatal*)   98

national socialism   16–17, 24, 257–258, 264, 270
support among smallholders   267
See also anti-Semitism; Arrow Cross Party; fascism; Hitler; Hungarism
National Socialist Hungarian Party (*Nemzeti Szocialista Magyar Párt*, NSZMP)   265, 267
National Unity Party (*Nemzeti Egység Pártja*, Hungary)   263
New Course   164–165
effects of   165–169
reversal of   169
See also Imre Nagy
New Economic Mechanism (NEM)   192–195
halting of   208
new patterns of stratification   205–210
working-class discontent against   193, 204–207, 211–213, 253
See also Kádár regime; socialist consumerism

Orbán, Viktor   275
OT. *See* National Planning Office (*Országos Tervhivatal*, Hungary)
ÖVP. *See* Austrian People's Party

Party of National Will (*Nemzet Akaratának Pártja*)   264
peasants   21, 32, 36, 42, 44, 55–56, 157, 231
and Hungarism   265, 268, 273
and worker discontent and support for MSZDP and MKP   28
opposition against forced collectivisation   59–60, 122(n2)
policies of the Rákosi regime towards   35, 62, 284
the New Course as a 'peasants' policy   167
See also worker-peasants (*kétlaki*)
Poland/Polish   13–14, 16–17, 19–23, 25, 27–29, 31–32, 36–37, 41–43, 48–49, 52–53, 57, 59, 64, 92, 96, 123, 170, 245, 251, 270, 286
Polish Peasants' Party (*Polskie Stronnictwo Ludowe*, PSL)   36, 46
Polish United Workers' Party (*Polska Zjednoczona Partia Robotnicza*, PZPR)   48, 53
Polish Workers' Party (*Polska Partia Robotnicza*, PPR)   29, 46, 48, 53

popular front   47, 49
   deportation of ethnic Germans by
      Hungarian government   222
   governments in Eastern Europe   36–38,
      47–48, 228, 231–232, 272, 282
   industrial working-class base of
      governments in Eastern Europe   44,
      57
   MKP's destruction of coalition   239,
      283–284
   opposition towards governments
      'popular front' rule in Eastern
      Europe   45–46, 51
   policies against fascism   34–35
Rácz, Sándor   187
Rajk, László   51, 170, 172, 184
Rákosi, Mátyás   62
   Gerő replacing   170
   Nagy replacing   165
Rákosi regime
   attempt to create a 'new
      working-class'   90
   criminalisation of absenteeism   152–153
   deepening crisis of   169–172
   See also socialism; Stalinism; working class
Red Army   19, 27–29, 31–32, 35, 44, 48, 161,
   222, 225
   atrocities towards civilians during
      World War II   30
   attitudes towards in Austrian-Hungarian
      borderlands   225–229, 231, 272
   opposition towards during revolution of
      1956   173, 177, 277–278, 283, 287
   support for popular front governments in
      Eastern Europe   13, 35, 41
   withdrawal from Burgenland   244
revolution
   Arrow Cross Party representing a
      'revolutionary promise'   273
   in production and shop-floor culture
      under Stalinism   65, 90, 124, 127, 197
   Horthy regime as counter-revolutionary
      reaction   259–261
   Hungarian revolution of 1956   91, 156,
      164, 172–191, 243–244, 250, 276–291
   myth of 1956 as 'counter-revolution'
      157–158(n6), 162–163
   revolutionary wave in Eastern Europe
      after World War I   14–15

World War II   32–33
   See also Kádár regime; Imre Nagy; workers'
      councils; working-class
Romania/Romanian   14–19, 28–29, 32,
   36–37, 46, 48–49, 52, 54, 56, 58–59,
   137(n54), 245, 259, 270

Slovakia   27–29, 40, 42, 45, 51–52, 270
socialism   191–192
   and heavy industry   126
   construction of   47, 53, 64, 97, 146, 154,
      284
   demise of   213, 247–256
   state   95, 120, 160, 194, 215, 247–256, 278,
      280–281
   support for   50, 162
   See also Kádár regime; New Course; New
      Economic Mechanism; Rákosi regime
socialist consumerism   138, 195, 200–205, 211,
   214, 255
Soviet Republic of Hungary   15
Soviet Union   18–19, 27, 34, 37, 42, 47, 49,
   63–64, 69, 96, 127, 170, 249–250, 258,
   270–271, 286
SPÖ. See Austrian Socialist Party
Stakhanovites/Stakhanovism   57, 64–66, 69,
   100, 107, 128, 242
   in Petőfi Coal Mine   110
   in United Lighting and Electrics
      Factory   104
   resentment of   66, 70, 77–78, 129
   See also Rákosi regime; working-class
Stalin, Joseph   29, 34, 37, 47–49, 55
   birthday of   104
   death of   59, 90, 285
   effects of death of   55, 59–60, 90–91,
      122(n2), 170–172, 285–287
   Khrushchev's denunciation of   170
Stalinism   50, 94, 96, 119–120, 126, 155, 191
   in Hungary   90, 113, 194, 283
   'Stalinism without Stalin'   49
   See also Rákosi regime
State Security Agency (Államvédelmi Hatóság,
   ÁVH)   49, 121, 277
strikes   223, 242, 268–269
   in Eastern bloc regimes   59, 122(n2), 165
   in revolution of 1956   156–159, 175,
      177–178, 180–181, 183–184, 186–188,
      289–290

led by women machine-operators 134
under Rákosi regime 121–122, 131
See also workers' councils; working-class
students 50, 56, 250
  in revolution of 1956 172–175, 177–178, 277, 285–289
Szakasits, Árpád 50
Szálasi, Ferenc 17, 29, 264–266, 271–273
  See also Arrow Cross Party; fascism; Hungarism
Sztálinváros. *See* Dunaújváros

Tatabánya 61, 131, 214(n97)
  coal mines in 71, 99, 130, 167, 197
  negative effects of Soviet-style industrialisation in 108–111, 136–138, 143–144
  revolution of 1956 in 156–159, 175–176, 178–179, 183–185, 280, 289
  tensions between urban and rural workers in 89
  See also worker-peasants (*kétlaki*)
Tito, Josip Broz 26, 29–30, 38, 48–51, 122(n2)
Torgyán, József 274
trade unions 36, 44, 58, 64–65, 76, 110, 114, 125, 142–143, 148–149, 172, 179, 194, 213, 223, 241, 255, 286
  research in Hungarian archives on 215–216, 219–220
Treaty of Trianon 14–16, 259, 262, 264, 266, 274, 276
  See also borders/borderlands; Hungarism

Újpest 52, 104, 197, 214
  factories in 106–107
  living standards among workers in 190–191
  reality of socialist consumerism in 136
  revolution of 1956 in 176–181, 186–189, 288–290
  support for First Five Year Plans amongst workers in 126

Warsaw Pact 178, 278, 289
Women 41, 164, 189, 226, 234
  in division of labour 124–127, 140–142, 120
  in textile industry 133–135
  job discrimination against 148, 167

methods of resistance against Soviet-style industrialisation 123, 134, 155
resistance to by male workers 76–77, 81–82, 85
state's effort to mobilise 66–68, 80–81, 84, 136, 196–198
support for Catholicism in Hungary 51–52, 90
See also gender; worker-peasants (*kétlaki*)
worker-peasants (*kétlaki*) 110, 126(n13), 146, 149
  as oil workers 85–86, 88–89
  in revolution of 1956 91, 182–183, 188–189
  opposition against forced collectivisation 87, 150–151, 153
  party-state's mistrust against 87, 145, 152
  perception of 153–154, 204–205
  See also gender; peasants; women; working-class
workers' councils 32, 44
  during the 1956 revolution 91, 156, 174, 176, 179–183, 186, 195–196, 288, 290
  election of 179, 277, 289–290
  the Central Workers' Council of Greater Budapest 186–188
working-class 15
  discontent with Soviet-style industrialisation drive 57–60, 62–68, 164–165
  forms of opposition against the Rákosi regime 71–74, 122–123, 127–135, 154
  Kádár regime's attempt to repair relationship with 92, 159, 162–63, 190, 197–198, 200–202
  leading role in the 1956 revolution 157, 164, 171–178, 182, 184–185, 195, 211–213, 287–288
  relations with popular front regimes in Central and Eastern Europe 40, 44–45
  role in post-1989 Hungarian politics 245, 253, 255–256
  support for Hungarist parties among sections of 258, 267–269
  See also gender; women; worker-peasants
World War I 13, 15
  Hungarian territorial losses after 231, 234

opposition against post-war
  settlement   14, 16
support for national-conservative ideas
  after   259, 261
See also Horthy regime; Hungarism; Treaty
  of Trianon
World War II   13, 31, 263
  deportation of ethnic Germans after
    end of   222
  Horthy regime blamed for   257–258, 273
  polarisation of Hungarian society
    after   160, 282
  population losses in Eastern Europe   33

Yugoslavia   14, 16, 23–24, 28, 30, 34, 36,
  38–39, 42–44, 46–49, 51–52, 54, 57–58,
  122(n2), 172, 270, 276–277

Zalaegerszeg
  factories in   189–190
  research in archives in   218
  revolution of 1956 in   174, 277, 287

www.ingramcontent.com/pod-product-compliance
Lightning Source LLC
Chambersburg PA
CBHW020352080526
44584CB00014B/987